THE

EARLY YEARS

OF

CHRISTIANITY.

BY E. DE PRESSENSÉ, D.D.,

AUTHOR OF "JESUS CHRIST: HIS TIMES, LIFE, AND WORK."

TRANSLATED BY ANNIE HARWOOD.

THE APOSTOLIC ERA.

NEW YORK:

CHARLES SCRIBNER & CO.,

654 BROADWAY.

1870.

PREFACE TO ENGLISH EDITION.

OF all the topics of the day, none is of graver importance than the early history of Christianity, and the foundation of the Church. Every thing points inquiry in this direction. A bold criticism claims the right to snatch from our hands the documents of this great history, and to scatter them in fragments to the winds. It is not enough for us to take refuge in our faith as in an inviolable sanctuary; we must establish that faith on solid ground, and produce its original titles. Our part is not to linger on the shore, lamenting the constraint which keeps us there, but rather to abjure the false dominion of a faith imposed by authority, to cross the stormy sea, and plant our feet in the enemy's country, on the much-cultivated soil of contemporary criticism. The fact is not to be disguised that science, hostile to Christianity, has long ago left the lonely height from which it was once wont to bend a pitying eye upon the ignorant masses. No lips take up in our day the cry, "*Odi profanum vulgus;*" every one feels that such a motto would be the confession of weakness. The law of most democratic reform has finally asserted itself in the world of thought; we are governed by the universal suffrage of minds. Therefore science has assumed, in its hostility to Christianity, a popular form. It has not contented itself with the light, quivering arrows, as piercing as they were brilliant, discharged in such rapid flight by the great satirist of the eighteenth century. It has forged other weapons; it has transfused into the vulgar tongue the results of criticism; it has coined a currency, which circulates from hand to hand, out of those heavy ingots which seemed immovable in their ponderosity. While in Germany, Strauss's "Leben Jesu" has been read and pondered in cottages and workshops, men in France, unaware of the very existence of that famous book, have been initiated into its conclusions. M. Renan's "Vie de Jésus"—circulated by thousands of copies—has given a new popularity to the results of negative criticism, by casting them into a poetic mold. Thus, from day to day, a form of skepticism is being developed which is so much the more dangerous because it conceives itself better informed. It is present in the very air we breathe; it finds its way into the lightest publications; the novel and the journal vie with each other in its diffusion; short review articles, skilled in giving grace and piquancy to erudition, furnish it with arguments which appear weighty, because they are so in comparison with the pleasantries of Voltaire. Such a condition of things is critical, and calls for grave and special consideration. If those who are convinced of the divinity of Christianity slumber on in false and fatal security, they must be prepared to pay dearly for their slothfulness ; and the Church and mankind—which have need of each other—will pay dearly for it also. The voice of skepticism will alone be heard, and the sweeping assertions of an unbelief—often more credulous than bigotry—will pass for axioms.

There can be no doubt of the ignorance which extensively prevails, even among the highly cultivated, as to the nature and origin of Christianity. This is the newest of themes, because that which has fallen into deepest oblivion. We are persuaded that the best method of defense against the shallow skepticism which assails us, and which dismisses, with a scornful smile, documents, the titles of which it has never examined, is to retrace the history of primitive Christianity, employing all the materials accumulated by the Christian science of our day ; for it must be well understood among us that there is in truth such a thing as Christian science in the nineteenth century. Those who have taken upon themselves, during the last few years, to initiate other countries into the scientific movement of Germany, have only brought into view one side. The other side deserves a like publicity ; and as this very subject of the early history of Christianity has been treated with a marked predilection by the greatest Christian divines of our age, we are bound, in approaching it, to remember their labors, and profit by all the treasures their patient researches have amassed.

This subject commends itself to us also from another point of view. We are the witnesses of an unparalleled triumph of ecclesiastical authority, which takes advantage of all the ground left at its disposal by the general indifference. Our century has seen that which would not have been endured by any previous age. It has received the gift—fatal or precious—of pushing every principle to its ultimate issues. The Roman—I will not say the Catholic—principle achieved its most signal victory when a new dogma was proclaimed by a single man. The intoxication of success has closed the ears of the Ultramontane party against the protestations—dull as yet—of the Christian conscience in the bosom of that very Church, whose rights have thus unscrupulously been trodden under foot. The approaching Council, if we may judge by the letters of convocation, is about to formulate as dogmas the most senseless pretensions of Ultramontanism—the infallibility of the Pope, the temporal power, and the negation of liberty of conscience. Discussion would be perfectly useless with the heads of this party, who will see nothing, hear nothing, that differs from their own opinion. "Let the dead bury their dead," and let us not concern ourselves with them, except when they seek to bury us also in the same tomb. But it would be a serious mistake to suppose that this intolerant faction has succeeded in overcoming all resistance. A formidable crisis has commenced in the history of Catholicism, and nothing will check it. Grave questions are proposed; it must be ascertained whence the Papacy has derived this vast authority which it has so boldly assumed. Let us produce its titles. It is cited before the bar of history. Now or never is the time to listen to that inflexible judge, whose sentence, thanks to the discovery of numerous documents, we can hear for ourselves. It is clear what interest must attach under these circumstances to an investigation of the history of primitive Christianity.

Nor has the subject a lower claim on Protestants. Before them also there are serious questions for solution, both in the domain of theology and in that of the Church. There is not a single religious party which does not feel the need either of confirmation or of transformation. All the Churches, born of the great movement of the sixteenth century, are passing through a time of crisis. They are all asking themselves, though from various stand-points, whether the Reformation does not need to be continued and developed. Aspiration toward the Church of the future is becoming more general, more ardent. But for all who admit the divine origin of Christianity, the Church of the future has its type and ideal in that great past, which goes back not three, but eighteen centuries. To cultivate a growing knowledge of this, in order to attain a growing conformity to it, is the task of the Church of to-day. This is the path in which it will find liberty and holiness—those two attributes so closely linked together, and so necessary to enable the Church to rise to the height of its true vocation. In the same direction it must move, in order to make that advance in its theology which prudence and necessity alike dictate, and which will consist only in an ever-deepening appropriation of apostolic doctrine. Thus by a concurrence of circumstances, which reveal the manifest will of God, the attention of our age is directed to the question of the origin of Christianity.

This great subject we have attempted to treat in the present work, going back always for our materials to original documents. It is indeed an enviable task to take up the history of the early ages of Christianity, thanks to the abundant sources of information now opened, and to the invaluable discoveries of manuscripts made during the past few years.

It is our aim to present as full a picture as possible of this period, commencing with the apostolic age, which is so little understood, either from religious indifference or because of the unintelligent veneration which surrounds it with a legendary glory, behind which its types lose all distinctness and originality. St. Peter, St. Paul, and St. John appear too often like those fabulous heroes placed by tradition on the threshold of the historic age, after whose era history, properly so called, begins. We feel the necessity of reconquering, as part of the domain of history, this primitive age of the Church. It will thus regain color and life.

It is not possible in this day, and in view of the recent attacks of criticism, to neglect the study of the first century, and to proceed at once to that of the second and third. Such a course would leave untouched delicate problems which demand a solution. We have placed in notes all that relates to the discussion of documents, without which no serious history of the Church would be possible. We have endeavored to depict, in its true colors, the great conflict of Christianity with the society of the old world, which assailed it—without by persecution, within by heresy; and which, though vanquished so signally, avenged itself in a manner by the leaven of error which it left within the bosom of the Church. To follow closely this triumph and this inner transformation—to watch all the shifting scenes of the drama, make the personages live again and speak their own words—to let constant streams from the original sources flow throughout the whole course of the narrative, so that all religious parties may find exact information in our book, even though they differ from our conclusions—such has been our aim. It will be much to have contributed any thing, by earnest effort, toward such an end. We confine ourselves in this work to the first three centuries of the Church, because the period which precedes the great Councils has a peculiar interest. The Church of this early period has not yet bowed under the yoke of a mechanical and external unity. Its various sections have each a distinct physiognomy, and we can speak of the Church of the East and the Church of the West; in short, we are upon the fruitful soil of freedom. We may add that this period is also the least known, because the official documents are few. In it all the elements of Christian greatness are manifest; in it are also present all the germs of error and enslavement which the following age will develop.

Interest in the glorious past of the Church is reviving in our day on every hand. Even in a literary point of view, there are few themes more fertile and more attractive. For ourselves, while we do not overlook this aspect of our subject, our great desire is to bring once more into the full light of day those immortal truths of Christianity, of which our age, even while it repudiates them, feels such a mighty need. We have observed singular analogies between this our generation and that Roman society which concealed so much corruption under a glittering gloss, and so many aspirations after the future under the mask of an ill-assured incredulity. Our faith in the divinity of Christianity is deep and absolute; it has inspired this book; it has never, however, laid any fetters on our freedom of examination. We believe because we have examined; and we have been careful, in our historical criticism, to set aside all preconceived ideas. We have endeavored to recognize always the sovereign authority of history—that is to say, of facts accepted as we find them before they have undergone any transformation from the spirit of system. We have faithfully stated the result of our researches on all points, ever remembering that our duty here on earth is not to take the mean of opinions received in one quarter or another, but to speak out all the truth as it appears to us. We may say, further, that we have not brought the paltry prepossessions of sectarians into the history of the ancient Church. We have pointed out its errors and blemishes, while we have done justice to its pure and primal glory; nor have we turned aside from the Church of the Fathers, to seek in some inaccessible hiding-place an unbroken tradition of spotless orthodoxy. In every period of its history—the first alone excepted—we find the visible Church in all its manifestations far below its own ideal. And yet, while we hold fast out preferences, we rejoice to repeat the ancient adage, *Ubi Christus, ibi Ecclesia.* This is no reason, however, why the Church should not aspire to rise higher and higher toward its ideal ; to realize that is ever increasingly its true idea. May it succeed in our day less imperfectly than in the past, and, casting aside all human trammels, and the darkness which clings around them, become conformed, both in doctrine and organization, to the very apostolic type! Most needful is such preparation for the impending conflict. Our highest wish will be fulfilled, if we may contribute in some measure to lead the Church back to its origin, as to the fountain of its life.

The reproduction in English of this "History of the Early Years of Christianity" is not a mere translation of the French edition, but the presentation of that work in a considerably altered form. We have, in the first place, dispensed with the long introduction treating of the history of religions prior to Christianity, partly because this has already appeared separately in England, and partly because a very full *résumé* is given of it in our book on "The Life, Work, and Times of Jesus Christ," to which the present work may be regarded as a sequel. We have, further, endeavored to bring the English edition into a smaller compass than the French, without curtailing it in any necessary or important branch. By this means we have condensed into one volume the whole history of the apostolic age. The next volume will comprise all the great conflict of the Church with paganism, and will be entitled "The Martyrs and Confessors." We hope to give, in a concluding volume, the entire history of Christian thought and doctrine, treating of all that bears upon theological and ecclesiastical questions during the same period.

The English work will thus have its own special character, and will be more concise than the French. By removing some branches from this rather overgrown forest, we hope to let in more light.

EDMOND DE PRESSENSÉ.

PARIS, *October* 27, 1868.

NOTE BY THE AMERICAN PUBLISHERS.—By the above statement it will appear that our author's plan was to embrace the entire subject in three volumes. Upon further reflection, however, he has concluded that both the requisite fullness of treatment and the proper division of the matter demanded FOUR VOLUMES; and the publishers, both English and American, concur in his proposal. The topics of the FOUR VOLUMES will, therefore, be as follows: I. APOSTOLIC ERA. II. MARTYRS AND APOLOGISTS. III. DOCTRINE AND HERESIES. IV. THE CHURCH WORSHIP AND CHRISTIAN LIFE. The author's expectation is, that the French volume will be ready for the English translation in November, which will be forthwith followed by its issue from our press.

INTRODUCTION
TO THE AMERICAN EDITION.

THE name of DE PRESSENSÉ, the eminent leader of evangelical Protestantism in France, is favorably known in England and America by his published works, especially his "Life of Christ," and his "Religion and the Reign of Terror." By his clear maintenance of Christian truth, his ripe scholarship, his fresh and pictorial style, and the tone of modern liberality that pervades his firm conservatism in behalf of fundamental verities, he has placed himself in the highest rank of modern defenders of the primitive Christian faith. Had he, like Renan, the advantage of the *zest of opposition* to ancient opinions, and of a factitious originality, arising from an unrestrained liberty of shaping, coloring, and grouping the facts and characters of history to his own fancy, Pressensé could bring to the work an insight not less clear, and a style not less vivid. But he holds himself solemnly bound to TRUTH alone, whether that truth be marvelous and picturesque, or commonplace and brown. Yet truth, like wisdom, is justified of her children. She is infinitely valuable for her own sake; she is often capable of an ever-varying freshness as viewed by successive ages; and the truths which Pressensé unfolds must forever possess for the earnest spirit an unsurpassable interest and an eternal youth.

While maintaining evangelical truth in its true spirit, Pressensé, with a genuine Protestant freedom, expresses individual views from which many devout Christians dissent, and in regard to which the publishers are not to be held as expressing opinions. He adopts, for instance the view of Van Oosterzee and others in regard to the divine nature of Christ, modifies the Anselmian theory of the atonement, and strenuously maintains immersion to be the sole mode of New Testament baptism. Some of the views furnish grounds even for denominational differences; but Pressensé speaks from that elevated stand-point which may induce even those who differ from him to give him a liberal hearing.

We may add, that this is the only edition issued from the press in this country, and that it is printed by agreement with an English publishing house, under the proper arrangements with the author and translator.

CONTENTS.

First Century—Book First.

FIRST PERIOD OF THE APOSTOLIC AGE, FROM PENTECOST TO THE COUNCIL OF JERUSALEM.—A.D. 30-50.

CHAPTER I.

COMMENCEMENT OF THE CHRISTIAN CHURCH.

CHAPTER II.

FIRST INTERNAL CONFLICT, AND FIRST EXTENSION OF THE CHURCH BEYOND JERUSALEM.

CHAPTER III.

CONVERSION OF PAUL. HIS FIRST MISSION.

CHAPTER IV.

THE TWO CONFERENCES AT JERUSALEM, AND THE DISPUTE AT ANTIOCH.

First Century—Book Second.

SECOND PERIOD OF THE APOSTOLIC AGE.—THE APOSTOLIC CHURCH UP TO THE DEATH OF ST. PAUL, FROM A.D. 50 TO 65.

CHAPTER I.

MISSIONS OF THE CHURCH UP TO THE CAPTIVITY OF ST. PAUL.

CHAPTER II.

MISSIONS AND PERSECUTIONS OF THE CHURCH FROM THE CAPTIVITY OF ST. PAUL TO HIS DEATH AND THAT OF ST. PETER.

CHAPTER IV.

THE STATE OF THE CHURCHES DURING THIS PERIOD. FIRST SYMPTOMS OF HERESY.

CHAPTER V.

CONSTITUTION OF THE CHURCHES DURING THIS PERIOD.

CHAPTER VI.

WORSHIP AND THE CHRISTIAN LIFE.

First Century—Book Third.

PERIOD OF ST. JOHN, OR CLOSE OF THE APOSTOLIC AGE.

CHAPTER I.

THE FALL OF JERUSALEM AND ITS CONSEQUENCES.

CHAPTER II.

ST. JOHN, THE APOSTLE AND PROPHET.

CHAPTER III.

THE DOCTRINE OF ST. JOHN.

CHAPTER IV.

THE CHURCHES IN THE TIME OF ST. JOHN.

Notes.

EARLY YEARS

OF THE

CHRISTIAN CHURCH.*

BOOK FIRST.

THE FIRST PERIOD OF THE APOSTOLIC AGE, FROM PENTECOST TO THE COUNCIL OF JERUSALEM, A. D. 30–50.†

CHAPTER I.

COMMENCEMENT OF THE CHRISTIAN CHURCH.‡

JESUS CHRIST came to restore the kingdom of God upon earth. He came not simply to offer salvation to every individual man. It was his design to found a holy community, from which, as from a new humanity reconstituted by him, filled with his Spirit and living by his life, the Gospel should go forth into all the world. The holy community thus founded is the Christian Church. It differs from all the religious institutions which preceded it. It is not limited, like the Jewish theocracy, to one special nation; it is not bounded by the frontiers of any

* See Note A, at the end of the volume, on the works of reference.

† See Note B, on the Chronology of the Acts.

‡ See Note C, on the principal source of the history of the Apostolic Age.

land. It forms the kingdom which is not of this world, and which is destined to triumph over all the powers of earth leagued against it. Placed beyond the external conditions of Judaism, the Church is primarily a moral and spiritual fact, the character of which is essentially supernatural. Born of a miracle, by a miracle it lives. Founded upon the great miracle of redemption, it grows and is perpetuated by the ever-repeated miracle of conversion. It is entered, not by the natural way of birth, but by the supernatural way of the new birth. Resting upon free convictions, the Church—the holy community of souls—wins them one by one, and conquers them in a hard struggle with the world and with themselves; it requires from each one an adherence, which implies the sacrifice of the will. It makes the most powerful appeal to the individual, just because it addresses itself to all the race. The Church, resting on no national or theocratic basis, must gather its adherents simply by individual conviction, and such a basis alone corresponds with the breadth of Christianity, because it alone places the Church beyond the narrow bounds of nationalities and of territorial circumscription. In truth, setting aside in man the contingent of race and distinctions of birth, all that remains is the moral personality, the individual soul to be brought into direct contact with God. Individuality is therefore the widest conceivable basis for a religious community. When Jesus Christ sent forth to the conquest of the world the few disciples whom he had gathered around him, and who formed the nucleus of the Church, he by that act abrogated the old theocratic distinctions, and implicitly founded the new community, in which there is neither Jew nor Greek, circumcision nor uncircumcision.

Strange conquerors, we must own, are these Galilean fishermen, without repute, without learning, the poorest of the poor, sent forth in their simplicity into the midst of a state of society in which dazzling splendor is combined with a power hitherto irresistible. Brute force will be let loose upon them, and they have neither might nor right to meet force with force; their weapons are to be of the Spirit only. Reviled and persecuted, they must offer no other resistance than the fortitude of their patience and the vigor of their faith; for let them at all avenge themselves on their adversaries, and they will do themselves irremediable wrong by dishonoring and striking a death-blow to their own principle. They are not suffered for one moment to forget that their strength comes from that higher and invisible world, of which they are the representatives upon earth, and which is at once their fatherland and their goal.

The Christian Church has a double vocation. It is called first to assimilate to itself more and more closely the teaching and the life of its divine Founder, to be joined to him by tender and sacred bonds, to grow in knowledge, in charity, in holiness. It is then to carry every-where the light and flame thus kindled and fed in the sanctuary of the soul, so that it may illuminate and vivify the world. To purify itself within, and to extend itself without, such is the twofold task of the Church, and the ages are given for its fulfillment.

There is, however, one period of its history which claims to be distinguished from the rest—namely, the apostolic age. Its peculiar mission was to preserve to the world the living memory of Christ. The primitive Church is of necessity the medium between us and him; through it alone can we know him; it is to us as the channel which conveys the water from the fountain. It is endowed, therefore, with the gifts necessary for the fulfillment of this mission. Of these gifts two especially are peculiar to it. It is the Church of the apostolate, and the Church of inspiration. On the one hand, it is the direct witness of Christ; on the other, it has received the Spirit of God in extraordinary measure, to enable it to lay a solid foundation upon which the Church of all ages may be built up. Our task is to study closely these two great facts of the apostolic age.

We say at once, that neither by the apostolate nor by inspiration was the primitive Church spared the salutary labor of the assimilation of the truth. It is a grave mistake to suppose that a definite constitution was given to the Church from its very commencement, by decrees promulgated by the Apostles, and that it was at once lifted on the wings of inspiration to the luminous height from which, subsequently, the eye of a St. Paul and a St. John surveyed the whole extent of the Gospel revelation. Many conflicts, many dissensions, many lessons of experience were to precede and to prepare this closing period of the apostolic age, which was the result and crown of all.

The revelations of the Old and New Testament were always given progressively, because it was the will of God to establish a real harmony between the truths which he communicated and the soul by which they were received. This inward, penetrating, progressive action of the Divine Spirit, reaching its ends without doing any violence to human nature, is far more beautiful than any sudden and irresistible operation. Between the two methods there is all the difference between grace and magic. Every one who admits that the ideal of the new covenant shines forth resplendent in the person of the God-Man, must equally admit that the complete blending of the human with the divine element is the great consummation of the Gospel design. This, which is to be the aim of every age, finds its first perfect realization in the age of the Apostles. Their era, therefore, may be regarded as having furnished, as it were, the theme of the history of the Church; for that history is but a free and vigorous development of the great results gained in the first century. The first subject, then, for our consideration, is this normal and ideal union of the human and the divine element in the life of the primitive Church.

We shall divide its history into three periods, each of these designated by the name of the apostle who exercised the greatest influence upon it. We have thus the period of St. Peter, that of St. Paul, and that of St. John.

In the first, the divine element predominates almost to the exclusion of the human, which is, in comparison, reduced to passivity. This is the period of the purely supernatural; it follows the first outpouring of the Holy Spirit, and precedes the great internal deliberations in the Church. In the second and third, the human element is more apparent, though always controlled and purified by the divine: great questions are stated and debated, Church organization begins, doctrine becomes more defined, and if miracles are still many, they are less abundant than before. The latter fact, so far from implying any inferiority in the closing periods of the apostolic age, seems to us to mark a real superiority. For in truth, when the supernatural element is so infused into human nature that it animates it, as the soul the body, it may be said that the union between God and man is fully realized, and the most glorious results of redemption achieved.

§ I. *Actual Foundation of the Church on the Day of Pentecost. Its First Mission and First Persecution.*

Fifty days after the resurrection of Jesus Christ, during the celebration at Jerusalem of the Feast of Pentecost, which was the feast of the ingathering,* the Holy Spirit came down upon the apostles and disciples, assembled to the number of a hundred and twenty in an upper chamber. Some representatives of the sacerdotal theory—always disposed to confine the Spirit of God to his sanctuaries—have maintained that this place, consecrated by so glorious an event, formed a part of the large attached buildings of the Temple at Jerusalem.† But this is an entirely gratuitous hypothesis, of which the text bears no trace. The Holy Spirit breathes where he will, and does not suffer himself to be restricted to any

* Pentecost was spoken of in the time of Josephus as the feast of the great assembly. ("Ant.," iii, 10, 6.) According to Jewish tradition, Pentecost was the anniversary of the promulgation of the Jewish law.

† Thiersch, "Die Kirche in dem Apostolischen Zeitalter," p. 66.

religious institution. The Pentecostal miracle was, moreover, the inauguration of the glorious era foretold by Jesus Christ, when adoration should be no longer associated with certain sacred edifices, but when the whole world should become again the temple of God. We must carefully distinguish, in this miracle, the religious fact from the attendant circumstances and figurative symbols. The "mighty rushing wind," the tongues like as of fire, which rest upon the Apostles' heads, are sublime types of the inward miracle: the wind symbolizes the invisible action and sovereign freedom of the Divine Spirit, (John iii, 8;) the fire its purifying virtue, (Isaiah vi, 6, 7;) and the form under which this fire appeared suggests its chief mode of operation in the moral world. Speech is, in truth, as has been well said, a divine eloquence which sways human freedom. Speech is the noblest medium between the Creator and the creature; as between the creatures themselves, by it the Gospel is to fight and conquer. We fully admit the marvelous character of that scene in the upper chamber at Jerusalem. The sovereign God, who rules in the world of nature no less than in the world of spirit and of grace, has undoubtedly the right to borrow from the former effective symbols to set forth to the eye the great facts of the latter. "He maketh the winds his angels, and the flames of fire his ministers." Heb. i, 7. We must rise at once, however, from the sign to the thing signified. In this, as in every other instance, the miracle belongs essentially to the moral and invisible world. It is wrought in the hearts of the disciples, who, according to the testimony of sacred history, "were all filled with the Holy

Ghost." Acts ii, 4. They had already received it in a measure, but they were not entirely filled with it till then. All the barriers between earth and heaven were removed. The fullness of God could now fill the human soul; by the Holy Spirit God himself could henceforth inhabit this living sanctuary, and the promise of the spiritual return of Christ was abundantly realized. Until this time, the young Church might be compared to a ship ready to depart, its sails spread for the wind. The breath from on high now blows upon it; it is no longer an inert mass, it is an animated body; it may set forth on its flight over all seas, and be they stormy or calm, it shall be ever advancing toward its appointed haven. This first outpouring of the Spirit of God was not restricted to the Apostles, for the sacred writer declares that all who were in the upper chamber were filled with it. Nor was it a simple illumination of the understanding: the Holy Ghost was first and most sensibly shed abroad in the *hearts* of the primitive Christians. His influence went down at once to the very center of their moral and religious life, that it might assimilate to itself one by one all their faculties. But this assimilation was not realized in a moment. They did not in one brief instant acquire all knowledge. That which they already knew was quickened, while the Spirit went on day by day to enrich them with understanding, and to "lead them into all truth." John xvi, 13.

His presence in their midst was marked by one miracle more extraordinary than those which had preceded it. The disciples began to speak in unknown tongues. This miracle, which, with some modifications, is repeated several times in the apostolic age, was in harmony with the essential character of this period, which we have called the period of the purely supernatural. The human element seems to pale and succumb in its first contact with the divine. The Spirit of God, on its descent from heaven, finds human language a vessel too small to contain it. The ordinary forms of speech are broken through; a language which is beyond all known forms takes the place of ordinary words. It is the burning, mysterious tongue of ecstasy. Thus we regard those unknown tongues, of which mention is made in the Church of the first century. To speak in an unknown tongue, was to use that ineffable language which has no analogue in human speech. The Pentecostal miracle had a special character, by which it was distinguished from kindred miracles; the disciples were understood by all who ran together on the first tidings of the prodigy wrought in the upper chamber. Was there in this exceptional language a marvelous power, which went from soul to soul, and triumphed over the diversity of idioms? or did these Jews, gathered at Jerusalem from all parts of the world, really catch the accents of their various dialects? The problem is beyond solution. It is, however, certain that the miracle, at least under this special form, was of no permanent character. Irenæus and Tertullian have erroneously asserted that the early Christians retained the use of the gift of tongues, and employed it in carrying the Gospel to the nations of the world.* The style of the sacred

* Irenæus, "Adv. Hæres., Book V, c. vi; Tertullian, "Contra Marc.," Book V, c. viii.

writers clearly shows that they had learned the Greek language in an ordinary manner, and did not possess it by miraculous gift and by inspiration, for they wrote it incorrectly, and in a form surcharged with Hebraisms. We know also that Peter had an interpreter at Rome.* St. Paul seems not to have understood the language of the inhabitants of Lystra and Derbe, who wished to sacrifice to him as to a god. Acts xiv, 11–14.

The miracle of Pentecost was an enacted prophecy of the happy time when all the diversities created by evil will be lost in the unity of love. Is not this prophecy receiving a constant fulfillment as Christianity masters, one after another, the languages of mankind, and makes them the media for conveying its immortal truths? "The Church in her humility," says the venerable Bede, "re-forms the unity of language broken before by pride." †

We know with what success Peter replied to the raillery of some unbelieving Jews, who had found their way into the wondering crowd. Three thousand persons were won to the Church by that first preaching of the Apostle. This rapid increase was soon to bring about an open rupture between the young Church and Judaism. The Sadducean party took the lead in the persecution. It has been declared to be very unlikely that the Pharisees, who had been the most bitter enemies of Jesus Christ, would have let themselves be thus outstripped by their rivals.‡ But it

* According to the testimony of Papias in "Eusebius," Book VII, c. xxxix.

† "Unitatem linguarum quam superbia Babylonis disperserat humilitas Ecclesiæ recolligit." See Note D, on the Pentecostal miracle.

‡ Baur, "Paulus," pp. 34, 35.

must not be forgotten that at this period the Church had not yet comprehended the doctrine of Christ in all its issues. It had not yet broken the outward bond with Judaism. The point on which it insisted most strongly was the resurrection of the dead; now this dogma was particularly odious to the Sadducees. Annas and Caiaphas, who presided over the council before which the Apostles were cited, were the well-known leaders of the Roman or Sadducean party. Acts v, 17. The only judge who showed himself impartial toward the Church was the Pharisee Gamaliel.

During all this early time the influence of the Apostle Peter predominates. The part thus taken by him has been urged as a proof of his primacy. But on closer examination it will be seen that he does but exercise his natural gifts, purified and ennobled by the Divine Spirit. Peter was the son of a fisherman named Jonas, of the village of Bethsaida, in Galilee. Matt. xvi, 17; John i, 44. He was among the disciples of John the Baptist, and was thus prepared to respond favorably to the call of Jesus Christ. He soon received his vocation as an apostle. His disposition was quick and ardent, but his zeal was blended with presumption and pride. Living in constant contact with the Master, as one of the three disciples who enjoyed his closest intimacy, he conceived for him a strong affection. His impetuous nature was, however, far from being brought at once under control. He had noble impulses, like that which prompted his grand testimony to the Saviour: "Thou art the Christ of God." Matt. xvi, 16. But he was also actuated by many an earthly motive, which drew down upon him the Master's sharp reproach. Once, under the influence of Jewish prejudice, he repelled with indignation the idea of the humiliating death of Christ. At another time he was eager to appear more courageous than all the other disciples, and again yielding to his natural impetuosity, he drew his sword to defend Him whose "kingdom is not of this world." It was needful that the yet incoherent elements of his moral nature should be thrown into the crucible of trial. His shameful fall resulted in a decisive moral crisis, which commenced in that moment when, pierced to the heart by the look of Christ, he went out of the court of the high priest and wept bitterly. He appears entirely changed in the last interview he has with the Saviour on the shores of the Lake of Tiberias. Jesus Christ restores him after his threefold denial, by calling forth a threefold confession of his love. John xxi, 15.

Nothing but determined prejudice could construe the tender solicitude of the Master for this disciple into an official declaration of his primacy. We are here in the region of feeling alone, not on the standing ground of right and legal institutions. Nor has the primacy of Peter any more real foundation in the famous passage, "*Tu es Petrus*." Jesus Christ admirably characterized by this image the ardent and generous nature of his disciple, and that courage of the pioneer which marked him out as the first laborer in the foundation of the primitive Church. The son of Jonas was its most active founder, and, as it were, its first stone. He was also the rock against which the first tempest from without spent its fury.* Be-

* In the course of this history it will be seen that the Church, for three centuries, did not attach the Romish sense to Matt. xvi, 18.

yond this, the narrative of St. Luke lends no countenance to any hierarchical notions.

Every thing is natural and spontaneous in the conduct of St. Peter. He is not official president of a sort of apostolic college. He acts only with the concurrence of his brethren, whether in the choice of a new apostle,* or at Pentecost,† or before the Sanhedrim. Peter had been the most deeply humbled of the disciples, therefore he was the first to be exalted. John's part being at this time inconspicuous, no other apostle is named with Peter, because he fills the whole scene with his irrepressible zeal and indefatigable activity.

The Christian mission during this period gained two altogether exceptional successes. A few weeks after the baptism of the three thousand converts of the day of Pentecost, five thousand souls were added to the Church as the result of the miraculous healing of the impotent man, and of another sermon of St. Peter. Acts iv, 4. The Church continued for a long time rapidly to receive adherents in numbers scarcely less surprising. This first offensive movement of Christianity was accomplished with a holy impetuosity and joyous enthusiasm. It has been asserted that the number of the conversions is too enormous not to indicate a mythical character in the sacred narrative.‡ Such an assertion does not take into account the extraordinary zeal displayed by the first Christians, the powerful inspiration by which

* "And Peter stood up in the midst of the disciples." Acts i, 15.

† "But Peter, standing up with the eleven, lifted up his voice." Acts ii, 14.

‡ Baur, "Paulus," p. 27.

they were animated, and the impressive miracles which accompanied their preaching. Acts v, 15, 16.

It would be a mistake also to imagine that all these new converts had reached the same stage of religious development. They differed in piety and in knowledge, but they had nevertheless received the Gospel with sincerity. In a short time the Church had gathered into itself more than ten thousand persons. This was assuredly a miracle not less amazing than that of the day of Pentecost.

To these triumphs Judaism replied by persecution. The Church has had time, during eighteen centuries, to become accustomed to this brutal and senseless appeal to force. We need not here dwell on the constitution of the Sanhedrim. We know that it was composed of seventy-one members, that it was presided over by the High Priest, and that from the time of the Roman conquest it constituted the religious tribunal of the nation. It was not always possible to distinguish with clearness the religious sphere from the civil, so closely had the two been united in the old theocracy. The Sanhedrim naturally assumed as its right to summon to its bar any who attacked the religion of the country. Now the apostolic preaching appeared, in the eyes of those who regarded Jesus Christ as a false prophet, to be an assault upon the national religion. A theocratic government is a government of constraint. Freedom of conscience would have been an unmeaning sound under the Jewish economy. But the abrogation of the ancient economy had abrogated the right of religious coercion. Persecution on the part of the Sanhedrim was now only an odious abuse of power. It must be further admitted that men like Annas and Caiaphas cared little for theocratic rights, for they belonged to the sect which repudiated the spirit of the ancient religion.

This first persecution revealed the deep-seated enmity which exists between skeptical Materialism and the Gospel. We shall often have occasion, in the course of this history, to show how intolerant is incredulity, and how impatient of the freedom of sincere belief. We shall see that the Sadducean spirit is always essentially a persecuting spirit. At this time we find that the people were not, as subsequently, in favor of the adoption of violent measures against the Church, for the persecutors feared to offend the multitude by maltreating the Apostles. Acts v, 26.

Immediately after the healing of the impotent man at the Beautiful Gate of the Temple, the magistrate in charge of the sanctuary, and who appears to have been a man of rank, since Josephus names him directly after the High Priest,* seizes Peter and John, and casts them into prison. A solemn meeting of the Sanhedrim is convoked, and the Apostles appear before this iniquitous tribunal, in which fanaticism sits side by side with skepticism. The grandeur of the scene is beyond description. The entire world is at this time held under terrible oppression. A heavy yoke bows the heads of all. Every effort has been made to break it—open revolt, treason, force, and cunning. But the chains have been only riveted the firmer upon the struggling race. Now, for the first time, despotism finds a barrier that will not break,

* Josephus, "Bell. Jud.," vi, 5, 3.

and meets with invincible resistance. It must bend before these ignorant and unlearned men, who have no weapons of war in their hands, no inflammatory words on their lips, but who oppose an indomitable faith to all the threats hurled against them. In this first conflict between conscience and force victory remains with the former. This day is liberty born into the world, never to be destroyed.

The president of the Sanhedrim asks Peter in what name he healed the impotent man. The Apostle replies with the utmost respect to the magistrates of his nation. He recognizes their authority like the most docile of their subordinates. Acts iv, 8. Peter is neither a rebel nor an agitator. He is a servant of God and of truth; therefore he is invincible upon the ground of religion. With what boldness does he avow, in the midst of that council, which a few days before had condemned Jesus Christ, the name of the crucified Lord! "If we be this day examined of the good deed done to the impotent man, by what means he is made whole; be it known to you and to all the people of Israel, that by the name of Jesus of Nazareth, whom ye crucified, whom God hath raised from the dead, even by him doth this man stand here before you whole." Acts iv, 8–10. The Sanhedrim deliberate on this reply, so firm and courageous. The result of their deliberation is to forbid the Apostles to speak or to teach in the name of Jesus. Acts iv, 18. By such a decision the first step is taken in the path of persecution. Had the judges of Peter and John gone no further than this prohibition they would have even then deserved the name of persecutors. To hinder the manifestation of a conviction, to restrain the efforts at proselytism made by a sincere faith, is to persecute the immortal soul; it is to deny its right, and to prepare the way for violent persecution, since conscience does not allow of concessions to fear or danger. A duty becomes all the more sacred when obstacles are placed in the way of its accomplishment. Disobedience to an unjust command is dictated by the same motives which, in the ordinary course of things, would lead to a scrupulous conformity to law. The Sanhedrim thought they were taking a safe and inoffensive step. From that step, however, they will be fatally led on to violent persecution. Peter and John appeal from the authority of this iniquitous tribunal to the authority of God himself and to his clear command: "Whether it be right in the sight of God," they exclaim, "to obey you rather than God, judge ye." Socrates had made the same appeal before the Athenian judges. We admire it in the mouth of the great philosopher, but how is its power enhanced as the utterance of those who are guided not merely by the inspiration of a noble heart and a true genius, but by the light of revelation.

The Apostles, as they had declared, pay no heed to an unjust prohibition. They resume their preaching with the same success as before. They are thrown into prison. Miraculously set at large, they begin again to proclaim the Gospel. Cited anew before the Sanhedrim, they preserve the same attitude. They are calm and immovable, as becomes the disciples of that Jesus whom "God hath exalted to his right hand to be a Prince and a Saviour." Acts v, 31. They would have been again incarcerated but for the intervention of Gamaliel, who takes up their defense, and gives wise counsel of toleration. The closing words of the speech of this venerable doctor, on the danger of fighting against God, show a great breadth of view. Acts v, 39. Was he expressing the general good-will of his sect toward the Christians, or did he personally stand aloof from the rest of the Pharisees, by a more independent spirit? Did his toleration cover, as has been asserted, contempt for the new religion, or was it founded on an exaggerated confidence in Judaism? Be the answer what it may, Gamaliel obtained from the Sanhedrim the liberation of the Apostles, after they had been scourged and again charged to speak no more in the name of Jesus. But they were men of purpose, and nothing could turn them from the accomplishment of their duty. Peter and John had shown, by their calm and firm attitude, that they were the conquerors in the struggle of force with conscience. Their readiness to endure all sufferings and ill treatment declared yet more clearly that their cause was not to be crushed. Heroic words, such as they had uttered, would be meaningless unless they were prepared to honor them by submitting to all the consequences of resistance. He who is resolved to suffer and to die for God cannot be vanquished. His noble endurance is also an ineffaceable disgrace to his persecutors, and every fresh victim to their rage makes persecution more detested. There is, then, no graver mistake than for a persecuted people to offer material as well as moral resistance; this is to subject themselves to the chances of strength, to the risks of a struggle of which the issue is always uncertain. He who takes the sword deserves to perish by the sword, for he implicitly admits the right of the strongest. Moral resistance, on the contrary, knows no chances, no risks. It is linked to an immortal principle, and destined to certain triumph.

The young Church thus persecuted took refuge in prayer. Hence the majestic calmness, the blending of gentleness and indomitable energy which distinguished it. In such conflicts the soul finds serenity only on the summits of faith. To what an elevation were the Apostles lifted in that sublime prayer which was inspired by the circumstances in which they had just found themselves. From the particular fact of the persecution, they rise to the general law of the religious history which it reveals. They see it in that opposition between the princes of this world and the Son of God, set forth in the prophetic strains of Psalm ii. They comprehend that the bloody and victorious strife of Calvary is to be ever renewed. They feel themselves close bound to Christ the crucified ; therefore they ask not to be delivered from persecution, but only to be faithful to him under their cross, and to be filled with his Spirit that they may the better glorify the name of the Holy Child Jesus. Acts iv, 24–30. God manifested his presence in their midst by a miraculous token. The place where they were was shaken. This miracle contained a promise for every time of persecution. The Church of the catacombs and the Church of the desert alike received its fulfillment, for in both there was given a marvellous manifestation of the presence of God.

§ II. *The Teaching and First Constitution of the Church at Jerusalem.*

From its very birth the Christian Church is called to defend itself against the attacks of its adversaries, and to contend for the claims of truth. The opposition to Christianity assume from the outset various forms. The first to be encountered is that of scoffing unbelief. This foe has not yet sharpened and polished the weapons with which, in subsequent times, it will wound by the hands of a Celsus and a Lucian. But was not the laugh of the scorner heard on the very day when the Holy Spirit descended upon the Church? Did not his voice cry, "These men are full of new wine?" And from the scorner's point of view it was a fair conclusion. The supernatural is absurd to those who discern nothing beyond the circle of the visible; and herein is its peculiar glory. The laugh of unbelief has never ceased in all these eighteen centuries to ring through the world. But ridicule alone was not enough. Calumny and false insinuations must be enlisted in the same cause. The miracles of the primitive Church were incontestable; they could not be brought in question, but they might, like those of Jesus Christ, be ascribed to witchcraft, and to the powers of darkness. The arts of magic were much believed in at this epoch, as in all periods of religious crisis. There was, therefore, profound subtilty in likening the Apostles to common magicians. Such an idea is evidently present in the question of the Sanhedrim to Peter and John, after the healing of the impotent man: "By what power or by what name have ye done this?" Acts iv, 7. The enemies of the Apostles did not admit that they were the organs of divine power. The influence, then, by which they made so much stir must be diabolical or magical. Side by side with this open unbelief, the primitive Church had to encounter the ignorance and prejudices of a people of formalists and materialists. They had to establish the claims of Jesus Christ; that is, of a humble and crucified Messiah, before a nation which was ready to believe only in a glorious king—a new Maccabeus.

To meet all objections, the Church had ready a simple and popular apology. We at once admit that they appealed without hesitation to the testimony of reason for all the facts coming within its competence. Thus, in reply to the absurd charge of drunkenness brought against the disciples, Peter urges that it is but the third hour of the day—the hour, that is, of morning prayer, before which the Jews never presumed to eat or drink. Acts ii, 15. But the advocates of Christianity do not pause long on such vindications. They have a line of argument peculiarly their own.

It is to be observed that the miracles are rather the occasion than the cause of the apology which accompanies them. Peter does not say, "Believe because of this amazing gift of tongues, or these miraculous cures." He says, on the contrary, "Believe in the reality, the divinity, of the miracles on the scriptural and moral grounds, which show their necessity and establish their lawfulness." These miracles certainly contributed to the rapid spread of the new faith by the impression they produced upon the people; but so little are they the pivot on which the apology of the Apostles turns, that they are not the proof, but rather the object of the proof. We except one single miracle, which is the essential miracle of Christianity. The resurrection of Christ is not merely a marvel; it is also a great religious fact. It is the glorious seal of redemption. Therefore it occupies the first place in the preaching of the Apostles. Peter constantly appeals to it both before the people and before the Sanhedrim. Acts ii, 32; iii, 15; iv, 10; v, 30. The Apostles regarded themselves pre-eminently as the witnesses of the resurrection. Nothing, in fact, gave so solid a foundation to the new religion as this splendid triumph of Jesus Christ over death. It was the proof of his divine mission and of that of the Church, and the seal affixed by the hand of God to teaching in his name. "Between us and you," the Apostles seem to say, "God has judged: by raising up Jesus he has sovereignly declared that he was indeed Christ the Lord."

Next to the proof drawn from the resurrection of the Lord, that which is most prominent in the discourses of Peter is the evidence from Scripture. He sets himself to show the harmony of the facts, in process of accomplishment, with Jewish prophecy. The first apologist of the Church could take no other ground. An appeal addressed to Jews by Christians of Jewish extraction must be made to a tribunal recognized by all, and this was no other than Holy Scripture. If the Apostles at Jerusalem succeeded in showing that the facts of which they were the witnesses had been foretold in the Scriptures, every upright Jew must be enlisted on their side. The

Christian apology did not rise, in this its first stage, to the height to which it was carried by St. John and St. Paul. In form and spirit it was limited and characterized by the views so prominently set forth in the first Gospel.

Thus Peter commences by showing that the miracle of Pentecost is the fulfillment of the prophecy of Joel, who foretold the outpouring of the prophetic Spirit at the time of Messiah's appearing. Acts ii, 17–20. He points out that the resurrection of Jesus Christ had been predicted in Psalm xvi, which could not have reference to David, since the sepulcher of that king was still to be seen in Jerusalem. Acts ii, 25–34. In his second discourse, as in his defense before the Sanhedrim, Peter shows that the sufferings and death of Jesus Christ as the Messiah, which were such a stumbling-block to the Jews, were set forth in the prophecies of the Old Testament. "This is the stone which was set at nought of you builders, which is become the head of the corner." Acts iii, 18; iv, 11, 12. The Apostle, like St. Matthew, uses great freedom in quoting the Old Testament. Absorbed with the idea, so true in itself, that the thought of Messiah runs through the whole of the sacred oracles, he often turns into positive prophecy declarations of Scripture which have only an indirect reference to Gospel facts.

In this first apology of Christianity many appeals are made to the conscience. The conclusion of Peter's discourses is always an invitation to repentance, and this invitation he urges by boldly charging home the great crime committed by the Jewish people: "You crucified the Lord of glory," he cries again and again to the murderers of Jesus Christ. He darts this terrible accusation like a barbed arrow into the hearts of his hearers, and thus he touches their vulnerable point. He pierces their conscience, and strong conviction is followed by multiplied conversions. Thus, the apology of the primitive Church is not simply defensive : it is able to take the offensive, and to carry the warfare into the hearts of its adversaries with all the authority of truth and the ardor of love. "The Apostles understood," says Calvin, "that the Gospel is also *fire and sword*."

In estimating the doctrinal teaching of the Apostles at this period, it is needful to avoid exaggerating or detracting from the influence of the new ideas, which were at the basis of their belief. If there is full evidence that they declared the truth of Christ in all its essentials, the evidence seems to us no less clear that they still enveloped that truth in Jewish forms.

It would be utterly unjust, however, to confound the primitive Church with this or that Jewish sect. It clung most closely to the prophetic portion of the Old Testament, that is to say, to the elements in the sacred book which best harmonized with itself. Never has transition been more admirably accomplished than that from the old covenant to the new, for the very simple reason that the latter struck all its roots down into the former. In the period which immediately followed the Pentecost the primitive Church was not called to break the tie which bound it to the temple. It still celebrated the Levitical worship. The assiduous attendance of the Apostles in the holy place is very notable ; and they scrupulously observe the ceremonial law, which, in their view, still stands in its integrity. If they admit that all the nations of the earth are to be blessed in the Seed of Abraham, they have not yet comprehended that in Christ Jesus all national barriers are done away, and that the privileges and the prescriptions of Judaism are alike abolished. They still believe in the necessity of circumcision. But, on the other hand, they are broadly distinguished from their nation at large, not only by reaction against the formalism of the Pharisees, but also by their faith in Jesus Christ. This, their simple and artless faith, has in it no speculative element. The divinity of Messiah is not formally stated in Peter's preaching, but it comes out spontaneously. What correspondence is there between the Messiah of the Ebionites, the Prophet of the "Clementines," and the Christ of St. Peter? On the one hand we have a simple man, like Adam or Moses; on the other, we have the Saviour represented as "seated at the right hand of God," (Acts ii, 33, 34;) "the Prince of life," (Acts iii, 15;) the One apart from whom there is no salvation, (Acts iv, 12;) Him who is spoken of in Psalm ii as the Lord's Anointed, and his first begotten Son. Acts iv, 26. Let it not be forgotten that these illustrious names are given to Christ at a time when his power had not yet been gloriously manifested in the extension and establishment of his Church. Evidently, by this recognition of the dignity and sovereignty of Jesus Christ, the Church cast away all Jewish prejudices. Enough stress has not been laid on the conclusion of Peter's sermons, which always sets forth faith in Christ as the infallible means of pardon and of regeneration. And again, is it not in his name that all are to be baptized? The relation between Christ and the sinner is represented by Peter, as it was by Jesus Christ himself. Of this unique relation between the soul and the Saviour, St. Paul and St. John, drawing their inspiration from the last discourses of the Master, will presently unfold to us the profound significance.*

Christian doctrine had, it is evident, at this time, no systematic form. It was subsequently to develop all its consequences, to define its outlines, and, in the repeated shocks of a salutary conflict, to cast away its Jewish garment. This first era of the Church was to be the period, not of conflict and debate, but of the manifestation of the direct, sovereign and extraordinary action of the Divine Spirit. The history of the Church itself, properly speaking, was not to begin till later. The first Christians had no thought of a history. They believed in an immediate return of Jesus Christ "to restore all things." They supposed that the end of the world was at hand, and that the last days foretold by Joel had begun to dawn. Acts ii, 17; iii, 19, 20. Thus they awaited those days of refreshing from the presence of the Lord which were to inaugurate the second coming of Christ.

Ecclesiastical organization was as far from being fixed, in this first period, as was the doctrine of the

* All these observations are called for by the bold statements of the Tübingen School. Schwegler, "Nach Apost. Zeitalt.," p. 10; Baur, in his book on St. Paul; Ritschl, "Enstehung der Altcatholischen Kirche," pp. 108, 109, affirm the identity of primitive Christianity with Judaism. They rest their assertion on such expressions as "Jesus, a man approved of God." Acts ii, 22. But they take no notice of all the other declarations which we have mentioned.

Church from being formulated. A Church must be founded before it can have a constitution. The river is as yet too near its source to flow in a regularly-channeled bed. We find, therefore, no office, properly so called, nor any fixed rule for the admission of new members. All offices are centered in the apostolate. The Apostles receive gifts for the community. Acts iv, 35. They attend to the distribution of alms, as well as to preaching. Acts ii, 42; vi, 2. When some subject of general interest is mooted, they convene a meeting of the faithful. It cannot be disputed that they exercised a large authority in the primitive Church. The apostolate at first united in one all the various offices, which were by degrees to become detached. It is, then, of great importance that we should rightly conceive the situation.

We must set aside, first of all, any ideas of sacerdotalism. It must not be forgotten that, at the period when the apostolic authority was used with most power in the Church, the Church still acknowledged the Jewish priesthood. Besides, Christianity recognizes no priesthood but that of Christ, communicated by faith to the Christian. The Apostles were not the sole organs of inspiration, for the Holy Spirit which was promised was granted to all the disciples assembled in the upper chamber a few days after the ascension. We have fully shown that on the day of Pentecost all the Christians were filled with the Holy Ghost. It is incontestable that in the primitive Church some private Christians, not invested with the apostolic office, had more influence than the majority of the Apostles; it is enough to cite the names of Stephen, Philip, and James. In what, then, consisted the apostolic office? Their name of messenger has nothing exclusive in it, since all Christians are the witnesses of Jesus Christ. Their number supplies us with one element for the resolution of the question. They were twelve. Evidently this symbolical number points to the twelve tribes of the chosen people. The Apostles are the ideal representation of the true Israel, and answer, in the spiritual ancestry, to the twelve sons of Jacob. They clearly do not represent the priestly tribe, but the twelve tribes; that is to say, the people of God as a whole. In other words, they are the nucleus of the Church, so made by Jesus Christ himself. Apostolical succession is not, then, the privilege of a certain portion of the body, but of the whole; the Christian Church itself carries on the apostolic office. There is nothing in such a conception derogatory to the authority of the Apostles. In them were concentrated, so to speak, all the gifts bestowed on the Christians of the primitive Church, for they were the immediate witnesses of Christ. This qualification of being a direct witness is that specially required by Peter, when the place of Judas is to be filled. Acts i, 21, 22. In short, an apostle is pre-eminently a witness of Jesus Christ, and officially so recognized; he is by this very characteristic the authentic representative of the primitive Church. His authority is not in any way defined; it varies in the case of various apostles, according to the nature of the gifts of each, but it is exercised most largely during this period, while the Church is yet young and unorganized. The primitive apostolate, founded upon personal contact with Jesus Christ, was not designed to be transmitted; it was to give place subsequently to a more spiritual apostleship.*

The conditions of entrance into the Church are at first extremely simple. No guaranty of preparation, of instruction and examination is required, because conversion has at this period an exceptionally sudden and supernatural character. The sign of initiation into the new society is baptism. The gift of the Holy Spirit is so far from being bound to the material act, that sometimes it precedes immersion. The formula of baptism was not pronounced in full; the neophytes were simply baptized in the name of the Lord.† The Church, though not separated from the temple, felt nevertheless that it constituted a body apart, to which adherence must be given. Its discipline shares in the miraculous character of this period, as is shown by the history of Ananias and Sapphira. Acts v, 1–11. Their death, which it may be observed does not necessarily imply their perdition, since there may have been a coincident awakening of conscience, is the effect of the direct and terrible discipline of the Divine Spirit. It reveals the will of God, that in his Church itself there should be a burning crucible, in which the pure gold should be twice purified.

The worship of the primitive Church is also of an exceptional character. The disciples are continually in the temple; they go up to it at the hour of prayer and of sacrifice. Yet they have also their secret

* Some have discovered a sort of anticipation of the diaconate in this office of the young men who carried out the bodies of Ananias and Sapphira. But this is quite a gratuitous supposition.

† Acts ii, 38. Ἐπὶ τῷ ὀνόματι Ἰησοῦ Χριστοῦ. Acts x, 48.

worship, celebrated in the upper room at Jerusalem.* This, if it borrows some forms from the synagogue, has nevertheless a stamp of originality. We recognize in it the essential elements by which it will be ultimately characterized. Teaching, adoration, song, prayer, and the eucharistic meal, are its principal features.†

We must be especially careful not to deprive it of its primitive simplicity. The teaching did not take the form of preaching, properly so called; it was an unstudied speech, springing from the heart. The Apostles were not the only speakers; the other Christians spoke as freely as they of the wonderful works of God. Acts ii, 4. The hymn and prayer borrowed their forms of solemn poetry from Old Testament prophecy; the whole assembly took part, but in what manner is not clearly described. Acts iv, 24. The eucharistic meal of the Church at Jerusalem bears no resemblance whatever to what is called the Sacrament of the Altar. The first Christians still held themselves in subjection to the ceremonial law; thus for them the altar was in the temple, and nowhere else. The Lord's Supper could not then have any possible analogy with a sacrifice. It was not kept distinct at this period from an ordinary meal; it was the conclusion of ordinary meals, as it had been the conclusion of the Passover feast. The commemoration of redemption took place every time that Christians gathered around the family table. St. Luke

* See Harnack, "Der Christliche Gemeinde Gottesdienst im Apost. Zeitalt.," pp. 69–131.

† In Acts ii, 42, "the apostles' doctrine" represents the element of teaching, and "the breaking of bread" the eucharistic feast.

says positively that it was observed from house to house.* The *Agapæ* were only introduced in the next period.†

From all these observations, it appears that the distinction between the ordinary and the religious life had no existence for the primitive Church, because its ordinary life was raised to a height truly divine. Hence the supernatural character of its piety. The Church is not satisfied, as afterward, with infusing the spirit of Christianity into all the various social relations; it translates the pure ideal at once into the real, and banishes poverty from its midst by the voluntary generosity of the rich. Acts iv, 34, 35. "As many as were possessors of lands or houses sold them." There was nothing absolute or compulsory in this community of goods; it was based upon free consent; but it was certainly for the time almost fully carried out in Jerusalem.‡ The history of the Church thus commences with a glorious Sabbath, in which every thing is marvelous and exceptional; this precedes the long week of toil and struggle which is even now far from ended, just as divine grace precedes human effort in the Christian life.

* *Κλῶντές τε κατ' οἶκον ἄρτον μετελάμβανον τροφῆς ἐν ἀγαλλιάσει.* Acts ii, 46.

† When Thiersch and Harnack assert that the first Christians observed the Sabbath from this time, they speak without proof. St. Luke declares that Christian worship was celebrated without distinction of days. *Καθ' ἡμέραν.* Acts ii, 46.

‡ The words of Peter to Ananias (Acts v, 4) prove that there was perfect freedom of action. This community of goods was not absolute, for we read that the Church was gathered together in the house of Mary, the mother of Mark. Acts xii, 12. Neander seems, however, to depreciate unduly the significance of the first community of possessions. "Pflanz," pp. 39, 40.

CHAPTER II.

FIRST INTERNAL CONFLICT, AND FIRST EXTENSION OF THE CHURCH BEYOND JERUSALEM.

§ I. *The Seven Deacons of the Church at Jerusalem. Stephen.*

THE Church could not always remain on the calm heights to which the Spirit of God had at first carried her. It was needful that the truth, of which she was the depositary, should be made her own by laborious assimilation; that she should follow it out to all its issues, and attain, as it were, her moral majority by breaking the bonds of Judaism. But this could not be achieved without many a severe struggle; there were inveterate prejudices to be subdued, which would only yield after a sharp resistance. The disputes which arose between the Hebrew and Hellenist Jews gave forewarning of the storm soon to burst upon the Church.

Christian charity had spontaneously found a noble mode of expression in the new society. In the first fervor of zeal the wants of all the poor members were supplied. It was only subsequently that certain jealousies began to arise about the distribution of the alms. The Church had been formed on the occasion of a great festival, when numbers of foreign Jews were assembled at Jerusalem. Among these a large proportion of its members were found. These Jews were designated Hellenist because they spoke the Greek language. They had lost some of their Jewish peculiarities under the influence of the lands in which they lived. The Church found among them the readiest proselytes. The Jews of Hebrew origin, whose national pride was stimulated to excess by the Pharisees, despised these Hellenist Jews. They regarded them as their inferiors, on the pretext that they consorted with Gentiles ; they were wont almost to rank them in the vanguard of paganism. These prejudices found their way into the Church, and the Hebrew widows had the largest share in the almsgiving, while the Hellenist widows were neglected. The Jews of foreign extraction complained loudly of this injustice. Thus within the very inclosure of Judaism arose the great question which was to excite so much controversy in the first century. It became necessary at once to decide if the differences of nationality were or were not abrogated by Christianity ; if the new religion was to perpetuate or to annul Jewish tradition. The Apostles engaged in no theoretical discussion ; they would not at this period have been capable of it, but they provided, by the institution of a new office, for the removal of any inequality in the distribution of alms.

Until now there had been in the Church no office but the apostolate ; the nomination of the seven Deacons at Jerusalem was the first new wheel introduced into the simple machinery. This primitive diaconate must be distinguished from that which was subsequently established in a definite form. The further we go back in the history of the Church the more indefinite in character are all ecclesiastical offices.

Their limits are not clearly or precisely laid down. The regular division of labor is not yet a necessity. The seven Deacons chosen to superintend the almsgiving are all men distinguished for their missionary zeal, and one of them for a time stands out even more prominently than the Apostles. In the primitive Church all speak and act as they are moved by the Holy Ghost—there are no hierarchical distinctions. But this condition of things ceases when the ecclesiastical organization is definitely completed; the various offices in the Church are then distinguished by a clear line of demarkation.*

The institution of the primitive diaconate shows how free and spontaneous is every thing in the apostolic Church. None of its ordinances are appointed like the Mosaic institutions; there is not even the semblance of any official declaration of them. They arise out of the necessities of new circumstances. The organization of the Church is as supple as it is simple, and accommodates itself to the various exigencies of its situation, avoiding only any concession to error or to evil. It is evident that this first ecclesiastical office springs from the apostolate, and is again cut off like a bough from the parent trunk; it is not imposed by the Apostles on the Church, nor conferred by way of sacramental transmission. The

*Vitringa, "De Sygnag. Vetere," Lib. III, pars ii, c. v, shows perfectly the difference between the seven Deacons of Jerusalem and the Deacons spoken of by Paul. He points out, in the first place, that the name "Deacon" is not given to the former. He then shows that while these had, as their special function, to superintend the almsgiving, that duty is not mentioned by St. Paul among those devolving on the Deacons of his day. Lastly, he rests upon the opinion of Chrysostom, "Homily XIV, in Act." 11, 3.

seven Deacons are not nominated by the Apostles, but chosen by the whole assembly. The imposition of hands which they receive bears no resemblance to a priestly consecration. It is the sign of their entry upon their office, accompanied with a solemn prayer.* To maintain, as do the advocates of hierarchical principles, that the Deacons were chosen by the assembly instead of being appointed by the Apostles because their duties were essentially temporal and administrative,† is to misconceive the part which belonged to them in the primitive Church ; it is to depreciate their office—one which was filled at first by the Apostles themselves ; it is to ignore, in fine, the fact which we shall presently establish, that all offices, without exception, were by election.

The seven men chosen to serve the tables were for the most part Hellenist Jews, as may be inferred from their names. We even find among them a proselyte named Nicholas.‡ His election indicates that the liberal tendency had already gained the ascendant, and that the primitive Church was not so much in bondage to Jewish prejudices as has been asserted. The most remarkable man among the seven Deacons is unquestionably Stephen. The sacred historian is sparing of personal details in his case, but the few scattered traits in the narrative

* Acts vi, 5, 6. We shall speak again of the question of the laying on of hands in the primitive Church.

† Thiersch, "Die Kirche im Apostolischen Zeitalter," p. 98.

‡ The fathers of the third century make this Nicholas the father of the Nicolaitan heresy. (Irenæus, "Contr. Hæres.," II, c. xxvii ; Epiph., "Hæres.," § 27.) We shall discuss this opinion when we come to speak of the heresies of the early Church.

suffice to give us the outline of one of the noblest and most beautiful figures of Christian antiquity. Stephen appears to us a man of ardent and energetic nature, formed for conflict, full of the fire of an enthusiastic conviction. His spirit is remarkable for breadth; he was the first Christian emancipated from Jewish prejudices. The love of truth consumes him; for it he is ready to make any sacrifice—not withholding his life. His death is the crowning evidence of the disinterested love by which he was impelled; for, like his Master, with the same lips which had hurled the anathema at hypocrisy and formalism he forgives his murderers, proving at once his holy indignation against sin and holy pity for the sinner. Stephen is the ideal witness for truth, and therefore he was the first of the martyrs. He was the forerunner of St. Paul, for he laid down the principles which the great Apostle was to develop and victoriously to defend. Is not this abundantly evident from the terms of the charge brought against him: "We have heard him," say the false witnesses, "speak blasphemous words against Moses and against God." "This man ceaseth not to speak blasphemous words against this holy place and the law." "For we have heard him say that this Jesus of Nazareth shall destroy this place, and shall change the customs which Moses delivered us." Acts vi, 13, 14. It is evident that the words of Stephen are represented in a false light; it is a calumny to accuse him of having blasphemed God or Moses, and of having declared the destruction of the temple by Jesus Christ and his disciples. But it is easy to discern the true beneath the false. Stephen had, doubtless, insisted, in his argument with the formalist Jews, on the transitory character of the old covenant. He may have commented on those discourses in which the Master showed how the Mosaic law was at once accomplished and abolished in himself. He may have repeated the Master's sayings with reference to the true spiritual worship, which has no more need of holy places; and he may have proclaimed the substitution of a new and final order of things for the old and evanescent. In the eyes of the Jews this is his high crime; this is also the glory of his mission. His defense before the Sanhedrim would alone suffice to show to what an elevation he had been raised by the Spirit of God.

At the first glance, Stephen's apology may seem too remote, too far fetched.* It is not immediately evident for what reason he traces in so much detail the history of the Jewish people. All is clear, however, when the drift of his argument is once perceived. In this position, as in all others, Stephen forgets himself, and thinks only of the truth of which he is the organ. He seeks not to be himself acquitted; he desires only to defend well his principles. He cares nothing for himself—the cause of Jesus Christ absorbs him wholly. Thus considered, nothing can be more admirable than his address. He has been charged with blasphemy against Moses and against the institutions and revelations of the old covenant. He proves that the blasphemy and impiety are not on his part, but on the part of his adversaries—the worthy descendants of a rebellious people, which through every stage of its history had

* Baur, "Paulus," 43-45.

received with a hard and uncircumcised heart the unwearying love of God.

Stephen makes good his statement by drawing a broad historic picture, in which he shows, in parallel lines, the goodness of God and the ingratitude of the people of the Jews. We feel that he has ever in view the last and highest manifestation of that ingratitude, and that he perpetually gives to the history a symbolic and prophetic meaning. He brings to mind, first, the origin of the nation and all the promises which rested on its cradle, all the blessings and deliverances which were granted to it in the person of Abraham. This recital shows, on the one hand, how deeply Stephen has been calumniated in the charge of blasphemy against the God of his fathers, and on the other, brings out the guilty obduracy of a people so richly blessed. The largest part of the address is taken up with the history of Moses, and this for the reason, that the contrast between the goodness of God and the unbelief of the chosen people never appeared in characters more strongly marked than at that time. This Moses, chosen to be the deliverer of Israel, miraculously saved by God and visibly prepared for this mission, is rejected by his own people on his first attempt to aid them. Acts vii, 26–29. He meets with the same reception when he returns from the desert, where God has trained him for his great work. Acts vii, 29–35. He has still to contend with the same slowness of heart to believe, after the miracles of the deliverance; and during the very time when he is speaking to God on the mountain, the people give themselves up to abominable idolatry. Who does not see that Moses is set forth by Stephen as a type of Messiah? That his hearers may by no possibility mistake, he calls him a redeemer,* and suddenly in the midst of his narrative, as if to illuminate the whole, he brings in the prophecy in Deuteronomy of the prophet like unto Moses, whom the Lord should raise up. Acts v, 37. Stephen thus transforms his apology into a bold accusation. He shows that if Moses has been blasphemed it has been not by him, but rather by the forefathers of his accusers and by those very accusers themselves, who have treated Jesus Christ as their fathers treated his precursor. Stephen sums up in a few words the later period of the history of his nation. He refers to the building of the temple, without a word of the condemnation with which he had been charged; on the contrary, he sees in it a striking proof of the favor of God toward the family of David. Acts vii, 46–50. He protests only against the gross materialism which has made this temple the national idol: "God dwelleth not," he simply reminds them, "in temples made with hands." The history of the Prophets furnishes him with new proofs of the unbelief of his nation. These heralds of Christ were treated as Christ himself had been treated. At this thought, the indignation long repressed seems to burst in a torrent from his heart, and he concludes his whole address with this tremendous apostrophe: "Ye stiff-necked and uncircumcised in heart and ears, ye do always resist the Holy Ghost: as your fathers did, so do ye." †

* Λυτρωτὴν, Acts vii, 35.

† The address of Stephen shows great freedom in the manner of quoting the Old Testament. Thus, in verse 14, he says that the

Such is the apology of Stephen—so simple, so noble; it contains, in an historic form, ideas the most fresh and sublime, and reveals an important development of Christian thought. And, strange to say, we owe this development to a man who is not an Apostle, and who appears in this crisis superior to the twelve. We have in this fact an irrefragable proof that nothing like a monopoly of revelation was enjoyed by the Apostles.

Fiercely interrupted by the rage of his hearers, Stephen is dragged out of the assembly. The fury of the Jews is so great that all the forms of justice are set aside; he is, in the wild commotion, stoned without a trial. His death is truly sublime.* His countenance beams with a heavenly light. It is the pure radiance of love. A vision of glory is granted him; he dies while breathing pardon on his murderers. His last prayer is addressed distinctly to Jesus Christ, and, by his final homage, he renders dying testimony to his divinity. It was fitting that this great truth should be thus proclaimed by the first of the martyrs—by the man who most fully comprehended the superiority of the new covenant over the old; for Christianity rises above Judaism just in proportion to the

family of Jacob consisted of seventy-five persons, while, according to Genesis xlvi, 27, it numbered only seventy. In verse 16 he says that Abraham bought the sepulcher at Sychem for a sum of money. But, according to Genesis, it was Jacob who did so. Gen. xxxiii, 19. See a beautiful paraphrase in Thiersch of the speech of Stephen. The typical point of view is, however, there given with exaggeration.

* His death is said to have taken place in the year 36, the time of the deposition of Pilate. Such a murder can be more readily understood in an interim of authority; but the sudden excitement of a mob is never stayed by scruples as to legality.

recognition of the divinity of Christ. There was great lamentation over Stephen. The pious men who carried him to his burial with tender respect simply obeyed one of the truest impulses of the human heart. And yet that very sentiment, in an exaggerated form, became subsequently the parent of wretched superstitions, and found its ultimate expression in the adoration of the dust of the martyrs.

The death of Stephen, like that of all the confessors, set to his testimony a truly sacred seal, and gave it redoubled power. It not only served Christianity in a general manner, but specially advanced that truth for which he had given his life. His cause was gained. The glorious thought which had inflamed his zeal was to be caught by a man who stood as yet among the enemies of the Church, but whom God designed to use for the casting down, with a strong hand, of the barrier between Judaism and the Gentile world. This was that young man whom the sacred writer points out to us, holding the garments of them that stoned Stephen. Saul of Tarsus had heard Stephen's defense with the indignation of a Pharisee of the Pharisees, but in the midst of his anger God had darted into his soul one of those piercing goads which cannot long be resisted. The memory of that day never faded from his mind. The redoubling of his persecuting zeal denotes the disquiet of his spirit. Of this we shall find further proof when we trace the story of his conversion. "If Stephen had not prayed," beautifully says Augustine, "the Church had not had Paul." *

* "Si Stephanus non orasset, Ecclesia Paulum non haberet." St. August., "Sermo" XCIV.

The persecution of which Saul of Tarsus was the instigator is an indication of the sudden change in the disposition of the Pharisees toward the Church. This sect, at first favorably disposed, took little part in the first persecution: now it takes the initiative in measures of violence, and soon surpasses the Sadducees in cruelty. In truth, the religious parties which lay their crimes to the charge of God, and pretend to avenge the cause of Heaven, are the most dangerous of all, because they hold themselves bound to no moderation in their transports of rage. The first result of this second persecution was the dispersion of the Christians. They were to learn more than one lesson in this exile. Salutary experience was to give confirmation to the words of Stephen, and the successes gained by the Church on foreign soil were to raise it above the exclusiveness of Judaism.

§ II. *The Dispersion of the Christians. The Gospel in Samaria. Simon Magus. Philip and the Eunuch.*

Persecution, by scattering the Christians, widened at once the field of their missionary activity and the range of their ideas. They went forth to encounter, for the first time, paganism—the eclectic paganism of that age, which united in its vague beliefs the East and the West. This new adversary awaited them in one of the cities of Samaria, to which certain of their number had directed their steps. Samaria was not, indeed, actually a pagan country. Its inhabitants were the descendants of that mixed population, formed of the remnant of the ten tribes and of a colony of foreigners, transplanted by the order of Salmanasar.*

* 2 Kings xvii, 24. Josephus, "Antiq.," Book XI, c. viii, 6.

When the Jews returned from Babylon, the Samaritans sought to take part in the rebuilding of the temple. Ezra iv, 1, 2. They were repelled with indignation. They then resolved to rear a temple to Jehovah on the Mount Gerizim.* The Samaritans shared, like the Jews, in the consequences of the revolutions in Asia Minor. Their temple was destroyed by John Hyrcanus.† But Mount Gerizim continued still to be to them a holy place.‡ They ultimately fell under the dominion of the Romans, and underwent the same political fluctuations as their neighbors. Many causes nurtured the hatred between the two neighboring nations. The Samaritans were wont to repudiate any community of origin with the Jews when they found it their interest to do so. "The Samaritans," says the historian Josephus, "deny their Hebrew origin when the Jews are in distress, but as soon as any prosperity comes to them, they are eager to appeal to their common ancestry in Joseph and Manasseh." ‖ It is easy to understand what a leaven of bitterness such conduct would prove in the hearts of the Jews. These could not forget that, to purchase the favor of Antiochus Epiphanes in a time of pressing peril, the Samaritans had declared that their temple was dedicated to the deities of Greece, and that they themselves practiced Greek rites.§ They had,

* Josephus, "Antiq.," XII, c. i, 1.

† Josephus, "Antiq.," XIII, c. ix.

‡ Josephus, "Antiq.," XIII, c. xiv, 1.

‖ *Εἰσὶ γὰρ τοιοῦτοι τὴν φύσιν, εν μέν ταῖς συμφοραις ὄντας τοὺς Ιουδᾶιους ἀρνοῦνται συγγενεῖς ἔχειν.* Josephus, "Antiq.," Book XI, c. vi.

§ *Τοῖς ἑλληνικοῖς ἔθεσιν αἱροῦνται, χρώμενοι ζῆν.* Josephus, "Antiq.," Book XII, c. v, 5.

however, in truth remained faithful to monotheism. As the great prophetic period had commenced just at the time of their separation from the Jews, they had been utter strangers to the whole of that magnificent development of the old covenant. They acknowledged the Pentateuch only, and, with the exception of a small minority, denied the resurrection of the dead.* It appears, also, from Epiphanes, that the mysticism of the Essenes found some adherents among them.† The Samaritans shared in some measure in the Jewish expectation of Messiah, (John iv, 25,) but their Messianic hopes were even more tainted with materialism than were those of the Jews, at least if we give credit to the few Samaritans who still live among the ruins of their country, and who appear to have faithfully kept the ancient traditions. According to them, Messiah is to reign over all nations, to restore the holy law, to rebuild the temple on Gerizim, and to insure the universal triumph of Moses.‡ The facility with which the magician Simon fascinated the whole Samaritan people with his sorceries is another proof of the earthly nature of their hopes.

We need not here show, (for we have done so elsewhere,) that from the stand-point of natural religion, the magician was the sole Messiah, the only deliverer that could be looked for. For those who have deified nature, the last resource must be her hidden power; pagan dualism, not rising to the conception of moral evil, by conjuring away the effects of the noxious pow-

* "Prophetis non credunt Samaritæ, resurrectionem mortuorum negant." (Origen, "In Numeros," Homily XXV, 1.)

† Epiphan., "Hæres," § 16.

‡ "Die Samariter. Ein Beitrag," by Joseph Grimm, 1854, p. 99.

ers of nature. Magicians had, therefore, an important part to play in these times of religious transition and aspiration. The predominance of oriental ideas, the influence of the Jewish conception of Messiah, all combined to increase their ascendency in these lands. The Samaritans had already yielded to the influence of a false Messiah named Dositheus. The testimonies of Christian antiquity with regard to this man are incomplete and contradictory. According to the oldest witness, Origen, Dositheus, a contemporary of Jesus Christ, declared himself to be the expected Messiah, and even laid claim to the attribute of the Son of God.* It is quite possible that the impostor may have turned to account the impression produced by the Saviour's passing through Samaria. His influence appears to have been maintained for some time, but within a limited circle.† Simon gained a far wider popularity. Legend has borrowed his name, and has invested his history with absurd fables. He even becomes a wholly typical character in some writings of Judaizing heretics of the second century.‡ Justin Martyr supposes him to have come to Rome, and regards him as the founder of a

* Ἔφασκεν ἑαυτὸν εἶναι, τον προφητευόμενον χριστὸν. Orig., "Comment in Johann," viii, 27. Καὶ αὐτος υἷος τοῦ θεοῦ. "Contra Celsus," vi, 17.

† Epiphanes gives us quite another notion. According to him ("Hæres.," 13) Dositheus was a Jew, the founder of the sect of the Sadducees, which passed into Samaria after receiving some check in Judæa; but he has evidently confounded the Dositheus of Origen with the Dositheus of the Talmud. (Grimm, "Die Samarit.," 117.)

‡ In the "Clementines" and the "Recognitiones," Simon represents heresy in general, and primarily St. Paul, who to the Ebionites was the supreme heretic.

new worship, but his assertion is evidently based on an historic error.* Many modern theologians have concluded from these myths that the whole history of Simon was only a tissue of legends. But it contains positive facts, guarantied by the unanimous witness of the Fathers, and confirmed by the recently-discovered writings of Hippolytus. "Simon," we read in the "Philosophoumena," "was of Gitton, a village of Samaria. He was a skillful magician; he sought to pass for God." † He had with him a woman of dissolute life named Helena whom he had found at Tyre, and to whom he allotted a prominent part in his system.‡ As to this system—if a confused medley of incongruous ideas be worthy of such a name—we must distinguish between its original form and the modifications which it underwent after Simon became acquainted with Christianity. As these modifications, however, touched no essential principle, we may fairly seek for its primary idea, in the tolerably complete exposition of his doctrines, contained in the "Philosophoumena" of Hippolytus. We find there valuable fragments of a book, composed, if not by Simon, by one of his immediate

* See Justin Martyr, "Apologia," edition of 1686, p. 69. Justin asserts that in his time the following inscription was to be read at Rome: "Simoni Deo Sancto." But it is now admitted that, instead of *Simoni*, the word is *Semoni*. Semo was the Sabine Hercules worshiped at Rome.

† *Μαγείας ἔμπειρος ὤν θεοποιῆσαι ἑαυτόν ἐπεχείρησε.* "Philosoph.," p. 161, comp. with Justin Martyr, "Apol.," p. 69, and Irenæus, Book I, c. xxiii. We see by the testimony of the "Fathers," that Simon of Gitton cannot be confounded with Simon of Cyprus, also a magician, of whom Josephus speaks. "Antiq.," XX, c. vii, 2.

‡ "Philosoph.," 174.

disciples.* St. Luke tells us that Simon was proclaimed by his followers to be "*the great power of God.*" † The book to which his name is attached gives us the exact meaning of these words. Simon recognized a first, hidden, invisible principle, of which the world is the eternal manifestation.‡ This first principle has two modes of manifestation: it reveals itself first as an active and spiritual, next as a passive and receptive principle. Dualism is thus at the outset clearly stated. § The receptive or passive principle deteriorates perpetually, and finally becomes altogether materialized. The courtesan Helena was the personification of this principle. The mission of Simon the sorcerer was to effect her deliverance, which was to be that of all mankind. He pretended, himself, to represent the active and spiritual principle, and thus to incarnate the great power of God. This sketch of his doctrine will suffice for the present. We shall look at it again under the new and complex form which it assumes, when, by alliance with Christian ideas, it becomes heresy.||

* Bunsen ("Hippolytus," vol. i, 43) proves the authenticity of these fragments, which are found in the "Philosophoumena," p. 163.

† *Οὗτός ἔστιν ἡ δύναμις τοῦ Θεοῦ ἡ καλουμένη μεγάλη.* Acts viii, 10.

‡ "Philosoph.," 163, 90.

§ *Δύο εἰσὶ παραφυάδες τῶν ὅλων αἰώνων ἀπὸ μιᾶς ῥίζης ἥτις ἐστὶ δύναμις, σιγὴ, ἀόρατος ἀκατάληπτος ὢν ἡ μία φαίνεται ἄνωθεν, ἥτις ἐστὶ μεγάλη δύναμις, ἄρσην. Ἡ δὲ ἑτέρα, ἐπίνοια μεγάλη θήλεια.* "Philos.," 173, 60.

|| "Philosoph.," 163, 85. Our exposition of the system of Simon differs at once from that of Neander, ("Pflanzung," i, 79,) and from that of Grimm, ("Samarit.," p. 156.) The former, who could not have any acquaintance with the "Philosophoumena," has too much identified that which Simon called "the great power of God," with the *Word* of Philo. The ideas of the magician are much more incoherent than those of the Alexandrine Gnostic. The system of ema-

We know enough of it to recognize in it the old Phœnician dualism, and the earliest features of Gnostic dualism. It contains the first rough, imperfect outline of the subtle doctrines which were destined to cause so much evil to the Church. The absurdity of the part which Simon allots to himself, the great indecorousness of that which he assigns to a courtesan, are less astonishing when we remember the country in which his strange system was conceived. This country was situated on the borders of that Phrygia which gave birth to the most infamous fables of paganism. Simon may be considered as pre-eminently the false Messiah. He held a doctrine of perdition, but this perdition was not the result of sin, since it was, like matter, eternal and fatal. Nor had salvation in his system any moral character ; it consisted

nation is far from being clearly expressed by him. On the other hand, we cannot share Grimm's opinion that Simon asserted himself to be the supreme and absolute deity. Grimm dwells, in the first place, on the testimony of Justin, who says that the Samaritans regarded him as the first god, ὡς τὸν πρῶτον θέον, (see Hippolytus, "Phil.," p. 161,) and on that of Irenæus, who affirms that Simon was worshiped under the name of Jupiter, ("Hæres.," i, 23.) But these testimonies simply signify that Simon declared himself to be the highest manifestation of the unknown God. We know that in the Greek Theogony Jupiter is not the first of the gods in date ; he comes forth from Saturn, the ancient and primitive deity. Simon pretended to incarnate the first principle emerged from the potential fire, without likening himself to the potential fire itself. The passage in the "Philosophoumena," which we have already quoted, ("Phil.," p. 176, 60,) dispels all doubts in this respect. The "great power of God" is there clearly set forth as the male principle sprung from the eternal root of being. No doubt, in the pantheistic point of view, the eternal and potential principle is found in its manifestations. But the manifestation of a principle cannot be absolutely identified with the principle itself. There is between them a sort of hierarchy and subordination.

only in subtle artifices, and the pretended Saviour was nothing but a magician. Thus, by diabolic art, the desire after redemption, so keenly alive at this period, was miserably cheated. Simon acquired a very great influence over the Samaritan people. He in a manner bewitched them.

It might be foreseen that the same vague aspiration which impelled the multitude eagerly to follow Simon, would make it attentive to the preaching of the Gospel. Such was the actual result when Philip, driven from Jerusalem by the persecution, preached Christ to the Samaritans, and confirmed his word by signs and wonders ; the people at once forsook the impostor, and thronged to hear the word of truth.

Simon, like a cunning tactician, followed the multitude, in the hope of regaining his authority. He was baptized with his former adherents. The Apostles, who had remained at Jerusalem, hearing of the success of Philip's preaching, sent two of their number into this new and fruitful field of labor. They chose Peter and John, who up to this time had displayed the greatest activity in the primitive Church. This decision was most wise : Philip had very probably suggested it in his letters. The work was too wide and important for his unaided efforts ; it was natural that those who had shown the greatest missionary zeal should come to his assistance. Peter and John, as soon as they arrive in Samaria, witness, in answer to their prayer, a descent of the Holy Ghost upon the Samaritan neophytes. The defenders of the hierarchy magnify this fact ; but in order to raise it to the height of a principle and general rule, it is needful to show that during the whole apostolic period the Holy Ghost never chose any other medium than the Apostles or their immediate delegates. Now it is certain that the Holy Spirit was often given to the new converts without their concurrence.* The wind bloweth where it listeth, and the grace of God is not confined to any official channel. If the Holy Spirit was not given to the Samaritans until after the arrival of Peter and John, we hold, with Neander, that the cause must have been a purely moral one. Their preaching rapidly developed the germ of the new life in the neophytes of Sychar, who had possibly at first embraced Christianity only in outward form. It is surely more honorable to the Apostles to suppose the results to have been wrought by the living power of their words, than by any outward and material act—the transmission of some mysterious, magnetic fluid from their persons. Such theories are truly derogatory, and lower the Apostles to the rank of the magicians, whose power they were come to destroy.

Simon betrayed in these circumstances the secret of his heart. By offering to buy the gift of God, he showed that he, like so many since his day, had confounded grace with magic; and it is just that the abominable traffic in holy things should bear his name. We see him for one moment trembling under

* Is it not evident that the Ethiopian eunuch baptized by Philip received the Holy Ghost in the desert? The conversion of St. Paul was completed at Damascus, and it was Ananias who conferred the baptism upon him with the laying on of his hands, after the scales were fallen from his eyes, in token of the inward illumination which could be the work only of the Holy Spirit. Acts ix, 18.

the tremendous rebuke of the Apostle. But history shows us that his repentance had no root. He was the founder of the first heresy. Legend says that he came to Rome, and there ignominiously died. It is possible that in the great confluence of East and West he may have been found in that capital of the world where all creeds met, and all impostors left their track. But this sojourn of Simon at Rome is not verified by any authentic document. In him Christianity encountered the father of Gnosticism and of heresy. The numerous legends which cling around his name reveal the terror he inspired.*

The foundation of the Christian Church in Samaria had a very happy effect upon the growth and expansion of Christian thought. Not only did the Jews cherish the strongest antipathy to the Samaritans, but they had raised a barrier of legal prescriptions of extreme severity between themselves and their hated neighbors. The Gospels give us numerous proofs of this fact. The most injurious name which the enemies of Christ can find for him is that of a Samaritan. John viii, 48. The woman of Sychar is amazed that a Jew will dare to converse with her. John declares positively that the Jews have no dealings with the Samaritans. John iv, 9. The Talmud shows that it is forbidden for an Israelite to break bread with a Samaritan: "He who takes the bread of a

* In the "Act. Pauli et Petri," Simon dies, the victim of a rash challenge. He had promised to rise to heaven. St. Peter, with a word, made him fall to the earth crushed before the eyes of Nero. ("Act. Pauli et Petri," 33, Tischendorf edit.) According to the "Philosophoumena," he had himself shut up in a tomb at Rome, declaring that he would rise again the third day. "But," adds Hippolytus, "he remains there until now." "Philosoph.," p. 176.

Samaritan is like him who eats the flesh of swine. No Israelite may receive a Samaritan as a proselyte; this accursed people shall have no part in the resurrection of the dead."* Thus the Apostles, when they went to preach the Gospel in Samaria, must needs have risen above the most inveterate prejudices of their nation. It was a great step toward realizing the true breadth of Christianity. The preaching addressed to the Samaritans was to lead them, by a transition of the Saviour's own appointing, to carry the Gospel throughout the whole world. The primitive Church thus entered upon the path opened by Stephen, and his martyrdom bore its first-fruits.

Peter and John return to Jerusalem, while the Deacon Philip is called, by a new manifestation of the will of God, yet further to extend the field of Christian missions. It is not a Samaritan, but a pagan, whom he next instructs in the truth. In crossing the desert which leads to Gaza, a city of the ancient Philistines, he meets with a stranger, who, as he journeys, is reading in his chariot a portion of the Scriptures. He was an Ethiopian eunuch, a great dignitary of the court of Meroë, treasurer of the Queen.† This man, a pagan by birth, had taken a long journey to worship the true God in the temple at Jerusalem.‡ Whatever might have been his religious character, he could never, as a eunuch, have passed the door of the

* Grimm, "Die Samarit.," pp. 109, 110.

† According to Pliny, the name of Candace was a dynastic name. ("Hist. Nat.," vi, 35.)

‡ Eusebius, "H. E.," ii, 1. The fact that he was reading the Scriptures cannot prove, as Olshausen asserts, that he was a Jew, for he might easily have them in the Greek version, then widely diffused.

congregation of the people of God. Deut. xxiii, 1. He was, perhaps, only a proselyte of the gate. But his soul, full of holy aspiration, was already open to the Gospel. He was reading that sublime chapter, Isaiah liii, in which the sufferings of Messiah are depicted in traits so touching and so true. Philip, by a few words of explanation, removes all his doubts, and carries conviction home to his heart. He eagerly embraces the truth. He becomes without delay a disciple of Jesus Christ, and without any consideration of Jewish practice, he receives baptism. "He found more," eloquently says Jerome, "in the desert fountain of the Church than in the gilded temple of the synagogue."* This scene, which was enacted far from human eyes in the depths of the desert solitude, is inimitably beautiful. It reveals the dispensation by which God seeks out in all places the soul which is seeking him, and leads his Church into full liberty by the exercise of his love.†

§ III. *Foundation of the Church at Antioch, and Conversion of the Centurion Cornelius.*

The dispersion of the Christians not only carried the Gospel into Samaria, but into the surrounding countries. Its seeds were scattered in many cities. Damascus, so important both from its geographical position and from its history, contained within its

* "Plus in deserto fonte Ecclesiæ reperuit quam in aurato synagogæ templo." (St. Jerome, "Eph.," ciii.)

† The old historians of the Church (Eusebius, "H. E.," ii, 1) attribute to the converted eunuch a great share in the mission carried on in his country. Ethiopia was not, however, won to the Church till the fourth century, by the preaching of Frumentius and Edesius. Still, it is possible the efforts of the eunuch may not have been fruitless.

walls a strong Jewish colony. It is not surprising that Christianity should have there early gathered a large number of adherents, and that its progress should have alarmed the Sanhedrim. Acts ix, 2. The new religion had also disciples at Lydda and Joppa, maritime towns of Phœnicia. Acts ix, 35,36. Some unknown Christians had even carried it into the Isle of Cyprus, so famous for its worship of Venus; they had thus planted the religion of holiness in one of the most infamous hot-beds of pagan corruption. Acts xi, 19. But in all these different places the new faith had been cradled in the synagogue. It had not yet come into direct contact with the pagan world; its first step in this direction was taken at Samaria, the second was at Antioch. The foundation of the Church of that city is a leading event, the consequences of which to the early Church were incalculable. Antioch, the ancient residence of the Kings of Syria, built on the banks of the river Orontes, in a fertile plain, had become one of the capitals of pagan civilization, one of the great centers where East and West mingled their brilliant and refined culture. The beauty of its buildings, its large population, its wide commerce, its artistic advancement and its wealth, made it, according to Josephus, the third city in the empire.* It was, on the testimony of Cicero, a city where men of cultivation abounded and where the liberal arts flourished.† The Jews had there, as in all other places, founded a colony, but the Christian mission did not confine itself within the bounds of

* Josephus, "Bell. Judaic," Book III, c. xxiv.

† "Celeber quondam urbs et copiosa, atque eruditissimis hominibus liberalissimisque studiis affluens." Cicero "Pro. Arch. Poeta," c. iii.

the synagogue. It was undertaken by some of those Hellenist Jews who had been converted on the day of Pentecost. The Gospel was preached at Antioch by disciples from Cyprus and from Cyrene, (Acts xi, 19, 20; comp. Acts ii, 10,) who belonged to the most liberal section of the Church at Jerusalem, and who had probably been especially attached to Stephen. The direct inheritors of the great thought which had animated the proto-martyr, they perceived, as he had done, that the new covenant rested upon a wider basis than the old. Thus they went at once to the heathen. "They spake unto the Grecians, preaching the Lord Jesus." Acts xi, 20. These were soon converted in large numbers, and the first Church outside of Judaism was founded. Thus the world's gates were opened to the Christian mission—those gates which, until then, Jewish prejudice had kept closed. From this day the new religion takes its true position; it invites Hellenism as freely as Judaism, the West no less than the East, and it rises for the first time to the comprehension of those words of the Master, "The field is the world." On the other hand, the foundation of the Church at Antioch foreshadows the transformation, or rather the development, of the primitive apostolate. It was founded without the assistance of the twelve Apostles. The opinion that Peter was the first Bishop of Antioch has no foundation,* and

* The tradition which attributes to Peter the foundation and government of the Church at Antioch is of very ancient date. Eusebius records it, ("H. E.," ii, 36,) and St. Jerome also ("De viris illustribus, 1;) and Origen confirmed it in these words: "Ignatium dico episcopum Antiochiæ post Petrum secundum." ("In Luc.," Homily VI, vol. iii.) The "Liber Pontificalis" only copies the "Fathers," as does Baronius, ("Annals," i, 245,) and with him all the Catholic

must be ascribed to episcopal preconceptions. According to St. Luke, the Church at Antioch owed its origin to the Hellenist Jews of Cyprus and Cyrene; the Church at Jerusalem did not send an Apostle to it, but a simple Evangelist, Barnabas. God designed thus to show that the apostolate of the twelve was not the only and necessary channel of his grace, but that Christian activity, putting forth its strength and evidencing its lawfulness by great and splendid results, received in those very results divine sanction. This new apostolate is conferred directly by the Holy Spirit, and is independent of any special institution. Stephen had already been invested with it; St. Paul was soon to unite in one person all its gifts, and to claim all its privileges; the Church was destined to see it perpetuated from age to age, less richly endowed, but still powerful to reform and to renew.*

The Church of Antioch was early distinguished for the abundance of its extraordinary gifts. It had numerous prophets. The new religion, released from the restraints of Judaism, there expanded in all its freedom and beauty. At Antioch it first became known by its true name. This was doubtless given

writers, (Lenain de Tillemont, "Mémoires," i, p. 167.) But the silence of the writer of the Acts invalidates all these witnesses. We shall show presently that the episcopate did not exist at this period. The origin of the legend is easily explicable. Episcopal notions soon necessitated the retrospective regularization of the Church at Antioch. From a hierarchical point of view it was impossible to adhere to the narrative in the Acts, which attributed the foundation of that Church to mere Evangelists. It was known that Peter had at the same period traveled into the neighboring countries. What more natural than to make him the first Bishop of Antioch?

* See Baumgarten, "Die Apost. Kirche von Jerusalem bis Rom.," i, p. 257.

it by the multitude, who witnessed its development and progress. The name *Christian* showed the dawning comprehension that the Church was not simply a Jewish sect. No one at Jerusalem, seeing the disciples in the temple, had thought of seeking for them a new name. This new name revealed the greatness of the revolution just wrought. It is important to observe that the earliest Church called out of the midst of paganism was the first to bear it. It was also from Antioch, as we shall see, that Paul set forth on his missionary journeys. Antioch was, in a manner, the Jerusalem of the Gentile world.

At this very time the Apostle Peter was led, by a miraculous dispensation of God, to shake off the yoke of Jewish exclusiveness. Notwithstanding the success of his mission in Samaria, he had not abjured his old notions; he still thought that all the prescriptions of the Mosaic law were in force. It was of the utmost importance that the Apostle whose activity and influence were paramount at this period, should be won over to the cause of a world-wide Christianity. God brought about this result in a most remarkable manner, by the coincident illumination of a special revelation and of personal experience. There lived at this time in the town of Cæsarea a Roman centurion named Cornelius, belonging to the Italian cohort, which maintained in those countries the authority of Rome. A heathen by birth, but conscious, like so many of his contemporaries, of unsatisfied religious needs, Cornelius had, from his first contact with the synagogue, forsaken the worship of false gods, and embraced the Jewish faith. Acts x, 1. But he had not found even in it satisfaction of heart. His upright and pious soul sought and required a more complete response to its cravings. It is probable that Cornelius may have already heard of the new religion and of St. Peter, for the angel who appears to him merely mentions the name of the Apostle, and Cornelius understands without further explanation. The vague rumor of Christianity which had reached him had perhaps rendered his prayers more fervent. However this may be, as he was in prayer, he suddenly saw in a vision an angel of God, who told him that his prayers were heard, and bade him send for the Apostle Peter. Acts x, 3–8. At the same moment Peter, who was at Joppa, received a revelation which was to prepare him to accede to the request of Cornelius.

This revelation seems, at the first glance, to have reference only to the distinction between clean and unclean animals. Acts x, 10–17. But all the institutions of Judaism were closely connected. The distinction between animals rested on the same principle as the distinction between days, places, and men. Till redemption had been wrought out, the original taint infected every thing in a world under the curse. It was only by exception that certain men, certain days, certain fruits of the ground, certain animals, were raised in part above the universal defilement. The Jewish people was the only fraction of humanity which was not profane; the distinction between the clean and unclean animals symbolized, therefore, one far more important, namely, the distinction between men. When Peter says, "I have never eaten any thing common or unclean," he speaks as a Jew; he is pointing to the legal distinction between men and things. The reply which he receives shows him the meaning of the new covenant. God, by the blood of redemption, has in truth purified all that was defiled. The distinction between a holy people and an unholy race is done away, like that between animals clean and unclean; and thus Peter may and must go and preach the Gospel to Cornelius the Roman.

We know what were the results of his preaching. The miracle of Pentecost was wrought afresh on these converts from heathenism, and Peter exclaimed, "Can any man forbid water, that these should not be baptized, which have received the Holy Ghost as well as we? Acts x, 47. In these words he boldly proclaimed Christianity to be wide as the world. The death of Stephen was bearing its fruits, and a career, wide as the world, was opening to apostolic missions. Paul had only to go forth into it. Thus the Church made progress, step by step, in its path of light, guided by the Holy Spirit, and taught by the lessons of experience. Revelation seemed at the same moment to come down from heaven, and to spring up in human hearts; so true is it that the Spirit of God, ever secure of attaining its ends without the aid of magic, never consents to do violence to that noblest of instruments, human freedom. But though gained at Antioch and at Cæsarea, the cause of Gentile Christianity was not yet triumphant at Jerusalem. We must now follow the discussion which arose on the conversion of the Centurion Cornelius.*

* Difficulties have been raised about the liberal action of Peter at Cæsarea and the timidity subsequently shown by him at Antioch,

§ IV. *The Church at Jerusalem at the time of the First Mission beyond Judæa.*

The Christians who had remained at Jerusalem had experienced no change in their religious convictions. They had taken no part in the missionary work in Samaria, Antioch, and Cæsarea. Living in the center of Judaism, in the immediate neighborhood of the temple, where they daily offered the sacrifices commanded by the law, it would cost them much to shake off their national prejudices. Thus they learned with astonishment that Peter had entered the house of a Gentile, had eaten with him, and treated him as a brother. They reproached him sharply. "Thou wentest in," they said, "unto men uncircumcised, and didst eat with them." Acts XI, 3. In other words: "Thou hast trampled under foot the most sacred prescriptions of the law; thou hast denied the religion of thy fathers, which, as a fundamental principle, commands absolute separation from strangers." Peter replied to the charge by an account of the conversion of Cornelius and of the foregoing revelations, setting before his brethren the same effectual demonstration which God had used to convince him, and which is the sovereign lŏgic of One whose word gives its own translation in marvelous and undeniable miracles. What answer could there be to such arguments, powerfully summed up in the words, "Forasmuch then as God gave them the like gift as he did unto us, who believed on

when he was reproved by St. Paul. From this contradiction it has been attempted to draw arguments against the authenticity of the narrative. Surely this is to lose sight of the inconsistency so characteristic of all human actions.

the Lord Jesus Christ, what was I, that I could withstand God?" Acts xi, 17. The Christians at Jerusalem were convinced. It must not be supposed, however, that the question was finally settled, and all dissent made impossible. We must ever remember the instability of the human mind, its vacillations and inconsistencies. First impressions rapidly wear off, and others come in their stead. The sacred story, by preserving the trace of these fluctuations of opinion in the primitive Church, gives a strong proof of its historical truthfulness. Let us further observe that the admission of Gentiles into the Church did not necessarily involve the complete abrogation of all distinctions of nationality under the new law. It was necessary to know if circumcision was or was not obligatory on all the new converts. This was the point of the question, and it was not yet ripe for solution. The acute dialectics of Paul, the broad discussions of the Council at Jerusalem, and the ardent polemics of the succeeding period, were all needed before its final decision.

The simple machinery of the primitive Church had just been completed at Jerusalem. A new office had been created—that of elders. Acts xi, 30. It is of great moment to us to determine exactly its origin and its functions; only by this means can we judge fairly the pretensions of the various ecclesiastical systems. The office of elder was not without precedent. We find it in those numerous synagogues in which the Jews, distant from Jerusalem, met on the Sabbath to read the Scriptures. We have elsewhere spoken of the simple and democratic constitution of the synagogues. Each one was governed by a sort of senate or council, whose authority was much like that of the judges appointed in each town on the conquest of the promised land. Deut. xvi, 18. The functions of this council were clearly defined. It was to regulate authoritatively all matters relating to worship, and was not restricted to simply administrative measures. The reading and explanation of the holy books belonged by right to its members. These were called "*zakanim*," or elders. This appellation, we learn from positive statements, indicated not so much maturity of age as of wisdom and intellectual merit.* The council of the synagogue had a president, called the ruler of the synagogue, or master, or rabbi; his influence was very great wherever the council was small, as in towns where there was but an insignificant colony of Jews.† But the ruler of the synagogue had no peculiar dignity which raised him above his colleagues in the hierarchy. He was the first among his peers, *primus inter pares*. Unquestionable passages prove that the same synagogue often had several rulers or presidents.‡ All the

* "Nullus est senex nisi qui sibi acquisivit sapientiam." Vitringa, "De Synag.," III, c. i, p. 616.

† Vitringa, II, 10.

‡ In Matt. ix, 18, we read of one of the rulers of the synagogue. So in Acts xviii, 8, 17, the rulers of the synagogue are mentioned at Corinth, where there was only one synagogue. (Vitringa "De Synag. Vetere," pp. 584, 585.) See also Justin Martyr, "Dial. cum Trypho," p. 366. *Ὁποῖα διδάσκουσιν οἱ Ἀρχισυνάγωγοι ὑμῶν μετὰ τὴν προσευχήν.* Traces of this identity of the rulers of the synagogue and the elders are met with in the "Theodosian Code." There we find these words: "Neque licentiam habebunt hi qui ab iis majores omnibus *Archiphericitæ* aut *presbyteri*, forsitan vel *magistri*, appellantur anathematismis hoc prohibere." Vitringa, "De Synagog. Vetere," page 590.

elders probably occupied the position in turn. Such an organization was essentially democratic ; it presents no analogy with the Levitical priesthood, or the episcopacy of the third century.

When we read in the Acts of the Apostles, without further explanation, that the Church of Jerusalem appointed for itself elders, it is clear that the office in question must be one already known, and the name of which would convey distinct ideas. Had it been otherwise, the sacred historian would have used a new word to designate an entirely new institution ; he certainly would not have connected the sacerdotal hierarchy in the Church with the democratic rule of the synagogue, when it would have been so easy to borrow from the Jewish priesthood its honorable titles. To suppose, as do the advocates of hierarchical theories, that the first elders were probably the first converted priests, who received a fresh ordination from the hands of the Apostles, is to build the whole sacerdotal system upon a pure hypothesis.*

The sacred historian gives no details of the nomination of the first elders. We may hence conclude that there was no formal institution of the office. The Apostles were often called away from Jerusalem. The young Church, though richly supplied with the gifts of the Spirit, could not dispense with some direction in its daily progress and in its worship. The wisest step was to borrow from the synagogue the institution of elders, so admirably adapted to the new dispensation. Besides, the seven deacons first appointed had been more than deacons. They had taught with power, and

* Thiersch, work quoted, p. 78.

fulfilled by anticipation the office of elders. Just as the diaconate had grown out of the apostolate, so the office of elders was in part an offshoot from the primitive diaconate, and thus the organization of the Church went on perfecting itself by the division of labor. The Apostles gave their sanction to the creation of the new office, but the narrative contains no trace of any solemn institution or special revelation. The Church had, in this respect, no other revelation to await than that of its own needs. It was not creating either a priesthood or a clergy, but simply a ministry adapted to the spirit of the new dispensation. It was doubtless acting in obedience to its guiding inspiration, but no direct intervention of God was necessary, as though a new priesthood was to be instituted. It is beyond question that the elders, like the deacons, were chosen by the whole assembly. Their part in the Church at Jerusalem cannot be exactly defined: they formed its council; they directed without coercing it; they read and explained the Scriptures, at times when no extraordinary gifts were manifested. In the second period of the apostolic age we shall find their functions assuming more importance. At that stage, also, the question of the identity of the bishop and the elder will come before us for solution. At Jerusalem, as in all the Churches of Jewish origin, elders alone were known. The name bishop appears only in the Churches of Greek origin.

Side by side with the elders we find the prophets. The gift of prophecy was distinguished from the other operations of the Spirit by its sudden and powerful character. The prophets of the primitive

Church were not called only to communicate to the Church revelations as to the future, such as those put into the mouth of Agabus. Acts xi, 28. Like the prophets of the Old Testament, they addressed themselves to the hearts and consciences of their hearers; the prophetic character manifested itself in the remarkable efficacy of their words. Barnabas, placed among the prophets, had been surnamed "The Son of Consolation." Edifying and consoling sermons were thus accounted as prophecies when they were accompanied with peculiar power.*

A short time after the return of Peter to Jerusalem persecution broke out anew, raised this time, not by the priests or the rabbis, but by the King, Herod Agrippa; it was employed by him as a means of gaining popularity. This prince succeeded in uniting under his scepter all the countries over which his uncle, Herod the Great, had reigned. Having crept to the throne by flattery, he kept his seat by the same means, servilely pandering to vulgar prejudices. The time was gone when the Church was in favor with all the people; persecution was beginning to become popular; it was to retain this character during three centuries, for nothing is more odious to the great mass of men than the law of holiness when its requirements are once rightly understood. James, the son of Zebedee, was beheaded by the King's commandment. Acts xii, 1, 2. He was the first apostle-martyr. His place was not filled up. Eusebius relates, on the authority of Clement of Alexandria, an incident of his martyrdom, which we see no reason to discredit. The false witness, who

* Neander, "Pflanz.," p. 59.

had deposed against James, was touched by the sight of the courage and constancy of the Apostle; he avowed himself a Christian, and was visited with the same sentence. As he was being led forth with James to death, he asked his forgiveness. The Apostle looked at him for some moments, then embracing him, said, "Peace be with thee." Both perished together by the sword.*

Herod was anxious next to strike a blow at the Apostle who had most powerfully drawn upon himself the attention of the people, and had thus enkindled the most bitter hatred. He caused Peter to be thrown into prison and condemned to speedy death. The alarmed disciples gathered in the house of Mary, the mother of Mark, to entreat help from God in this terrible crisis. Threatened with a blow which would overturn one of the pillars of the Church, they lift up earnest prayers to Heaven. Suddenly Peter himself, delivered by a miracle, knocks at the door of the house, and comes to teach them the omnipotence of prayer, which they were yet slow to believe, as their incredulity of his presence proves. Soon after Herod died, smitten with righteous judgment from God. He had gone to Cæsarea to decide some differences with the inhabitants of Tyre and Sidon, and to celebrate games in honor of the recovery of Claudius. He was received with the utmost enthusiasm. Appearing on the second day of the games arrayed in a silver tunic, on which the rays of the early morning shed a dazzling brightness, he excited universal admiration, and his flatterers even carried

*'Ο *δὲ ὀλίγον σκεψάμενος, εἰρήνη σοὶ εἶπε, καὶ κατεφίλησεν αὐτόν.* Eusebius, "Hist. Eccl.," ii, 9.

their adulation so far as to call him a god. In that very moment he was smitten with a loathsome disease; eaten of worms, he died, exclaiming, "I, the god, am about to die; death has already seized him whom men called immortal." * This event produced a deep impression upon the Church, which saw in it the direct intervention of God for its protection and the chastisement of its enemies.

According to tradition, St. Peter went to Rome after his deliverance, and the excitement caused in the Jewish colony by his preaching provoked the severe measures taken by Claudius against the Jews.† But the presence of Peter in the Council at Jerusalem, which took place very shortly after, disproves this assertion. He probably continued to preach the Gospel through all the regions of Asia Minor, where his influence was still so great during the following period. The defenders of the hierarchy affirm that after the persecution under Herod Agrippa, the Apostles divided the world among them, and drew their field of labor by lot.‡ To what

* *Καὶ ὁ κληθεὶς ἀθάνατος ἤδη θανὼν ἀπάγομαι.* Josephus, "Antiq.," XIX, c. viii, 2. Josephus states that Herod, at the moment he was hailed as a god, saw a screech-owl, which he regarded as an omen of evil.

† Thiersch's work quoted, p. 97. Baronius, "Annals," i, 273. Lenain de Tillemont (i, p. 70) places the journey of the Apostle to Rome before his imprisonment; but how then explain the silence of the Acts? The testimony of the "Fathers" on this point is altogether wanting in precision. Eusebius, (ii, 14, 15,) in order to prove the presence of Peter at Rome in the time of Claudius, rests upon the tradition (proved to be untrue) of his contest with Simon Magus. The "Liber Pontificalis" declares explicitly that he did not go to Rome under Claudius. "Hic Petrus ingressus in urbem Romam sub Nerone Cæsare."—"Liber Pontificalis," p. 11.

‡ Leo, "Sermo," I. Baronius, "Annals," i, 273.

lengths will not the desire lead to paint the past with the colors of the present, and to substitute for the spirituality of the early days an official character and the machinery of a hierarchy! It is not possible to go further than this in the untrue rendering of facts. The opinion which attributes to the Apostles, at the same time, the compilation of the creed which bears their name, is equally without foundation. The day of Pentecost was not yet far enough removed for the reduction of faith to rule.

The same preconception, and the same disposition to transfer the institutions of the third century of the Church into the first, have led to an imaginary recognition of the episcopate in the entirely moral preeminence which James,* the Lord's brother, enjoyed

* The question whether James, the Lord's brother, is another than James the son of Alpheus, one of the twelve Apostles, is one of the most controverted points of criticism. In maintaining the identity of the two it is urged that James the son of Alpheus, being clearly related to Jesus Christ, through his mother, (John xix, 25,) the name of brother may be only an extension of the term of kindred. Galatians i, 19, is also brought forward, in which James, the brother of the Lord, is named among the Apostles. But these reasons appear to us insufficient. It is evidently a dogmatic bias which has led to the attempt to change the natural signification of the word ἀδελφός. As to the designation "Apostle," applied by St. Paul to James, it presents no difficulty if the gradual extension of the ideas of the apostolate be admitted. The oldest tradition in the Church favors our opinion: it represents James as the Lord's own brother. Eusebius ("Hist. Eccl.," ii, 25) is as explicit as possible upon this point. James, in his Epistle, does not describe himself as an Apostle. John says that the Lord's brethren had not believed on him when James, the son of Alpheus, was already in the ranks of the Apostles. John vii, 5. Finally, in Acts i, 13, 14, the brethren of the Lord are distinctly mentioned in addition to the Apostles, consequently they were not one and the same. See Winer "Realworterbuch," vol. i, p. 217.

in the Church at Jerusalem. This, however, is capable of a most simple explanation. His relationship to Jesus Christ had an inestimable value in the eyes of the first Christians, who felt themselves under no obligation to repudiate the natural and indestructible feelings of the human heart. The character of James, his piety, and the very form which it assumed, all contributed to increase his influence at Jerusalem. Profoundly attached to the religion of his fathers, he had watched, not without alarm, the first contests between Jesus Christ and the representatives of the ancient worship. He had only gradually learned to take broader views; the resurrection of the Saviour seems to have vanquished his latent hesitation; but this hesitation did not spring from pride or obstinacy; his scruples were those of a strong but unenlightened piety, which was startled by any change introduced into the order established by God. The testimony concerning James of an old historian of the Church gives us a key to the position he filled. "James, the brother of the Lord," we read in Eusebius, who quotes Hegesippus,* "known universally by the surname of 'The Just,' shared with the Apostles the direction of the Church. He was holy from his mother's womb. He drank neither wine nor strong drink, and abstained from all meat. . . . He alone might enter into the holy place;† for his raiment was simply of linen. He was accustomed to go into the temple alone. There he was found prostrate before God, seeking forgiveness for the sins of the people. His knees were

* Διαδέχεται τὴν ἐκκλησίαν. "Hist. Eccl.," ii, 23.

† Τοὺτῳ μόνῳ εξῆν εἰς τὰ ἂγια εἰσιέναι. "Hist. Eccl.," ii, 23.

worn like those of a camel, so constantly were they bent before God in intercession for the people. Because of the excellence of his justice he was surnamed 'The Just,' the *Oblias*,* which signifies the bulwark of the people, and righteousness." Those who pretend that Christianity was originally very little distinguished from Judaism lay much stress on this passage.† They forget that Hegesippus is unfolding before us the whole life of James from his childhood to his death. Set apart as a Nazarite from his earliest years, he adhered scrupulously to the practices of the sect. But there is nothing in the description of Hegesippus to forbid the supposition that after his conversion he may have used greater freedom, though he, with the whole Church of Hebrew origin, continued to observe the institutions of Moses. His conduct in the Council at Jerusalem, and his Epistle, abundantly prove that, in his view, the Christian was not in all points like the Nazarite. It is, nevertheless, certain that he remained in heart attached to Judaism, and that the new religion was primarily, in his eyes, a fulfillment of prophecy. His patriotism was wholly unlike that of the proud Pharisees of the time, for he was best known by his fervent prayers for Jerusalem, and his tears over the sins of his people. He was a determined enemy of false Judaism, a true child of Abraham, one of those who yearned for the divine Isaac. None was a more forcible preacher of repentance than he. James was, in a manner, the John the

* Διὰ τὴν ὑπερβυλὴν τῦς δικαιοσύνης αὐτοῦ ἐκαλεῖτο Δίκαιος καὶ Ὠβλιάς. Ibid.

† Schwegler, "Nachapost. Zeitalt.," i, 137.

Baptist of the apostolic age—a new forerunner making the paths straight for the law of liberty. He was a Jew after God's own heart, gladly accepting the realization of his promises, and thus accomplishing the transition from Judaism to Christianity. He is, in fact, the purest type we have of the Israelite indeed; he thus truly belongs to the new covenant, the mission of which is to bring to perfection all that existed in germ in the old. The Lord's brother repeats, in his life, the Sermon on the Mount; by holiness he prepared the way for progress, freeing the law of the spirit from the law of the letter, as the ripened grain shakes off the enveloping husk.

It is not then necessary, in order to explain the influence of such a man, to have recourse to apostolic investiture.* Respected and beloved by the people, who witnessed his zeal in the temple, he exercised great moral authority over the Church at Jerusalem, of which he was in truth the representative. According to Clement of Alexandria, James was like a ruler of the synagogue in the Church at Jerusalem—that is to say, the first among his equals. It is probable that he obtained this consideration by the sole ascendency of his piety. Hegesippus clearly states that he took part in the government of the Church at the same time with Peter and John. His right was equal to theirs; and it did not need for its exercise either a constituted hierarchy or apostolic succession.

The Church at Jerusalem continues, during this period, a religious center for all the Christians. From it go forth the first missionaries; it sends

* This is the assumption of Thiersch.

spontaneously delegates into the countries where the Gospel has already gained some ground, as in Samaria and at Antioch. In later times important conferences on the question of the admission to baptism of Gentile converts will be held within it. It could hardly have been otherwise in the first period. This central position resulted from the situation of the new Churches, from their weakness and inexperience. But it would be a grave misconception to regard Jerusalem as the Rome of the first century; this would be to forget altogether the difference of the times.

We have seen, after the brief phase of the Church's history when all was miraculous and supernatural, the commencement of internal division. The teaching and martyrdom of Stephen, the mission in Samaria, the formation of the Church at Antioch, the conversion of Cornelius, all these events, which followed each other rapidly, brought into full view the question of the relations of Christianity with Judaism. The discussion is to take still broader ground, through the influence of St. Paul; it will be at times envenomed by the evil passions of the false teachers of Galatia and the schismatics of Corinth, but we shall see it, nevertheless, steadily advancing to its solution, by means of wholesome experience and brotherly consultations, in which the free and living character of the inspiration of the new covenant will strikingly appear; but we shall find no radical opposition between the disputants; and the theories which suppose two irreconcilable forms of Christianity in the apostolic Church will prove to be as fabulous as the legends of tradition.

CHAPTER III.

CONVERSION OF PAUL. HIS FIRST MISSION.

§ I. *Saul of Tarsus. His Preparation and Conversion.*

EVERY great truth which is to win a triumphant way must become incarnate in some one man, and derive from a living, fervent heart that passion and power which constrain and subdue. So long as it remains in the cold region of mere ideas it exercises no mighty influence over mankind. The truths of religion are not exceptions to this law. God, therefore, prepared a man who was to represent, in the primitive Church, the great cause of the emancipation of Christianity, and whose mission it was to free it completely from the bonds of the synagogue. This man was St. Paul, and never had noble truth a nobler organ. He brought to its service an heroic heart, in which fervent love was joined to indomitable courage, and a mind equally able to rise to the loftiest heights of speculation and to penetrate into the deepest recesses of the human soul. All these great qualities were enhanced by absolute devotedness to Jesus Christ, and a self-abnegation such as, apart from the sacrifice of the Redeemer, has had no parallel upon earth. His life was one perpetual offering up of himself. His sufferings have contributed, no less than his indefatigable activity, to the triumph of his principles. Standing ever in the breach for their defense—subject to most painful contradictions, not only from the Jews, but from his brethren—execrated by his own nation—maligned by a fanatic and intolerant section of the Church, and threatened with death by those Gentiles whose claims he so boldly advocated—he suffered as scarcely any other has suffered in the service of truth; but he left behind a testimony most weighty and powerful, every word sealed with the seal of the martyr. Paul was the first missionary to the Gentile world, and he thus effectually inaugurated the universal triumph of Christianity. It was needful that the door of the Church should be opened to the thousands of proselytes from Corinth, Athens, Ephesus, and Rome, who came up to it and knocked. But the great Apostle of the Gentiles was not satisfied with this irresistible argument from facts; he added to it reasoning equally able and eloquent, and, armed with dialectics perfectly adapted to the habits of mind of his opponents, he victoriously established his principles.

The epistles in which these reasonings have in part come down to us, bear on every page the impress of his heart and mind; they show us the whole man, and the very style depicts in vivid characters his moral physiognomy. His polemics are especially admirable, because with him a negation always leads to a weightier affirmation; he never destroys without replacing, and, like his Master, abolishes only by fulfilling. He is not only an incomparable dialectician in the subversion of error, but he is able also to discern all the consequences of a truth, and to grasp its marrow and inner substance. This great controversialist is, therefore, at the same time, the first representative of that true Christian mysticism which St. John was so fully to develop. St. Paul triumphed over Judaism only by putting in its place Christianity in all its breadth and beauty. What holiness, strength, nobleness of character he displayed in the course of his ministry will appear as we trace his history. St. Paul is the type of the reformer in the Church; in every fresh struggle for the Church's freedom, his will be the track in which courageous Christians will follow. No true reformation can be wrought in any spirit other than that of Paul—a spirit equally removed from the timidity which preserves that which should be destroyed, and the rashness which destroys that which should be preserved.

When God is forming a powerful instrument for the accomplishment of his designs, the process of preparation is long and gradual. Every circumstance is brought to bear on the education of the chosen witness, and every experience, even of wrong and error, is made to enhance the power and completeness of the testimony rendered. When a man is called to effect some great religious reformation, it is important that he should himself have an experimental acquaintance with the order of things which he is to reverse or transform. The education of Paul the Pharisee, was to him what the convent of Erfurt was to Luther. It was well that he who was to break the yoke of Jewish legalism should himself have first suffered under its bondage. Thus, while the question of the emancipation of Christianity had been stated by men belonging, like Stephen, to the most liberal section of Judaism—the Hellenist Jews—it was to receive its final solution from a man who had himself felt the full weight of the yoke.

Saul belonged to a Jewish family, rigidly attached to the sect of the Pharisees. His name, which signifies "The desired one," has led some commentators * to suppose that he, being born, like Samuel, after hope long delayed, was, like him, specially consecrated by his parents to the service of God, and, therefore, sent from his early childhood to Jerusalem to study the sacred writings in the most famous school of the age. However this may be, it is evident that his mind had a natural bent toward such studies. He may have received some intellectual development in his own city. Strabo tells us that literary and philosophical studies had been carried so far at Tarsus that the schools of Cilicia eclipsed those of Athens and of Alexandria.† It appears, however, from the evidence of Philostratus, that a light and rhetorical school of learning predominated at Tarsus ; more attention was paid to brilliance of expression than to depth of philosophical thought.‡ The life of the East there reveled in boundless luxury, and the corruption of manners reached its utmost length. The young Jew, endowed with a high-toned morality, may well have conceived a deep disgust for this pagan civilization ; and these first impressions may have tended to develop in him an excessive attachment to the religion of his fathers.

* Neander, "Pflanzung," i, 138.
† Strabo, "Geography," xiv, 5.
‡ Philostratus, "Life of Apollonius of Tyana," i, 7.

We may, probably, attribute to his abode at Tarsus the literary culture displayed in his writings. He familiarly quotes the Greek poets, and poets of the second order, such as Cleanthes, (Acts xvii, 28,) Menander, (1 Cor. xv, 33,) and Epimenides, (Titus i, 12.) According to the custom of the rabbis of the time, he had learned a manual trade, and as the Cicilian fabrics of goats' hair were famous for their strength, he had chosen the calling of a tent-maker.

Jerusalem was the place of his true education. He was placed in the school of Gamaliel, the most celebrated rabbi of his age. Acts xxii, 3. We know how fully the scholastic spirit was developed among the Jews at this period. To the schools of the prophets had succeeded the schools of the rabbis; the living productions of the Divine Spirit had been replaced by commentaries of minutest detail, and the sacred text seemed in danger of being completely overgrown by rabbinical glosses, as by a parasitic vegetation.

While an ingenious and learned school, formed at Alexandria, had contrived by a system of allegorical interpretation to infuse Platonism into the Old Testament, the school at Jerusalem had been growing increasingly rigid, and interdicted any such daring exegesis. It clung with fanatic attachment to the letter of the Scriptures, but, failing to comprehend the spirit, it sunk into all the puerilities of a narrow literalism. Its interpretations lacked both breadth and depth; it surrendered itself to the subtilties of purely verbal dialectics. Cleverly to combine texts—to suspend on a single word the thin threads of an ingenious argument—such was the sole concern of the rabbis. Gamaliel appears to have been the most skilled of all the doctors of the law. He is still venerated in Jewish tradition under the title of "Gamaliel the Aged." The "Mishna" quotes him as an authority. We are inclined to believe that he may have been less in bondage than the other doctors of his day to narrow literalism, and that he may have maintained a spirit more upright and elevated. His benevolent intervention on behalf of the Church at Jerusalem distinguishes him honorably from those implacable Jews, who were ready to defend their prejudices by bloody persecutions. The fact of his having had a disciple like Saul of Tarsus, who must have been through his whole life characterized by a grave moral earnestness, leads us to suppose a true superiority in the teaching of Gamaliel. He had not got beyond the stand-point of legalism, but this he at least presented in its unimpaired and unabated majesty. He was not a man to delude the conscience with subterfuges, and his disciples were therefore disposed to austerity of life, and were distinguished by a scrupulous fidelity to the religion of their fathers.

Saul of Tarsus embraced the teaching of his illustrious master with characteristic earnestness and ardor, and, it must be added, infused into it all the passionate vehemence belonging to his nature. At the feet of Gamaliel, he became practiced in those skillful dialectics which were the pride of the rabbinical schools, and he thus received from Judaism itself the formidable weapon with which he was afterward to deal it such mortal blows. Here he gained a profound knowledge of the Old Testament. Gifted with a strong and keen intellect, he in a few years acquired all the learning of his master. He thus amassed, without knowing it, precious materials for his future polemics; but his moral and religious development in this phase of his life is of more importance to us than his intellectual acquirements. With all his knowledge, he might have become, at the most, the first of Jewish doctors, surpassing even Gamaliel, and shedding some glory on the decadence of his people; but he could never have derived from that vast learning the spirit of the reformer, which was to make him immortal in the Church. It is in the depths of his inner life we must seek the distinctive character of his early piety; he has himself accurately described it when he says, that being "taught according to the perfect manner of the law of the fathers," he "was zealous toward God." Acts xxii, 3. In other words, he carried into his exalted Judaism a truly religious spirit, and he was animated by a sincere desire to serve God. Herein was the germ of a possible transformation; and it was through this, his moral nature, that the transformation would subsequently be wrought.

In times of spiritual crisis, when mankind is breathlessly awaiting a great religious revolution, the common hope and expectation are manifested in two extremes of conduct. Some men openly abandon ancient forms: others cling to them with desperation, and demand from them with feverish impatience the satisfaction of the new cravings of their souls; their morbid excitement is in itself an evidence that they have not escaped the universal restlessness. They push to its furthest logical issues the principle in which they wish to believe; it is clear that they are themselves dissatisfied with its existing application, and seek in this way to appease their unquiet hearts. Such a cleaving to the past is, in truth, an aspiration after something beyond, an appeal for a new religious life. If we look closely at Saul of Tarsus while he is still a Pharisee, we shall discern in his manner of bearing the yoke a prophecy that he will one day cast it off. We find no likeness in him to those self-complacent Pharisees whose hypocrisy Christ painted in colors of fire. He does not seek to deceive God and men by vain forms, nor flatter his conscience that he has satisfied the law when he has paid tithe of mint, and anise, and cummin. This young Jew is a zealous and scrupulous observer of all the ordinances of Moses; he receives them with all seriousness; he practices them with all sincerity and exactness. Let us listen to his own words: "I profited in the Jews' religion above many my equals (in years) in mine own nation, being more exceedingly zealous of the traditions of my fathers." Gal. i, 14. He declares again that he was "as touching the law, blameless." Phil. iii, 6. A faithful, scrupulous, zealous observer of the law above all his contemporaries; such, then, was Paul. Who cannot discover beneath this extraordinary zeal the secret disquietude, the dull, oppressive uneasiness of which we have been speaking? In heart, Saul of Tarsus was seeking from Judaism that which it had not to give. He sought salvation in it; and salvation to him, as to every upright man upon whose soul there has never broken the bright light of divine forgiveness, could be nothing else than perfect conformity to the will of God. The law was precious in his eyes as the revelation of that will, and he strove to keep it under the awful sanction of the words, "Cursed is every one who continueth not in all things which are written in the book of the law to do them." Gal. iii, 10. Hence his restless eagerness, his extraordinary zeal, in the observance of all the commandments of Moses.

He seems to us, in some portions of his Epistles, to be recalling the memories of his early life. When he speaks of the powerlessness of legalism, he does not pause long on the development of the doctrine; his argument takes a dramatic and personal form. We feel that he is touching what were the live wounds of his soul before his conversion. The seventh chapter of his Epistle to the Romans is full of these sorrowful memories. When he depicts to us, with marvelous psychological insight, that singular effect of the law in revealing evil to us, and giving it an accursed charm by presenting it as the forbidden fruit, (Rom. vii, 8, 9,) is he not calling to mind the time when, after having recognized the commandment of God—the moral ideal set before his conscience—he had been consumed by a vain zeal to realize it, and had only gained in the struggle an agonizing conviction of the incurable corruption of human nature? Evil attracted him simply because it was a violation of the law of God.

Is it not the same Saul of Tarsus who exclaims, in deep sorrow of heart, "When the commandment came, sin revived, and I died: and the commandment, which was ordained to life, I found to be unto death." Rom. vii, 9, 10. He reveals himself to us, perpetually renewing a fruitless struggle; willing to keep the law, and in the measure of his desires finding the measure of his powerlessness; doing not the good that he would, and the evil which he would not, that doing. Tossed to and fro in this inward conflict, this war of the flesh and the spirit, which can have no issue till a new principle has been implanted in the heart, he exclaims in despair, "O wretched man that I am, who shall deliver me from the body of this death?" * Is it possible to doubt that the goad of the Lord had already touched his conscience? To him the law was a real scourge; no man ever groaned more heavily under the rod of the pitiless schoolmaster, whose mission is only fulfilled when he has brought his scholar bruised and helpless to the cross. Nor must we forget that the unregenerate nature was far from being wholly vanquished in Saul of Tarsus. Energetic and impetuous in character, he was easily carried away into violence, and, doubtless, deeply as he felt his moral misery, he did not cease to pride himself on the high position he occupied in his sect. It is not, then, surprising that at the time of the first conflict between Pharisaism and the Church at Jerusalem, Saul should

* It has often been questioned whether this portion of the Epistle to the Romans refers to Paul's moral condition before or after his conversion. It seems to us that feelings of discouragement and despair, such as are expressed here, are inconceivable in a Christian who knows the secret of victory, and who has received from God the principle of a new life. Let us not forget, however, that the Christian is never perfect, and that he falls back by his inconsistencies, under the dominion of the flesh. At such times his old feelings return, and the moral contradiction described in this chapter is not without analogy in the history of days of decline and fall in his Christian life. But it is none the less true that this picture of the impotent wrestlings of the soul finds its complete realization only in the unconverted man.

have approved and encouraged the persecution. The internal fever which consumed him—the desire to believe himself satisfied—his passionate attachment to every thing Mosaic—all contributed to make him an implacable enemy of the courageous confessor, who had ruthlessly shaken all his prejudices, and done violence, from his point of view, to all the glorious past of Israel. Saul of Tarsus was not a persecutor like Caiaphas. He was not defending either his person or his interests. He believed himself to be defending his God, and the fierce emotion excited by the words of Stephen inflamed his anger all the more, because it confirmed the testimony of his conscience.

His contact with Stephen may be regarded as the leading event of his life. From the day in which he heard Stephen speak—or rather, from the day in which he saw him die, with a calmness so sublime—Paul was beside himself. He abandoned the quiet studies of a doctor of the law ; he could not go on pursuing them till he had silenced that importunate voice within, which declared them to be of no avail. He felt that if Stephen's words were true, all the scaffolding of his legal virtues and Judaistic learning would fall to the ground. He was at heart more troubled than he was willing to appear ; a secret doubt gave him no rest, and he sought to shake it off by persecuting those who had called it forth. Hence that redoubled zeal which marks the moral crisis at its culminating point. "He breathed out," as the sacred writer tells us, "threatening and slaughter," (Acts ix, 1,) and "made havoc of the Church, entering into every house, and hailing men and women committed them to prison." Acts viii, 3. In every synagogue, he himself says, "I punished them oft, compelling them to blaspheme." He thought that by thus coercing the new converts to open retraction, he would obtain an unanswerable argument against the new religion, and would confirm his own convictions. But nothing appeased him, and his violence went on growing with his doubts. A moment came when it broke through all bounds, and not content with persecuting the Church at Jerusalem, he started for Damascus, with letters from the high priest to the elders of the synagogue, authorizing him to lay violent hands on the Christians in that city. And now God's appointed time was come.

While we thus regard the conversion of Paul as the issue of a long and painful preparatory period of inward crisis, we in no way detract from the importance of the remarkable miracle which was its immediate cause. If certain dispositions of mind were required by Jesus Christ as preparatory even for a miracle affecting the body alone, such as the healing of blindness or paralysis, how much more necessary must they be for a miracle wholly spiritual. The latter can only be received in its full power and meaning by a man whose heart has been prepared by God. This important truth comes out with a high degree of evidence from the narrative of the conversion of the Apostle.

As he was on the way, and already near Damascus, suddenly there shined round about him a light from heaven, and accompanying the brilliant flash a voice was heard with the shock of thunder. The companions of the Apostle saw the dazzling brightness, but could discern no distinct image; they heard the voice also, but caught no words.* Awe-struck, they fell to the ground. Acts xxvi, 14. They were witnesses only of the outward miracle; but within the external was another manifestation of a far higher order, which was perceived only by Saul, because he alone was prepared to receive it. In the bright light Jesus appeared to him, and in the confused noise he heard the voice of Christ making to him the most solemn appeal.† Paul's subsequent repeated and distinct references to the events of this day as establishing his right to the apostolate, on the ground, directly and positively stated, that he had seen Jesus Christ, set aside absolutely the theory of

* Acts ix, 7. Compare Acts xxii, 9.

† Baur ("Paulus," pp. 70, 71) lays stress upon the slight discrepancies which may be observed between Luke's narrative and the accounts which St. Paul himself gives of this transaction, and draws the conclusion that Luke's recital is only legendary. But these discrepancies are quite unimportant, and vanish before a close examination. We have carefully noted the various versions of the event in our representation of it. The supposed discrepancies are three in number. According to Acts ix, 7, the companions of Paul heard "a voice," while in Acts xxii, 9, we are told they "heard not the voice of Him" that spake. The two statements seem to us reconcilable by supposing, as we have done, that Paul's companions heard inarticulate sounds, but not distinct words, ("*the voiee of him that spake to me.*") According to Acts ix, 7, the same men saw no man; according to Acts xxii, 9, they saw the light. Here again we have a reference only to the external aspect of the miracle. It is possible to see a light, and yet to see no man. Finally, according to Acts ix, 7, the companions of Saul "stood speechless;" according to Acts xxvi, 14, they fell "to the earth." There is no necessary contradiction between the two statements. We have not even alluded to the naturalistic explanation of the miracle, according to which Saul of Tarsus was struck to the ground by a thunderstorm. It is beneath discussion.

a mere vision.* Paul did actually see Jesus, and hear him; but the fact that he alone did so on this occasion shows how entirely the perception of a miracle may depend on the moral condition. Every miracle has a twofold aspect—one external, and belonging to the whole world; the other spiritual and divine, discernible only by the inward eye.

Let us endeavor to give some account of the mysterious scene which transpired on the road to Damascus, the consequences of which were so momentous to the Apostle and to the Church. Saul of Tarsus is already secretly troubled in mind. He has closely observed the first Christians, has watched their pure and holy lives, and their still more remarkable deaths. The remembrance of Stephen is constantly present with him. He has, at the same time, proved the utter impotence of the old law; he is exhausted with inward struggles, and yet trembles at the thought of repudiating his past life. All these mingled emotions are tumultuous within him as he journeys toward Damascus. His conscience is ill at ease; his spirit is at once depressed and stirred within him. At this crisis Jesus appears to him, and asks, "Saul, Saul, why persecutest thou me?" The question wakes a deep echo in his soul; and when the voice goes on to say, "I am Jesus, whom thou persecutest," Saul is vanquished; he falls lightning-struck to the ground; he feels that he has long been kicking against the piercing goad. Light bursts in upon him; his doubts are dissipated; he sees, he believes. Stephen was not deceived; Jesus Christ is the very Lord of glory, and it is he whom

* See 1 Cor. xv, 8.

Saul had been about to persecute at Damascus. The shock of such a discovery is overwhelming. Saul is utterly crushed by it. He is himself no longer: not his bodily eyes alone, but the eyes of his soul are covered with a vail of blackness. He feels that this is the crisis of his spiritual life, and he gropes in the thick darkness, discerning clearly but this one thing, —that he has been persecuting Christ. Like a little child, he suffers himself to be led by the hand into the city, where, according to the promise given him, he is to receive new light.

It would be a grave mistake to suppose that Saul's conversion was completed on the road to Damascus. His pride was then broken; his doubts were scattered; but he did not at once rise from that tremendous blow which had severed his life in two. He then, indeed, received his calling as an Apostle, (Acts xxvi, 16–18,) but he had not then any conception of its greatness or of its cost. He must needs pass through a painful initiatory process. For three days he remains in utter darkness, and can neither eat nor drink. He has not told us the history of those three days, but it is easy to conceive what they were to him. He passed them, doubtless, in deepest humiliation, overwhelmed both by the remembrance of his sins, and by a sense of the grace he had received. He experienced all the depths of a true repentance; and, writhing under the consciousness that he had persecuted his Saviour, he reached the full and abiding conviction that he, the persecutor, the blasphemer and injurious, was the very chief of sinners. 1 Tim. i, 15. When, in a forcible figure, he represents the first stage of conversion as burial with Christ, set forth in the act of baptism, he may have been calling to mind those three days when, separated from men, without a ray of light breaking the awful obscurity, he was, for all the things of earth, as one dead. But deliverance had been promised him ; God had in a vision foretold its approach. At the same time, a disciple named Ananias was commanded to go and lay his hands upon him.* His eyes are opened, he receives the Holy Ghost, and is baptized ; and thus that work of sovereign grace is completed, of which he was to be at once the mightiest witness and the most amazing monument.†

The best preparation of a great servant of God for his work is stern solitude. Saul of Tarsus, before entering on his ministry, was sent into the wilderness, like Moses and John the Baptist, and like Jesus himself. He lived for some years in Arabia, (Gal. i, 17,) in silence and seclusion, maturing his soul by prayer, and recovering his moral equilibrium after the violent shock he had experienced. From Arabia he returned to Damascus, burning with the desire to confess Jesus Christ. He preached the Gospel in the very synagogues in which before he had sought to stir up bitter adversaries against the Church. His preaching thus gave great offense. The intolerant Jewish

* Baur, in his mythological interpretation, regards Paul's recovery of sight as a symbol of the illumination produced by a new doctrine. ("Paulus," 71.) It is evident that such a system of interpretation does violence to the text.

† Lenain de Tillemont asserts that Ananias was a priest, and probably a bishop of Damascus. ("Hist. Eccl.," c. i, p. 210.) There is nothing whatever in the narrative to lead us to suppose he was even an elder of the Church. As to his being a priest or bishop, the idea is simply absurd at this period.

party, furious at the loss of their leader, let loose upon him the popular passions, and he only escaped death by precipitate flight. He then went up to Jerusalem. For the first time since his conversion he entered that city in which he was known only as the most cruel of persecutors, as the most ardent adherent of Pharisaic legalism. A severe ordeal was in reserve for him in the isolation in which he was for a long time kept by the distrust of the Church. Instead of affectionate welcome, he met only with suspicious fear. Men would not believe in a conversion so astonishing. At length he succeeded in attaching to himself Barnabas, a proselyte of the Isle of Cyprus, a man of broader spirit than the native Jews, and by him he was brought into the society of the Christians. But he received no directions from the Apostles; he only saw Peter, and James the brother of the Lord, and his own account of his interview with them is altogether incompatible with the notion that he sought from them any initiation into evangelical doctrine, (Gal. i, 19;) on the contrary, he declares that he did not receive his doctrine from them, but was directly taught of God. Gal. i, 11, 12. It was at this period that, in a trance in the temple, he received, for the second time, the command to go to the Gentiles. Acts xxii, 17–22. But he was pressed in spirit to preach the Gospel at Jerusalem. He longed, as at Damascus, to confess his crucified Lord and Saviour in the very places where he had blasphemed and persecuted him. He addressed himself to those same Hellenists for whom Stephen had labored, thus taking up, at the very point where it had been left, the work of him for whose death he had clamored.

Such a marvelous change was well adapted to teach the Church the fruitfulness of the martyr's death, and to enhance in its eyes the power of that grace which could transform the murderer of Stephen into his successor. Saul encountered the same hostility which he had himself once helped to provoke against his bold forerunner, and he was forced to flee to escape a premature death. He went first to Cæsarea, and then to his native city, where Barnabas came to seek him, and took him to Antioch, where was the first Church gathered out of the Gentiles. Here Saul found himself in an atmosphere most favorable to his religious development; here he preached the Gospel during one year, and contributed to that happy movement in advance, by which the Church became distinguished in name from Judaism. Saul made another short visit to Jerusalem, to carry thither the offerings which the Church at Antioch sent in anticipation of the famine predicted by Agabus, and which actually took place in the reign of Claudius. On their return from this journey, Saul and Barnabas, in consequence of a direct revelation of the Holy Spirit, received with the laying on of hands the charge of carrying the Gospel to the Gentiles. This is, properly speaking, the true commencement of Paul's apostolic work. It is important that, before we go further, we should clearly comprehend its character.

We know how frequently Paul insisted upon his privilege as an apostle, and with what vehemence he repudiates any inferiority in this respect in comparison with his colleagues in the apostolate. "Am I not an apostle?" he says in his first Epistle to the

Corinthians, (1 Cor. ix, 1 ;) and adds in the second, "I suppose I was not a whit behind the very chiefest apostles."* On the other hand, we know that this equality claimed by him was disputed by the Judaizing party. We may conclude from this opposition that his apostolate was not altogether of the same nature as that of the first apostles. Let us inquire in what way it was similar, and in what superior to theirs.

We have seen that the apostolate was not a new priesthood, but the ideal representation of the Church. The apostle was the Christian of the early Church in an official character ; he was to raise the Christian vocation to its supreme dignity ; he was thus, pre-eminently, the witness of Jesus Christ, for the special mission of this first generation of Christians was to preserve to the world the living memory of the Redeemer. St. Paul, in this respect, in no way differs from the twelve ; like them, he is one of the accredited witnesses of the great fact of salvation, only his credentials are of a peculiar kind. The essential condition for taking rank among the twelve first apostles was, "to have been with the Lord Jesus all the time that he went in and out among them, beginning from the baptism of John unto that same day that he was taken up from them." Acts i, 21, 22. Paul could not adduce any external connection with the Saviour in the days of his flesh ; he had not seen the historic Christ, so to speak ; he had seen only the ascended and glorified Christ. This sight of him, however, was not a mere vision ; it was miraculous and positive, and it confers on St. Paul an

* 2 Cor. xi, 5. Comp. Rom. xv, 15, 16 ; Gal. i, 1.

authority in no way inferior to that of the twelve apostles. But it is equally true that, in this respect, he more nearly represents the numerous generations of Christians who have had no outward relations with the incarnate Saviour. Again, he stands apart from that symbolic number of the twelve, which points to the ancient tribes of Israel. He is the apostle of the Church, as it bursts the confines of Judaism ; the apostle of mankind, rather than of a nation. Lastly, he did not receive his office by transmission : Ananias, who laid his hands on him, was a simple believer. His apostolate was conferred on him by a direct revelation ; it stands in no relation to any positive institution, but it carries its own glorious witness in its results. Paul represents essentially the reforming portion of the Church ; he inaugurates the apostolate of the demonstration of the Spirit and of power, that from which almost all other Christian offices ultimately spring, that which breaks, when needful, the framework of imperfect ecclesiastical organization, and lives by a life independent, both in its origin and continuance, of mere institutions. Let us not forget, however, that St. Paul, while he was the representative of the Church in its free development, derived a special authority from the direct mission which, by revelation, God had conferred upon him.*

* M. Scherer, in an article on the apostolate in general, and on that of St. Paul, (" Revue du Theologie," tom. iii, 6th edit.,) ascribes all that the Apostle says as to his authority to a false conception entertained by him of the apostolate at large. It seems to us that he might easily have avoided so extreme a conclusion by admitting that enlargement of the primitive apostolate, which was to lead to the true apostolical succession, the inheritance of the Christian Church as a whole.

One preliminary question remains to be noticed. Paul declares, in his Epistle to the Galatians, that the Gospel he preaches comes not from man. "I neither received it of man," he says, "neither was I taught it, but by the revelation of Jesus Christ." Gal. i, 11–13. Are we to conclude from these words that Paul received by direct revelation the whole divine history of salvation? We think not. God never works useless miracles; he does not communicate by supernatural means that which can be acquired without such aid. There is no reason why we should not believe that St. Paul obtained his acquaintance with the substance of the Gospel in his interviews with Ananias and the other disciples at Damascus. It is probable, also, that he may have himself drawn from fuller sources. Perhaps he may have had in his hands one of those written declarations of the things most commonly believed, to which Luke alludes, and which were in very early times circulated in the Churches. When Paul speaks of his Gospel, he intends by the word his own manner of presenting the truth, and especially his profound view of the old and new covenant—of the law and justification by faith. These great truths he did not receive from any man—they were given him by the Holy Ghost. We see, indeed, that the revelation which he received in the Temple at Jerusalem bore directly on his mission to the Gentiles, (Acts xxii, 21;) it thus presupposed an enlargement of his religious views. Paul himself tells us that the mystery revealed to him in these last days had reference to the calling of the Gentiles. Eph. i, 9, 10. His deep experience of the weakness of Judaism, combined with the marvelous and sudden deliverance granted to him, was adapted, under the enlightening influence of the Divine Spirit, to bring him to a complete apprehension of the relation of the two covenants. Had not the great antithesis of the law and grace been realized in his life before it was expressed in his writings?

§ II. *St. Paul's First Journey.*

Until the time when he was sent forth by the Church at Antioch, Saul had confined himself to preaching the Gospel to the Jews and proselytes. He did not enter on his great mission-field among the Gentiles till this first journey, which was, therefore, one of great importance to himself and to the Church. It called forth differences of opinion which led, ultimately, to the Council at Jerusalem; and the result of that council was the first solution of the question which had already raised more than one stormy contention among the Christians. Saul and Barnabas left Antioch accompanied by John, whose surname was Mark. Acts xiii, 5. He was a disciple from Jerusalem, the son of that Mary in whose house the Church met to pray for Peter's deliverance from prison. Acts xii, 12. He appears to have been a convert of Peter, who calls him his son. 1 Peter v, 13. He was subsequently Peter's interpreter.* From his antecedents we may gather that he was, at this time, strongly imbued with the prejudices of a Judaizing Christianity. He was not yet on the same level of enlightenment with Paul, and a separation between them soon ensued. It is possible that on

* Eusebius, "Hist. Eccl.," Book III, c. xxxix.

his return he may have contributed, by the reports he brought, to occasion the controversy between the Apostles and the narrow Christians of Jerusalem. The differences between them cannot have been slight, since Paul preferred to separate from Barnabas rather than to accept his kinsman again as a colleague. From his Epistles we learn, however, that the difference was only transitory, for Mark subsequently appears again among the companions of Paul. Philemon, 24 ; 2 Tim. iv, 11 ; Col. iv, 10. Barnabas being a native of Cyprus, the delegates from Antioch first visited that island. They passed through its whole extent. After a short stay at Salamis, they went to Paphos, a town rebuilt under Augustus. It was in this place, defiled by the infamous rites of the worship of Astarte, that Paul won his first conquest over heathenism. The highest dignitary of the island, Sergius Paulus,* was one of those who, disgusted with the polytheism of the West, was seeking in the religions of the East, and especially in Judaism, the satisfaction of vague aspirations. This state of mind had rendered him susceptible to the sorceries of the Jewish magician Elymas, who, like Simon of Samaria, turned to account, by base deceptions, the religious cravings of the age. Sergius Paulus had not, however, yielded entirely to the seductions of the

* Sergius Paulus is called ἀνθύπατος. This title corresponds to proconsul. He served under the governor of the senatorial provinces, while the governors of the provinces, receiving their authority directly from the emperor, were called proprætors. The island of Cyprus was at first, under Augustus, a senatorial province, ("Dio Cassius," 53, 2,) but it was afterward given to the senate, (ibid, 54, 4). Luke's designation of Sergius Paulus is strictly accurate, (Wieseler, "Chron. des apostolisch. Zeitalt," p. 225.)

impostor, for when Saul and Barnabas arrived, he at once sent for them to come to him. Elymas endeavors to turn away the Proconsul from the faith; but, at Paul's severe rebuke, he is struck with sudden blindness, and learns, at the sharp cost of experience, what is the difference between the sorceries of the magician and a true miracle. The Proconsul is converted to Christ, not so much by the miracle of which he had been the witness, as by the beauty of the doctrine preached to him.*

From the island of Cyprus Paul and Barnabas cross into Asia Minor. They only pass through Perga, where Mark leaves them, and go on to Antioch in Pisidia, an important town, built, like the other Antioch, by Seleucus Nicator. A large Jewish colony is there resident. To this Paul first addresses himself. He always, in his missionary journeys, follows the

*Acts xiii, 12. The sacred historian from this time uses the name Paul instead of Saul, (Acts xiii, 9.) Jerome's ingenious interpretation of this is well known: "Apostolus a primo ecclesiæ spolio proconsule Sergio victoriæ suæ tropæa retulit, erexitque vexillum ut Paulus ex Saulo vocaretur" ("De Viris Illustrit.") The name Paul was borrowed (this Father supposes) from Sergius Paulus, in token of the Apostle's victory, and as a trophy of this first triumph over paganism. But Jerome has not observed that Luke does not say that the name of Saul was changed on this occasion; he simply mentions, in a general manner, that Saul was also called Paul. We have no right to identify the time when this name appears in the narrative with that of its first adoption by the Apostle. Other commentators have supposed the name Paul, which signifies small, humble, mean, to have been assumed by Saul after his conversion, and they bring forward 1 Cor. xv, 9 in support of their view; but had this been so, Luke would have spoken of this change of name in connection with Saul's conversion. We are disposed rather to think that Paul was the Greek form of the name Saul, and that the Apostle, ufter entering upon his mission among the Gentiles, began to use it habitually.

order adopted by God himself in the gift of his revelations. He held it his duty to preach the Gospel first to those who had received in the law and the prophets a direct preparation for it. We know, besides, what tender affection he felt for his people, and what a lofty patriotism blended with the breadth of his enlarged Christianity. The synagogue at Antioch seems to have been considerably frequented by the Gentile population ; at least so we may gather from the composition of the audience which received the Gospel from the lips of Paul. Acts xiii, 44, 45. Judaism was thus confronted with paganism, and the Christian Church was to learn, by a significant and decisive fact, in what quarter it would find the readiest accessions. For the first time the two great religious sections of mankind were summoned on the same day to take their position in relation to Christianity. It is a critical moment in the history of the apostolic age.

When Paul has received the invitation to speak the word of exhortation, he turns to his countrymen and addresses to them an appeal most earnest and touching. The plan of his discourse, of which evidently we have only the leading points, is admirably adapted to his purpose. Speaking to Jews, he takes his stand on the ground of the old covenant. He first shows the historic descent of Christ. Just as the kings succeeded the judges, so the Son of David has succeeded the kings, and has inaugurated a new kingship. Acts xiii, 23. The last of the prophets, John the Baptist, recognized him as the Messiah. Acts xiii, 25. If objection be taken to his ignominious death, that death itself Paul shows to be part of the prophecies concerning him. Every Sabbath, in every synagogue, the prophetic oracles declaring it are read. And beyond this, he is risen again, and has been seen of his disciples; and this glorious fact, foretold by the prophets, is a pledge of the fulfillment of the promises. Acts xiii, 32, 33. So far Paul follows substantially the same method as Peter. In addressing Jews he could not, indeed, well do otherwise, but his conclusion is startlingly new. For the first time he proclaims the impotence of Judaism, and preaches salvation by faith alone. "By him," he says, "all that believe are justified from all things, from which [they] could not be justified by the law of Moses." He concludes by reminding his hearers how awful is their responsibility.

This discourse produced a deep impression; but while the Gentiles were filled with joy, there were murmurings of indignation among the Jews. These could no longer be restrained when, the next Sabbath, a large concourse of Gentiles came up to the synagogue. Paul had given his countrymen a grand opportunity of vindicating themselves from the heavy charge which had rested on their nation ever since the crucifixion of Christ. Far from embracing it, they sanction by their conduct the crime of their brethren, and betray once more the obstinate pride of their race, at the very moment when the ignorant Gentiles eagerly receive the Gospel. Paul and Barnabas are filled with holy indignation; this confirmed resistance of the Jews draws from them those words of incalculable import, "Lo! we turn to the Gentiles!" A new era opens upon the Church. The grateful Gentiles throng around the Apostles—conversions are multiplied—but at the same time, persecution, stirred up by the Jews, breaks out in fury, and Paul and Barnabas are compelled to quit the country, leaving behind them a host of neophytes. As they depart they shake off the dust of their feet, and this symbolical act is a fresh proof that the severance between the Church and the synagogue is complete.

At Iconium—a neighboring city—similar scenes are enacted. The Gospel is preached with acceptance to the Gentiles, but the exasperated Jews league themselves with some fanatics, (Acts xiv, 3–6,) and the Apostles escape death only by flight. They continue their journey no further in Asia Minor; but on returning they pass through Derbe and Lystra, cities of Lycaonia, built not far from the mountain chain of Taurus.

The people of this region were rude and ignorant; they still clung to ancient paganism with its absurd fables. They were distinguished by their fanaticism, and carried into their religious ideas the same wild passion as their neighbors, the people of Phrygia. The worship of Jupiter and Mercury was in favor in these provinces. In the familiar fable of Philemon and Baucis, these two divinities appear in Phrygia. A temple to Jupiter had been built at the gates of Lystra. Such a people would be sure to love the marvelous. The miraculous healing of the impotent man by Paul excited, therefore, the most lively enthusiasm. On all hands the cry was raised, "The gods are come down to us," (Acts xiv, 11, 12,) and Paul and Barnabas were hailed under the honored names of Mercury and Jupiter. The Apostles, not understanding the language of the country,* were unconscious of this idolatrous homage till they saw the priest of the false gods approaching them with garlands and oxen for sacrifice. Indignant and distressed, they ran in among the people, rending their clothes according to the Jewish custom, and disclaiming the impious worship offered them. "Sirs, why do ye these things?" they exclaim; "we also are men of like passions with you." Acts xiv, 15. They then press upon their hearers a belief in the true God. We observe in these words of Paul that beautiful idea, so often brought out by him, that even before the coming of Christ God's care had not been concentrated solely on the Jews, but that he had, in the benefits of his providence, given to the Gentiles also a revelation designed to prepare them for yet higher blessings. Acts xiv, 17, 18. It was henceforward not difficult for the Jews of the neighboring cities to stir up against the Apostles a multitude already ill-pleased. Paul was stoned, and dragged out of the city for dead, and his subsequent recovery was nothing less than a miracle. After rapidly passing again through the cities where they had preached the Gospel, and presiding at the election of elders, Paul and Barnabas set sail from Attalia to return to

* The people used, before Paul and Barnabas, the language of Lycaonia. Acts xiv, 11. In the same tongue they call Barnabas Jupiter, and Paul Mercury. And yet Paul and Barnabas have no suspicion of the thing at the time. The feelings of the people seem to have been explained to them. Acts xiv, 14. It is clear they did not comprehend the language. It was rather a Greek patois than a language; it is probable that the people knew Hellenic Greek, since Paul's discourse seems to have been at once understood.

Antioch. Their first missionary journey was ended, and its glorious results were summed up in the grand declaration that "God had opened the door of faith unto the Gentiles."* Acts xiv, 27.

This journey gave striking confirmation to all the revelations which Paul had received. He knew now, from the conversion of Sergius Paulus and the success of his preaching at Antioch in Pisidia, that deep spiritual needs were felt by the Gentiles, and that the heathen world was, after its manner, looking for redemption. But, at the same time, he had come into sharp contact with popular fanaticism, and had learned the cost of opposing it, and he had also proved by experience the obstinate resistance of his proud and opinionated countrymen. He had gained clearer ideas of the vocation wherewith he was called, with its inevitable accompanying perils and pains, and, doubtless, had already a sure presage of martyrdom as the final seal of faithfulness to the truth.

* Baur ("Paulus," p. 91,) sees in the narrative of Paul's first journey nothing more than a skilful imitation of the miracles and discourses of St. Peter during the first era of the apostolic age. Thus the punishment of Elymas is the reflection of that of Simon Magus, and the healing of the cripple at Lystra, of the cure of the paralytic at the Beautiful Gate of the Temple. As to Paul's discourses, they are but feeble echoes of those of Peter. On this latter point, we content ourselves with referring to the analysis we have given of Paul's sermon at Antioch in Pisidia. It is very natural that in the first part of the discourse, when speaking to the Jews, he should employ a mode of argument similar to that which Peter uses in addressing the same opponents. As to the miracles of Paul, what difficulty is there in supposing that two magicians and two paralytics should have crossed the path of the Apostles. An attentive observation of the sacred narrative will also discover positive differences between the two series of facts. What history could stand before such criticism as this?

But the glorious victories he had just gained, and the "marks of the Lord Jesus," which he already bore in the body wounded for his sake, gave him a right to be heard at Jerusalem, as at Antioch. God had confirmed his apostleship in a manner not to be mistaken. He was ready for the great internal conflict of the Church, after having so mightily served the common cause in the conflict with outlying heathenism.

CHAPTER IV.

THE TWO CONFERENCES AT JERUSALEM, AND THE DISPUTE AT ANTIOCH.

§ I. *The Two Conferences.*

THE Christian Church had reached a critical moment. It had already long passed out of the peaceful upper chamber at Jerusalem. Important questions had arisen which clamored for solution. It must be decided if a Judaizing Christianity or a Christianity of broader principles was to govern the Churches gathered from among the heathen. A great step in the path of emancipation had been taken when circumcision had been declared not obligatory in the case of Gentile converts, and they had thus been placed on the same level with Jews by birth. This innovation had been introduced by Paul, and it implied that he possessed authority equal to that of the twelve Apostles. Hence arose two critical questions on which minds were deeply stirred and greatly divided. The first referred to circumcision. Is it lawful, it was asked, to abrogate an institution consecrated by the practice of the Church? The question was not now confined, as in the instance of the conversion of Cornelius, to an isolated case, or the baptism of a single family; it embraced all the thousands of the uncircumcised. The second question was touching the apostleship of Paul. Had he the right to use such large liberty in his chosen field of action? Might he thus, without even consulting with the Church at Jerusalem, introduce such important changes? In other words, was he truly an apostle? Of these two questions, the one was of general interest, the other personal to Paul. The first demanded open deliberation in presence of the whole Church; while the second, which was of a more delicate nature, might more fitly be discussed in private. Two conferences, therefore, took place simultaneously at Jerusalem, the one private, among the Apostles themselves, (Gal. ii, 1–11,) the other public, and with the assistance of the whole Church. Acts xv, 6.

But before following in detail these important deliberations, we shall do well to place ourselves, as far as possible, in the midst of the various conflicting influences which gave occasion to them. It has been asserted that the conflict was essentially one between St. Paul and the other Apostles, who, we are told, had not in any respect advanced beyond the limits of Judaism. This theory is contradicted alike by the explicit declarations of St. Paul and by the narrative of Luke. We have already sketched the history of the Church at Jerusalem up to this period. We have seen that, while still continuing to observe the ordinances of the law, the Church regarded itself as forming a separate society, the basis of which was faith in Jesus Christ. It had already constructed its first simple organization. It had also, in principle, recognized the calling of the Gentiles, though without a full comprehension of all the consequences of that concession. The majority of the Christians of this

Church were under the influence of James, the Lord's brother. The opposition raised against Paul at Jerusalem cannot be ascribed to any of the Apostles. He tells us, in his letter to the Galatians, how readily they gave to him the right hand of fellowship. Gal. ii, 9. But the primitive Church had not more power than any other to preserve itself wholly from the intrusion of sectarian influence. The presence of a few hot-headed bigots was enough to sow the seeds of discord. It would be impossible to suppose that none such found their way into the Church, in the multitude of the early-baptized converts. The spirit of Pharisaism is indestructible upon earth ; it can assume any form, and it is not, therefore, surprising to find it in the very Church which was the object of Pharisaic persecution. These men of narrow soul, taking advantage of the respect and affection shown by the Christians to Judaism, sought to transfuse into the new religion the pride and prejudices of the Jews of the decline. Actuated by their national exclusiveness and intolerant bigotry, they showed a fanatic zeal for the ancient privileges of Israel. Paul does not hesitate to call them false brethren. Acts xv, 1 ; Gal. ii, 4. They heard with indignation of the results of his first missionary journey. Some of them went privily to Antioch, to spy out the conduct of their great adversary, to oppose his views, and to arrest, if it might be so, the liberty of practice introduced into the Churches formed under his influence. They attacked at once the person and the principles of the Apostle, questioning his authority, and obstinately maintaining the permanent obligation of circumcision. Acts xv, 1. It was impossible for

Paul and his followers not to offer an energetic resistance to such interference, and it was probably by his advice that the Church at Antioch determined to carry the question before the Church at Jerusalem. Let us not lose sight of this circumstance, which is important, as it proves that the Church at Jerusalem had no share in raising the discussion, and that those who were the first agitators had no right whatever to speak in its name; that, on the contrary, the Christians at Antioch had full confidence in it. St. Paul himself distinguishes between the public and the private conference. "I communicated," he says, "to them of Jerusalem,* but *privately* to them which were of reputation,† that Gospel which I preach among the Gentiles."

The moment was full of grave issues for the Apostle; it was a decisive crisis, from which his authority must come out either seriously compromised or sanctioned before the Church. As he himself says, the point to be resolved was, "if by any means he should run, or had run in vain," (Gal. ii, 2;) in other words, if his apostleship was to be recognized or not. Paul brought forward the question in a manner which admitted of no compromise or equivocation. He had with him a young converted Greek, named Titus, who had never been circumcised. By bringing him to Jerusalem he came to an overt rupture with the Judaizing party; he affirmed his right, and used the disputed freedom.

It is not difficult to form an idea of the points de-

* This refers to the public conference.

† Κατ' ἰδίαν. Gal. ii, 2. This is an allusion to the private conference.

bated in the private conferences. The later polemics of St. Paul give us valuable hints on this subject, for his adversaries constantly repeated the same charges against him. The great objection to his apostleship was drawn from the difference existing between him and the primitive Apostles. He had not, like them, lived with Jesus Christ; for he was yet a fierce persecutor of the Church when the twelve were already governing it with authority. Paul met this objection by declaring that "God accepteth no man's person," (Gal. ii, 6;) and that, in the choice of his instruments, precedent forms no law.

To those who demanded that he should have received his vocation by direct transmission from the hands of the twelve Apostles, he replied with equal frankness and boldness, "They added nothing to me." * He sought, for the steps he took, no authority from those who had gone before him. The question, which was at first simply a personal one, soon became general. Paul raises it to the height of those great principles which animated all his ministry. He appeals, in support of his apostleship, to that free, sovereign grace of God, which is not limited by precedent, merit, or institution. The same grace which made him a Christian made him an apostle. Having done the greater, it was assuredly able to do the less. His title is in no way inferior to that of the twelve. Without grace, Peter would have been no more an apostle than he; with it, their calling was the same. Gal. ii, 8. If the question is raised, by what signs shall they recognize this second apostolate? the Apostle's reply is, that in these signs there is nothing ar-

* Οὐδὲν προσανέθεντο. Gal. ii, 6.

bitrary. They are to be as clear as the light of day. The grace which makes the Christian is demonstrated by its efficacy, by its results. And so, likewise, is the grace which makes the apostle. Let him be tried by this test. "He that wrought effectually in Peter to the apostleship of the circumcision, the same was mighty in me toward the Gentiles." Gal. ii, 8. Paul placed the Churches founded by himself side by side with those founded by Peter. The first Apostles could point to the work in Jerusalem and in Samaria; he to the mission work at Antioch, Paphos, Iconium, Derbe, and Lystra, and to all the young and flourishing Churches founded by him. What higher demonstration of efficacious grace could there be than such signs as these, and who would dare to dispute the legitimacy of so fruitful an apostleship?

This argument of Paul appeared irresistible to the men, who, from the extraordinary consideration they enjoyed, may be regarrded as the arbiters in the dispute. It is impossible, except under the bias of very strong preconception, to pretend to gather from the history that Peter, James, and John were at the head of the adversaries of Paul, when Paul himself so distinctly draws the line between them and the "false brethren," who had calumniated him, and so explicitly declares their readiness to recognize his apostleship. Gal. ii, 9. The result of the conference is clearly indicated by the Epistle to the Galatians. The Apostles divide among them the field of Christian missions, or rather, they accept the division already made by God. While Peter and James continue to devote themselves chiefly to the Jews, Paul and Barnabas turn to the Gentiles; but in this division of labor they are none the less united, and James and Peter urge Paul to remember the poor Churches in Palestine, and to send to them the offerings of the young Churches gathered out of paganism. What an admirable method for preserving unity in diversity! Love serves as an effectual bond among the Churches, and there is no need to lay upon them the yoke of an external and legal uniformity. The importance of this conference cannot be questioned: it effected the recognition of the full apostleship of Paul, it gave, by anticipation, sanction to the ministry of all whom in any age God has called to break the bondage of custom and traditional routine.

Besides these private conferences, the Church at Jerusalem had public conferences, not on the question of the apostleship of Paul, but on the admission of Gentiles into the Church. To these has been given, by emphasis, the name of the Council of Jerusalem. No better method could have been taken to bring into strong light the contrast between this first council and all that have succeeded it. It differs as widely in its composition, as in the mode of its deliberations and in its results. It is no clerical council pronouncing authoritative decisions on points of doctrine. Not only the apostles, but the elders, and the whole multitude of the believers, take part in the conference, because all have an equal interest in the question at issue.* The Council of Jerusalem is essentially democratic in character. At a time when the level of the religious life was so elevated, there was no fear that the gravest interests of the

* Σὺν ὅλῃ τῇ ἐκκλησίᾳ. Acts xv, 22.

Church would be compromised by a free discussion. The Church had not as yet opened its doors to the motley throng of merely nominal Christians. If it is asked what right had believers, who were neither Apostles nor elders, to sit in the first council, the answer is ready, without an appeal to the general constitution of the Church at that period. It is sufficient to remember that every one of these Christians was prepared to endure martyrdom for the faith. Those who are ready to die for the Church have the truest qualification for its government. A fair consideration of the part taken by the Apostles in the council at Jerusalem, cannot but dispel many false conceptions of the apostolic office. If they had really constituted a sort of autocratic college, governing the Church, and deciding all questions of doctrine and practice by their personal infallibility, they would on this occasion have assembled themselves, and sent forth to the Church their authoritative decision on the point in dispute. They would have inaugurated the method adopted by their so-called successors, and determined, without appeal, the mode of admission of converted Gentiles. In place of any such act of apostolic authority, we find a free discussion, in which the Apostles take part only like the other Christians, without enforcing their opinions by any appeal to their peculiar prerogatives. On the contrary, the man of most influence in the council, he whose advice prevails, is not an apostle: he is James, the Lord's brother, one of the elders of the Church at Jerusalem. The advocates of a hierarchy maintain that Peter presided over the council. They base their opinion on the fact that he was the first of the Apostles to give expression to his views. In this, as in so many other instances, they mistake, for the privilege of office, that forwardness of speech and action which really proceeded from his natural impetuosity and ardor. In this case, however, it is not correct to assert that Peter opened the conference; the discussion had already gone to a considerable length before he spoke. "And when there had been much disputing, Peter rose up." Acts xv, 7.

The breadth of spirit which characterized the deliberations of the Council of Jerusalem is worthy of all admiration. We have already shown the importance of the point to be decided. It cannot be questioned that there were strongly marked differences of opinion in the assembly, even leaving out of view the extreme fanatical party. Between Paul and James the divergence was great, though both were equally devoted to Jesus Christ. Peter, whose mind had already been enlightened by a special revelation, occupied an intermediate position. The great body of the Christians sided with James. If each one had clung without concession to his own peculiar views, a lamentable schism must have resulted from these conferences; but the discussion was conducted in a spirit of Christian liberty, which obviated all danger. It commenced evidently with hot and confused disputation, (Acts xv, 7,) in which, doubtless, the accusers of Paul and Barnabas took the chief part. This was the first shock of contradictory opinion. It was natural that Peter, who had seen the descent of the Spirit upon the converted Gentiles, should promptly interpose in the discussion. He simply stated the facts of which he had been the witness, and pointed out the conclusions to which they naturally led. Since God, he says, put no difference between Christians brought out of heathenism and those who had scrupulously observed the customs of Judaism, why impose upon them a legal ceremonial, a yoke which the Jews themselves had not been able to bear? Salvation is not attached to the ceremonial law; it is the gift of the grace of God. Acts xv, 7–12. Peter, without entering on the crucial question of circumcision, contented himself with laying it down as a principle, that the ceremonial law, as a whole, should not be made binding on converted Gentiles.

Paul and Barnabas immediately follow Peter as speakers. They narrate the great results of their mission in Asia Minor. They describe, no doubt in fervent language, the eagerness of the Gentiles to listen to the Gospel, and contrast it with the resistance of the Jews. They point to Sergius Paulus converted at Paphos; they dwell on the zeal and love of the Churches they have left as bright lights in the midst of the darkness and corruption of Asiatic paganism. Acts xv, 12. The assembly is thrilled with gladness. None of the Christians well-known for their special attachment to Judaism have, however, as yet expressed an opinion. It was of the greatest importance that their feeling should be known, for they formed the majority. James, the Lord's brother, was the representative of those sincere but scrupulous disciples who did not feel themselves free to discontinue ceremonial observances. He thus fulfilled, on this occasion, the special mission devolving upon him; he served to bridge over the gap between the old law and the new, between legal bondage and Gospel liberty. We feel, as we listen to him, that he has not yet reached the same standpoint as Peter and Paul. The prophetic oracles, with reference to the calling of the Gentiles, have more weight in his mind than the great principles of the new covenant. Acts xv, 15–18. The natural conclusion from the speeches of Peter and Paul would have been the complete abrogation of all legal prescription in the case of the Gentile converts. James does not go so far: he desires that Christians of Jewish extraction should still observe all the ordinances of Judaism. They, therefore, need no directions, since they have the law of Moses, which is read in every city in the synagogues on the Sabbath day. Acts xv, 21. For the Christians converted from paganism James proposes a middle course. He does not insist on the necessity of circumcision, and on the observance of all the ceremonial laws; he only asks that they submit to the conditions imposed on proselytes of the gate, in proof of their renunciation of heathen practices.* "Let us write unto them," says James, "that they abstain from pollutions of idols, and from fornication, and from things strangled, and from blood." The first of these interdictions is explained by the horror the Jews had of idolatry, and every thing connected with it. The second was called forth by the deep corruption of pagan manners. In the prevalent laxity of morals, debauch was scarcely accounted a crime, and the Gentile conscience was in this respect especially perverted. The epistles of Paul bear abundant evidence that

* Thiersch, p. 127.

such an injunction was greatly needed.* The third interdiction, that of things strangled and of blood, had reference to the commandments given by God to Noah immediately after the Deluge. Gen. ix, 4, 5. A distinction was thus made between the ordinances given to Moses and the revelation of God's will to Noah. The latter represented the minimum of Jewish requirements, the observance of which was demanded of proselytes of the gate. The recommendation of James was, therefore, a middle course, designed to avoid any actual rupture between the parties.

It has been said that James made no real concession by this proposition—that, in fact, he secured the triumph of the Judaizing party. But was it nothing to place Christians converted from paganism, and who had only fulfilled the conditions required of proselytes of the gate, on the same level with the proselytes of righteousness and the Jews by birth? Was it nothing to consent to admit the uncircumcised into the Church? Let it be remembered that the whole discussion originated in the question of circumcision, and it will be evident that the solution proposed by James, while it gave legitimate satisfaction to the Christian Jews, completely won the cause for Paul and Barnabas. The whole conference agreed in the course proposed, and it was decided to send delegates to Antioch, provided with a circular letter containing the resolution unanimously taken at Jerusalem. This letter is a model of Christian toleration. It is not weighted with anathemas; it does not even

* A vain attempt has been made to discover in this second interdiction a deep meaning, turning on second marriages, or on marriages within the degree prohibited in Leviticus, (Lev. xviii.)

use the tone of command ; it is not the promulgation of a decree. After explaining the cause of the disputation, it goes no further than to tell the Churches they would *do well* to conform to the resolutions passed at Jerusalem. Acts xv, 29. The letter recognizes the inspiration of the Holy Spirit as shared by all who took part in the council.* It was after prolonged deliberation that the assembly reached a result, which is, nevertheless, thus attributed to divine influence. The first Christians were not mistaken ; they had felt that the Spirit was in their midst. The calm and brotherly manner in which they had been able to conduct their deliberations testified to his presence ; and as they had faithfully sought the light, it had been evoked from their consultations as pure and bright as if it had descended from heaven by a direct revelation. No two things could be more unlike than the canons of a council of the fourth century and the decisions of the council at Jerusalem. Passed in free conference, they appealed only to Christian freedom.

We shall be much mistaken, however, if we suppose that the question of the relation of the two covenants was finally determined by these conferences. The obligation to observe the law was still laid on Jewish Christians. The concessions made to the Gentile converts would not long suffice. There is no ground whatever, therefore, for attributing any permanent value to the decree of the Council of Jerusalem. This decree was a temporary compromise in the interests of the peace of the Church. Acts xv, 28. Paul

* Baumgarten, vol. II, p. 141 ; Lange, vol. II, p. 184 ; Neander, vol. I, p. 206.

does not scruple, subsequently, to discuss freely one of the points at issue, that touching meats offered to idols. He declares, in his first Epistle to the Corinthians, that the liberty of the Gospel, rightly understood, banishes the scruples of a weak conscience, and that the Christian has a right to eat whatever is set before him. 1 Cor. x, 27. He admits, however, that every Christian should restrain himself, if need be, in the exercise of this freedom, rather than offend a weak brother in the faith. The ancient Church never recognized any permanent obligation in the decrees of the Council of Jerusalem. St. Augustine says: "For a time the Church divided itself into two sections, one composed of the circumcision, the other of the uncircumcision, which, while both resting on the Corner-stone, were distinguished by very marked characteristics; but that time being passed, what Christian would hold himself bound to abstain from birds strangled?"*

§ II. *The Dispute at Antioch.*

Immediately after the council at Jerusalem, Paul returned to Antioch with Barnabas. He was quickly followed thither by Peter. At this time must have occurred that contention between the two Apostles which is narrated with such courageous frankness in the Epistle to the Galatians. Gal. ii, 11–15. Peter, whose agreement with Paul had been so complete in the conference at Jerusalem, showed at first no scruple in associating freely with the converted Gentiles.

* "Quis jam Christianus observat ut turdas vel minutiores aviculas non attingat, nisi quarum sanguis effusus est." St. August., "Contra Faust.," book XXXII, c. xiii.

But on the arrival of certain Judaizing Christians from Judæa, he suddenly altered his conduct; he separated himself from those whom before he had treated as brethren, and drew away several disciples, Barnabas among others, by his example. What could account for such a rapid change? How could such scruples be revived after the council at Jerusalem, and what was the errand at Antioch of these messengers from James, whose part in the conference had been so distinctly one of conciliation? For these questions we can find no solution, so long as we regard moral and religious history as governed only by the inflexible logic of pure reason. But looked at in the light of the changeableness of human nature, its strange inconsistencies and failings, the events which transpired at Antioch are only too easily to be explained. The Council of Jerusalem was far from having solved the great problem of the primitive Church. It in no way followed, from its decisions, that the Jewish and Gentile converts were absolutely on a par, since the former were still bound to observe the ordinances of Moses. The barrier was lowered, not removed. Thus, no sooner was the decision communicated than it received various interpretations. Paul drew from it inferences which were undoubtedly by implication contained in it, but which were not equally evident to the eyes of all. He deemed that henceforward Jewish Christians might freely sit at table with converted Gentiles, a practice which would be a formal abrogation of one entire portion of the law of Moses. Clearly nothing could be more logical, when once the principle had been admitted, that converted Gentiles had the right to enter the Church without being circumcised. But James had not foreseen this application of the resolution. He had, indeed, provided by anticipation against it, by insisting on the obligation of Jews by birth to conform to the law of Moses as it was read in all synagogues. Acts xv, 21. We can well imagine that he may have heard with alarm of the broad interpretation given at Antioch to his decision, and may have sent messengers from his Church to put an end to an innovation which appeared to him at variance with the policy of conciliation of which he had been the wise promoter. It is probable that the delegates from James had neither his largeness of heart nor his conciliatory spirit. They were stronger partisans than he, and they carried into their mission a spirit of intolerance for which they were alone responsible. Peter, who did not wish to break with the Church at Jerusalem, allowed himself to be drawn into a concession, to be regretted as a failure alike in good faith and moral courage. The defenders of the primacy refuse to see in this act any thing more than a venial error in conduct; one which in no way affects his doctrinal infallibility. They forget that Peter, in refusing to eat with converted Gentiles, gave sanction to a false doctrine. In fact, a doctrinal question was at stake in this question of Christian practice; by his act Peter denied the equality of Christians of different origin, and thus espoused a positive error. All the subtleties of ingenious argument cannot avert the conclusion that Peter's pretended infallibility made shipwreck at Antioch. Paul withstood him to the face; he showed that his conduct was unreasonable and blameworthy, and he thus in open combat successfully defended one of the most important consequences of the decree of the council. He was preparing for the time when, like a scaffolding reared only for a temporary purpose, this transitory order of things would give place to the complete abrogation of the ancient law. The sequel of this history will show that the contention between Peter and Paul was as short as it was sharp. The great Apostle was on the eve of undertaking another missionary journey. He wished to visit the Churches which he had founded; he did not yet know how, under God, this purpose would expand, and he would be called to carry the Gospel into the very center of Western heathenism.*

* See Note E, at the end of the volume.

BOOK SECOND.

SECOND PERIOD OF THE APOSTOLIC AGE.—THE APOSTOLIC CHURCH UP TO THE DEATH OF ST. PAUL, FROM A. D. 50–65.

CHAPTER I.

MISSIONS OF THE CHURCH DURING THIS PERIOD.

§ I. *Second Missionary Journey of St. Paul.*

AFTER the conferences at Jerusalem Paul made but a short stay at Antioch. He was anxious to visit the Churches which he had founded, and to carry the Gospel into new countries. According to his original plan, Barnabas was to be his companion ; but the latter was not willing to separate from Mark, and Paul judged it not reasonable to take with them again the young disciple, who had left them in Pamphylia. He did not wish to have his own liberal views hindered in their manifestation by a timorous comrade, still under the thraldom of Jewish prejudice. A sharp contention followed, and Paul and Barnabas parted. The latter repaired with Mark to the Island of Cyprus, of which he was a native, while Paul returned into Asia Minor, accompanied by Silas. We shall see presently how fresh fellow-laborers joined him as he went. The support of such men, devoted to his person and his doctrine, was very necessary, while he was thus plunging into conflict with the dark depths of paganism. The Apostle could scarcely have undertaken, unaided, the tremendous task of founding Churches and directing their first steps in a path so untrodden. The sense of isolation could not have failed also to weaken his hands, for his heart was as full of tenderness as of courage. His associates threw themselves completely into his work; they shared its responsibility, and acted rather as friends, co-workers, and disciples, than subordinates. They yielded to his influence, but they did not wear it as a yoke. Silas, or Silvanus, who departed from Antioch with Paul, occupied a distinguished position in the Church at Jerusalem. He was one of the delegates who carried to Antioch the resolutions of the conference at Jerusalem; and from this circumstance it may be inferred that he had shown a liberal and conciliatory spirit in the deliberations. He served as a sort of link between the Church at Antioch and the Church at Jerusalem. Through him the latter was therefore directly associated with the work of Paul among the Gentiles. Paul's choice of him as a companion was thus both wise and prudent. Silas remained faithful to this mission of conciliation, for we subsequently find him associated with St. Peter. 1 Peter v, 12.

Paul manifests in this second journey all the great qualities which make him the type of the Christian missionary. Feeble in health, with many infirmities, his bodily strength is soon exhausted, but his zeal never, and his very weakness gives more touching pathos to his appeals. Gal. iv, 14, 15. That voice, broken by suffering, pleads with irresistible accents.

He is not merely the great orator; he seeks to win souls one by one, and where words are too weak, he uses the eloquence of tears. Acts xx, 19, 20. He preaches the Gospel with equal earnestness to the poor and unlearned, to the proconsul and the king; and employs as persuasive arguments in the prison where he teaches the slave Onesimus, as on the Athenian Areopagus, or at the judgment-seat of Festus. Not content with the extraordinary toils of his ministry, he supports himself by the work of his own hands, and, after a hard day of missionary labor, he may be seen providing, by tent-making, for his own subsistence, that he may be chargeable to none of the Churches. 1 Cor. ix, 12. Acts xviii, 3. Freely he will give that which freely he has received. This Christian, so free from prejudices, so liberal in spirit —this Apostle of a free salvation—nevertheless practices himself a severe asceticism, so much the more to be admired because he accounts it no merit and makes it no ground of pride. His one desire in keeping his body in such subjection is to conquer sin and to glorify his Master. Nor may we forget that all these unceasing labors are wrought in the midst of persecution and contradiction from without, while within is the perpetual pressure of that mysterious trial, that thorn in the flesh, designed to chasten and prove him, which, in his powerful language, he calls "a messenger of Satan sent to buffet him." *

* There has been much discussion as to the nature of this trial. It cannot have reference, as has been supposed, to the sufferings inseparable from apostleship, or Paul would not have desired exemption. Nor can we see in it merely the lusts of the flesh, especially after such a declaration as we have in 1 Cor. vii, 7, 8. It was, probably, physical suffering reacting upon the soul through the nervous organism.

His tact as a missionary is no less admirable than his zeal. Never was worker so wise as he in "redeeming the time"—taking advantage, that is, of favorable occasions and circumstances. When he arrives in a city, he immediately finds means of access to the largest possible numbers. He preaches sometimes in the synagogues; sometimes, as at Philippi, by the road side; sometimes, as in frivolous Athens, in the place of public resort. He adapts himself to the customs of every country, and far and wide proclaims the name of Jesus.

Paul began his missionary journey by visiting the Churches which he had founded in Syria and Cilicia. These were very prosperous, and daily increasing in the number of their members. In Lycaonia the Apostle took to himself a young disciple, converted during his previous journey, a young man full of faith, and endowed by God with many excellent gifts. The son of a Jewish mother, he had been taught from his childhood in the Scriptures. 2 Tim. iii, 14, 15. His father being a Gentile, he had not been circumcised. Paul deemed it well to observe scrupulously the decisions of the Council at Jerusalem, so as to give no ground for unjust suspicions; he accordingly circumcised Timothy, considering him according to Jewish custom, as of Hebrew origin. The young missionary also received the laying on of the hands of the assembled elders of his Church, (1 Tim. iv, 14,) as Paul had received it at Antioch before departing on his first mission. It was the prompting of the Divine Spirit, which led the brethren to give to Timothy this truly apostolic commission; they had a prophetic foresight of the service he would render to the Apostle in his great work. Timothy was, indeed, to Paul as a second self; the bond between them was like that of father and son. Paul's letters bear witness to the closeness of their relations. "I have no man like-minded," he writes to the Philippians. Phil. ii, 20. "I am mindful of thy tears," (2 Tim. i, 1–4,) he writes to him, speaking of their separation. Timothy was not less attached to the Churches than to Paul. He combined the energy of youth with the maturity of experience. Phil. ii, 22, The gravest and most delicate missions were safe in his hands. Paul had full confidence in him, and sometimes devolved upon him some of the most difficult duties of his office, such as presiding over the organization of new Churches. Timothy, like his beloved master, spared not himself in the service of Christ; he endured hardness to such a degree as even to injure his health. 1 Tim. v, 23. In his youth, his gentleness, his unshrinking devotedness, his utter forgetfulness of self, he presents to us one of the purest examples of primitive Christianity. He was the Melanchthon of the apostolic Luther.

Paul had also with him, at the beginning of this journey, another companion not less faithful: he was a Christian of Greek parentage, as we gather from his name—Epaphras, or Epaphroditus.* We shall see him again at Paul's side in the Roman prison. Col. iv, 12; Philemon 23. He appears to have possessed remarkable gifts; for Paul, having passed rapidly

* There seems to us no good ground for questioning the identity of the Epaphras of the Epistle to the Colossians with the Epaphroditus of the Epistle to the Philippians. (ii, 25.) Such a contraction of ancient names is most common.

through Phrygia, left Epaphras behind, and he there founded the flourishing Churches of Colosse, Hierapolis, and Laodicea.* The first of these cities, built on the banks of the Lycus, had been at one time a place of much consideration, and although now in its decline, it was still important. Laodicea, not far from Colosse, was beginning to eclipse it in commercial prosperity. Hierapolis was famous for its cave consecrated to Cybele. These three cities belonged to a country notable in the ancient world for a religious zeal approaching to frenzy. The worship of Cybele, or the Great Mother, had fostered the direst abominations of heathenism. It displayed that hideous blending of sensuality and cruelty which characterizes all merely natural religions. Apuleius has made us acquainted with the abominable rites of the Phrygian priests, and with the excesses of the fanatical eunuchs called "*Galli*," whose convulsive dances and deafening music were of world-wide repute. It might be easily foreseen that Christianity would with difficulty preserve its own purity in so tainted an atmosphere.

Paul merely passed through Phrygia, but made a longer stay in Galatia. There he found a race entirely new to him. The Galatians were not pure Asiatics, but a Western race, of Gallic and Celtic origin, which had settled in Asia Minor three centuries before Christ, and which, although modified by long sojourn in the East, yet retained in many respects their original type. The people of these countries

* Nowhere in the Acts do we read of any sojourn of Paul's at Colosse, while it is positively said in the Epistle to the Colossians that they received the Gospel from Epaphras. (Col. i, 7.)

were at once warlike and democratic; they had for a long time governed themselves, and under the imperial dominion had retained their own rulers. Paul, ever ready to be all things to all men, threw an unwonted vivacity into his preaching in order to make an impression on their warm and sensitive natures. In writing to them afterward, he says that Christ was set forth before them as vividly as if they themselves had seen him crucified. Gal. iii, 1. He thus won his way into their hearts, and the bodily sufferings under which he labored completed the conquest of their sympathies. He was to them as an angel, even as Christ Jesus, and their growing enthusiasm soon knew no bounds. "I bear you record," says the Apostle, in recalling that happy time, "that if it had been possible ye would have plucked out your own eyes, and given them to me." Gal. iv, 15. But this quick sensibility to impressions might be as easily turned in an opposite direction, and he was soon to learn to his cost the vacillation of these impetuous natures.

The mission in Galatia seems a sort of preparation for the transition into Europe. The time had come for Paul to set his foot on the classic ground of philosophy and ancient art. For entering on a field of labor so wide and so new, a direct call from God was necessary. Paul was preparing to pursue his mission in Asia, when he was turned aside by a very remarkable vision. A man of Macedonia appeared to him, saying, "Come over into Macedonia, and help us!" This man was the representative of those powerful nations of the West which had accomplished such great things, and agitated such great thoughts in the domain of politics, and of free speculation, and which now, growing old and feeble, writhing in the restlessness of doubt at the foot of their world-famous altars of art and beauty, were turning tired eyes toward the East, seeking there a deliverance of which they had no longer any hope in themselves. This cry, *Come over and help us!* was it not the groaning of Greece, enslaved and fallen? and did not the same despairing entreaty come up from all quarters of the Roman empire? Was not the strange yearning of the West toward the religions of the East itself an unspoken prayer for help? This, then, was a favorable moment for carrying the Gospel into Europe. The ruler of the world at this period was Claudius, the puppet of mistresses and favorites, who had laid upon the whole empire a yoke of deepest humiliation, because the slavery imposed was accompanied with no redeeming ray of glory. Neither by the arts of peace or war did Claudius achieve any thing honorable to himself or to the world. Under this condition of things, the historians of the time describe the deepening agitation of men's minds, ever in restless quest of the new. The sick man turns upon his bed in feverish impatience, and seeks in religions beyond his own new medicines for the soul's long malady.* But in spite of such favoring dispositions, the preaching of the Gospel would have to encounter in Europe a host of obstacles. The refined culture of ancient Greece, ever devoted to the worship of form, idolatrous of beauty alike in language and in art—the terrible corruption of manners—the political and religious despotism of Rome,

* Tacitus, "Annals," xi, 15.

which, with its marvelous organization, had agencies in every city, large or small, to discover and to impede any hostile movement—such were some of the main obstacles in the path of the missionary of Christ. But Paul was not the man to shrink before them; and there was power enough in the doctrine which he preached to triumph over philosophers and rulers, over human force and human science.

It was at Troas Paul had the vision which decided him to go over into Macedonia. It was also at Troas he associated with himself another helper—Luke, the physician, who was to be the inspired chronicler of the apostolic age. Luke was, according to Eusebius,* a native of Antioch, and in all probability a Gentile by birth, and one of the Apostle's converts. We shall find him henceforward constantly by Paul's side, his companion in prison and up to the eve of martyrdom. None caught more thoroughly than he the spirit of the Apostle; none was more capable of truly representing his life, and preserving to us the features of that noble form. The legend which speaks of him as a painter, only errs by clothing a moral quality in a material form. Luke shows himself a true and inimitable painter in his representation of the Christians of the first century.

From Troas Paul went by Neapolis to Philippi. This city, built by Philip II., on the borders of Macedonia and Thrace, and rendered illustrious by the famous battle in which the Roman republic finally succumbed under Brutus, had become a flourishing Roman colony, the most important in the whole

* Eusebius, "Hist. Eccles.," iii, 4.

country.* It was governed, like all the colonies, by magistrates called *decemvirs*, who exercised all the rights of sovereignty in minor causes. They had lictors at their command.†

In entering on this new field, the work of Christian missions was coming into collision not simply with Jewish fanaticism, or popular superstition as in Asia, but with the Roman administration, so admirably constructed for the universal suppression of liberty. Immediately on arriving at Philippi, Paul repairs to the river side, where the Jews were accustomed to assemble every Sabbath. There he found only a few women. To these he preached the Gospel with all his wonted earnestness and power; and in the house of one of them, Lydia, a seller of purple from Thyatira, the first nucleus was formed of that Church which was to be the jewel in his apostolic crown. Into this humble family there soon came a poor servant-girl, whose condition sheds light upon the paganism of that day. The mysterious malady, known as possession, was not peculiar to Judea. In this time of momentous crisis, the intervention of the powers of the unseen world was more than usually direct and sensible. It seems as if the barrier between that world and ours was broken down. The evil spirits, whose existence is so clearly revealed in the New Testament, act at such epochs in a special manner on persons predisposed to their influence by an unhealthy moral and physical condition. Natural phenomena, such as somnambulism, assume a pecul-

* This is the most natural sense to attach to the words: ἥτις ἐστὶν πρώτη.

† Στρατηγοῖς (Acts xvi, 20) ῥαβδοῦχοι.

iar character, and are aggravated by the addition of actual possession. The girl healed by Paul was the subject of this diabolical somnambulism. She had some gifts of divination, like somnambulists in all ages. Her fellow-citizens, therefore, regarded her as possessed with the spirit of Python, which was one of the names of Apollo, the god of oracles. But in addition to this gift of divination, there was in her case positive possession, as is clear from the language of Paul, who commands the evil spirit to come out of her. As the unhappy girl follows Paul and Silas about the streets, crying, "These men are the servants of the most high God, which show unto you the way of salvation," (Acts xvi, 17,) the Apostle, who will not receive demoniacal support at any price, heals the girl. This becomes the occasion of a violent persecution. The masters of the sick girl, enraged at the loss of the gains they made by her divination, stir up the populace, and drag Paul and Silas before the *decemvirs*, charging them with introducing into the city a religion not sanctioned by the laws. The magistrates yield to the popular clamor: they throw the accused into prison, and the jailer, the pliant instrument of the fury of the crowd, casts them into a dark dungeon, and makes their feet fast in the stocks. A long and painful night begins; but the prisoners feel free and happy in their chains. "That gloomy prison," to use the language of Tertullian, "was to them what the desert was to the prophets—a holy retreat; one of those solitary places in which by preference Christ reveals his glory to his disciples. While their body was in fetters, their soul, sublimely free in spite of grating doors and guarded passages, was pressing on the way to God. The flesh feels no ill when the spirit is in heaven." * They are singing at midnight the praises of God. Suddenly an earthquake bursts the prison doors. The terrified jailer, fearing the retribution awaiting him if his prisoners escape, draws his sword to kill himself. The voice of Paul arrests him. "Do thyself no harm," cries the Apostle, "for we are all here." The soul of the rough man is moved by the generosity of these strange prisoners, who thus return good for evil. The sight of Paul and Silas rejoicing in their chains has already touched his conscience. Words which, doubtless, he had previously heard from their lips receive a new significance; in place of the dread of man, there springs up in his heart fear of the judgment of God. There is a convulsion in his inner nature corresponding to the convulsion in the world without, and he utters that cry of the broken heart whose salvation is nigh, "What must I do to be saved?" We know the Apostles' reply. The jailer and his family at once receive the sign of the new birth, and the Church of the Philippians gains a noble victory in the very place in which its founder was to have been consigned to ignominy and silence.

Paul's imprisonment had been the result of a tumult of the people. His cause had not been tried. The *decemvirs* having, like other Roman magistrates, but little leaning to religious fanaticism, now send their lictors to bring the Apostles out of the prison. But Paul protests indignantly against the unlawful

* "Hoc præstat carcer Christiano quod eremus prophetis. Nihil crus sentit in nervo, cum animus in cælo est." (Tertullian, "Ad Martyres," c. ii.)

treatment they have received. He boldly declares himself a Roman citizen—a name which, according to Cicero, casts a shield of protection over all who could use it to the uttermost parts of the world, and even in the midst of barbarous nations.* The *Porcia lex* forbade the beating with rods of a Roman citizen. The magistrates, alarmed at such a message, came themselves to release the Apostles; and we learn from the example of Paul on this occasion to rise above the narrow and petty notions which interdict Christians from boldly asserting their rights as citizens. Such views tend, in their practical issue, to sap the whole divine basis of society.

Paul left at Philippi a Church which had received the baptism of persecution, and which was strengthened in its attachment to his person by witnessing his courageous endurance of suffering.

Of this attachment the Philippian Church soon gave him touching proof, by sending generous aid to him at Thessalonica, whither he had gone to carry the Gospel. Phil. iv, 16. He had hastily passed through Amphipolis and Apollonia in order to reach this important city. It had been built by Cassander, who had given to it the name of his wife. Standing at the base of a mountain, not far from the sea, it was the capital of the second district of the province of Macedonia. It had become very flourishing under the Romans, especially by its commerce, and the Jews, who had flocked to it in large numbers, had there built a synagogue. Paul preached the Gospel to them three Sabbath days, and some of them

* "Illa vox et imploratio: Civis Romanus sum! sæpe multis in ultimis terris opem inter barbaros et salutem tulit."

believed, and consorted with the Apostle. But the preaching was much more successful among the Greeks. Paul, in his first Epistle to the Thessalonians, gives an admirable account of his mission among them. He came to them, as we there see, still bearing in body and spirit the wounds he had received at Philippi. 1 Thess. ii, 2. The fanatical Jews at Thessalonica soon again kindled the flame of persecution against him, and it was evident he would find no respite or peace. In the midst of many conflicts, therefore, his ministry was accomplished; but his courage never faltered, and the power of God was magnified in his servant's weakness. 1 Thess. i, 5. Enfeebled by suffering, he yet proves irresistible in his arguments with the unbelieving Jews. But his own experience of much affliction has given a deepened gentleness to his ministry, and full of tenderness for souls scarcely escaped out of heathen darkness, he cherishes them "even as a nurse her children." 1 Thess. ii, 7. He finds in these Thessalonians much readiness to receive the truth, and a childlike enthusiasm for the new religion, very beautiful, and productive of the happiest results while restrained within bounds by his presence, but dangerously akin to fanaticism. Hence the earnest warnings in his Epistles to the new converts not to neglect the fulfillment of their daily duties, in undue impatience of all the trammels of earthly life.

These ardent young Christians displayed heroic courage in the conflict stirred up by the Jews. 1 Thess. i, 6. Paul was probably led by the persecutions which burst so rapidly upon this newly-formed Church to dwell much on the glorious issues of Christianity, the triumph of the Lord, and his near return. 1 Thess. i, 10.

It was, indeed, a terrible storm which broke over the Church at Thessalonica. Paul's implacable adversaries hired men of low character, who by their calumnies of the Apostle set all the city in an uproar. Wresting the words he had spoken with reference to the kingdom of Christ and his speedy coming to reign, (Acts xvii, 7,) they accused him before the Prætor of conspiring against Cæsar. They thus took advantage at once of the Roman law, and of the passions of the people—a cunning proceeding which proved only too successful.

When they could not find either Paul or Silas, they assaulted the house of an inhabitant of the city, named Jason, who, being probably a convert through their preaching, had received them into his house. The magistrates committed Jason to prison, and he was only released on giving bail. The Apostles were sent away by their friends by night to Berea, a town about ten miles distant from Thessalonica. Here they met with a better reception from the Jews; they even gained some adherents in the upper classes of society. Acts xvii, 12. But the synagogue of Thessalonica, irritated by a course of conduct, which in its eyes seemed only wicked obstinacy, contrived to stir up the Berean populace also against Paul and Silas. Some devoted friends conducted Paul at once to Athens, while Silas, Timothy, and the rest of their company, remained for awhile behind.

What Athens was to the ancient world is well known. "From Athens," says Cicero, "philosophy and religion, agriculture and laws, have gone forth into the whole world."* At Athens paganism had attained all the perfection of which it was capable. The religion of Greece, which was a religion of artists, since its essence was the worship of the beautiful, had there found its best interpreters in the great sculptors, whose immortal works were the embodiment of ideal beauty. In strange paradox, it was also at Athens that paganism had been more deeply undermined by philosophy. Socrates and Plato had there taught the adoration of a deity more adapted than the Olympian Jupiter to meet the demands of conscience. Nor must we forget that not far from Athens were celebrated the Eleusinian Mysteries, so closely connected with the worship of the divinities, who, according to the belief of the Greeks, had the control of death and of the judgment of the soul after the earthly life. The secret source of this worship was the vague dread of eternity, and the feeling of the insufficiency of a purely æsthetic religion to lighten the dark abode of death.

The Athenian people were more concerned than most to appease the gods. Philostratus puts these words into the mouth of Apollonius of Tyana: "It is wise to speak well of all the gods, especially at Athens."† This disposition had grown, as Greek polytheism had fallen into deeper and deeper decay. In its subjection to the Romans, the brilliant city was at once more frivolous and more devout than ever before. The rostrum was voiceless; the great poets had been succeeded by frigid versifiers. The places of Plato

* "Unde humanitas, doctrina, religio, fruges, jura, leges, artes in omnes terras distributæ putantur." (Cicero, "Pro Flacco," 26, 62.)

† "Philost.," vi, 3.

and Aristotle were filled by feeble philosophers. While the Epicurean mocked at the gods, the Stoic asserted the uselessness of metaphysics. The Athenian people, indolent and skeptical, lounged about the public places, seeking to beguile their ignoble leisure, but chafed all the while in spirit by a restlessness that would not be allayed.

Such were the conflicting influences at work when the great Apostle arrived in Athens. As he passed along the streets of the queenly city, where the masterpieces of pagan art met his eye at every step, a sacred sadness seized his soul, and he eagerly desired to preach Christ to these poor idolators. After having proclaimed the Gospel in the synagogue, he sought access to the Epicurean and Stoic philosophers. The Athenians, whose curiosity was easily excited, brought him to the Areopagus, to hear him speak of these new gods. It has been erroneously imagined that Paul was arraigned by the Athenians, and that his address was a defense of himself rather than a general apology for Christianity. He was indeed taken to the spot, where causes were customarily tried, but it was only that he might more easily harangue a large assembly. Paul had before him the marvelous Acropolis, adorned with the miracles of the chisel of Phidias; above him the temple of Theseus, the most ancient monument in Athens; and wherever his eye turned, it rested on the altars of false gods. It is worth observing, that the temples which were nearest to him, in the Areopagus itself, were dedicated to those subterranean deities which inspired so much terror in the Greeks, and which expressed the protest of outraged conscience against the too facile poetry of their state religion. These temples were, in fact, according to Pausanias, devoted to the Furies and to Pluto.* The worship of these terrible and mysterious deities implicitly contained an acknowledgment of the unknown God. It is of little consequence whether the famous inscription, which the Apostle makes his starting-point, really had all the significance which he seems to ascribe to it. It was, in any case, a faithful expression of one aspect of Greek polytheism, and he had a perfect right so to make use of it.

The testimony of Pausanias and of Philostratus confirms that of St. Paul as to this inscription.† Of all the interpretations which have been given of it, the most plausible appears to us to be that of Diogenes Laërtius. He says, that in the time of a plague, when men knew not which God to propitiate in order to avert it, Epimenides caused black and white sheep to be let loose from the Areopagus, and wherever they lay down, to be offered to the respective divinities. "Hence it comes," says Diogenes Laërtius, "that altars are still found in Athens which do not bear the name of any known god." ‡ This fear of neglecting angry and unknown gods clearly revealed that in the hearts entertaining it there was a deep

* "Pausanias," p. 27; Xylander Edit.

† *Βωμοὶ θεῶν ὀνομαζομένων ἀγνώστων.* Pausanias, i, 1; Philostratus, vi, 3.

‡ Diog. Laërtius, "Epimenides," i, 1. St. Jerome says that the inscription was thus worded: "Diis Asiæ et Europæ et Africæ, Diis ignotis et peregrinis." ("Ad. Tit.," i, 12.) But this opinion has no solid ground. Eichhorn maintains that it referred to an ancient god, whose name was lost. This opinion might be accepted if we had not the explicit testimony of Diogenes Laërtius. (See De Wette's "Comm. on the Acts," in which the question is admirably treated.)

consciousness of the insufficiency of their religion; for if they had truly believed in the gods they knew, they would have been assured that when these were appeased there was nothing more to dread. But they had a vague conception that another yet more powerful deity was angry with them. The worship of the subterranean gods took its rise in the same consciousness. "That they had reared an altar to an unknown god," says Calvin, "was a sign that they knew nothing certainly. It is true they had an infinite multitude of gods, but when with these they associated unknown gods, they by that act confessed that they knew nothing of the true Deity." *

It is not our purpose here to analyze Paul's address; we shall treat of that when he comes to speak of his doctrine. It is impossible not to notice, however, the skill with which he finds the point of contact between the truth and his hearers. Observing their extraordinary devotion, he traces it to its principle—the deep necessity felt by the human heart of union with God. He reads on the altars of paganism the avowal of its impotence, and he borrows the words of a pagan poet to show how grand is man in his origin, and how infinite are his aspirations. That living and true God, whom they in their ignorance are feeling after, has just revealed himself in an amazing manner by the gift of his Son; and faith in the Christ is the one way of escape from the terrible judgment which awaits the unpardoned sinner at the resurrection day. The Greeks listened to the Apostle so long as he confined himself to philosophic generalities, but they could not endure the faintest allusion

* Calvin, "Commentaries," vol. ii, p. 798, Paris edition. 1854.

to a judgment to come. The doctrine of immortality was contrary alike to the pantheism of the Stoics and to the atheism of the Epicureans. It was natural that Greek paganism, on its first contact with the severe religion of Jesus Christ, should elude its appeals, and seek refuge in graceful frivolity. The Greek feels no indignation; he does not persecute like the synagogue; he simply returns with a scornful smile to the diversions of the public square—a striking illustration of the distance which divides mere intellectual curiosity from a serious love of truth. The bow, however, so steadily drawn by the Apostle, has not been ineffectual. The true worshiper of the "unknown god" perceives that, in truth, this God whom Paul declares to them is He; and among the new disciples, one is a judge of the Areopagus. In the metropolis of paganism, Paul has spoken words mightier and more beautiful than any which had ever fallen from the lips of philosophers or poets—words which will be a living power when temples and statues are in ruins. Their ruin is indeed already imminent. In preaching the true God, Paul has pronounced the death-doom of polytheism, and the sentence is without appeal.

From Athens Paul repaired to Corinth. This city, washed by two seas, the Ionian and the Ægean, united, through the activity of its commerce, the pomp and luxury of Asia with the civilization of Greece. It had been celebrated in all ancient times for the cultivation of the arts and sciences.* Destroyed by Mummius, 146 years before Christ, it had been rebuilt by Julius Cæsar, and had become the

* Herodotus, ii, 167.

capital of Achaia. Corinth, at the period when Paul visited it, had recovered all its ancient splendor. It surpassed even Athens ; for while the city of Pericles represented the most exalted side of paganism—pure and noble art, great philosophy and great poetry—Corinth represented its material and voluptuous side; and such luster is ever the most conspicuous in an age of decay.* Its beautiful climate, its wealth, the extraordinary concourse of foreigners within its walls, all contributed to the corruption of manners. Thus, amid the licentious cities of the old world, Corinth was distinguished for its immorality. The worship of Aphrodite was there observed in all its shamelessness. To live like a Corinthian was a proverbial expression for a career of debauchery. What a miracle was the foundation of a Church in such a city! Paul's labors here commenced less brilliantly than at Athens. He began by working in the shade. His first converts were a humble family of Jews, fugitives from Rome, in consequence of the decree of banishment issued by Claudius against their nation. Priscilla and Aquila were fellow-countrymen of the Apostle's, coming, like him, from Pontus ; like him, they also maintained themselves by making tents of the substantial fabrics of their country. A close friendship arose between them ; Paul lodged under their roof, and supported himself by working with them. Not for a day, however, did he lose sight of his missionary work. Every Sabbath he went up to the synagogue, and in the interval he preached the Gospel to the Gentiles. It is evident, from his first Epistle to the Corinthians, that he addressed himself

* Lange, work quoted, ii, 233.

chiefly to the lower orders of society. 1 Cor. i, 26. He had not here a brilliant auditory, as on the Areopagus; he did not see the first magistrates and philosophers of the city thronging around him. He presented the truth to the Corinthians in all its naked simplicity; he would not pander to the tastes of the degenerate Greeks, enamored of human eloquence and outward show. "My speech and my preaching," he subsequently says, "was not with enticing words of man's wisdom." 1 Cor. ii, 4. The simple setting forth of the Cross was the substance of his teaching. Oppressed, as he may well have been, by the sight of the enormities of paganism shamelessly enacted before his eyes, he tells us that he preached the Gospel in weakness, and in fear, and in much trembling. 1 Cor. ii, 3. Nevertheless, he gained many adherents, and, among others, Stephanas, Crispus, and Gaius. 1 Cor. xvi, 15; 1 Cor. i, 14. The Jews at Corinth, with a few exceptions, offered him an obstinate resistance; he was even constrained to an open rupture with them. He separated himself from them, after addressing them in terrible words of denunciation, justly provoked by their blasphemies; and he founded a true synagogue in the house of a disciple named Justus, where he continued to preach. His discourses produced such an effect that the chief ruler of the Jewish synagogue was won to the Gospel. The Apostle did not in general baptize the new Christians, leaving this duty to his companions, or to the elders of the young Church. He was no representative of an ecclesiastical hierarchy, which makes it its first concern to initiate men into outward observances; he was concerned solely with the moral and religious effect of his teaching, leaving aside as subordinate all questions of form.

After he had thus preached the Gospel during a year and a half, the Jews, taking advantage of the arrival of a new proconsul, accused him of professing a strange and unauthorized religion. Happily for Paul, this proconsul was a man of a tolerant and enlightened disposition; he was Gallio, brother of the famous Seneca, by whom he was declared to be the mildest of men.* He refused, with the disdain of a lettered Roman, to interfere in these questions of religion, which appeared to him all miserable chicanery. He shared the proud contempt of his countrymen for the Jews, and he did not scruple to leave Paul's accusers to the violence of the inhabitants of the city, who held them and all their race in abomination. Paul soon after quitted Corinth. It was from this city that he wrote his two Epistles to the Church of Thessalonica.† Timotheus and Silas, who rejoined the Apostle at Corinth, brought him news from Thessalonica, and their communications led him to write, warning that Church against such an undue preoccupation with the prophetic aspect of revelation as might lead into error.

Paul, before leaving Corinth, had his head shaved,

* "Nemo mortalium unus tam dulcis est quam hic omnibus." (Seneca, "Præf. Natur. Quæst.," I, iv.

† Reuss, "Geschichte der Heilig. Schrift., N. T.," pp. 67, 68. It has been erroneously stated that the first epistle was dated from Athens; but this is not possible. We see, in fact, (1 Thess. i, 7,) that the Churches of Achaia are spoken of. The passage in 1 Thess. ii, 18, also implies that some time had elapsed between the journey of Paul to Thessalonica and the date of the letter. Baur's objections to the genuineness of the second epistle are entirely dogmatic and of no critical value.

in fulfillment of a vow made some time previously. We cannot but wonder to see the great Apostle of the Gentiles submitting to this legal observance. We must not forget, however, that this was an age of transition, and that Judaism was only gradually vanishing before Christianity, as shadows before the sun. Paul, also, while he borrowed an ancient custom from the religion of his fathers, did so not as under the yoke of Mosaic observances, but in the use of his Christian liberty. While holding as a fundamental principle that the whole life is one act of worship, and that whatever is done must be done unto the Lord, he yet admitted a sort of individual discipline, by which portions of the life, characterized by greater austerity than the rest, might be set aside, so that the soul, freed from the fetters of the material, might the more readily rise into a purer region. 1 Cor. vii, 5. The vow of the Nazarite, so common among the Jews, seemed to St. Paul the faithful symbol of this exceptional consecration of a portion of his life to God. This vow enforced, as we know, abstinence for a time from all fermented drinks, and the free growing of the hair uncut. Those who were under the vow were regarded as specially consecrated to God. Num. vi, 1–8. Commentators have been much perplexed by the fact that Paul had his head shorn at Cenchræa, and not in the temple at Jerusalem, according to Mosaic prescription.* For ourselves, we regard this deviation from Jewish ritual as in perfect harmony with his principles; he felt no scruple in modifying legal practices, because he held

* "And the Nazarite shall shave the head of his separation at the door of the tabernacle of the congregation." (Num. vi, 18.)

himself to be under the law of liberty. The Apostle, who, writing some months later to the Corinthians, says, "Know ye not that your body is the temple of the Holy Ghost?" (1 Cor. vi, 19,) and who, consequently, no longer believed in the existence of any particular sanctuary, was thus raised above all the ordinances which had reference to the temple. He felt himself as fully at liberty to have his head shorn at Corinth as at Jerusalem, if circumstances rendered it desirable. He thus vindicated the voluntary self-discipline of his religious life from the appearance of a timid subservience to ritual law.*

From Corinth, Paul went to Ephesus, with Aquila and Priscilla. After a short stay, he left them there, and himself went up, by way of Cæsarea, to Jerusalem, there to keep the Feast of Pentecost.† He did

* The vow of Paul has been the subject of long and confused disputations. It has been maintained, first, that the vow was not made by him, but by Aquila; but the adjective κειράμενος evidently refers to the principal subject of the sentence. Neander, ("Pflanz.," i, 348) resting on a passage of Josephus, ("De Bello Judaico," ii, 15,) supposes a modification of the vow of the Nazarite among the Jews of that period; but the passage of Josephus does not at all signify that the head was shaved elsewhere than in the temple. Lange maintains that Paul had his head shorn before quitting the Gentile lands, in order that his new growth of hair might be undefiled; but such a notion is utterly at variance with Paul's principles. Baumgarten (ii, 326, 327) makes unfair use of the symbolical manner in which the Apostle speaks of the long hair of a woman, (1 Cor. xi, 19,) and sees in St. Paul's vow a token of his spirit of humility and submission; but this is a forced and over-subtle explanation. As to the idea of Salmasius, that what is here meant is some such vow as those spoken of by Juvenal, (Satire xii, 815,) which consisted in devoting the hair of the head to the Deity, it is utterly baseless.

† Paul goes up by sea to Jerusalem, Now the inexperience of navigation would render such a voyage impossible in the spring. The feast to be observed could not, therefore, have been the Passover;

not stay either there or at Ephesus, but returned to Antioch, whence he had twice gone forth on his great missionary journeys. During his sojourn at Jerusalem and at Antioch, Aquila and Priscilla heard at Ephesus of a Jewish stranger who was producing a deep impression by his discourses in the synagogue. This was Apollos, who was to play so important a part in the early Church, and whose influence at Corinth was to rival even that of St. Paul. He came from Alexandria, where he had heard the learned teachers who endeavored to fuse and harmonize the Mosaic religion with the Greek philosophy. From this school he had doubtless acquired much aptitude in penetrating into the meaning of sacred symbols. He had probably gained some knowledge of the new religion in a recent journey in Palestine ; but he had, as yet, very elementary notions of the Gospel, for he had come in contact only with disciples of John the Baptist, and had received only the baptism of John. He succeeded, however, even with these imperfect lights, in convincing the Jews at Ephesus. He was a man nobly gifted, deeply versed in the sacred Scriptures, full of fervor and enthusiasm,* courageous,† and possessed of remarkable oratorical power, which he had been able freely to exercise in one of the great centers of Greek civilization.‡ From Aquila and Priscilla Apollos learned the way of truth more perfectly ; and thus furnished, he went at once to Corinth, where his eloquence§ produced an

and of the other Jewish festivals, the Pentecost alone would have a religious interest for such a man as Paul.

* *Δυνατὸς ὢν ἐν ταῖς γραφαῖς.*

† *Ζέων τῷ πνεύματι.*

‡ *Ἤρξατο παῤῥησιάζεσθαι.*

§ *Λόγιος.* Acts xviii, 24, 28.

unparalleled effect. We shall soon meet with him again, and shall see how party spirit, without Apollos' own concurrence, wrested his noble gifts to the disadvantage of Paul, whose language had neither the correctness nor the beauty of that of the young doctor of Alexandria. The author of the Epistle to the Hebrews is, nevertheless, perfectly in harmony with the Apostle Paul, though acting, according to the custom of the apostolic age, with complete independence.*

§ II. *Third Missionary Journey of St. Paul.*

Paul began his third missionary journey by visiting the Churches he had founded in Phrygia and Galatia. He had the grief of finding that in the latter country, where he had been so readily received, his adversaries had succeeded in partially nullifying his influence and in giving currency to Pharisaic legalism. He went on to Ephesus, sorrowful and wounded by signs so unexpected of ingratitude and changeableness. His first care was to write a letter to the Churches of Galatia. Every line evidences the painful surprise he felt at being thus distrusted by those who had at first devoted themselves to him with enthusiastic affection.

Ephesus now became the principal center of his apostolic work. No other city could have been chosen so well adapted to be the focus from which light might radiate over the whole of Asia. The capital of ancient Ionia, it had been the cradle of

* See, with reference to Apollos, Bleek, "Brief an die Hebræer," i, 422.

that famous Ionian civilization, which, transplanted into Greece, and correcting the effeminacy of Eastern manners by the moral energy of the West, while retaining all the flexibility and brilliancy of the Greek genius, had found full and harmonious development at Athens. At Ephesus, situated not far from the Ægean sea, between Smyrna and Miletus, the oriental type predominated; but it had also come under the influence of the West, by the numerous communications maintained through its commerce with Greece. It had, however, faithfully adhered to the worship of the old gods of Asia; the only change it had made was to give the name of Diana to the Astarte or Artemis of the Asiatic religions. These, as is well known, consisted substantially in a voluptuous adoration of nature; and sensuality was an element inseparable from their religious rites. The temple of Diana of the Ephesians was of world-wide celebrity. Burned by Erostratus, it had been rebuilt with greater magnificence. Pausanius declares no other temple could be compared to it for grandeur;* the glory of Diana of Ephesus threw into the shade all the other divinities of the East and West. At a time of crisis, when all eyes were turned toward the East, a divinity which formed a sort of link between the religions of the East and West could not fail to acquire extensive popularity. It was said that the statue of the goddess had come down from heaven; it was carved in wood, rough and ungraceful, like the mummies of Egypt. It was customary among the pagans to carry about with them small images of the

* *Μέγεθος τυῦ ναοῦ τὰ παρὰ πᾶσιν ἀνθρώποις κατασκεύασματα ὑπερηκότος.* (Pausanias, p. 141.)

temples in which they worshiped;* thus the making of shrines had become a very large and profitable trade. The people of Ephesus were distinguished for their love of pleasure. "The whole city," says Philostratus, "resounded with the music of flutes accompanying the dance, and the streets were full of men disguised as women."† The corruption of manners had here reached its climax.

Ephesus was, like Corinth, and to a greater degree than Antioch, one of the centers of the pagan world, where all sects and all opinions met and came into collision. There, as in all the large cities, was a Jewish synagogue; in this Paul preached for three months; but here, as at Corinth, he came to an open rupture with his countrymen, and abandoned the struggle with the invincible obduracy of the Pharisaic spirit. He continued to teach the Gospel in the house of one Tyrannus, a public teacher of rhetoric, who had a school at Ephesus, and who had doubtless been convinced of the folly of his system by the preaching of the Apostle. Thus Christianity gained a readier victory in a school of pagan literature than in the school of the doctors of the law; and those who read Moses and the prophets showed themselves less prepared to receive the Gospel than the Greeks, nurtured on Homer, Hesiod, and Pindar. So true is it, that external revelation is a dead-letter to those whose hearts are hardened.

Besides the unbelieving Jews of the synagogue,

* "Asclepiades philosophus deæ cœlestis argenteum breve figmentum quocumque ibat secum solitus efferre." (Ammianus Marcellinus, xxii, 13.)

† Philostratus, "Vita Apoll.," iv, 2.

Paul met at Ephesus with some proselytes, who were in a singular position. They had been among the multitudes who flocked to the baptism of repentance administered by John in the river Jordan. They had heard of the miracles of Christ, and had recognized him as the true Messiah, without, however, getting beyond the point of view of their first master, the Baptist. They had left Palestine before the resurrection of the Saviour, and knew nothing of the great facts upon which the Church was founded; they were still in the position of the disciples before the Feast of Pentecost. The germ of faith in their hearts rapidly sprang and grew under the teaching of Paul; they soon received the symbol of the new birth, and the Holy Spirit marked his presence in their midst by signs and wonders.

There was also a third class of Jews at Ephesus. These were exorcists, who worked on the credulity and eager expectations of the people, and endeavored, like Simon of Samaria and Elymas of Cyprus, to make gain by sorcery. They attempted to cast out devils by the repetition of mysterious formulas, which they ascribed to Solomon.* They succeeded sometimes in producing a certain impression on the diseased imaginations of the sufferers from possession, but their cures were not lasting; had they been so they would certainly have set them in the balance, against the miracles wrought by the Apostles. Some of these magicians, seeing the miracles which Paul worked in the name of Christ, imagined he had the secret of some more efficacious formula than

* *Καὶ αὕτη μέχρι νῦν παρ' ἡμῶν ἡ θεραπεία πλεῖστον ἰσχύει.* (Josephus, "Ant.," viii, 2. See Olshausen, "Comment.," i, 400.)

those they were in the habit of using. They endeavored to cast out the demons in the same manner, pronouncing, like the Apostle, the sacred name of Jesus. Their attempt proved a miserable failure. The unhappy man upon whom they made the experiment, in one of those mysterious crises of supernatural lucidity common to such cases, cried out, "Jesus I know, and Paul I know; but who are ye?" and, leaping on the false exorcists with demoniacal strength, wounded and overcame them. The powers of darkness are not to be vanquished by words and formularies; they yield only to a divine influence, passing from soul to soul.

This incident in the history of Paul draws a well-marked line of distinction between miracle and magic.* The event had a very happy effect upon the Greek proselytes, who were already attracted by the Gospel, but were not yet free from their superstitions. Ephesus was, indeed, famous for the practice of the arts of sorcery; Apollonius of Tyana there excited the greatest enthusiasm. If Paul wrought more miracles in this than on his other missions, it was because no other method would have been equally effectual in arresting the attention of so corrupt and idolatrous a city. The lesson thus severely taught the Jewish exorcists was further of use in preventing any possible identification of the power of God manifested in the apostles, with the sorceries of the impostors. Many of these, reproved by their own conscience,

* Justin speaks of devils cast out by the name of Jesus: *Κατὰ τοῦ ὀνόματος αὐτοῦ πᾶν δαιμόνιον ἐξαρκιζόμενον νικᾶται.* ("Dial. cum. Tryph.," c. lxxxv. Comp. Origen, "C. Celsum," i, 25.) We have here a superstition of the second century, which reminds us of the error of the Jewish exorcists.

brought their cabalistic books and burned them publicly, just as, in later times, a penitent people cast all that reminded them of their life of worldliness into the flames kindled at Florence by the voice of Savonarola. An important Church was founded at Ephesus, which was to be in the close of the apostolic age that which Jerusalem and Antioch had been at its commencement.

For three years Ephesus was the chief abode of the Apostle. During this time, however, he made a journey of considerable extent in Europe. His first purpose was to visit Corinth, to set at rest the unhappy contentions in the Church of that city. He went by sea, and turned aside from the direct course to visit Crete. It is easy to suppose that the Gospel had been already conveyed to that island by some Christians, and that Paul's mission there, like Peter's at Samaria, was to carry on a work already commenced, and prosperous. His stay was but short. This island, famous for its wealth, and for the number of its towns, presented peculiar difficulties to Christianity. The national character of its inhabitants had been depicted in severe colors by one of its poets, Epimenides, surnamed the prophet, who accused them of being altogether given up to sensuality and falsity. Titus i, 12. The very name of Cretan had become synonymous with liar.* A Church was established in the midst even of this depraved people; but Christianity had many a conflict to wage with the recurring influences of the old corrupt nature.

From Crete Paul went on to Corinth, where he stayed but a short time. During this visit he wrote

* Κρητίζειν.

his First Epistle to Timothy, whom he had left at Ephesus, and who in his youth and inexperience found himself at issue with serious errors, the first indications of those Gnostic heresies which subsequently struck such deep root in this soil, where all the religions of the East and West had in turn striven for predominance. Paul shortly after this visit returned to Ephesus. He there wrote his Epistle to Titus, giving him the benefit of his advice in the difficult task of conducting a Church. Shortly after his return, he sent Timothy into Macedonia to visit the Churches there, and to make collections for the Christians in Judea.* He himself, on the serious reports received

* 1 Cor. xvi, 10, 11. After careful examination we have accepted Wieseler's supposition, (pp. 280–329,) shared by M. Reuss, ("Gesch. der Heil. Schr. N. T.," pp. 74–76,) as to the date of Paul's voyage to Crete, of the First Epistle to Timothy and that to Titus. This theory only acquires any degree of certainty when the question of Paul's second captivity has been thoroughly examined. This will come before us as we proceed. For the present we are content with showing the probability of the facts being as we have represented. First, it is certain that Paul did not remain continuously at Ephesus during two years and a half, for we learn from 2 Cor. xiii, 1, that before writing his Second Epistle to the Corinthians he had twice visited their city. His first visit coincides with the foundation of the Church. His second journey can only be placed in the interval between his arrival at Ephesus and his departure from that city, for he alludes to it in 1 Cor. xvi, 7; and his First Epistle to the Corinthians was written from Ephesus. It is evident, therefore, that during this time Paul traveled, and traveled in Europe. His voyage to Crete is then possible at this period; and if, as we shall subsequently show, that voyage cannot be assigned to any other period in his life, the possibility becomes a certainty. We may add that the Epistle to Titus contains more than one indication of the date of its composition. Apollos is mentioned in it as one of Paul's companions, who had joined himself to Titus. (Tit. iii, 13.) Now Paul had just made his personal acquaintance at Corinth, and he is not after this found in his company. Does not the name of Tychicus, who is a disciple of

from Corinth, wrote a letter to the Church of that city, earnestly reproving it for its schism, for the irregularity of conduct which threatened its destruction, and also for the dangerous heresies which even went so far as to deny, under pretense of spirituality, the resurrection of the body.*

This letter was written under most touching circumstances, for Paul was at that very time obliged to hide himself to escape the malice of his enemies. He had been suffered for a long time to labor without hinderance in the propagation of the Gospel at Ephesus, but persecution of singular violence suddenly broke out against him. He encountered a kind of opposition which was more than once temporarily to arrest the progress of the Church, and to

Asia Minor, indicate that the Apostle had just been laboring in that country? He appears again in company with the Apostle at the time of his last journey to Jerusalem. (Acts xx, 4.) M. Reuss places the composition of the Epistle to Titus during Paul's short sojourn at Corinth, and Wieseler on his return to Ephesus. The latter supposition appears to us the more probable, for on M. Reuss's hypothesis, the letter to Titus would have been written very shortly after Paul's leaving Crete. With reference to the First Epistle to Timothy, the Apostle's manner of addressing him gives the impression that Timothy is still very young. We shall touch presently, in treating of the heresies of the Church of the first century, on the objections to the authenticity of the pastoral letters.

* This letter was not the first, as we find in 1 Cor. v, 9 allusion to an earlier one. We may observe that these heresies, corresponding exactly with those contended against in the pastoral epistles, are pointed out by Paul in an epistle, the genuineness of which is never called in question. Is there not in this a powerful refutation of the system which pretends that the heresies mentioned in the pastoral epistles could have had no existence at this period, and which on that ground argues their spuriousness? Is there not also in this fact a confirmation of our supposition as to the date of the Epistles to Timothy and Titus?

shed rivers of Christian blood. The new religion disturbed not only the minds of men, but their secular interests. Paganism was not simply a system of general corruption, but also of universal traffic. The temples of the false gods had a multitude of dependents, who lived by the altars, and who, while they shared the popular superstition, also speculated on it for their own advantage. The preaching of the true God, no longer confined within the precincts of the synagogue, but making itself heard in the public squares, and gaining its thousands of adherents from among the idol worshipers, could not fail by its success to strike alarm into all those who made their gains out of the pagan worship. At Ephesus the priests were not the only persons whose interests were compromised by the preaching of the Gospel. A considerable traffic was carried on in small statues of the goddess and images of her temple. The silversmiths made immense sums from this craft; the whole city was interested in the worship of Diana, for the votaries of the goddess brought streams of wealth within its walls. Nothing, then, was more easy than to excite the passions of the populace against the Apostle, and by the fury of his enemies we may infer how great had been the success of his mission. A silversmith, named Demetrius, was the instigator of the tumult. His violent harangue, addressed to his workmen, presents a strange mixture of cynicism and superstition. He passes without transition from the profits of his trade to the compromised glory of Diana of the Ephesians. "Not only this our craft is in danger to be set at naught, but also the temple of the great goddess Diana shall be despised, and her magnificence be destroyed, whom all Asia and the world worshipeth." Acts xix, 27. Thus the true ground of fanaticism—self-interest—is brought to light. The vail of religion, in which it loves to envelope itself, is torn away, and the people of Ephesus come forward to make common cause for their riches and their faith. Demetrius succeeds in stirring up a serious tumult. The people rush to the theater, clamorously calling on the name of their favorite goddess. Two of Paul's companions are caught. The courageous Apostle never hesitates. He will speak to this crowd, bellowing in the circus like a beast hungering for its prey. It was, doubtless, with the impression of these events, fresh in his mind, that he wrote in the letter addressed at this time to the Corinthians, "I have fought with beasts at Ephesus." This lively image was an admirable representation of the scene in question. A roaring lion is the truest symbol of an enraged mob.* His friends would not suffer him to make himself a

* 1 Cor. xv, 32. Some Commentators have been disposed to take this expression literally. But Paul, as a Roman citizen, could not be sentenced to this ignominious torture. Nor have we the record of any further persecution than that mentioned in Acts xix, 29. Is it possible to suppose that when, in the Second Epistle to the Corinthians, (xi, 23–28,) he is recalling all his sufferings, he should have passed over in silence an event so important as fighting with wild beasts? On the other hand, if these words of the Apostle are referred to the tumult raised by Demetrius, they have a very impressive meaning. Doubtless he was not himself in the theater; but did not the fierce yells of the mob reach his ears? Was he not involved directly in the combat? Was it not, in fact, between him and the people of Ephesus, and was not he the cause of the exasperation? There is no argument against placing the conclusion of the First Epistle to the Corinthians after the riot, as Paul still remains one day in the city. (Acts xx, 1.)

sacrifice to the crowd. The Asiarchs, who were deputies of the towns of Asia Minor, charged with the provision and control of the public games, sent to entreat him not to adventure himself in the theater; possibly they were favorable to him; they were at any rate responsible for all that occurred in the place of public entertainments. The riot came to a singular conclusion. The Jews, alarmed at this violent reaction of idolatry, by which they might themselves be seriously compromised, put forward one of their number named Alexander to speak, doubtless with a view to show that their cause was not to be identified with that of Paul.* But their tactics turned against themselves, for they thus provoked an increase of excitement, and for two hours nothing could be heard but the cry, "Great is Diana of the Ephesians!" The Town Clerk had the utmost difficulty in quieting the people by flattering their passions, and at the same time holding over them a salutary terror of the imperial power, which was wont to inflict severe punishments on the seditious. Paul, in consequence of these events, immediately quitted Ephesus. The treatment he had there received was full of significance. It was prophetic of the persecutions awaiting Christians from the whole heathen world. It taught the Church how hard it is to change a corrupt condition of society. The vociferations in the circus at Ephesus would be re-echoed again and again, during the first three centuries, in the clamor-

* De Wette, in his "Commentary on the Acts," asserts that these Jews who put forward Alexander were Christian converts from Judaism. But the expression τῶν Ἰουδαίων does not permit this interpretation. Our hypothesis seems to us the most reasonable.

ous cry, "*The Christians to the lions!*" It was the first deep roar of paganism against Christianity.

From Ephesus Paul went on into Europe. He had shortly before sent Titus to Corinth, in order to ascertain the precise effect produced in that Church by his letter. 2 Cor. xii, 18. After having vainly awaited his return at Troas, (2 Cor. ii, 12, 13,) he left to visit the Churches of Macedonia. These he found flourishing, full of devotion to himself, firm in their faith, purified by persecution, and disposed to contribute generously to the collections he was making for the Christians in Palestine. 2 Cor. viii, 1, 2. This was a great consolation to the Apostle in the midst of his own afflictions; for in Macedonia, as in Asia and Achaia, he encountered the bitter and persistent hostility of the Jews, and was at times overwhelmed with the greatness of his labors and the weariness of incessant conflict. 2 Cor. vii, 5. At length Titus rejoined him, and told him of the salutary effect produced by his first letter on the Christians at Corinth. The irregularities which had caused so much scandal were put away: love for the Apostle had revived, and better days seemed about to dawn on the Corinthian Church. Equilibrium could not, however, be at once restored in a community which had been so violently agitated, and the adversaries of the Apostle made one more attempt to regain their lost influence by redoubling their attacks on Paul, and denying his right to the apostolate. He himself, in the second epistle, written under the impression of his interview with Titus, gave free expression to the feelings which filled his heart. Joy at the repentance of the Corinthians, and indignation at the unjust attacks on himself, form the burden of this letter. In reply to his assailants, he pleads the facts of his apostolic career—a touching and beautiful apology. He depicts in glowing colors his labors, his sufferings, his triumphs; and after the incomparable picture of his missionary life, gives a glimpse into the most sacred secrets of his spiritual history. In no part of his writings, full as all are of originality, has Paul left so deep an impress of his individuality. The epistle concludes with some practical suggestions relative to the collections for the Church at Jerusalem. This letter was sent to Corinth by Titus, who was to receive the latest offerings of the Corinthian Christians. Paul himself remained some time longer in Macedonia, and it was probably at this period he made the missionary journey into Illyria, of which he speaks in his Epistle to the Romans. Rom. xv, 19. He there stayed, as he had arranged, with Titus, in the city of Nicopolis, built by Augustine in memory (Titus iii, 12,) of the battle of Actium. Thence he returned to Greece, and spent three months in Achaia, chiefly at Corinth, where he wrote his Epistle to the Romans, which we shall find equally valuable as an historical document, enabling us to trace the commencement of the Church at Rome, and as a doctrinal statement of Paul's views upon Christianity.

Paul, in his indefatigable zeal, contemplated a missionary journey into the far West. He desired to carry the Gospel into Spain, (Rom. xv, 24;) but before doing so, he was anxious to revisit Jerusalem, to hand over the liberal collection which had been made, through his efforts, in the Churches of Macedonia and Achaia, and to draw yet closer the bonds which united him to his colleagues in the apostleship. Rom. xv, 25–27. But at the very time he was preparing for these new and distant enterprises, he had a presentiment that in going up to Jerusalem he would encounter graver perils than any he had yet known. In truth, he had come to an open disruption with the Jews in all the great cities of Asia and of Greece. He had made no compromise with them, and he knew, by painful experience, what he might expect from their fanaticism in the very center of their power. Even in the Epistle to the Romans these presentiments are apparent; the Apostle urges the Christians at Rome to pray that he may "be delivered from them that do not believe in Judæa." Rom. xv, 31. His friends shared his apprehensions, which were also repeatedly confirmed by prophetic revelations. Thus this journey from Europe up to Jerusalem was one succession of most pathetic farewells. These began at Troas, whither the Apostle had gone by sea from Philippi. On the eve of his departure, he assembled the Christians of that city in one of the *agapæ* so common in the early Church, and which were concluded by the celebration of the Lord's Supper. Parting words of exhortation and of consolation were prolonged far into the night. The miracle wrought upon Eutychus, who being killed by a fall from an upper window into the street was restored to life by the embrace of the Apostle, was a token of consolation and encouragement for the sorrowful Christians at Troas. The most affecting scene took place at Miletus, where the Apostle landed after coasting along Asia Minor. He had appointed this as the meeting-place for the elders of that Ephesian Church in which his ministry had borne such noble fruits. Every thing contributed to the solemnity of this interview. Paul had an ever-deepening conviction that bonds, afflictions, and perhaps death, were awaiting him. He went up to Jerusalem as to an altar of sacrifice. He knew that the Church of Ephesus was threatened with dangerous heresies. Acts xx, 23–31. Before him were its representatives—men to whom he was deeply attached. We can imagine how bitter was the separation under such circumstances. The words of the Apostle are full of pathos and sublimity. The most tender human feelings find expression as freely as the manly courage of the martyr, and the solemn warnings of the pastor. Paul calls his hearers to witness the faithfulness with which he has preached the Gospel at Ephesus, "keeping back nothing." He tells them that they must depend no longer on him, for "he shall see their face no more," and he adjures them to watch over the young Church as over a frail plant exposed to the storm. Paul is evidently fully conscious of the difficulty of the transition from the apostolic age to the period when the Church is to walk without the guidance of its founders. His address is full of pathetic warnings, which will be only too fully justified by history. "And now," he says, in conclusion, "I commend you to God, and to the word of his grace, which is able to build you up, and to give you an inheritance among all them that are sanctified, through faith which is in Jesus. I have coveted no man's silver or gold. Yea, ye yourselves know that these hands have ministered to my necessities, and to them which were with me. I have showed you in all things how that so laboring ye ought to support the weak, and to remember the words of the Lord Jesus, how he said, "It is more blessed to give than to receive." * After thus speaking, Paul fell on his knees, and prayed fervently for that Church so threatened with peril. Then, amid sore weeping, he took leave of the elders of Ephesus. They knew, as they sorrowingly accompanied him to the ship, that upon those shores he would never stand again, and their parting had all the bitterness of a final farewell.†

No remarkable incidents marked the journey to Jerusalem, except that Paul's presentiments as to his coming captivity were confirmed by positive predictions. At Tyre he met some disciples who, warned by the Spirit of the dangers awaiting him, entreated him not to pursue his journey to Jerusalem. At Cæsarea, in the house of Philip the Evangelist, a prophet named Agabus yet more clearly foretold his captivity by a symbolic action, which reminds us of the manner of the ancient prophets. 1 Kings xxii, 11. He was once more besought by his friends to change his purpose, but he remained immovable, ready, as he said, not only to be bound, but also to die, if need be, for the name of the Lord Jesus. Presenti-

* This saying of the Lord is not recorded in our Gospels.

† Baur regards this address as a fabrication of the second century. He grounds his opinion on the mention of the heretics of the Church at Ephesus. We shall reply to this objection when speaking of the heresies of the primitive Church. The Apostle's presentiments also seem to Baur in contradiction with other declarations, such as Rom. xv, 32. May we not suppose, however, fluctuations of feeling in the heart of the Apostle? (See "Paulus," p. 177.)

ments and prophecies were soon to receive signal fulfillment.

The Apostle arrived at Jerusalem, surrounded by his most cherished companions, men belonging to the different Churches founded by him in Greece and Asia. They were the representatives and pledges of the universal triumph of Christianity. They were the first-fruits of the new Israel, to be gathered in from the ends of the earth. Paul was received with the greatest affection by the elders of the Church. It was quite evident, however, that the great body of Judaizing Christians were still prejudiced against him. With a view to conciliation, he consented, on the advice of James, not exactly to take upon himself the vow of the Nazarite, but to pay the legal charges for four Christians of Jewish origin, who were about to fulfill their vow in the Temple, at the very time of his arrival in Jerusalem.* This step was not a politic artifice on the part of Paul, an attempt at diplomatic conciliation, as has been objected. He merely acted out the decisions of the Council at Jerusalem. Himself a Jew, he observed the Jewish custom, according to the decree which had been passed with his concurrence a few years previously. He followed also that other law which he had laid down for himself, of being to the Jews as a Jew, that he might win

* To pay the charges for the sacrifices intended for the fulfillment of the vow of the Nazarite was regarded as an act of great piety. (Josephus, "Ant.," xx, 6, 1.) We cannot suppose that Paul himself on this occasion took the vow of the Nazarite, for the fulfillment of that vow required a much greater length of time. (Numbers vi, 8, 9.) His purification would be required for the offering of any sacrifice in the Temple, no less than for the fulfillment of the Nazarite's vow. (1 Samuel xvi, 5.) See Wieseler, "Chronol. des ap. Zeit.," pp. 104, 105.

all by wise conciliation, instead of offending all by a sudden revolution. It was this step, however, so pacific in intention, which most of all exasperated his enemies; they regarded it as an insult alike to the Temple and the law of Moses. When the Apostle entered the Temple to signify, according to custom, the days when the purification would be accomplished, and the offerings would be presented for the Nazarites, some Jews from Asia, who had come up to Jerusalem to keep the feast, stirred up the multitude against him, on the pretense that he had brought Greeks into the Temple. This accusation was a baseless calumny, for he had not taken with him any of his foreign companions. It has been asserted that these Jews were the Judaizing Christians who formed the nucleus of the Church at Jerusalem.* But this is a gratuitous supposition; the Jews from Asia did not belong to the Church at Jerusalem, but undoubtedly to one of those fanatical synagogues, from which Paul had already met so much opposition. Be this as it may, however, the calumny artfully set in circulation excited the ever mobile passion of the crowd. The people of Jerusalem showed themselves as fanatical as those of Ephesus. Ignorant attachment to the Temple of the true God produced the same effects as the worship of the impure goddess Diana. In truth, the adherents of the Judaism of the decline clung to their worship for the very same reasons as the priests and silversmiths of Ephesus; they thought first of all of the honor and profit to be derived from it. They made the name of Jehovah a covert for their unworthy passions

* Baur, "Das Christenthum der drei ersten Jahrh.," p. 65.

and sordid interests; thus proving that idolatry may be found in all religions and under all forms. When the tumult was at its height, the tribune who commanded the fortress at Antonia, situated not far from the Temple, brought down the soldiery to repress the riot, which seemed likely to throw the whole city into an uproar.

More than once already the excitable crowd had risen at the voice of the unknown agitators. A recent event gave great probability to the fears of the tribunes. Josephus tells us that an Egyptian had come to Jerusalem, saying that he was a prophet. He persuaded the multitude to follow him on to the Mount of Olives, on the promise that he would make the fortifications of the city fall down at his word, and would lead back his followers through the breach. Felix dispersed the tumultuous assembly by force of arms, but the Egyptian had succeeded in making his escape.*

The Tribune Lysias at once took it for granted that the present riot was excited by the return of the Egyptian, whom he supposed Paul to be. Acts xxi, 38. As he was being led away to prison, the Apostle asked leave to speak to the people who were following him with shouts and cries. Having received permission to address them from the steps of the citadel, he attempted no evasion, but, with heroic courage, related in a few graphic words the change wrought in him by his conversion, as though to say to this fanatical people, "There was a time when I was a persecutor of Christians, as you are, but I have seen my guilt, and I charge you with the same."

* Ὁ δὲ Αἰγύπτιος αὐτὸς ἐκ τῆς μάχης ἀφανὴς ἐγένετο. Josephus, "Ant.," xx, 6.

At the first mention of his mission to the Gentiles the hoarse cries of anger burst forth afresh and drowned his voice, as on another occasion—how fresh in the memory of Saul of Tarsus!—the voice of Stephen had been drowned; and the Tribune, to save him from the violence of the people, commanded that he should be brought into the castle.

CHAPTER II.

MISSIONS AND PERSECUTIONS OF THE CHURCH FROM THE CAPTIVITY OF ST. PAUL TO HIS DEATH AND THAT OF ST. PETER.

§ I. *Various Phases of St. Paul's Captivity.*

AS he crossed the threshold of the citadel Paul entered on a captivity which was to terminate only with his life. Let us endeavor to follow him through its various phases. The Tribune Lysias was much embarrassed by the presence of this prisoner, whose crime was unknown to him. He thought his guilt might be most easily ascertained by putting Paul under torture in its least cruel form. This was an expeditious method recommended by the Roman law, but only to be applied to slaves, or in cases of exceptional seriousness.*

Lysias thought he had before him a common agitator, a low ringleader of a despised people. He felt no hesitation in inflicting a degrading penalty on a man whom he regarded as worse than a slave. Paul, however, appealed to his rights as a Roman citizen, and the very name sufficed to cover him with a powerful shield. The next day the Tribune brought

* "Edictum divi Augusti extat: quæstiones neque semper in omni causa et persona desiderari deberė arbitror, sed cum capitalia et atrocia maleficia non aliter explorari et investigari possunt quam per servorum quæstiones, efficacissimas eas esse ad requirendam veritatem existimo." (Wieseler, work quoted, p. 376.)

his prisoner before the bar of the Sanhedrim, hoping to discover the cause of the hostility of the Jews to him. The Jews were vehemently desirous to have the whole matter left in their hands. Religious offenses were still within their province, and they might thus have avenged themselves on Paul, without all the delays of Roman jurisdiction.* It was important for Paul that these tactics should be frustrated. If the Sanhedrim were unanimous in finding him guilty of profaning the Temple, he might be at once given over to his implacable enemies. He therefore sought to divide them by setting forth in strong language his belief in a resurrection. Such a challenge could not fail to kindle strife between the Pharisees and Sadducees. Paul cannot be accused of duplicity, for there were in truth certain views common to him and to the Pharisees, and his opposition to their spirit of formalism was too well known to permit any misconception of his attitude toward them. We do not hesitate, however, to prefer his defense in the presence of the clamorous crowd, or before Felix and Festus, as being less politic and more noble. The violent words of Paul to Ananias, compared to the conduct of the Saviour under similar circumstances, make us sensible of the vast distance between the Master and the disciple. The Apostle still carried a human heart within his bosom, and he had ever to be on his guard against the outbreak of his impetuous disposition.† The sitting of the Sanhedrim ended in

* Wieseler, p. 378.

† There has been much dispute among commentators as to how Paul could have said of the High Priest, "Οὐκ ᾔδειν." Acts xxiii, 5. It has been maintained that Paul spoke ironically, "*I know him, but do not recognize him.*" It has also been conjectured that the High

a great dissension between the Pharisees and the Sadducees. The exasperation of the latter against Paul seemed so great that the Tribune once more interposed, and to save Paul's life remanded him to prison. On learning of a nefarious plot laid by the Jews against the captive, Lysias sent him away to Cæsarea.

The Procurator Felix, to whose tribunal Paul was now brought, was a freedman of the Emperor Claudius, brother of Pallas, the favorite of Agrippina. He belonged to that class, famous for its baseness and immorality, which then governed the world by governing the Cæsars, purchasing power by flattery, and using it with tyranny to recover the price paid for it. Tacitus has characterized Felix with one stroke of his incisive pen, when he says, "At once a debauchee and a tyrant, he performed functions little less than royal with the spirit of a slave." * In order to establish his position in Judæa, he married Drusilla, daughter of Herod Agrippa. He made his government odious to the Jews, indulging himself, as we further learn from Tacitus, in every sort of crime.† He had continually to suppress attempts at sedition, headed sometimes by robbers called sicarii, sometimes by false messiahs. He acted with the greatest severity toward the chiefs of the nation, in consequence of riots between the Jews and the Syrians in Cæsarea.‡ Such a man was likely to hold Paul and his accusers in an even balance, and to treat both

Priest being illegally in office, Paul designed to give him a rebuke. These explanations are too ingenious. It is better to suppose that Paul really did not, at the first moment, recognize the High Priest.

* "Per omnem sævitiam ac libidinem jus regium servili ingenio exercuit." Tacitus, "Hist.," v, 9.

† "Annals," xii, 54.

‡ Josephus, "Ant.," viii, 7.

with the impartiality of a common hatred. It is more than probable that if Paul had not been able to appeal to his rights as a Roman citizen he would have been left to perish in some obscure dungeon, or would have been put to death as a leader of sedition. But it was not possible for even a Felix to treat a Roman citizen with this cruel indifference. He was compelled to hear his cause. His marked antipathy to the rulers of the Sanhedrim was a circumstance favorable to the accused. The charges brought by the Jews against Paul were as false as they were bitter. They accused him, by the mouth of their advocate Tertullus, with being the chief of a sect which they represented as politically dangerous, stirring up sedition in Judæa and throughout the world. They knew well that nothing would be more sure to irritate the cruel Proconsul than such suspicions as these. They mentioned also the profanation of their Temple as a pretext for bringing the accused within their own jurisdiction. Paul refuted their accusations point by point, by the clear and simple narration of his last journey to Jerusalem. Felix was convinced of his innocence, but, willing to pacify the Jews, he remanded him to prison. He subsequently gave him at intervals several mock hearings, in which he sought rather to gratify his own curiosity and that of his wife Drusilla, than to do justice to Paul. Reproved in his conscience by Paul's solemn reasonings of righteousness and judgment to come, he left him for two years in prison, secretly hoping that Paul and his friends would in the end offer a large sum for his release.

The captivity of the Apostle at this time was not

rigorous. It was not, however, the merely nominal imprisonment known as *custodia libera*, which allowed the prisoner the right of living in the house of a consul, a prætor, or a magistrate. This sort of detention was granted only to the most illustrious offenders, and Paul was not of this number. We know positively that he was committed to the guard of Roman soldiers ; but there were many degrees in military captivity, and the magistrate could at will relax or tighten the bonds.* Felix commanded that Paul should be treated leniently, and be allowed free intercourse with his friends. Acts xxiv, 23. The Apostle thus received frequent communications from the Churches. Can we suppose that he was himself entirely silent during these two years passed at Cæsarea, so near to his beloved Churches in Asia Minor—those Churches for which he had expressed such tender anxiety to the Ephesian elders ? Had he not forewarned them at Miletus of the dangerous inroads that would be made by oriental Gnosticism on these Christians, already beset with so many snares, and blown about by such various winds of doctrine ? Was it not high time to put them on their guard against perils so serious ? These considerations seem to us to justify the supposition that the Epistles to the Ephesians and to the Colossians, and the lost Epistle to the Laodiceans, were written during this period of captivity at Cæsarea.† The Epistle to Philemon may

* Wieseler, work quoted, pp. 380, 381.

† Most commentators assign to these Epistles a later date, namely, the early part of Paul's captivity at Rome. Wieseler does so on the ground of the great freedom he enjoyed during that portion of his captivity. But the imprisonment at Cæsarea was sufficiently lax to

also well have been written at this date. Paul had met in his imprisonment with a poor fugitive slave belonging to a Christian at Colosse. Full of the thought that in Christ there is neither bond nor free, he had devoted himself with most affectionate solicitude to this unhappy outcast of society, and, according to his own beautiful expression, had in his bonds begotten him to the faith. He thus gave the strongest demonstration of the absolute equality which exists between Christians, and he secured the future emancipation of the slave by sending him back as his own son in the faith, and consequently as a brother of his master, to the house from which he had fled.*

Felix was removed from Cæsarea, and Festus came in his place. The new governor, like his predecessor, had to wage warfare with the Jewish brigands, who under the name of Sicarii laid waste the country. He had also some serious differences with the Temple authorities at Jerusalem.† Probably the hostility

allow direct and frequent communications with the Churches. (See Reuss, "Geschichte der H. Schr. N. T.," p. 98.)

* It appears to us, in spite of Neander's opinion, infinitely more probable that Onesimus should have fled from Colosse to Cæsarea than from Colosse to Rome. The fact that Paul was, in his captivity, the companion of a slave, proves that his confinement was not so light as at first it was at Rome, and we have thus an incidental argument in favor of our supposition. Wieseler (p. 455) endeavors to identify the Epistle to Philemon with that to the Laodiceans spoken of in Colossians iv, 16. He does so on the ground that the Epistle to Philemon is also addressed to Archippus, who in the Epistle to the Colossians (iv, 17) is mentioned as an inhabitant of Laodicea. But this latter fact does not appear clearly from the text. Besides, it is difficult to understand how a mere letter of recommendation could be spoken of as an epistle addressed to an entire Church.

† Josephus, "Antiquities," xx, 8–10.

between him and the priest's party broke out soon after his entry upon office. It may have even begun to manifest itself at the time of his journey to Jerusalem. Acts xxv, 1. In that case the tergiversations in the treatment of the Apostle would be explained. Festus at first shows himself favorable to the Jews; and willing to do them a pleasure, leaves Paul in prison. Then suddenly he turns against them, and haughtily refuses to allow the prisoner to be brought before the Sanhedrim. The High Priest is therefore compelled to go down to Cæsarea to sustain the accusation. The Jews, finding it hopeless to get Paul brought before their own tribunal, as guilty of crimes exclusively concerning their religion, change their tactics, and accuse him of stirring up rebellion against the Emperor. This appears from the defense of the accused, who strongly asserts his innocence on this point. Acts xxv, 8. Wearied of this interminable trial, indignant at being made a tool to serve the policy of the Roman procurators in their relations with the Jews, Paul takes a decisive step, and appeals to the Emperor. This was of course the highest jurisdiction, and there was no power in the empire the decisions of which might not be revised and reversed by this supreme authority.* Henceforward Paul's cause was

* Dio Cassius uses the following words with reference to these appeals to the Emperor: *Δίκαζε δὲ, καὶ αὐτὸς ἰδία τὰ τε ἐφέσιμα καὶ τὰ ἀναπόμπιμα ὅσα ἂν παρὰ τε τῶν μειζόνων ἀρχόντων ἀφικνῆται, μήτε γαρ αὐτοδικος μήτ' αὐτοτελὴς οὕτω τις παράπαν ἔστω ὥστε μὴ οὐκ ἐφέσιμον ἀπ, αὐτοῦ δίκην γίγνεσθαι.* ("Dio Cassius," ii, 19, 53.) Speaking of Augustus, he says, "He judged appeals and causes sent up to him even after the decision of the very highest authorities, for there was no independent or supreme judge from whom there could be no appeal to him."

withdrawn from the inferior tribunals. It must be pleaded and receive its solution at Rome.

The judicial ceremony, therefore, which was enacted at Cæsarea a few days later, can only be regarded as a sort of amusement given by Festus to his illustrious guests—an amusement worthy of a *blasé* Roman, to whom the enthusiasm and faith of St. Paul were but a curious phenomenon. The King Agrippa, before whom Paul appeared, was Herod Agrippa, son of the nephew of Herod the Great, of the same name. Brought up in the palace of the Cæsars, he had attained to his high rank by flattery, and had received from the munificence of the Emperor, to whom he had been an assiduous courtier,* with the title of king, the tetrarchies formerly held by Philip and Lysanias. Like all favorites, he used his power despotically, making and unmaking the high priests at his pleasure. Versed in all intrigue, he lived a life of shameless license, in incestuous connection with his sister, the famous Bernice, who was subsequently to try the power of her charms on Vespasian and Titus.

Attention has often been drawn to the sharpness of outline with which these various personages are sketched by the sacred historian. On the one hand we see the Roman of the decline, essentially a materialist, treating religious questions with contemptuous irony, and charging Paul with madness when he speaks of the resurrection of the dead, and carries his hearers into that invisible world which has no existence for the pagan. Acts xxv, 19; xxvi, 24. On

* Λαβὼν δὲ τὴν δωρεὰν παρὰ τοῦ Καισαρος. (Josephus, "Antiquities," xx, 7, 1.)

the other hand, Agrippa perfectly represents the man who knows the truth without loving it, and who, while giving to it the assent of his reason, refuses to yield to it his heart, and to break the chains of licentiousness. Acts xxvi, 28. In contrast to these two types of the ancient world, how nobly does Paul stand forth as the representative of the new religion! He gives an account, grand in its simplicity, of his past life, of his conversion, and his mission to the Gentiles. Acts xxvi, 4–23. His only crime is, that he has obeyed the call of God; for this alone have the Jews sought to kill him. He has no other apology to offer than his absolute devotion to the truth. The history of his ministry is the most eloquent commentary on the reply of Peter to the Sanhedrim: "We cannot but speak those things which we have seen and heard." Was it possible for him to resist commands so direct from God? Festus and Agrippa recognize fully the innocence of Paul, but he has appealed to Cesar, and he must needs be sent to Rome.

The incidents of his voyage are familiar to us all. In the midst of perils of the sea, he manifests the same calmness, the same courage, the same zeal for souls, the same unvarying forgetfulness of self. After the shipwreck, and a sojourn of three months in the island of Malta, made use of by the Apostle for the foundation of a Church, he lands on those shores of Italy which he was to water with his blood, and receives at Puteoli the brotherly welcome of the Christians of the country. Forty miles from Rome, in the little town of Appii Forum, Paul is met by some Christians from the capital of the world; a still larger number are awaiting him at a little inn called the "Three Taverns,"* thirty miles nearer the metropolis. Thus escorted, he enters the city by that Appian way which had witnessed so many triumphal processions amid its tombs. Little did any dream that this prisoner, conducted by a centurion, and surrounded by a group of poor and mean men, was the greatest conqueror who had ever trodden that path, and that no victory could be comparable with that he was to win over all the combined powers of the pagan world, which found their focus in the imperial city. The Centurion who brought Paul to Rome belonged to one of the legions of the prætorian guard.† He handed over his prisoner, according to his duty, to the prætorian prefect under whom he served. All the criminals who had appealed to the jurisdiction of Cæsar were put in charge of this high dignitary of the court. The prefect, at this time, was Burrhus, a man of distinction and moderation, and of severe morals, whose happy influence restrained even Nero in his career of crime.‡ He treated Paul with indulgence, probably in consequence of the favorable letters received from Festus, and also on the report of the Centurion, who had become the friend of his prisoner. Paul was allowed to remain under the guard of a soldier in a house hired by himself, and had free communication with his friends. This lenient captivity lasted for two

* Tres Tabernæ.

† We must thus understand the words: *σπείρης Σεβαστῆς*. (Acts xxvii, 1.) Wieseler mentions that detachments of this prætorian guard were often sent on distant missions.

‡ Tacitus, "Annals," xii, 2.

years, during which Paul was not inactive. He first of all called the chief of the Jews together for solemn conference, thus showing how full was his heart of that charity which hopeth all things. Was not his very presence in that prison the living proof of their obduracy? and were not the chains which bound him riveted by their fierce fanaticism? Here, as every-where else, Paul found them the implacable enemies of Jesus Christ, and of his Church. The last recorded words of the Apostle addressed to them seem like the echo of the anathema pronounced by Christ on the Pharisees shortly before his death. Acts xxviii, 25–27. These stern utterances are the final judgment of the Apostle upon the Jews as a nation.*

After being thus repulsed by the rulers of the synagogue at Rome, Paul turned once more with success to the Gentiles. As in the prison at Cæsarea he had preached the Gospel to a poor slave, his companion in captivity, so now he endeavored to win to Christ the soldiers who guarded him by turns. His bonds were by this means to become famous through the whole prætorium. Phil. i, 13. In the same manner, he embraced every opportunity afforded him to fulfill his apostolic commission among the inhabitants of the great city, and his captivity contributed much to the increase of the Christian Church in Rome.

This state of things lasted till the year 62. Then every thing was changed. From Paul's letter to the Philippians we learn, first, that the party of Judaizing Christians had commenced their intrigues against him; they did not hesitate even "to add affliction to

* See Baumgarten, work quoted, second part, c. ii.

his bonds." Phil. i, 15, 16. The greatness of Paul's soul, his absolute disinterestedness and sublime charity, were brought out under these circumstances. In presence of the colossal paganism which was ever before his eyes in Rome, minor differences must be lost sight of, and help must be accepted from all who preached Jesus Christ, even if they preached only from unworthy motives, and to provoke contention and strife. Phil. i, 18. The captivity of the Apostle became increasingly strict. We cannot but wonder at the all but interminable delays in the hearing of his cause at Rome. But he had already waited two years at Cæsarea; and Nero, who began to show a disposition to tyranny, was not likely to be more eager than his proconsuls to do prompt justice. Nor must we forget that his trial could not come on till his accusers had arrived, for their charge must be laid before the imperial tribunal. At the time of year when the Apostle reached Rome the sea voyage was impracticable. Some months, therefore, must elapse before his trial could begin.

The Jews had no interest in hastening the matter to a conclusion; on the contrary, they might wish to allow time for the impression favorable to Paul, produced by the reports of Festus, to wear away. They awaited some auspicious moment for gaining the ear of the Emperor. They doubtless thought such a moment had arrived when Octavia Poppæa was raised to the rank of empress, for she openly protected them, and Josephus asserts that she was a proselyte.* It was easy to obtain her intervention in a cause which so closely concerned her *protégés*. The wise

* Θεοσεβὴς γὰς ἦν. (Josephus, "Ant.," xx, 8, 11.)

Burrhus, prefect to the prætorians, was just dead, and had been succeeded by Fennius Rufus and the wicked Tigellinus, the creature of Poppæa.* Paul was directly in the power of the natural protectors of his most deadly enemies. He had little hope of obtaining justice from Nero at a time when, according to the expression of Tacitus, the young Emperor was inclining to crime.† In his letter to the Philippians, the Apostle had already expressed forebodings of the fatal issue of his trial. He still thinks there is a possibility of his being set at large, but the thought of approaching death is ever present with him. Phil. i, 19–26. He is ready that his blood should be poured forth—a holy libation upon the sacrifice of the faith of the Churches.‡ But it is the second letter to Timothy which is especially full of the presentiments of immediate death. It is like the dying testament of the Apostle. The hour of martyrdom is at hand; already he is left alone, forsaken by all who did not share his courageous and disinterested faith. The disciples from Asia Minor have gone back to their country. 2 Tim. i, 15. Demas has saddened his heart by a cowardly defection. 2 Tim. iv, 10. Luke alone is with him. The malice of enemies becomes daily more declared. He has been summoned to stand before the bar of Cæsar unsustained by any human aid. 2 Tim. iv, 16. But his word has been mighty, none the less; and, with the help of God, he

* Wieseler, pp. 403, 404.
† Tacitus, "Annals," xiv, 52.
‡ Phil. ii, 17. For a full description of the Apostle's spiritual position at this time, see Neander's "Practical Commentary on the Epistle to the Philippians," p. 71.

has been enabled to confess Christ before heathen Rome, and before the Emperor.

But though he has thus once been delivered out of the mouth of the lion, (2 Tim. iv, 17,) he knows he shall not escape a second time, and he gives his last exhortation to his most faithful friend. His heart is full, as at Miletus, of anxious care for the Churches. The heresy which then he feared has already begun to make havoc among them, (2 Tim, ii, 17; iii, 13; iv, 3,) and dangers are rife within and without. The Apostle points out to those who shall survive him the important work which will devolve upon them. He forewarns them of inevitable suffering and persecution, and epitomizes his own experience of the Christian vocation in all its height of privilege and depth of self-sacrifice in the noble words, "If we suffer, we shall also reign with him." Was not his whole career one "bearing about in the body the dying of the Lord Jesus," filling up that which was behind in the afflictions of Christ in his flesh, for his body's sake, the Church? Was not the living sacrifice already consumed by the fire of a fervent love? With what beautiful simplicity does he make the last surrender of himself when he says, "I am now ready to be offered, and the time of my departure is at hand;" (2 Tim. iv, 6;) and as he adds, "Henceforth there is laid up for me a crown of righteousness," can we not see its brightness already circling the aged brow? This prisoner of the Lord Jesus has for his crown the many Churches founded by his ministry. Those honorable sufferings, which give such irresistible weight to his testimony, are like the thorns under which the brow of the Redeemer bled. There is but little left for Nero to do to perfect the crown of martyrdom, and to set on the apostleship of Paul the last and most sacred seal of blood. He has fought a good fight, he has finished his course. "Having given himself to God," says Chrysostom, "Paul desired to bring with himself the whole world as an offering. To this end he traversed sea and land, Greece and the barbarous countries, every-where plucking up the thorns of sin, that he might sow the seed of the Gospel; and every-where transforming men into angels.* "*Qui vocatus a Domino*," adds St. Jerome in his forcible language, "*effusus est super faciem universæ terræ*." †

We shall presently consider Paul in the light of the first of the great teachers of the primitive Church; hitherto we have regarded him only as the man of conflict and of action, the missionary and the controversialist. If we inquire into the peculiar character of the missions undertaken and directed by him, we shall find that they differ somewhat from those of the foregoing period. The Divine Spirit works not less mightily in Paul than in Peter, but the part of the human agent is more distinctly observable. The thousands converted on the day of Pentecost and in Solomon's porch were acted upon by a sudden and irresistible influence, produced by the first outpouring of the Holy Spirit. Conversions in masses like these do not recur in this second period of the Church. The proselytes are many, but they

* Ἐπειδὴ καλῶς ἑαυτὸν καθιέρωσε καὶ τὴν οἰκουμένην προσήνεγχε. (Chrysost., "De laudib. Pauli apost.," Homily I.)

† Hieron., vol. iii., p. 1412. See Note F, at the end of this volume, on the captivity of Paul.

are made one by one, through the personal efforts of St. Paul. The longer he remains in any place, the more important is the Church there formed. Results seem proportioned in their magnitude to the amount of direct personal effort. When we come to examine his teaching, we shall see how wise he was in his adaptation of the means he employed to win souls, and how admirably he sought and found the point of contact between those he addressed and the Gospel he preached. His ministry is accompanied with miracles, but he has less frequent recourse than earlier preachers to this method of persuasion. In many places he founded Churches by the power of his word alone. In these missions of the Apostle to the Gentiles, therefore, the Divine Spirit works more directly upon the conscience and less by external manifestations. Man cannot derive any glory to himself from this fact, for though God's method of intervention assumes a different form, it is none the less to this sovereign intervention of grace that the most beautiful fruits of the Apostle's labor are to be ascribed.*

§ II. *Mission of the other Apostles during this period.*†

While Paul was carrying the Gospel from Asia Minor into Europe, and to the very center of Western

* See Note G, at the end of the volume.

† See Fabricius, "Salutaris lux Evangelii toto orbi oriens," Hamburg, 1731, pp. 94, 95. Eusebius is here the principal source of our information. Nicephorus Callixtus, in the second book of his "Ecclesiastical History," supplies us with some authentic information. (Nicephori Callixti, "Ecclesiasticæ Historiæ," Libri XVIII.) The sort of romance of Abdias on the apostolic age has no kind of value.

paganism, the other Apostles were not inactive in the field of Christian missions. We possess few certain details of their labors. We only get glimpses of them through the prismatic lens of legend. It is, however, possible to make out, beneath the capricious adornments of fable, some positive facts of their history, which present traits of indisputable accuracy. There is no evidence that the Apostles, with the exception of Peter and Paul, took all the part in the primitive missions which is ascribed to them by the Church of the third century. The Episcopal notions of that age have colored the history of the first century. Just as to St. Peter was attributed the foundation and government of the Church at Antioch, which, as we have seen, was formed without his assistance, so it is very possible that an attempt should have been made in later times to refer to the Apostles the propagation of the faith in countries where the weight of the labor really rested on simple evangelists. We must, therefore, accept with reserve the testimony of historians, and never forget that their conception of the apostolate is not in all points identical with that of the primitive Church. They regard the

(Abdiæ, "Babylonæ Episcopi de Historia certaminis apostolici," Libri X. Edidit Wolfgangus Lazius, 1552.) It is a collection of absurd fables, with a strong monkish coloring. The Apostles are there made to celebrate mass, and preach sermons with three heads, before undergoing the most barbarous tortures. These absurd narratives have as their basis the "Acta Apostolorum Apocrypha." (Tischendorf edition, Lipsiæ, 1851.) See Thilo, "Codex Apocryphus N. Test.," Lipsiæ, 1833, and the "Codex Apocryphus" of Fabricius. We shall make much use of these writings when we presently trace the history of oral tradition in the second century. The "Acta Canctorum," and too often the "Memoires" of Tillemont, reproduce all these fables.

Apostles as true metropolitan bishops, and cannot suppose a Church founded without their participation.

After the Council at Jerusalem, the Apostles disperse to meet no more. James, the brother of the Lord, continues to exercise paramount influence over the Church of that city; the holiness of his life, the form of his piety, the largeness of heart with which he fulfills his mission of conciliation, all contribute to strengthen it. Far from appearing as an adversary of Paul, James welcomes him, on his last visit to Jerusalem, with brotherly affection, and advises him to join himself to those Christian Jews who were about to fulfill in the Temple the vow of the Nazarite. We have no further details of his life from this time till his martyrdom; but we possess his epistle, from which we shall presently gather his doctrine. In it we shall find faithfully reproduced all the traits of his noble character—his piety, at once scrupulous and elevated; his stern and practical spirit; and, in the oriental coloring of his language, the reflection of the old prophets of Israel.

Jude, the brother of James, and consequently of the Lord, also took an active part in the propagation of the Christian faith. It is not possible to determine from his epistle what was the principal sphere of his work. It may, however, be inferred, from his vehement denunciation of false teachers, that he had come in contact with the heretics of the Churches of Colosse and Ephesus, and that he resided in the countries where the first germs of Gnosticism appeared.* History gives no exact statement with reference to the other Apostles. The various traditions, however,

* See Note II, at the end of the volume.

connected with their names, enable us to follow the track of the missionaries of the primitive Church. It is of far less importance for us to know their names, and to be sure that they were really apostles, than to verify their triumphs over the paganism of the East and West. Accepted with this precaution, tradition sheds light upon the path of apostolic missions.

Paul, in his rapid journeys through Asia, could not have preached the Gospel to all the inhabitants of those wide regions. He had succeeded in founding, in a short space of time, important Churches, but these were surrounded by unbelieving and superstitious masses. It was, therefore, very necessary that the missions of the other Apostles should occupy, to some extent, the same ground gone over by him. According to the testimony of tradition, Cappadocia, Galatia, and Bithynia were evangelized by the Apostle Andrew, Peter's brother.* He is said to have also penetrated into Scythia, and thence into Thrace and Macedonia.†

The Churches of Colosse, Laodicea, and Hierapolis, founded by Epaphras and St. Paul in Phrygia, shed abroad the pure light of truth in that classic land of superstition. But the epistles of the Apostles themselves show how severely the triumph of Christianity was there contested. The work begun had to be constantly renewed; therefore, the Apostle Philip went to settle in that country. He took up his abode at Hierapolis with his daughters, one of whom had the gift of prophecy.‡ His influence appears

* Niceph., "Hist. Eccl.," ii, 39. † Euseb., "Hist. Eccl.," iii, 1.

‡ Nicephorus, "Hist. Eccles.," ii, 39. Ὃς κεκοίμηται ἐν Ἱεραπόλει. (Eusebius, v. 24.) According to Eusebius, two of Philip's daughters

to have been great over the whole Church of Asia Minor.

The Christian mission does more than consolidate the work already commenced; it has an irresistible power of expansion. Matthew carries the divine message into Arabia; his Gospel was subsequently found in the language of that country.* He is soon followed by Bartholomew and Nathanael, who had at first accompanied Philip into Phrygia.† Matthias devotes himself to Ethiopia;‡ James, the son of Alphæus, to Egypt. Simon Zelotes evangelizes Mauritania and Libya; he is said even to have visited Britain,§ but this rests on the doubtful authority of Nicephorus. Mesopotamia is believed to have been traversed by Judas Thaddeus, who had his station at Edessa, where the new religion met with a very favorable reception.‖ The extreme eastern point of the primitive mission seems to have been the western frontier of India. Thomas is supposed to have preached the Gospel in the district adjoining Par-

continued virgins; while, according to Clement of Alexandria, they married. ("Stromat.," iii, 6.) Perhaps Eusebius confounded Philip the Apostle with Philip the Evangelist.

* Ὁ Πάνταινος εἰς Ἰνδοὺς ἐλθεῖν λέγεται ἔνθα λόγος αὐτὸν εὑρεῖν τὸ κατὰ Ματθαῖον εὐαγγέλιον. (Eusebius, "Hist. Eccles.," v, 10.) Sophronimus understands by the Indians the inhabitants of Arabia Felix. (Fabricius, "Lux Salutaris," p. 104.)

† Eusebius, v, 10. Nicephorus (ii, 39) asserts that he had temples built in Asia; this gives us a measure of his historical value.

‡ Nicephorus, ii, 40. The Ethiopian mission has been often ascribed to Matthew. His name might easily be confounded with Matthias.

§ Nicephorus, ii, 40.

‖ This is the origin of the legend about the correspondence between Jesus Christ and Abgarus, King of Edessa. (Eusebius, i, 13.)

thia.* It is certain that very early traces of Christianity are found in India. In the time of Constantine, a missionary who returned from that country asserted that he had met with Christians professing evangelical doctrine in its most ancient form.

If we endeavor to derive from the tradition of the Church any thing more than these very general indications about the Apostles, we enter the vague region of fable. We know from Eusebius that Philip died at Hierapolis, and that his tomb was there to be seen.† The apocryphal Acts of the Apostles are prolific in details of their sufferings. According to these legendary accounts, Andrew was sentenced to crucifixion by the Proconsul of Arabia, who was enraged at the conversion of his wife.‡ Matthew is said to have been burned; § Thomas to have been pierced through with a lance; || and Bartholomew beheaded.¶ It is impossible to ascertain whether these traditions have any historical foundation. Be this as it may, it is certain that the first Christian missionaries in these remote countries fell in the midst of their enemies, and the obscurity of their death is the best guaranty of their heroic fidelity. "These lights of the world," eloquently says a distinguished theologian, "have disappeared from our sight, but we behold the world illuminated by them.

* Nicephorus (ii, 40) says of Thomas: Ὃς καὶ τὸν ἐπ' Αἰθιοπίας καὶ Ἰνδοὺς κλῆρον λαχών. Origen, according to Eusebius, (iii, 2,) ascribed the mission among the Parthians to Thomas; but their country bordered on India. The narrative of the missionary contemporary with Constantine is found in Philostorgius, iii, 4.

† Eusebius, iii, 1.

‡ "Acta Apost.," Tischendorf edition, p. 128.

§ Ibid., p. 129. || Ibid., p. 239. ¶ Ibid., p. 249.

They sought not their own glory, but they are known to God; and thousands of souls saved by their word owe to them their entrance into heaven."*

We have more precise information as to the life of St. Peter after the Council at Jerusalem. From that time, however, his part is as inconspicuous in actual history as it is brilliant in legend. Paul fills the whole scene. Nothing could give stronger proof of Peter's growth in humility than the fact of his consenting to take the second place, after having, more than any other, contributed to lay the foundation of the Church by his courage and energy. It is clear that he has come under the strong influence of Paul; of this his epistle is the surest evidence. Unless we repudiate all proof, external and internal, it is impossible not to admit that the good understanding between these two Apostles is no invention of the writer of the Acts. Peter, however, according to the agreement voluntarily made at the Council at Jerusalem, devoted himself almost exclusively to the preaching of the Gospel among his countrymen. He passed by the great Churches founded by Paul in Phrygia and Asia Minor,† and chose as his center of action a city of once unrivaled celebrity—Babylon—where we find him shortly before his death. 1 Peter v, 13. According to Josephus, thousands of Jews had emigrated to that city. ‡ The Jewish colony in Babylonia must have been very important, since two strongholds were necessary for the safe keeping of

* Lange, Kirchen Geschichte, vol. ii, p. 403.

† The Epistle of Peter, addressed to these Churches, does not prove, as has been asserted, that he was at their head. We need only to remember how strong was at this time the sense of Christian oneness.

‡ Josephus, "Ant.," XV, iii, 1.

the offerings destined for the Temple at Jerusalem, and an escort of several thousands guarded the sacred treasure as far as Judæa, lest it should fall into the hands of the Parthians.* It is clear from these details given by the Jewish historian, that the synagogues of Babylonia continued in close connection with the religious center of their nation. After the destruction of Jerusalem, the rabbinical school of that country acquired very great influence. The Apostle Peter, therefore, found there a vast field of labor ; he had an entire people to evangelize. The advocates of his primacy, in their eagerness to prove, at any price, that he resided at Rome during the greater part of his apostolic career, maintain that when in his Epistle he speaks of Babylon, he intends the mystic Babylon of the Apocalypse, or pagan Rome. But, in the first place, the Epistle of Peter was written before the Apocalypse and the persecution under Nero, that is to say, before the time when pagan Rome was to the Church what Babylon had been to the Jews of old. Up to this time the Christians had had much more to suffer from the Jews than from the Gentiles. It is worthy of remark, also, that the style of Peter in his Epistle is not raised to the lyric tone of ancient prophecy, and its conclusion is as simple as possible. There can, then, be no reason for attaching a far-fetched symbolic meaning to a designation perfectly clear in itself. Peter had succeeded in founding a Church at Babylon ; † this Church had become a center of light to all the Jew-

* Josephus, "Ant.," XVIII, ix, 1.

† This is the sense we attach to the words ἡ ἐν Βαβυλῶνι συνεκλεκτή.

ish colony. Silas, one of the companions of Paul, joined Peter at Babylon, and the description given by him of the critical condition of the Churches in Asia Minor doubtless led the Apostle to address to them a letter of consolation.* Persecution was, in truth, imminent; like a violent tempest, it was giving precursive tokens of its approach, and it was well that words of earnest exhortation should be multiplied on the eve of so terrible a conflict. Peter pleaded with holy eloquence, magnifying, like Paul, the greatness and glory of Christian endurance, and himself preparing to seal with his blood his witness to the truth. In his Epistle we feel that he has reached that full maturity of the Christian life which is itself an anticipation of heaven. The power of the grace of God is magnified in the greatness of the change wrought in him. This hot and hasty man, who could one day draw his sword against Malchus and the next deny his Lord, now displays the patience and gentleness of his Master; this ignorant and prejudiced Jew has risen to the height of a broad and spiritual Christianity. The equilibrium of his nature has been restored, his zeal refined, his energy at once brought under control, and fortified against the weaknesses of the flesh. To use his own image, the pure gold has been tried in the fire, (1 Peter i, 7,) and, as we see the transformation in Peter's character, we feel that there is no nature so headstrong and rebellious that

* Baronius ("Annals," An. 45) gives the year 45 as the date of the Epistle of Peter; but it is evident that it was really written much later, for Silas was with Peter when he wrote, and Silas did not leave Paul till after his first journey into Europe, that is to say, after the year 52. Acts xviii, 18.

its alloy cannot be purged by the process of the Divine Refiner.*

Did Peter go from Babylon to Rome? This is a much disputed question. It is impossible to answer it with certainty, but we incline to a reply in the affirmative. It is very necessary to guard against party prepossessions. If an historian, wedded to the hierarchical theory, has an interest in proving the sojourn of Peter at Rome, an historian espousing opposite opinions may erroneously imagine he has an interest in showing the contrary. Both are therefore bound to weigh with scrupulous impartiality the testimony of Christian antiquity. For ourselves, we find it impossible to suppose that Peter was at Rome under Claudius and at the commencement of the reign of Nero. Besides the reasons we have already pointed out, we lay stress on the incontestable fact that the name of Peter does not once occur in the epistle written by Paul to the Romans, nor in any of the other letters of that Apostle dated from Rome. Admitting the hypothesis of Baronius and writers of his school, such an omission would be inexplicable; but, on the other hand, we are inclined to believe that Peter did spend the last year of his life at Rome. We fully admit the uncertainty and contradictoriness of tradition on this point. We do not attach much importance to the indirect allusion in the epistle of Clement.† The passage of Ignatius which refers to the martyrdom of Peter is apocryphal. His contest with Simon Magus, described in the "Apocryphal Acts," is obviously

* See Note I, at the end of the volume, on the Second Epistle of Peter.

† Clement, "Epistle to the Corinthians," c. v.

legendary and absurd.* Dyonisius, of Corinth, positively affirms Peter's sojourn at Rome; but his testimony is invalidated by a palpable error, for, against all historical evidence, he attributes to Peter a share in the foundation of the Church at Corinth,† which, beyond question, was the work of Paul alone.

The fragment of the preaching of Peter, quoted by Cyprian, belongs to a document which, though very ancient, is nevertheless apocryphal.‡ Irenæus § and Tertullian, || who both assert that Peter died at Rome, write at a period when many of the fables of the first century found ready currency. In spite, however, of all these errors of detail and absurd combinations, the unanimity of tradition as to Peter's stay at Rome appears to us of weight. It is so much the more worthy of credence, because several of the "Fathers"—for example, Tertullian and Irenæus—had no interest in establishing the primacy of the Bishop of Rome. We find, then, no difficulty in admitting that Peter passed the closing days of his life in the capital of the empire, and we see no conclusion deducible from this fact in favor of the hierarchy.¶ The Church of Rome had been founded many years before, and had long been molded by the powerful in-

* "Acta Petri et Pauli," p. 1.

† See the passage in Dyonisius: *Ἄμφω (Πέτρος καὶ Παῦλος) καὶ εἰς τὴν ἡμετέραν Κόρινθον φυτεύσαντες ἡμᾶς, ὁμοίως ἐδίδαξαν· ὁμοίως δὲ καὶ εἰς τὴν Ἰταλίαν ὁμόσε διδάξαντες, ἐμαρτύρησαν κατὰ τὸν αὐτὸν καίρον.* (Eusebius, "Hist. Eccles." ii, 25.)

‡ Cyprian, "De non iterando baptismo."

§ Τοῦ *Πετροῦ καὶ τοῦ Παύλου ἐν Ρωμῃ εὐαγγελίζομενων.* (Irenæus, "Adv. Hæres," iii, 1.)

§ "Ubi Petrus passioni dominicæ adæquatur." (Tertullian, "Præscript.," 36.)

¶ The opposite opinion to that we have expressed is very fully stated in Blumhart's "History of the Establishment of Christianity."

fluence of Paul. Peter went to Rome to preach the Gospel, and he soon paid with his life the penalty of his faithfulness to Christ. He was never Bishop of Rome, and was not called to confer any episcopal dignity, for the simple reason that the old democratic organization of the Church was at that time, as we shall show, in full vigor. The influence of Peter at Rome was further diminished by his ignorance of the Latin tongue; for, according to Eusebius, Mark, who had accompanied him from Babylon, acted as his interpreter. From Rome, Mark went to Egypt, and a tradition, which there seems no reason to discredit, ascribes to him the foundation of the Church at Alexandria, which was subsequently to become the metropolis of high Christian culture.*

Many legends are linked with the names of the other disciples of the Apostles, and to each has been assigned a large share in the missions of the first century; but it is absolutely impossible to discriminate between the false and the true in this medley of fable.† There is no need to have recourse to the embellishments of tradition, in order to bring out the grandeur of the apostolic labors. Unadorned history amply justifies these words of Eusebius: "The apostles and disciples of the Saviour, scattered over the whole world, preached the Gospel every-where."‡ The blessed light which had risen in the East was diffused over a large portion of the world.§ "In thus establishing

* Eusebius, "Hist.," ii, 16. Εἰς τὴν Ἀλεξάνδριαν παῤῥησίᾳ τὸν Χριστὸν κηρύττων. (Nicephorus, ii, 44.)

† See Fabricius, "Lux Evangelii," pp. 115–117.

‡ Eusebius, "Hist. Eccles.," iii, 1.

§ See in Fabricius a list of Churches founded in the apostolic age, pp. 83–92.

the kingdom of Jesus Christ," says Theodoret, "the Christians made use of no carnal weapons; they employed no other force than that of persuasive words to demonstrate the excellence of his divine laws. They fulfilled their missions in the midst of dangers, enduring violence and wrong of every description in the cities through which they passed, being scourged, tortured, cast into dungeons, subjected to every kind of suffering. But though the bearers of these divine laws might be killed, the laws themselves were deathless. They proved only the more potent after the death of those who promulgated them, and in spite of the resistance of the Romans and the barbarians, they continued in undiminished force; and from the graves in which the Romans sought to bury the memory of these fishermen and tent-makers, that memory sprang into new and nobler life." *

§ III. *Mode of Primitive Evangelization. Origin of the First Three Gospels.*

Having now described the missions of the primitive Church in their rapid and fruitful expansion, we must characterize the method adopted at this period in the propagation of the truth. "Faith cometh by hearing," says St. Paul, (Rom. x, 17,) and he sums up, in these words, the leading principle and practice of the apostolic Church, which was much more occupied with preaching the Gospel than with the composition of new sacred books. The Apostles were, for the most part, unlettered men, and they would not be likely to write except under pressure of necessity.

* Οὐχ ὅπλοις χρησάμενοι ἀλλὰ πείθοντες. (Theodoret, "Therapeut. gent.," p. 115; "Opera," vol. iv, p. 610.)

Their Master had left them no instructions on this point, and he himself had written nothing. He had founded the Church by his word.* Again, the expectation of his speedy return in glory was then general. They thought that at any moment he might appear in the clouds to judge the world. They had, therefore, no motive for concerning themselves with a distant future, and for committing to writing memories which were still living in the heart of the Church. The Church itself, but partially freed from the bondage of Judaism, found in the sacred books of God's ancient people a solid foundation for its faith; and the incontestable truth of what they believed was sufficiently confirmed to the Christians by the declarations of the prophets. Endowed with the richest gifts of the Spirit, they were perpetually conscious of the pure and life-giving breath of inspiration. Paul boldly declared that the new covenant was not in the letter, but in the Spirit. 2 Cor. iii, 3–7; Rom. vii, 6.

None of the expressions by which preaching is spoken of in the New Testament can apply to written documents. That which is intended is always the living word, the solemn proclamation of the truth from the lips of witnesses.† When the Gospel is spoken of, the reference is not to a book, but to the substance of the apostolic preaching—to the good tidings of salvation, as the etymology of the word signifies. "The Apostles of Christ," says Eusebius,

* We have mentioned the absurd legend given by Eusebius about the correspondence of Jesus Christ with the King of Edessa. (Eusebius, "Hist. Eccles.," i, 13.)

† Λόγος. (James i, 22.) Λόγος ἀκοῆς. (1 Thess. ii, 13.) Κηρύγμα. (Titus i, 3; 1 Cor. ii, 4; 1 Tim. i, 11; 2 Tim. ii, 2.)

"purified in life, and adorned with all the virtues of the soul, but rough and uncultivated in speech, upheld simply by the power of Christ, through which they worked so many miracles—preached the kingdom of God to the whole world. They were not concerned to write books, being put in charge with a far grander and superhuman ministry."*

For a long time the Church preferred the living to the written word. "If I met," says Papias, "a brother who had known the Apostles, I asked him carefully what they had said—what Andrew, Peter, Philip, Thomas, James, John, and Matthew had said. I thought I could gather more from a living testimony than from books."† It was very natural that, at a time when the first generation of Christians was still alive, their words should have been preferred to their writings. The Apostles themselves attached more importance to their preaching than to their letters; they thought they could gain a stronger influence over the Churches by their presence than by their epistles, else they would have been willing to remain at a distance from them, and would not have so frequently expressed a desire to visit them again. Rom. xv, 32; 1 Cor. xvi, 5, 6; 2 Cor. xiii, 10. "Having many things to write unto you," says John, "I would not write with paper and ink, but I trust to come unto you, and speak face to face, that our joy may be full."‡

It is in no degree our intention to detract from the

* *Σπουδῆς τῆς περὶ τὸ λογογραφεῖν μικρὰν ποιούμενοι φροντίδα.* (Eusebius, "Hist. Eccles.," iii, 24.)

† *Οὐ γὰρ τὰ ἐκ τῶν βιβλίων τοσοῦτόν με ὠφελεῖν ὑπελάμβανον ὅσον τὰ παρὰ ζώσης φωνῆς.* (Eusebius, "Hist. Eccles.," iii, 39.)

‡ 2 John 12. On this question see Gieseler, "Historisch-kritischer Versuch über die Enstehung der Evangelien," p. 70.

importance of the written Gospels, but to throw, as far as may be possible within the limits imposed by our subject, some light on the question of their origin. It is proved that during many years the word of God was freely propagated by the living voice, and that the most flourishing Churches the world has known were founded by the preaching of the early missionaries. It was of vital importance, however, that the great facts of Christianity should be transmitted to posterity through a safer medium than mere oral tradition. After being set forth in several writings, which were not handed down beyond the first century, (Luke i, 1,) they were cast into a permanent form in our canonical Gospels, which bear so manifestly the seal of inspiration. We shall not do more here than indicate the origin of the first three Gospels, which date from this period.*

The origin of the Gospel of Mark is thus stated by Papias, who is himself only the echo of John the Presbyter, or the Elder: "Mark, having been Peter's interpreter, wrote down carefully, but not in order, the words and actions of Jesus Christ. His one great concern was to give, unaltered and unadulterated, that which he had heard."† Clement of Alexandria adds, that Mark wrote his Gospel at the express

* On the question of the sources of the synoptics, see my work, "Jesus Christ: His Life and Times," Book I, c. iv.

† *Μάρκος μὲν ἑρμηνευτὴς Πέτρου γενομένος ὅσα ἐμνημόνευσεν ἀκριβῶς ἔγραψεν, οὐ μὲν τοι τάξει.* (Eusebius, "Hist. Eccles.," iii, 39; vi, 14.) It has been maintained that these words could not apply to our Gospel of Mark, which has, say the objectors, as much order as the rest. Let us observe, however: 1st. That the discourses of the Saviour are not grouped in Mark as in Matthew. 2d. That we do not find in it the chronological order followed by Luke. 3d. That there are in Mark strange omissions; for instance, there is no account of the birth

request of the hearers of Peter.* Luke himself clearly informs us of the motive which led him to write an account of the Gospel history. "Forasmuch as many have taken in hand to set forth in order a declaration of those things which are most surely believed among us, it seemed good to me also, having had perfect understanding of all things from the very first, to write unto thee in order, most excellent Theophilus." Luke i, 1–3. Matthew, according to Eusebius, wrote his Gospel in Hebrew on the eve of starting on his distant missions. Papias says, "Matthew made a collection in Hebrew of the discourses of the Lord Jesus, and each interpreted them as he was able."†

§ IV. *First Roman Persecution of Christianity. Persecution in Judæa. Death of James, the brother of the Lord.*

Persecution always followed step by step in the track of Christian missions, endeavoring to sweep away their glorious results by torrents of blood, and

of Jesus Christ. The expression *οὐ τάξει* seems, therefore, justified. (Tholuck, "Glanbwürdigkeit der evangel. Gesch.," 2d ed., p. 242.) There are a number of Latinisms in Mark's Gospel which confirm the testimony of Papias as to its being written at Rome.

* Eusebius, iii, 24.

† *Ματθᾶιος μὲν οὖν Ἑβραΐδι διαλέκτῳ τὰ λόγια συνεγραψάτο. Ἡρμήνευσε δ' αὐτὰ ὡς ἦν δυνατὸς ἕκαστος.* (Eusebius, "Hist. Eccl.," iii, 39.) According to Schleiermacher, the meaning of the last phrase was, that each gave his own interpretation of the discourses of Christ. It appears to us, that by comparing the word *ἡρμήνευσε* with the word *ἑρμηνευτῆς*, applied to Mark, we arrive at the sense we have given. From this passage it appears that we have only a translation of the first Gospel. This explains those points in the narrative which to the direct statement of an eye-witness present real difficulties, as for instance, Matt. xxi, 2, 5, 7.

succeeding only in watering and fructifying the buried seeds. We have already seen the outbreak of persecution in Judæa, giving to the Church its first martyrs. Paul had to encounter it in all his missionary journeys. We have left him at Rome loaded with chains, and awaiting his judgment. Up to the year 64 A. D., hostility to Christianity did not assume an official character. Opposition was offered, now in one city, now in another, but the Church was not as yet put under the ban of the empire. Its growth, however, had been so rapid, and its success so marked, that a terrible collision was inevitable with that imperial power which was the stronghold of all that Christianity came to destroy, and in which was personified that ancient order of things, the very basis of which Christianity was to undermine.

This sanguinary collision took place in the latter part of the reign of Nero. Paganism could not have found a fitter representative than this Emperor. Persecutions against the Church must needs break forth at Rome, for the doctrine of the Church was on one essential point directly antagonistic to the theories of the ancient world. In that world, religion was closely associated with political organization. Polytheism had produced, as its natural result, State religions, which trampled on the rights of conscience. The individual had no personal guaranty, and must, under every circumstance, sacrifice himself to the State. Freedom of thought could only exist in the presence of religions thus established, by means of reservations and artifices strongly savoring of hypocrisy. The light in which religion was regarded by pagan antiquity is forcibly described by Cicero: "No one," he says, "has a right to have particular gods; no one may introduce new or strange gods not recognized by the law of the State." * Now the Christians most evidently did proclaim a new god within the empire. This accusation had been already brought against Paul at Philippi. "These men," it was said of Paul and Barnabas, "teach customs which are not lawful for us to receive, neither to observe, being Romans." Acts xvi, 21. Christianity was not formally denounced as an unlawful religion until later, but its character of novelty placed it, from the first, at issue with the law. It might, perhaps, have even longer escaped the attention of the Cæsars if these had not been rendered, by a concurrence of events, peculiarly hostile to religious innovation. The Emperors were repeatedly troubled at this period by the inroads of strange superstitions. They were thus made conscious of the agitation of men's minds, and of the dull discontent which was pervading the ancient world. They had repeatedly taken severe measures for the repression of these dangerous novelties, with a view to restore the dignity of the national religion. A *senatus consultum* was passed in the reign of Claudius, which commanded the priests to attend vigilantly to the renewed observance of the ancient ceremonies of the *Haruspices*—"lest," as we read in the recital, "the ancient usages of Italy fall into desuetude through the prevalence of foreign superstitions." † It is clear that the imperial policy was eminently unfavorable to the introduction of ori-

* "Nisi publice adscitos." (Cicero, "De Legibus," ii, 8.)

† Viderent pontifices quæ retinenda firmandaque haruspicum ne vetustissima Italiæ disciplina per desidiam exolesceret. (Tacitus, "Annals," xi, 15.)

ental religions; it was awake and on its guard; Christianity, therefore, was in grave danger. By a strange contradiction, the new religion was rendered obnoxious equally by the features in which it resembled, and in which it differed from, Judaism. On the one hand, it was, by the mass of pagans, confounded with Judaism; on the other hand, the Jews themselves were its most bitter and most subtle foes and calumniators. The Jews were, as we know, objects of hatred and contempt to the pagans. Their spirit of insubordination constantly awakened the suspicions of the imperial power. Suetonius informs us that Claudius had issued a decree banishing all Jews from Rome, as a punishment for their constant agitations.* It was, then, no recommendation to the Church to pass for a Jewish sect. But while thus confounded by the majority of the Gentiles with this execrated people, it was vehemently repudiated by the synagogue, which found means at Rome, as elsewhere, to stir up the passions of the populace by artful insinuations against the Christians. The Church was thus at once implicated in the unpopularity of the Jews and made the victim of Jewish intrigues. But there was a deeper reason for the passionate opposition so quickly shown to the new religion, in the incompatibility of the principles of the Christian life with the corruption of the ancient world. Paganism felt itself judged and condemned by a purity of faith and prac-

* Judæos, impulsore Chresto, assidue tumultuantes, Roma expulsit." (Suetonius, "Claudius," 25.) The hypothesis of a tumult incited by the Christians is not tenable. The Church of Rome did not acquire any importance till after this date. Suetonius is, then, in error when he accuses the Christians of rebellion; but the decree issued by Claudius cannot be brought in question.

tice of which, till then, it had not had even a conception. Christianity cleaves like a lightning flash the thick darkness of antiquity. At once irritated and humiliated, Roman paganism will treat the Church as Jewish formalism has treated the Lord Christ. "Away with him," rang the cry through the streets of Jerusalem; "Away with him," was now re-echoed from the walls of Rome.

The determining cause of the persecution under Nero was the astonishing success of the new religion in the capital of the world. It had been tolerated so long as it could be ignored. The apocryphal letter from Pilate to Tiberius, which is said to have led that Emperor to propose to the senate to admit the God of the Christians into the Roman Pantheon, has no marks of authenticity.* It is certain that the Emperors took no heed of Christianity till they were constrained to do so by the popular voice. The first persecution was in reality a satisfaction given to the hatred of the populace. We find no trace of edicts proscribing Christianity in a general manner. Legal persecution was not declared until subsequently. Nero played the part enacted by Pilate in the crucifixion of Christ. He sacrificed the innocent to the blind fury of a misled crowd. He added to his villainy by casting on the Christians the imputation of having set fire to the city. But he only chose them as his victims because public execration was loud against them. "To put to silence the rumors raised against himself," says Tacitus, "Nero laid his

* This letter may be read in the Apocryphal Gospels, Tischendorf edit., p. 411. See also Tertullian, "Apologia," c. xxi; Eusebius, "Hist. Eccl.," ii, 2.

own crime on certain persons rendered odious by their heinous offenses, and whom the people called Christians; on these he inflicted the most cruel punishments."* It was this blind and cruel popular hatred which gave occasion for the first persecution. It is important to ascertain the grounds of this animosity, and to investigate the calumnies brought against the Christians.

These calumnies have no connection with the subtle and perfidious accusations of the philosophers. We are brought face to face with popular prejudices in their grossest form. It would be a serious anachronism to transplant into the first century, and into the midst of the Roman populace, the learned objections of a Celsus or a Lucian. Tacitus himself puts us on the track of the charges which, in the year 65, were current in Rome against the Christians. "They were convicted," according to his statement, "not of the burning of Rome, but of the crime of hating the human race." † We discern in this accusation the confusion, so common, of the Church with the synagogue. The Jews did actually merit this accusation by their intractable pride and arrogant contempt of all other nations. This prejudice against the Christians, arising from a mistaken identification of them with their bitterest enemies, was probably strengthened by warnings uttered by them of a coming terrible judgment of God. They proclaimed the con-

* "Ergo abolendo rumori Nero subdidit reos, et quæsitissimis pœnis affecit quos, per flagitia invisos, vulgus Christianos appellabat." (Tacitus, "Annals," xv, 44.)

† "Haud perinde in crimine incendii quam odio humani generis convicti sunt."

demnation of sinful humanity; they painted its doom in prophetic pictures; they borrowed the strong colors of the ancient seers to produce a salutary terror. They spoke, doubtless, of those flames of judgment which should consume a godless world. It was easy, by materializing that which was spiritual, to represent them as dangerous conspirators, capable of causing the conflagration they predicted, and of bringing about by their own efforts the accomplishment of their prophecies. Their preaching must have been thus travestied to furnish the shadow of a pretext for the absurd accusation brought against them.

When Tacitus adds, that they were odious for their crimes and abominations,* he doubtless alludes to the infamous reports so long circulated against the Christians, to which Justin Martyr subsequently gave an indignant denial. "Do you believe," he exclaims, "that we devour men, and that, after our evening meal, we extinguish the lights to cover with darkness a hideous debauch?" These very calumnies are repeated in detail in the "Octavius" of Minutius Felix. "Must we not groan," says the champion of paganism, "when men belonging to a wretched, illegal, desperate faction rise up against the gods? a sect loving darkness, hating the day; it is silent in public, but loud in its secret retreats; it despises the gods and mocks at sacred things. Its members call each other brothers and sisters to add incest to idolatry. They drink the blood of a child, divide its members among them, make a covenant over this horrid sacrifice, and are pledged to silence by their

* "Flagitia pudenda."

common participation in crime." * "We are accused," says Tertullian, "of practicing infanticide in our sacred rites, of then feeding on the flesh of the victim, and concluding our feasts with incest." † These quotations from the "Fathers" are a true commentary on the words of Tacitus. In the next century we shall meet again with these vile accusations, with the addition of other yet more treacherous insinuations; but it is obvious that those now cited were the basis of all the rest. It is easy to see that they are a gross misrepresentation of Christian worship, and, in particular, of the Lord's Supper, in which the sacred symbols of the body of Christ were dispensed. The Church had cunning adversaries who knew how to malign her artfully, and who, observing the absence of all outward display in her worship, brought against her the charge of atheism. When we remember that through Poppæa the Jews of Rome had at this time the favor and the ear of Nero, we shall wonder the less at the success of their intrigues. One of the most ancient writers of the Church, Melito of Sardis, undoubtedly had these underhand practices in view when he said: "Nero and Domitian, incited by the councils of certain malicious persons, have endeavored to bring reproach on our religion. They have bequeathed to their successors these false accusations against us." ‡ These

* "Homines deploratæ illicitæ ac desperatæ factionis. Latebrosa et lucifugax natio....se promiscue appellant fratres et sorores." (Minutius Felix, "Octavius," c. viii, ix.)

† "Dicimur sceleratissimi de sacramento infanticidii et pabulo inde et post convivium incesto." (Tertull., "Apol.," vii.)

‡ Ὑπὸ τίνων βασκάνων ἀνθρώπων ἀναπέισθεντες. (Routh, "Reliquiæ Sacræ," i, p. 117.)

calumnies would have produced no effect, however, if the Church had not increased in Rome in a remarkable manner. "This detestable superstition," says Tacitus, "broke out on all sides, not only in Judæa, but in the city of Rome itself. Tacitus might have added that it had found its way even into the palace of the Cæsars, for St. Paul wrote to the Philippians at the same period: "My bonds in Christ are manifest in all the palace, and in all other places." Phil. i, 13. The presence at Rome of the great Apostle of the Gentiles had been the principal cause of the rapid propagation of the new faith.

It was not possible that the Gospel should be disseminated in the metropolis of paganism without exciting vehement opposition. It could not, for the reasons already pointed out, engage public opinion without inflaming it against itself. Was it not in the world as a burning brand which was to set on fire the rotten edifice of a voluptuous and skeptical society? The self-interested devotees of paganism, men like Demetrius the silversmith, were even more numerous at Rome than at Ephesus. The Church had but to show itself, to be accursed. Nothing is more easy of explanation than this hatred of the Roman people to Christianity, and their eagerness to heap upon it undeserved reproach.

But though the first persecution was popular, it is none the less chargeable on the crowned tyrant who provoked it. Eusebius eloquently says, "Nothing was wanting to Nero but to add to his other titles that of being the first emperor who declared war against Christianity." * His object was to divert

* Eusebius, "Hist. Eccl.," ii, 25.

from himself the suspicions of the people, who justly accused him of having set fire to a great part of the city to gratify a fantastic whim. He caused the Christians to be seized and tortured to compel them to confess a crime of which he himself was guilty. He thought that the spectacle of their death would compensate for that of the conflagration of the city, which had been amusing to none but himself. Blending buffoonery with cruelty, he devised the plan of clothing the Christians in the skins of wild beasts that they might be torn by the dogs. The Emperor assumed at this time an air of the greatest condescension, appearing in the circus in a plebeian garb, and mixing familiarly with the people. Some Christians were crucified; others, having been rubbed over with pitch, were made to serve as torches to light up the imperial gardens.* This fearful persecution did not extend beyond Rome. It was contrived for the amusement and exculpation of the Emperor, and was one of the awful caprices of that mad despot, who studied crime as a work of art.†

This first persecution produced a deep impression through the whole Church. Nero became to the Christians the type of Antichrist, and Rome a new Babylon, "the mother of harlots, drunken with the blood of saints." We trace this sentiment in all its vividness in the representations of the Apocalypse, which show us thousands of martyrs around the throne of God, crying for vengeance on the great whore seated on the seven hills. Nero seemed to the

* "In usum nocturni luminis." (Tacitus, xiii, 44.)

† Orosius (vii, 7) asserts, without giving any proof, that Nero's persecution was general.

Church a sort of personification of the infernal powers leagued against her, and she could scarcely believe at his death that he had disappeared for ever. If we credit the Sibylline oracles, the Church lived in constant expectation of seeing him return from the far East to enter afresh into bloody warfare with the saints.*

St. Paul was probably put to death during this persecution, at the same time as St. Peter. According to a doubtful tradition, the latter was crucified with his head downward. Clement of Alexandria relates that Peter's wife went before him to death, and that the Apostle, calling her by name, addressed to her these simple and touching words, "*Remember thou the Lord.*" † Caius, who lived at the commencement of the third century, says that he saw at Rome the tombs of the two Apostles, and we have no reason to question his testimony.‡ Among the mass of legends associated with the death of the two Apostles is one which, without possessing any historical value, has real beauty. We read in the "Acts of the Saints," that as Peter was trying to leave Rome to escape martyrdom, Jesus Christ suddenly appeared to him. Peter said, "Lord, whither goest thou?" The Lord replied, "I go to Rome, to be crucified." The Apostle understood that the words were to be fulfilled in him.§ It was truly Jesus who suffered and was crucified in the persons of his disciples in that fearful persecution. From this assurance they drew all their comfort and strength.

While paganism was thus waging cruel warfare with the Church, Judaism in Palestine was persistent

* "Orac. Sibyll.," iv, 116. † Clement, "Stromat.," vii, 736.
‡ Eusebius, ii, 25. § "Acta Sanctorum." (Junius, iv, 432.)

likewise in its hatred. James, the brother of the Lord, was put to death a short time before Peter and Paul. Neither his great popularity nor the unanimous respect he inspired, could avail to save him. The Pharisees were his implacable adversaries. He was, as we have said, a Jew after God's heart, and therefore raised immeasurably above the Judaism of his day; for it was impossible to embrace heartily the old covenant without being led on to the new. Piety so sincere and lofty as his was the crying condemnation of Pharisaism—a condemnation so much the more direct because conveyed under the very form of the old religion.

According to the statement of Hegesippus,* as the influence of James went on increasing day by day, the Scribes and Pharisees sought to lead him into a denial of his faith before the whole people assembled for the Passover feast. "Persuade the multitude," they said, "not to fall into error with regard to this Jesus.† We have all confidence in thee, also the people know that thou art a just man, and regardest not the persons of men." They brought him into the Temple and questioned him before the multitude. "Tell us, O thou just one," they said, "tell us what is the doctrine of Jesus?"‡ "You ask me," replied James, "of Jesus the Son of man; he is in heaven, at the right hand of the Almighty, and he will come

* The account of Hegesippus is to be found in Eusebius, "Hist. Eccl.," ii, 23. We quote it from the text as given by Routh, "Reliquiæ Sacræ," i, pp. 209–211.

† *Πεῖσον οὖν σὺ τὸν ὄχλον περὶ Ἰησοῦ μὴ πλανᾶσθαι*, ("Reliquiæ Sacræ," i, p. 210.)

‡ *Τίς ἡ θύρα.* Literally, "What is the door?" that is to say, what admits to the sect? in other words, what is its doctrine?

again in the clouds." At these words the many Christians who were in the crowd uttered a loud hosanna. The enemies of James, furious at finding their crafty design turned against themselves, fell upon him, threw him down from the top of the Temple steps, and began stoning him. While the just man was praying for his murderers with his dying breath, a fanatic workman fell on him, and with heavy blows from a stick dispatched him.* The death of James was followed by a violent persecution of the Churches in Palestine. The letter which was addressed to them at this time by one of the disciples of Paul, probably Apollos, and known under the name of the Epistle to the Hebrews, was designed to strengthen the hearts of the Christians in Palestine under the ordeal of a fiery persecution. Still clinging, as they did, to Jewish prejudices, local and ceremonial, it was to them peculiarly grievous to be driven from the Temple, and compelled to relinquish the regular observance of the worship of their fathers.† It was needful that they should learn from the author of the Epistle to the Hebrews to distinguish between vanishing types and the eternal realities of true religion. Great trials were yet awaiting them, for already the imperial armies were marching upon the Holy City, to make of its ruins the signal monument of the justice of God.

* It cannot be denied that in the detail of Hegesippus's narrative there is a certain theatrical air; but in substance the story seems authentic. (Neander, "Pflanz.," ii, 181.) The passage in Josephus ("Archælog.," xx, 9, 1) has no more impress of authenticity than that referring to Jesus Christ.

† See Note J, at the end of the volume, on the author of the Epistle to the Hebrews.

CHAPTER III.

VARIOUS FORMS OF CHRISTIAN DOCTRINE IN THE SECOND PERIOD OF THE APOSTOLIC AGE.

§ I. *Fundamental Unity in Diversity.*

THE apostolic age did not arrive at once at the full consciousness of the treasures of truth committed to it. After its first period, which was, like a blessed childhood, all calmness and simplicity, it entered upon an era of prolonged conflicts. Did these conflicts make, as some have asserted, a schism among the Apostles, and did they lead to the formation of two hostile Churches—the Judaistic Church, under the conduct of Peter and James, and the Church freed from the synagogue, under the leadership of Paul? Can we discover two contradictory doctrinal systems, as widely divided the one from the other as were subsequently the heresy of the Ebionites and the orthodox faith? This is the question before us for solution.

We have already several times incidentally approached it; we must now give it full consideration, for it is the great theological question of the day. Raised by a scholar of the first rank, distinguished for his laborious research, and the head of a numerous school, it presents itself under continually varying forms. In order to show its full bearing, it will be necessary first to state the view of primitive Christianity taken by those who differ from ourselves.

According to Baur, we have in the apostolic age two religious parties in radical opposition within the bosom of the Church. On the one hand, the twelve Apostles range under their banner all the advocates of the perpetual obligation of Judaism; on the other hand, Paul represents the party of emancipation. The former are faithful to the true intention of Jesus Christ, who preached only a spiritualized Judaism, in all points corresponding to Ebionitism. Paul introduces an entirely new element. The contest is declared at Jerusalem and at Antioch, and is carried on in all the Churches. There is no trace of reconciliation between the Apostles during their life, but Paul, in his Epistle to the Romans, makes the first advance toward conciliation by his strong declaration of love for his nation, and his prediction of its glorious future. He takes a second step in the same direction when, on his last visit to Jerusalem, he joins himself to some Jewish Christians, who had taken upon them the vow of the Nazarite. But this attempt at reconciliation was too premature to lead to any result. The Judaizing party were inveterate in their hatred to the great Apostle, who is plainly referred to in the following century, in the "Clementines," under the name of Simon Magus. Even in this curious document, however, tokens of an approaching reconciliation may be discerned. The Judaistic party makes some concessions. In the first place, baptism is substituted for circumcision; then Peter is represented as the Apostle of the Gentiles. The reputed Epistle of James continues this good work by combating the spirit of Judaism in its exaggerated form, no less than the Pauline school. This school responds to these advances. The Epistle to the Hebrews is designed to harmonize the views of Paul with Judaism, interpreted, or rather allegorized, after the Alexandrine method. The Epistles to the Ephesians and to the Colossians take the same ground, for they tend to show that the death of Jesus Christ has effected a reconciliation between Jews and Gentiles, the two great sections of mankind. But the document which most evidently bears the trace of these conciliatory intentions is that ascribed to Luke, and known as the Acts of the Apostles. The writer endeavors to effect a sort of retrospective reconciliation between the Apostles, and he does it with consummate skill, by representing Peter as a satellite of St. Paul, and putting into his mouth utterances worthy only of the Apostle to the Gentiles. The tradition relating to Peter's sojourn at Rome, his connection with Paul, and their common martyrdom, belong to the same system. The pastoral letters which so forcibly denounce the dangers of anti-Judaic Gnosticism, as well as the letters to which the names of the apostolic Fathers are attached, are animated by the same spirit. The final result of all these attempts at conciliation is the composition of the fourth Gospel, which resolves all contradictions. It rises into the lofty regions of transcendental philosophy, leaving far below all past differences. To the writer of that Gospel, Jews and Gentiles come into one and the same category; they both belong to the kingdom of darkness, which is perpetually at war with the kingdom of light.*

Such is the system which, during almost twenty

* See note K, at the end of the volume.

years, has been perpetually under discussion in Germany. We have already refuted many of its statements. Never did the criticism of internal evidence assume such license. Its proofs are, in truth, drawn not from writings of which it is the business of the critic to fix the date, but from the preconceived system of the theologian. All that does not coincide with that system is prejudged and rejected. A purely hypothetical chronology is thus assigned to the monuments of the apostolic age. The most speculative theories are readily admitted as axioms, by which other hypotheses may be established. The results arrived at by sound criticism with reference to the principal writings of the New Testament suffice to undermine the very foundation of all this skillful theorizing. Indeed, the very elaborateness of the system suggests doubt. How can we suppose such wise diplomacy in the first two centuries of the Church? The New Testament, according to the Tübingen school, must have been written after the manner of the protocols of a congress—a singular explanation, surely, of that sublime simplicity which lends to it all its charm and power. We have already shown, in giving an account of the conference at Jerusalem, and of the dispute at Antioch, that the violence on either side was not on the part of the Apostles, but was excited by fanatical Jewish agitators. The picture we shall draw of the heresies of the primitive Church will give still more demonstrative evidence of this important fact. Besides, an attentive study of the various forms of apostolic doctrine proves that nothing can be more false than the theory that they were essentially at variance, so that there really existed two systems of

Christianity, that of James and Peter, and that of Paul. The hypothesis of a decided opposition between the Apostles being once set aside, there remains no reason for supposing any of those retrospective attempts at conciliation by which the historical facts of the first century are said to have been transmuted. We do not deny that the reconciliation of the Christians of Jewish origin with those gathered from among the Gentiles was gradual, but we see no ground for postponing it to the second century, in opposition to the testimony of the Acts, and that of Paul's Epistles.

Reduced to their true proportions, the divergences between the sacred writers no longer present themselves as radical or irreconcilable; on the contrary, they form the regular steps of a ladder, which enables us to rise gradually to the culminating point of revelation. Among these types of doctrine, two are distinguished by their originality and their broad results; the other two represent no less an important aspect of the truth, to which it was well that a sort of independent prominence should in this way be given, because it would not have been definable with sufficient clearness in the wide synthesis of doctrine presented by St. Paul and St. John.

The attempt to represent the doctrine of James and of Peter, as opposed to that of Paul, really arises from a false view of the relation of the Old and New Testament. Those who hold that the old economy germinally contains the new, see no antagonism between the doctrine of James and that of the Apostle of the Gentiles. It is too commonly forgotten that the Judaism of James had no analogy with Pharisaism.

It was, as we have said, the true ideal Judaism which was in harmony with the designs of God—a Judaism, consequently, which contained all the principal elements of Christianity. Developed and expanded by the acceptance of the Gospel, it could not differ essentially from the doctrine taught by St. Paul. James had been brought to a profound comprehension of the old covenant; he had grasped its spirit, and the fundamental principle which was to survive the theocratic forms in which it had been incarnated, as the life of the soul subsists after its bodily tenement has crumbled into dust. This fundamental principle was in its essence the conception of right, of justice, of duty, of conscience. James, in transferring this to Christianity, only introduced into it a permanent element of all true religion. On the other hand, Paul understood the Gospel too well not to perceive its point of contact with the Old Testament, and from the height on which he stood, the unity of the divine plan could not escape his notice. If, then, we admit the existence in the primitive Church of two types of doctrine, we nevertheless deny that these constituted two different systems of Christianity. The theologians who trace the commencement of Gnosticism to Paul, and of Ebionitism to James, are guilty of a strange anachronism. To us it is clear that both Apostles draw from one common source—the teaching and the life of Christ. In all there is manifest the influence of one and the same Spirit.

With these reservations, we do not for a moment deny the presence of differences among the sacred writers; unity prevails, but diversity exists. Nor do we at all dispute that of the two principal doctrinal types of the apostolic era the second is immeasurably broader and richer than the first; but the first has, nevertheless, its own peculiar value, and is admirably adapted to meet the moral necessities of every age. The diversity thus recognized is perfectly explained by the method of the Gospel revelation, which comes to us not in the form of a code, but is borne to us, as it were, wave upon wave, on the flood of the life of the primitive Church.

Each of the sacred writers preserves his individuality and speaks his own language. The imperfections of detail in each are like his peculiar accent; they testify to his being a free organ of the Spirit of God, not a mere passive instrument. They all melt into the great central light of truth produced by the collective testimony of the Apostles. It is this collective testimony which alone is authoritative, and which sets us free from the rabbinical yoke of isolated words under which the Church has been too long in bondage.

We cannot consent, moreover, to regard the writers of the New Testament only as the first of theologians. They moved in a sphere superior to theology; they possessed, as no other generation of Christians has done, the Spirit of God. Nor did they arrange their views in systematic form. "St. Paul," it has been very justly observed, "does not decide questions by metaphysical principles, and does not pride himself on scientific exactness." * So true is this, that it is impossible to reduce into complete unity the various elements of his teaching. Systems, properly so called,

* Ritschl., "Alt. Cath. Kirche," p. 67.

were not formed till a later period. Taken as a whole, the apostolic doctrine, which, while passing through various phases from James to John still remained the same in substance, may be regarded as the highest and fullest expression of truth. It is the rule and the standard of Christian theology, which has not to seek out new elements, but to gather up and classify those which are supplied, with all the inexhaustible abundance of a well of living waters, in the canonical books of the New Testament. But it is important to trace in the sacred writings the admirable progression of truth, to observe the unity underlying their variety, and to give to each its own place and rank, if we wish to have a living and spiritual conception of inspiration instead of a mere mechanical notion.

Three types of doctrine are presented to us in this second period of the apostolic age. Each of these is characterized by the solution it gives to the question of the relation of the two covenants. The old covenant was based upon two great institutions, the law and prophecy. James regards the new covenant as the expansion of the law; Peter sees in it, primarily, the fulfillment of prophecy. As prophecy was a sort of anticipation of Christianity, Peter is by his view brought into closer sympathy with Paul, whose influence upon him is also very evident. Paul is much less concerned with showing the relations of the two covenants, than with bringing out their differences. The new covenant is to him essentially a new fact, the proclamation of pardon, the sovereign manifestation of grace—in one word, the Gospel.*

* Schmid, "Biblische Theologie," ii, 90.

He is not in opposition either to James or Peter. He accepts the fundamental idea of James, but disengages it from all restrictions. The law, which seemed to abolish by grace, receives from that very grace a new sanction; it comes forth from the Gospel as from a crucible, purified and spiritualized. Peter's view is also just and true. Judaism is truly fulfilled by Christianity, and Paul sets forth with much philosophy its preparatory value. If, then, the Apostle of the Gentiles was constrained more than once to oppose primitive Judæo-Christianity, he nevertheless gave it all legitimate satisfaction in the full synthesis of his doctrine. He in this way deprived it of any ground for holding itself as a school apart. He abolished by comprehending it. It could not henceforward live again except as heresy, external to the Church. The reconciliation was brought about in the most natural manner in the apostolic age by the harmonizing of two elements of truth, designed thus to combine and complete each other.

§ II. *Doctrine of James.**

The main idea running through the whole Epistle of James is that of the permanence of the law and of moral obligation under the Christian dispensation. The law is taken by the sacred writer in its deepest sense; it is to him the expression of absolute good. He does not speak, in fact, so much of particular precepts of the law, as of the law regarded as an indivisible whole, and restored to that unity which is inseparable from spirituality. James ii, 11; iv, 11.

* In addition to the works already quoted, see Neander's "Practical Exposition of the Epistle of James."

The royal law is a law of love,* a perfect law, and a law of liberty.† James identifies it with the Word of God: "Be ye doers of the word."‡ If he does not use this expression in the metaphysical sense in which St. John employs it, he attaches to it, nevertheless, a very broad signification. The Word is the manifestation of God, or the sum and substance of the revelation of himself in religious history. Clearly the Word preached by Jesus Christ is pre-eminently *the* Word of God; § it is, therefore, the supreme law, raised infinitely above the law of Moses. This is no mere external commandment; it is a spiritual law, to be engrafted into the heart of man.|| It is to be observed, that James preserves a complete silence as to the ceremonial law; he says not a single word about it; he makes no allusion to circumcision, to the rites of the Mosaic worship, or to the sacrifices. Had he been truly the representative of the school of Judaizing Christians, so opposed to the spirit and teachings of Paul, he would certainly have protested in his letter against the growing freedom of Christian practice. We find James, in his Epistle, just as we have seen him in the Acts: he does not attach any universal obligation to the observance of the Mosaic law; he himself conforms to its rites only because of his nationality; and he insists alone on the great and

* Εἰ μέντοι νόμον τελεῖτε βασιλικὸν. James ii, 8.

† Νόμον τέλειον, τὸν τῆς ἐλευθερίας. James i, 25.

‡ Γίνεσθε δὲ ποιηταὶ λόγου. James i, 22.

§ "Which is able to save your souls." James i, 21.

|| Τὸν ἔμφυτον λόγον. James i, 21. M. Reuss erroneously detracts from the significance of this expression by regarding it merely as an allusion to the parable of the sower. ("History of Christian Theology in the Apostolic Age," I, 378.)

eternal principle of all morality—conformity to the will of God.

Thus understood, the law, so far from being opposed to faith, is intimately associated with it; James never separates them. True to his practical point of view, he brings out the indissoluble union of faith and works. Deeply convinced that moral obligation is as real under the Gospel as under the old covenant, he deprecates any teaching which, under pretext of magnifying salvation by faith alone, should lessen the importance of good works. He does not pretend that these suffice for man's justification.* They are produced by a living faith, as the ear is produced from the living blade. "Show me thy faith without thy works," he exclaims, "and I will show thee my faith by my works." James ii, 18. So far from pleading, as he has been accused of doing, the cause of works as opposed to faith, he powerfully defends the rights of faith. He repudiates faith apart from works, because it is then no longer faith; *it is dead in (or by) itself.*† When he says that Abraham was justified by works, he hastens to add that "*faith wrought with his works.*"‡ It is not true to assert that James regarded faith simply as confidence in God—the opposite of doubt and wavering—and that in this respect he does not advance beyond the conception of the Old Testament.§ He argues that faith should be characterized by holy love, and should thus be distinguished from the faith of devils, which is a light

* James speaks of righteousness as imputed: ἐλογίσθη εἰς δικαιοσύνην. James ii, 23.

† Νεκρά ἐστι καθ' ἑαυτήν. James ii, 17.

‡ Ἡ πίστις συνήργει τοῖς ἔργοις αὐτοῦ. James ii, 22.

§ This is M. Reuss's idea. i, 378.

without heat, enlightening without transforming: "they believe and tremble." James ii, 19. To believe without trembling is to rest entirely on the love of God; it is to love him, and such a faith will be manifested by love. There shall be judgment without mercy for him who hath showed no mercy; *mercy rises above judgment.** Hardness toward others is the more unpardonable in a Christian, because he has himself been the object of infinite compassion. This divine compassion requires that we forgive as we have been forgiven, and leaves us without excuse for harshness and uncharitableness toward our fellow-creatures. The great fact of God's pardon granted to men is clearly stated elsewhere by James. He says of the sick over whom is offered the prayer of faith, that "if he have committed sins, they shall be forgiven him." James iv, 15. If, then, in the eyes of the sacred writer, the gravest sin is the want of mercy, it follows that the best work is that of showing compassionate love to our neighbor. Love is the center of the moral life, as it is the center of the divine life. Thus faith and works are closely connected; they flow from the same source. Faith is the acceptance of the love of God; works are its realization and reflection. We have in this, as in the old economy, a law, but it is the law of love proclaimed with new power; the two economies meet and form a perfect whole.

In faith divorced from works, James combated intellectual dogmatism, the *opus operatum* of doctrine, as Paul had combated the *opus operatum* of legal formalism. Both are the champions of true religion,

* Κατακαυχᾶται ἔλεος κρίσεως. James ii, 13.

which has for its basis the royal law of love. We find in James the doctrine of grace very clearly taught. "Every good gift, and every perfect gift, is from above, and cometh down from the father of lights." "Of his own will begat he us with the word of truth." James i, 17, 18. The Spirit of God dwelleth in Christians;* it is he who gives them grace to walk in the way of holiness. We have here a mystical element introduced, which raises us far above mere Judæo-Christianity.

The great argument urged to prove an irreconcilable difference between the Epistle of James and the form of doctrine presented by Paul, is the entire silence of the former on all the historical facts of the Gospel. He says nothing of the death and resurrection of the Saviour or of his miracles. But if these facts are nowhere distinctly mentioned, they are every-where implied; the views—so clear, so beautiful—of God's forgiveness and mercy expressed by James would be unmeaning without them. The Gospel history silently but surely underlies the whole epistle. Is it not in view of the cross, where the deepest distress has issued in the most glorious triumph, that James pens the noble words with which his letter opens, "My brethren, count it all joy, when ye fall into divers temptations?" James i, 1. Is not his enlarged and spiritualized conception of the law derived from the words of the Master? With James, as with St. Paul, the object of faith is Jesus Christ, whom, in recognition of his majesty, he calls "the Lord of glory."† The duty of the Christian is, according to him, to

* Τὸ Πνεῦμα, ὃ κατῴκησεν ἐν ἡμῖν. James iv, 5.

† Τοῦ Κυρίου ἡμῶν τῆς δόξης. James ii, 1.

await the "second coming of the Lord." * With such declarations as these before us, it is impossible to regard James as an adversary of St. Paul. Doubtless the doctrine of James, as compared with that of the great Apostle, is very rudimentary. There is a vast distance between the vigorous dialectics of the author of the Epistle to the Romans, and the sententious language of the Epistle of James, in which the thread of the argument is constantly broken, or is concealed under the somewhat monotonous stateliness of the oriental style. But the main thought of the writer comes out the more prominently, because it is not incorporated in a broad dogmatic system. The earnest moral tone of this Epistle, with its graphic and striking images, commends it as a healthful tonic to the Christian conscience.

The sacred writer designed his letter for Churches of which he knew the internal condition. It has been wrongly asserted that he had in view only a Judaized and Pharisaic form of Christianity, altogether alien to Pauline doctrine.† We believe that it was also his intention to oppose certain exaggerations of the teaching of Paul, which had gained currency in the countries bordering on Palestine. A sapless and fruitless Christianity, in which doctrinal controversies took the place of good works, threatened to overspread the Churches in which the opposing parties had come into collision. This is the danger which James is anxious to avert. He condemns these aberrations by the general principle set forth in his

* Ἕως τῆς παρουσίας τοῦ Κυρίου. James v, 7.

† Neander's Introduction to his "Practical Exposition of the Epistle of James."

epistle; and his arguments go to maintain, not (as has been pretended) the severe asceticism of some writers of the Old Testament, but the permanence of moral obligation under the two economies. It was needful to remind those who were Christians in word only, that they would have to appear before the just Judge. James brought into full relief the severe side of Christianity, without detracting at all from the divine mercy. On the contrary, he reads in that mercy itself a law not less stringent than the law of Moses, and accompanied with the same solemn sanction. Thus closely did he connect the Gospel with the Old Testament, and thus admirably fulfill, not for his contemporaries only, but for all generations, his special mission as the man of a transition period.

§ III. *Doctrinal Type of Peter. The First Two Gospels.*

While James regards the Gospel as the consecration of the law in an enlarged and spiritualized form, it specially commends itself to Peter as the fulfillment of prophecy. He thus comes closer to the heart of revelation, inasmuch as the prophecy of the Old Testament had much more direct reference than the law to Messiah and his work. Thus the person of Jesus Christ occupies a far larger place in the Epistle of Peter than in that of James. The position taken up by the Apostle is very clearly described in the first chapter of his epistle. Of this "salvation," he says, "the prophets inquired and searched diligently, who prophesied of the grace that should come unto you: searching what, or what manner of time the Spirit of Christ which was in them did signify, when it testified beforehand the sufferings of Christ, and the glory that should follow. Unto whom it was revealed, that not unto themselves, but unto us they did minister the things which are now reported unto you by them that have preached the Gospel unto you with the Holy Ghost sent down from heaven." 1 Peter i, 10–12. If we collate these words with the first sermons of Peter, we shall find they take up the habitual theme of his preaching at Jerusalem; and if we remember further, that we are to seek the special doctrinal characteristic of the various sacred writers in the solution given by them to the question of the relation of the two covenants, we shall feel that we cannot attach too much importance to this passage of the Epistle of Peter. He affirms most explicitly the unity of the old and new covenants. The Spirit of Christ which lives in the Apostles was also the animating Spirit of the Prophets, who were the true forerunners of the Evangelists, since they foretold both the sufferings and the glory of Messiah. 1 Peter i, 11. True religion rises before his eyes like a vast and splendid temple—prophecy its foundation, the Gospel its top-stone. Supremely desirous to show the close bond which unites the two eras of revelation, he does not feel called upon to give at the same time prominence to the differences between them; in his letter we have, therefore, no trace of anti-Judaizing polemics. On the other hand, he moves in a sphere raised far above a narrow Judæo-Christianity. The religion of Christ appears to him a full and glorious development of Judaism. For the exclusive choice of one nation there has been substituted the election of all the redeemed; national election has given place to moral election, which is not confined to the limits of Judæa, but extends to those who once were not the people of God. 1 Peter ii, 9, 10. To the special priesthood has succeeded the universal and royal priesthood of all who are Christ's. 1 Peter ii, 5–7. The hope of the Church reaches far beyond the horizon of the theocracy. It is fixed no longer on an earthly inheritance, like the land of Canaan, it is changed into the lively hope of "an inheritance incorruptible, and undefiled, and that fadeth not away, reserved in heaven." 1 Peter i, 4. If the Apostle says nothing of the law, and of the preparatory part assigned to it, it cannot be justly argued that he is designedly silent, fearing to reawaken bitter disputations in the divided Churches.* He is silent on this point, simply because his great purpose is to bring out the harmonious relations of the two covenants rather than the differences between them.

Peter is not, like James, satisfied with simple allusions to the person of Jesus Christ; he has not, however, the same broad and full conception as St. Paul of his nature and work. He does not go back beyond the ages to adore the eternal Son, in the bosom of the Father or ever the world was; though some divines have discerned an allusion to his preexistence in one expression in the first chapter.† He does not speak of Christ's part in creation. He does not go into any analysis of the work of redemption.

* Reuss, ii, 586.

† *Τὸ ἐν αὐτοῖς Πνεῦμα Χριστοῦ.* 1 Peter i, 11. It is a matter of question whether the Apostle here intends to speak of the agreement of the prophetic spirit with the Spirit of Christ, or of the sending forth of the Divine Spirit under the old covenant by the eternal Word. (See Schmid, "Biblisch. Theol.," ii, 184.)

He simply sets forth the fact without endeavoring to explain its mystery. There can be no ground for saying that he rejects the mystical interpretation given by Paul; he neither denies nor accepts it; he passes it by. His simple affirmation is, that Christ "bore our sins in his own body on the tree, and that by his stripes we are healed." 1 Peter ii, 24; iii, 18. In his writings, however, we find, though in a less dialectic and more popular form, all the elements of the doctrine of Paul with reference to the Lord Jesus Christ. Peter speaks of him as invested with divine honors.* It is by his precious blood that Christians are redeemed; the blood "as of a lamb without blemish, and without spot." 1 Peter i, 19. His resurrection was to them a being begotten again from the dead. 1 Peter i, 3. Of him and to him are all things in the present, the past, the future. 1 Peter i, 11; iv, 1; i, 4. Even in the dark abode of the dead the effects of his power and love have been felt. He went and preached unto the spirits in prison in the interval between his death and his resurrection.† The Apostle thus gives us a wonderful glimpse of a mysterious aspect of the work of redemption. Jesus Christ is set forth as the supreme object of faith. Peter does not enlarge upon the nature of faith any

* *'Ιησοῦ Χριστοῦ, ᾧ ἐστιν ἡ δόξα καὶ τὸ κράτος εἰς τοὺς αἰῶνας τῶν αἰώνων.* 1 Peter iv, 11. "To whom (Jesus Christ) be praise and dominion for ever and ever."

† *Τοῖς ἐν φυλακῇ πνεύμασι πορευθεὶς ἐκήρυξεν.* 1 Peter iii, 19, 20. We find it impossible to give any other meaning to this passage. It is easy to see the broad distinction between this apostolic doctrine and the idea of purgatory. Here there is no suggestion of a purification by suffering, but simply of a preaching of redemption to those who had never heard of Christ.

more than upon the nature of redemption. Here also he affirms the fact without explaining it ; but the exalted manner in which he sets before Christians the example of the Saviour, (1 Peter ii, 21 ; iv, 1,) and beseeches them to bear his likeness, and sanctify him in their hearts, (1 Peter iii, 15,) shows that he did not intend by faith simply confidence in God, but that he comprehended it in its deepest sense—that of a real union with the Saviour. Speaking to Christians under persecution, and exposed to great trials, he constantly brings them into the presence of the cross of Christ; and if he does not expressly tell them, as does the author of the Epistle to the Colossians, to fill up the sufferings of Christ, his whole epistle breathes the same spirit. The sublime conclusion of the fourth chapter gives very convincing proof of this. We find, lastly, in Peter's writings, the same sentiments so tenaciously held by Paul as to the election and foreknowledge of God. 1 Peter i, 2 ; ii, 9. Such a conception is closely connected with his general view of God's workings. It was this divine foreknowledge which conceived in its unity the plan of salvation, and determined its successive developments from the earliest prophecies of the old covenant to its full consummation.

We have more than once observed traces of the influence of Paul in the form of Peter's doctrinal teaching. No fact of the apostolic age appears to us more easy of explanation than the influence exercised by the great Apostle of the Gentiles. But if Peter reproduces some traits of Paul's doctrine he never surrenders his own individuality. There must be singular obtuseness of spiritual perception in those who see in his beautiful epistle only a copy, or a mosaic of Paul's teaching. The Spirit of God has set his seal on almost every word of this letter, so rich in consolation, and so well adapted to the Church militant in the hour of most sharp and deadly conflict.

Having thus defined the doctrinal type of James and of Peter, we may at once recognize their impress in our first two Gospels. It is well known that Mark gives a summary of the preaching of Peter; this Gospel, so brief and graphic, presents us with the most vivid picture of the life of Christ. Written for the Church at Rome, it is marvelously adapted, in its condensed force and dramatic style, to the practical genius of the Latin race: *Festinat ad res.* It also corresponds very exactly to what we know of the doctrine of Peter. That Apostle, in his great desire to show that Christianity was the fulfillment of prophecy, was led to dwell mainly upon the facts of the Gospel history; he gave comparatively little attention to its speculative side. It was, therefore, natural that the Gospel written under his immediate influence should bear markedly and exclusively an historic character.

The Gospel of Matthew, which was written in Palestine and in the Hebrew language, for the Jewish converts, reminds us of the doctrine both of James and of Peter. The new religion is there presented as a law more perfect than that given from Sinai. The Sermon on the Mount is the principal source from which James draws his conceptions of the permanence of moral obligation. On the other hand, Matthew seeks to establish, with scrupulous care, the relation of the Gospel history with ancient prophecy. He does not lose a single opportunity of giving prominence to this harmony, and he discerns it in the most minute details no less than in great and important facts. This is his one all-pervading thought, and it gives him a strong and perfectly distinct individuality.

As a whole, the first two Gospels are no more favorable to Judæo-Christianity than are the epistles of James and of Peter. The high dignity of Messiah is recognized in the most explicit manner. His divinity is clearly asserted in such declarations as these: "All things are delivered unto me of my Father; and no man knoweth the Son but the Father; neither knoweth any man the Father save the Son, and he to whomsoever the Son will reveal him." * Jesus Christ himself is represented as the direct object of faith. Matt. x, 32, 37. The right of forgiving sins, which belongs to God only, is sovereignly exercised by him, as recorded by the first two Evangelists. Matt. ix, 6. What subordinate meaning can be attached to such words as these: "Lo, I am with you alway, even unto the end of the world." Matt. xxviii, 20. All the prophetic utterances concerning the glorious return of Christ are full of a declaration of his divinity; nor can these be justly regarded as in harmony only with the spirit of Judæo-Christianity, since they occupy, as we shall see, a large place in the doctrine of Paul.† The pretended opposition between the writings of the early Apostles and those of Paul vanishes before a close examination. The consideration, upon which we shall now enter, of the

* Matt. xi, 27. Comp. Matt. iii, 17; xiii, 41.

† Reuss, ii, 58.

doctrine of the great Apostle, will yet more completely show the fallacy of this theory.

§ IV. *Doctrine of St. Paul.**

Never did the connection between the thought and the life, the heart and the head, appear more manifestly than in the case of St. Paul. He is a remarkable illustration of the well-known saying, *Pectus est quod facit theologum ;* it is the heart which makes the theologian. His theology sprang all living from his heart ; it glowed with the fire that consumed him. His own moral life struggled for expression in his doctrine ; and to give utterance to both at once, Paul created a marvelous language, rough and incorrect, but full of resource and invention, following his rapid leaps of thought, and bending to his sudden and sharp transitions. His ideas come in such rich abundance that they cannot wait for orderly expression ; they throng upon each other, and intermingle in seeming confusion ; but the confusion is seeming only, for through it all a powerful argument steadily sustains the mastery. The tongue of Paul is, indeed, a tongue of fire.

The vocation of the Apostle of the Gentiles was to effect the final emancipation of the Church from the Synagogue ; he did not, therefore, feel himself bound to use the same caution as Peter and James, in the transition from Judaism into Christianity. He

* Besides the works on Biblical theology already mentioned, we direct attention to the monograph of Usteri, entitled "Entwicklung des Paulinischen Lehrbegriffs." The author may be accused of having made St. Paul far too much resemble Schleiermacher. His great merit is that of having made the first attempt to present a complete view of Paul's doctrine.

did not unloose with a timid hand the knot of this question; he boldly cut it. While he taught substantially the same Gospel as St. James and St. Peter, he did not set himself, as they did, to exhibit exclusively the positive side of the new religion; he repudiated emphatically every thing that was alien to it. In great religious reforms the simple affirmation of truth is not enough; there must be the corresponding formal negation of error, so that no misconception may be possible. Paul, therefore, laid the ax to the root of the tree which was to fall—to the root of that narrow and impotent legalism, which had overspread the Church with its deadly shadow. We shall see, however, at the same time, that while Paul used argument as a sharp and unsparing weapon, he used it also as the plowshare, which cleaves the earth only to make it fruitful. Every one of his negations led to a richer affirmation; and as his polemics took a wider field, his theology became more and more enriched with new and important truths, which, under divine inspiration, he drew from the inexhaustible treasury of the teaching of Christ. This was the sole and sufficient source of all Paul's doctrine; as a whole and in all its parts, that doctrine corresponds perfectly to the teaching of the Master, of which it was the logical deduction and development.

The theology of Paul has been repeatedly impoverished by the spirit of system, which has sought in it only the justification of its own dogmatic preferences. It has not been comprehended in its fullness in any of the creeds of the past. Between these formal creeds and the doctrine of Paul, there is as great a distance as between the testimony of the Apostles, and the always uncertain researches of human science. The Pauline doctrine is characterized by the marked predominance of the moral element. This is never lowered as in Pelagianism, which, in attempting to fit its morality to the measure of man, dwarfs it miserably, and takes away all its ideal character. But neither, on the other hand, does the doctrine of Paul merge the human in the divine as does Augustinism. It maintains the balance between grace and freedom ; it boldly asserts both the one and the other, and thus guards against any exclusive tendency. The harmonious fusion of the moral and the religious element is in our view the distinctive feature of this theology, which thus fulfills, while it abolishes, the old covenant. Accepting the central idea of James—the permanence of moral obligation on the conscience under the new covenant—St. Paul sanctifies and vivifies it by his doctrine of justification by faith. Thus all the supposed contradictions disappear. There is no better method of demonstrating the fundamental agreement between St. Paul and St. James, than a just appreciation of the essentially moral character of Paul's religious teaching.

The first principle in the doctrine of Paul is that of righteousness. Righteousness is the expression of the true relations which ought to subsist between the creature and the Creator. "Know ye not that the unrighteous shall not inherit the kingdom of God?" 1 Cor. vi, 9. The new covenant has not abrogated this essential principle of all religion and morality. On the contrary, it has given it emphatic sanction ; it has inaugurated the reign of true righteousness.*

* Νυνὶ δὲ χωρὶς νόμου δικαιοσύνη Θεοῦ πεφανέρωται. Rom. iii, 21.

The moral principle is, therefore, the basis of both covenants. Every thing turns, every thing rests, upon it. Righteousness is not taken by Paul in an external and legal sense, as if it consisted simply in the fulfillment of certain precepts. It is founded on a universal law, graven in the heart of man by the hand of God himself. This law is written deep in the conscience, and is therefore found in the Gentile no less than in the Jew.* Righteousness, thus regarded, is not only the conformity of our will to certain commands of God; it consists in the conformity of our being to the being of God. Man is called to become an *imitator of God.*† This is the moral ideal, the epitome of duty in which all is comprehended.

Starting from this deep conception of righteousness, St. Paul seeks its realization in religious history. He recognizes, first of all, the fact that humanity is in an abnormal condition, and that it has been plunged by an act of rebellion into sin and condemnation. He then endeavors to show in what way the fallen race is reinstated in righteousness; he is thus led to mark clearly the difference between the old covenant and the new, while he clearly indicates the preparatory value of the former. The fall, and the state of man since the first transgression—the Mosaic law and its design in Providence—redemption and its results—all these are successive chapters of the theology of

* "They show the work of the law written in their hearts." Οἴτινες ἐνδείκνυνται τὸ ἔργον τοῦ νόμου γραπτὸν ἐν ταῖς καρδίαις αὐτῶν. Rom. ii, 14, 15.

† Γίνεσθε οὖν μιμηταὶ τοῦ Θεοῦ. Ephes. v, 1. This precept is addressed to Christians, but it is evident that the moral ideal thus set before them is the moral ideal in itself.

Paul. We shall find him perpetually making all the various branches of his doctrine converge to the great idea of righteousness as the center and pivot of the whole.

We are all familiar with Paul's forcible description of the general corruption of mankind. Taking as his text those words in the Psalms, "There is none righteous, no, not one," he draws with inimitable power the picture of the degradation of the fallen race.* In order to render it yet more striking, he borrows his colors from the corrupt state of society around him. The first portion of his Epistle to the Romans is devoted to an unsparing demonstration of the fallen state of humanity. On the one hand the Apostle shows us the pagan world, abandoned to impure and hateful lusts, dishonoring man by its abominations after having attempted to dishonor God by its idolatries, changing the truth of God into a lie; (Rom. i, 23–32;) on the other hand he attacks the unbelieving Jew, and holding over his head as a sword that very law in which he glories, he says, "Thou that makest thy boast of the law, by breaking the law dishonorest thou God?" Rom. ii, 23. After this clear and concise declaration of the sins of the Jewish and Gentile world, Paul may fairly draw his conclusion as to the universality of sin.†

This melancholy fact has its own natural and inevitable consequences. It is clear that if man had adhered to righteousness—that eternal and divine righteousness, which ought to regulate his relations with God—he would have found that happiness

* Θὐκ ἔστι δίκαιος οὐδὲ εἷς. Rom. iii, 10.

† Πάντες γὰρ ἥμαρτον. Rom. iii, 23.

which is the fruit of righteousness. The perfect observance of the law of God results in a happy life. If all the works of man had been good—that is to say, if the whole of his moral life had been in conformity with the will of God—he would have been justified by his works. Righteousness would have been realized, and the harmony between the Creator and the creature maintained. Paul rejects justification by works, because the conditions of such justification have never been really fulfilled, and our boasted good works are still defiled by sin.*

The violation of the law of God brought condemnation on all the children of men. They are all under the wrath of God; (Rom. ii, 5;) they have all come short of the glory of God.† All the consequences of sin are summed up in one word—death. This word undoubtedly points, in its primary significance, to the separation of the body and soul, and the destruction of the physical life; but it has a less restricted sense. It may be understood also of separation from God, and of the evils consequent on that separation; (1 Cor. xv, 21;) of the ruin wrought by sin in our nature—Man is "dead in trespasses and sins."‡

Are we to take this declaration of St. Paul in its strictest sense? Did he intend to say that every spark of the divine life was quenched in us by the fall? Did he teach the absolute corruption of human

° Paul, in his theory of justification by faith, always assumes our sinful condition. It is in our actual state of sin that we have need of pardon.

† Ὑστεροῦνται τῆς δόξης τοῦ Θεοῦ. Rom. iii, 23.

‡ Ὑμᾶς ὄντας νεκροὺς τοῖς παραπτώμασι καὶ ταῖς ἁμαρτίαις. Ephesians ii, 1.

nature? We think not. Undoubtedly, as far as salvation is concerned, these words are to be taken in their fullest significance. Fallen man has no more power to save himself than a dead man to raise himself to life. The Apostle admits, however, that man still retains some traces of his original nature. He says, "When the Gentiles, which have not the law, do by nature the things contained in the law, these, having not the law, are a law unto themselves." They "show the work of the law written in their hearts." * In his discourse at Athens he speaks of the consciousness of the divine life as present in the unconverted man. "For we are also," he says, "his offspring." † The same conclusion may be drawn from the graphic representation given by the Apostle of the conflict which takes place in the heart before conversion—that painful struggle between the flesh and the spirit, which reveals the existence of the divine principle in powerful reaction against sin. Rom. vii, 14–24. But up to the moment when the grace of God gives deliverance the conflict always ends in the defeat of the higher principle. The natural man is the slave of sin, the slave of the law in the members—in one word, the slave of the flesh. Rom. vii, 23.

This does not imply that the body is the seat and principle of evil. By such a doctrine Paul would have sanctioned by anticipation Manichæism and all the dualistic theories of the ancient world. Instead of opposing, as he did, oriental asceticism, he would

* Ὅταν γὰρ ἔθνη τὰ μὴ νόμον ἔχοντα φύσει τὰ τοῦ νόμου ποιῇ, . . . ἑαυτοῖς εἰσι νόμος. Rom. ii, 14.

† Τοῦ γὰρ καὶ γένος ἐσμέν. Acts xvii, 28.

have favored and commended it. Col. ii, 20–23; 1 Tim. iv, 8; Rom. xiv, 6. His conception of righteousness is too broad and deep to permit him to identify the principle of evil with the corporeal principle. He is, further, careful to guard against any misconception by numbering among the works of the flesh such sins as hatred, variance, envyings, which clearly have no connection with sensuality. Gal. v, 10–21; 1 Cor. iii, 3. The opposition between the flesh and the Spirit is not so much between the material and the spiritual part of the nature of man, as between the lower or earthly and the higher or heavenly element in the soul.* The lower or earthly element predominates in the unconverted man, though even in him may be found some vestiges of the higher life. Rom. viii, 17. This predominance of the lower element causes the gravest perturbations in our nature, and leads almost of necessity to the bondage of the soul to the body. This is the most striking and universal evidence of the fall, the commonest manifestation of sin. The Apostle is, therefore, justified in characterizing it by that which may be regarded as its most palpable feature, and in calling the law of sin *the law in our members*."† Evil is not an accidental and isolated fact in our life; it has become a tendency, an inclination, a law.

We shall be yet more convinced that it is impossible to accuse Paul of dualism if we consider the solution which he gives of the tremendous question of the origin of evil. It was, according to him, the

* This is the distinction between the *ψύχη* and the *πνεῦμα.* 1 Cor. ii, 14, 15.

† Ἕτερον νόμον ἐν τοῖς μέλεσί μου. Rom. vii, 23.

rebellion of the first man which introduced evil into the world; in other words, the principle of evil must be sought not in the body but in the will. Sin is a free act; it in no way bears the character of a physical necessity. It is the breaking of the normal bond between the creature and the Creator.* St. Paul gives no explanation of the mode of the transmission of sin; he contents himself with pointing out how the powers of evil have been let loose upon mankind. It would be impossible to derive from his words a complete theory of original sin; he does no more than affirm the universality of the condemnation, and the universality of the sin introduced into the world by the first transgression.†

After having thus demonstrated that the whole race of Adam is exposed to the wrath of God on account of his unfulfilled law, the Apostle draws in broad outline the history of the work of salvation. He has set aside all the claims of Judaism to occupy a place apart in the midst of the general condemnation. By exploding all the pretensions of human pride, and destroying all its false titles to the favor of God, he has cleared the ground; and he may now triumphantly establish the doctrine of free salvation, which is, in his view, the very essence of Christianity.

* The first sin is a transgression: παραβάσις, a disobedience; therefore a moral fact.

† The famous passage, (Rom. v, 12–15,) ἐφ' ᾧ πάντες ἥμαρτον, was long translated, under the influence of Augustinism, *in whom* (Adam) *all have sinned.* This interpretation, which does violence to the grammar, is now almost universally abandoned. The true sense is this: Death has passed upon all men, *because all have sinned.* St. Paul adds, that the transgression of Adam brought that of his descendants; but he is content with the general statement of the fact. He does not say that the sin of Adam was imputed before it had been committed.

A race so deeply fallen can only be raised again by free grace. From before the creation of the world God conceived the plan of salvation;* from all eternity it was determined in the counsels of his mercy. This is the secret, the mystery of his gracious will.† The first cause of salvation is, then, the sovereign freedom of God. It rests upon an act of his good pleasure; its principle is the everlasting love of the Father, which embraces not one peculiar people, but the whole of humanity, the Gentile nations no less than the Jews. This glorious mystery was, however, only revealed in the last times.‡

The creation of the world was the first manifestation of the eternal and infinite love. It was, in truth, by the Son of God, who is the highest personification of love, that all things both in heaven and earth were created. "By him and for him were all things."§ Redemption is only the restoration of the primitive design of creation, the reparation of the confusion wrought by sin, the bringing in again of true righteousness. All that was comprehended in the plan of creation found a place afresh in the plan of redemption. It was the good pleasure of the Father to reconcile all things through him, by whom and for whom all had been created.‖

This eternal decree of divine love has been taken by many distinguished theologians in a sense so nar-

* Πρὸ καταβολῆς κόσμου. Eph. i, 4.

† Τὸ μυστήριον τοῦ θελήματος αὐτοῦ κατὰ τὴν εὐδοκίαν αὐτοῦ. Eph. i, 9.

‡ Ἐν τῷ μυστηρίῳ τοῦ Χριστοῦ, . . . εἶναι τὰ ἔθνη συγκληρονόμα. Eph. iii, 4, 6.

§ Τὰ πάντα δι' αὐτοῦ καὶ εἰς αὐτὸν ἔκτισται. Col. i, 16.

‖ Δι' αὐτοῦ ἀποκαταλλάξαι τὰ πάντα εἰς αὐτὸν. Col. i, 20.

row as to exclude altogether the moral principle; they have only escaped pantheism by a happy inconsistency, occasioned by their deep piety and their sincere desire to guard the rights of God against the assumptions of human pride. We hold, however, that their system finds no sanction in the theology of Paul. There is a vast difference between Augustinian predestination and the predestination spoken of by St. Paul. According to Augustine, God in his sovereignty has decreed the salvation of a small fraction of mankind. Calvin adds, that on the same ground he has decreed the eternal perdition of the rest of the race. We find nothing corresponding to this in the writings of Paul. According to him, salvation proceeds from a decree of sovereign love; it is thus a matter of predestination—that is, it has, as its first cause, the all-powerful will of God. It is a generous and free gift. Divine love precedes, therefore, any act of ours; it does not originate in any human merit; it has no other spring than the infinite compassion of God. God loved man, not because of his actual excellence or possible merits, but because he was pleased thus to love him. It is in this sense that man is predestinated to happiness. Thus the salvation comes " neither of him that willeth, nor of him that runneth." Rom. ix, 16. It is neither a recompense nor an exchange, for then its whole order and principle would be inverted; it would proceed from the creature and not from the Creator. It is a gift of free grace; but it is none the less in harmony with the laws of divine righteousness; they even receive in its realization a new and more sacred seal.

St. Paul does not regard salvation simply in an

abstract and general manner ; he insists on its individual application. The salvation of every man, as of the race, has its origin in the eternal love of God, and not in human merit. It is only realized, however, under certain conditions inseparable from the conception of righteousness, which is always kept inviolate in the theology of the Apostle. The eye of God —to which all futurity is open, as are the secrets of all hearts, and with whom there is no time—sees from all eternity the unfolding and complete development of every individual life. Election is nothing else than this eternal foreknowledge of God, embracing the destiny of every man, and discerning the part which every man will take with reference to salvation ; or, to be more exact, it is the application of the decree of infinite love to every soul which has not obstinately rejected mercy. The initiative in the reconciliation ever belongs to God ; it always flows from his eternal purpose of mercy, and it is impossible to find a shadow of merit in the creature, whose part it is simply to suffer himself to be saved. The very word election sets aside the idea of any thing arbitrary in the salvation of the individual, for it implies a choice, and an intelligent choice.

Against this interpretation of the idea of the Apostle, the famous ninth chapter of the Epistle to the Romans is adduced ; but it is a violation of all the rules of sound exegesis to isolate one portion of Scripture and to endeavor to explain the whole Bible by one page, instead of explaining that page by all the rest. Let us observe, in the first place, that in that chapter the Apostle is speaking not of the election of individuals but of nations. His design is to oppose the Jewish notion that a national election creates for a people an inalienable and permanent claim to salvation ; and he appeals, in controversion of this prejudice, to the free grace of God. Rom. ix, 11. The proposition thus sustained by the Apostle is the great principle of Christianity. At the close of the chapter, instead of entering into a metaphysical discussion, he silences all objections by invoking the absolute sovereignty of God : "O man, who art thou that repliest against God?" He crushes his imagined opponent by thus directly bringing him into the presence of that supreme power on which man is absolutely dependent. His position is unassailable even on the limited ground thus voluntarily assumed by him ; but is there no broader ground in his theology? Has he not shown in the passage already quoted that this supreme power is at the same time supreme love? Has he not declared that God was pleased to reconcile all things to himself by Jesus Christ? Why should the one statement be sacrificed to the other? Why should not the one explain and complete the other? In the ninth chapter of the Romans, Paul follows the legitimate method employed in all discussions ; he says to his adversaries, "Even admitting that God is only sovereign power, your mouth is still shut." But he has told us elsewhere what is this sovereign power, and violence is done to his doctrine if it is accepted only in part. Unquestionably man, regarded as a frail creature and compared with the omnipotent Creator, is but as the earthen vessel before the potter who has fashioned it. But Paul has told us what precious treasure is contained in that earthen vessel; he has shown us the divine spark within. This vessel of clay is a being created in the image of God, endowed with liberty, called to holiness. Therefore, to save that which he has so made, God shakes the heavens and the earth. Those who find the whole Gospel in some impassioned turn in the dialectics of St. Paul, or in some bold but incomplete image, misconceive the moral beauty and the depth of his doctrine; they overturn all the fundamental ideas of conscience, and deprive Christianity of its true basis and point of contact in ourselves. The best means of refuting any such partial notions is to retrace with the Apostle the successive developments of God's plan in the world. Such a careful examination will give emphatic evidence that the clay out of which was wrought this frail vessel called man was not simply borrowed from the lower world and kept in subjection to the inflexible laws of nature.

The work of restoration begins immediately after the fall. It is divided into two great periods. The first, which extends to the coming of Christ, is the time of God's patience. The world is under sentence of condemnation; but judgment is not fully executed, because God will give sinners space for repentance;* he subjects the fallen race to a gradual education to prepare it to receive the Saviour. This education was not the same for the Jews as for the Gentile nations. The former were intrusted with the great privilege of being the depositaries of the oracles of God.† They received a positive revelation; but, although divine, this revelation was not absolute

* Ἐν τῇ ἀνοχῇ τοῦ Θεοῦ. Rom. iii, 25.
† Ἐπιστεύθησαν τὰ λόγια τοῦ Θεοῦ. Rom. iii, 2.

and final in its character. Its one design was to prepare the way for the Redeemer. The Apostle notes two distinct periods in the history of Judaism—the patriarchal period and the Mosaic. In the former, a divine sanction had been by anticipation given to the constituent principles of the new covenant. In fact, the promise of salvation preceded the law, and Abraham was justified by faith in that promise. Rom. iv, 15–22; Gal. iii, 16–27. The law was only brought in by Moses. It was enough, therefore, in order to set aside legalism, to go back to the sources of Judaism, in which a divine seal was attached to justification by faith and free salvation.

It is impossible not to admire the broad grasp which the Apostle takes of the intention and significance of the Mosaic dispensation. In that very law, so strenuously urged against him, he finds fresh proof of the necessity of Christianity. He shows that it has been the most active agent in fostering the desire for salvation, and he fully recognizes its divine authority; so far from depreciating it, as the Gnostics subsequently do, he lauds and magnifies it. "The law is holy, and the commandment holy, just, and good." * But, if it is holy, it is at the same time terrible, for it demands nothing less than absolute obedience on the part of man. "Cursed is every one that continueth not in all things which are written in the book of the law to do them." Gal. iii, 10. This character of awfulness was necessary that it might accomplish its great mission in the work of preparation. It proclaims commands and thunders threatenings, but it communicates no moral strength to

* Ὁ μὲν νόμος ἅγιος, καὶ ἡ ἐντολὴ ἁγία. Rom. vii, 12.

man.* It places him, impotent and awe-struck, in the presence of the holy God. If, on the one hand, it is a restraint on evil, preventing its excess, on the other, it is also a goad, urging into activity the desire of sin. This it excites and develops; it removes from sin its character of ignorance, and constrains it to an open avowal of itself; placed face to face with sin, the law shows it to be what really it is, a positive transgression of the will of God; by the law sin becomes *exceeding sinful.*† Thus it gives rise to terrible conflicts in the heart, and fills man with deep distress; the law overwhelms the sinner, humbles him, lays him low in the dust, wrings from him a cry of anguish, which is the strongest expression of the need of redemption. Let us remember that, according to the doctrine of Paul, the law has not annulled the promise.‡ The promise still rises above the threatenings of the law, and saves man from despair; it directs his prayer toward God and the more he is crushed under the law, the more is he accessible to the consolations of the promise. So far, therefore, from being in antagonism to the covenant of grace, the law is the schoolmaster to bring man to Christ.§ In these few words, by what might be called a stroke of genius, (if it were not traceable to a higher inspiration than that of any mere human intellect,) the

* "It was weak through the flesh." Rom. viii, 3.

† "Sin, taking occasion by the commandment, wrought in me all manner of concupiscence, for without the law sin was dead." Rom. vii, 8.

‡ "And this I say, that the covenant which was confirmed before of God in Christ, the law, which was four hundred and thirty years after, cannot disannul, that it should make the promise of none effect." Gal. iii, 17.

§ Ὥστε ὁ νόμος παιδαγωγὸς ἡμῶν γέγονεν εἰς Χριστόν. Gal. iii. 24.

Apostle epitomizes his profound views of the law. The whole of the Mosaic dispensation was thus admirably adapted to nourish the desire for salvation.

The work of preparation was not confined to the Jewish people. We find traces of it also, according to St. Paul, in the history of the Gentile nations. To them God spoke by the voice of nature, (Rom. i, 18–21,) and by the voice of conscience. Rom. ii, 14, 15. The law written in the human heart was the schoolmaster to bring them also to Christ—one invested with less authority than the law of Moses, because of the darkening of the moral sense in man, but exerting, nevertheless, a very decided influence. In his discourse to the Athenians, Paul declares that God has "determined for all nations of men the times before appointed and the bounds of their habitation." * It follows, that he rules over their destinies and directs the events of their history; and, as his purpose is the same for all sections of humanity, he seeks to make the Gentiles, no less than the Jews, conscious of the need of redemption. He uses, however, means altogether different in the two cases. While, among the Jews, their desire after salvation was fostered by direct revelations, it was awakened among pagan nations by the absence of revelation. It was the will of God that these should feel after him for themselves, that they might prove, from their own experience, whether thus groping after him they could "haply find him." † The Gentiles were brought by

* Ὁρίσας προστεταγμένους καιρούς καὶ τὰς ὁροθεσίας τῆς κατοικίας αὐτῶν. Acts xvii, 26.

† Ζητεῖν τὸν Θεὸν, εἰ ἄραγε ψηλαφήσειαν αὐτὸν καὶ εὕροιεν. Acts xvii, 27.

these prolonged and fruitless efforts to a consciousness of their own impotence ; and they admitted, by erecting an altar to the unknown God, how unavailing had been all their endeavors. For them then, as for the Jews, the fullness of time had come, and prepation having thus been made, the purpose of God had only to receive its fulfillment by the coming of Christ.

§ V. *God "spared not his own Son, but delivered him up for us all."**

The whole work of redemption is summed up in these words. They testify that it is in its very essence a manifestation of the love of the Father, of that eternal love which formed the design of saving us, and of renewing us in true righteousness. Before describing the work of Christ, Paul is very explicit as to its nature. We have already said that he recognizes the eternal existence of the Son of God, "the image of the invisible God, by whom and for whom all things were created, who was before all things, and by whom all things consist." † This Eternal Son took

* Τοῦ ἰδίου υἱοῦ οὐκ ἐφείσατο, ἀλλὰ ὑπὲρ ἡμῶν πάντων παρέδωκεν αὐτόν. Rom. viii, 32.

† Εἰκὼν τοῦ Θεοῦ. Col. i, 15–17. The expression πρωτότοκος (first-born of every creature,) has often been used in disproof of the divinity of Christ. M. Reuss himself regarded it as an inconsistency in the language of Paul. We find no difficulty in it. In the writings of Paul, words constantly receive a special and partial significance from the context. Here, the sense of the word πρωτότοκος is defined by the general meaning of the passage in which it occurs. The accent is not upon τοκος, but upon πρωτος. Paul regards the Son as the eldest of all beings. His right is pre-eminently the right of seniority ; but it does not follow because he is before all other beings that he is not himself eternal. The word τόκος in no way excludes the idea that He was begotten from all eternity. It would be as

upon him a body like our own. Being in the form of God, not having to win by conquest a Godhead which was already his by right, he humbled himself, taking the form of a servant, and being found in fashion as a man.* In this state of humiliation, or rather of self-annihilation, there still dwelt in him "all the fullness of the Godhead bodily." Col. ii, 9. Thus the Apostle unhesitatingly applies to him the title of God; he calls him "God over all, blessed for ever." † While thus recognizing the divinity of Christ, the Apostle admits, however, a certain subordination of the Son to the Father. This cannot, in our view, be restricted to the time of his manifestation upon earth, and be supposed to originate solely in his temporary abasement, since Paul declares that in the end of time, that is, when the Son shall have reassumed all his glory, he will even then himself be subject unto God, that God may be all in all.‡ Is not this subordination implied in the very name of the Son, the image of the Father, and the brightness of his glory? From all eternity he has received all the fullness of the Godhead, but still he has received it. Now, he who receives is subordinate to Him who gives; his subordination to the Father may have been more marked in the days of his humiliation;

reasonable to argue against the divinity of Christ from the word *υἱός* as from the word *τόκος*.

* Ὃς *ἐν μορφῇ Θεοῦ ὑπάρχων οὐχ ἁρπαγμὸν ἡγήσατο τὸ εἶναι ἴσα Θεῷ* (he did not regard equality with God as a prey to be taken) *ἀλλὰ ἑαυτὸν ἐκένωσε*. Phil. ii, 6, 7. Comp. 1 Cor. x, 4; viii, 6; Rom. viii, 3; Gal. iv, 4; 2 Cor. viii, 9.

† Ὁ *ὢν ἐπὶ πάντων Θεὸς*. Rom. ix, 5; Titus ii, 13. See Reuss ii, 101.

‡ *Καὶ αὐτὸς ὁ υἱὸς ὑποταγήσεται τῷ ὑποτάξαντι αὐτῷ τὰ πάντα*. 1 Cor. xv, 28.

nevertheless, it subsisted before all time, and will subsist when time shall be no more.

St. Paul speaks no less clearly with reference to the humanity than to the deity of Christ. If he is declared to be the Son of God according to the Spirit, he is no less the seed of David according to the flesh.* God sent his own Son in flesh like that of sinful men,† that is to say, in all the frailty and feebleness of earthly life, to suffer and to die. 2 Cor. xiii, 4; i, 5; Phil. ii, 8.

But Christ did more than simply assume human nature; he became the head of a new humanity, and its representative before God. Paul establishes a parallel between the first Adam and him whom he calls the second Adam. "If by the offense of one," he says, "many be dead, much more the grace of God, and the gift which he hath given us by his grace, of one man, shall abound unto many." Rom. v, 15. Thus, the second Adam comes to repair the wrongs done by the first. Between him and man there is a bond of strict solidarity. The difference between the first Adam and the second does not consist simply in this, that the first Adam brought sin and condemnation upon earth, while the second Adam wrought the world's redemption. "The first Adam was made a living soul, but the last Adam is a quickening spirit."‡ In other words, the second Adam possesses in himself the creating spirit which gives and sustains life.

* Γενομένου ἐκ σπέρματος Δαυὶδ κατὰ σάρκα, τοῦ ὁρισθέντος υἱοῦ Θεοῦ ἐν δυνάμει κατὰ πνεῦμα. Rom. i, 3, 4.

† Ἐν ὁμοιώματι σαρκὸς ἁμαρτίας. Rom. viii, 3.

‡ Ὁ πρῶτος ἄνθρωπος Ἀδὰμ εἰς ψυχὴν ζῶσαν, ὁ ἔσχατος Ἀδὰμ εἰς πνεῦμα ζωοποιοῦν. 1 Cor. xv, 45.

He is able, therefore, to restore life to those who have lost it, and to kindle a new and living flame in the cold hearts of a condemned race. It remains for us to see in what way he restored the true relations between man and God, which are those of perfect righteousness.

Redemption is not, with Paul, simply the declaration of the love of God and of his pardon; it is a positive work, a great and bleeding sacrifice. Jesus Christ "*was delivered for our offenses.*"* It is clear from the epistles of the Apostle that the death of Christ is the basis of our salvation, that his blood was shed for us, and that his sufferings have effected our reconciliation with God. "I have determined," he says emphatically, "to know nothing among you save Jesus Christ and him crucified." 1 Cor. ii, 2. In order to understand the close relation which he establishes between the sufferings of Christ and the work of redemption, it must be remembered that the cause of man's ruin was the transgression of the first man. "By one man sin entered into the world." "By the disobedience of one many were made sinners." Rom. v, 12–19. Sin has thus interrupted the normal relations between man and God; it is needful that these should be restored. Now, of these true relations obedience is the essence. It is therefore necessary that the representative of the new race should present it prostrate before God in unreserved submission, and should thus cancel the effects of Adam's rebellion. The redemptive act is essentially one of obedience. "It is by the righteousness of one that all shall receive the righteousness which gives

* Παρεδόθη διὰ τὰ παραπτώματα ἡμῶν. Rom. iv, 25.

life." * The death of Christ being a proof of absolute obedience is the supreme reparation of the rebellion of Adam. The second Adam saves us because he was "*obedient* unto death, *even the death of the cross*." † Thus is the harmony re-established between man and God. But while the discord of the moral world was thus resolved by the second Adam, the condemnation resulting from sin was as effectually removed by him. Here it is that his suffering becomes so important an element in his work. Death had been the consequence of sin. "By sin death entered into the world." Rom. v, 12. In the language of Scripture death is the wages of sin, ‡ the terrible sanction attached to the law of God, the solemn vindication of his disregarded authority. Christ, in submitting to death, submitted to the conditions under which humanity had placed itself by sin; he thus became its true representative. By dying for us he was made a curse for us; he was made *sin*, for, in so far as it was possible for a sinless being, he endured the penalty of sin. "He who knew no sin was for our sake treated by God as a sinner, that by him we might be made righteous before God." §

This death, being undeserved, was on his part a free sacrifice, and an act of obedience; hence, its redemptive value. In making his death an offering to God, an act of free and holy love, Christ reunited the broken link between man and God; his death thus

* Ἑνὸς δικαιώματος εἰς πάντας ἀνθρώπους εἰς δικαίωσιν ζωῆς. Rom. v, 18.

† Γενόμενος ὑπήκοος μέχρι θανάτου, θανάτου δὲ σταυροῦ. Phil. ii, 8.

‡ Τὰ γὰρ ὀψώνια τῆς ἁμαρτίας θάνατος. Rom. vi, 23.

§ Ὑπὲρ ἡμῶν ἁμαρτίαν ἐποίησεν. 2 Cor. v, 21.

produced life and salvation. He, the Holy One and the Just, received the wages of transgression, but he yielded himself to death only to extract its sting, which is sin; by dying he gained the mightiest of victories over the powers of evil. He took upon him our condemnation; but, so assuming it, he transformed and subdued it. "He condemned sin in the flesh." * The righteousness of God is written in letters of blazing light upon his cross, since, having come down to our sin-stained earth and joined himself to the human race, he must needs die in spite of his holiness. That holiness, however, at the same time made his death a satisfaction of the divine justice—a reparation of Adam's disobedience.

After a careful study of the declarations of St. Paul, we find ourselves unable to derive from them any other conception of redemption than this The death of Christ is a demonstration of the righteousness of God, since it gives proof that the representative of the sentenced race of man cannot save it without submitting to the penalty of sin; but the penalty thus endured is accepted by God as a sufficient reparation, because of the perfect obedience which it manifests. It is in this sense a redemption, a propitiation; this is the entire theory of Paul. Theology may find some links wanting in this dialectic chain; it may attempt to explain and to enlarge upon the great doctrinal statements of the Apostle, but it has no right either to suppress or to add any. The judicial theory, according to which the suffering of Christ consisted in the feeling of rejection and of the wrath of God, is altogether alien to the conception

* Περὶ ἁμαρτίας κατέκρινε τὴν ἁμαρτίαν ἐν τῇ σαρκί. Rom. viii, 3.

of Paul.* He always represents the Father as acting in harmony with the Son. "God," he says, "was in Christ reconciling the world unto himself." † If he was in Christ he could not be against him. The judicial theory of Anselm is in contradiction with the general views of Paul on salvation. In Anselm's system it is no longer free grace, a realization in time of the purpose of eternal love. The law of retaliation receives, on this theory, the supreme sanction of the cross; forgiveness is robbed of its freeness. We are on the ground of legal right, not on that of mercy. It is, further, an erroneous conception of the work of redemption which disjoins the death of the Saviour from his life; the two are closely connected—the former the consummation of the latter. If he was *obedient unto death*, he was not obedient only in death. If He who knew no sin was treated as a sinner in the crucifixion, so was he no less in all the sufferings going before his death, and his death appears to us as the culminating point of the redemptive work which comprehends his whole life on earth.‡

* In favor of this view, Gal. iii, 13, is quoted: "Christ hath redeemed us from the curse of the law, being made a curse for us," (*γενόμενος ὑπὲρ ἡμῶν κατάρα.*) But the Apostle is careful to add in explanation, "For it is written, Cursed is every one that hangeth on a tree." It is the outward fact of the crucifixion, therefore, which is the mark of the curse. It is so as suffering and death; it is so in itself, without the addition of the idea of damnation. Schweizer, in the third number of "Studien und Kritiken," (1858,) regards this curse as simply the anathema of the synagogue which repudiated Christ; and by the same act cut off and set at large the Jewish Christians. But this explanation is altogether inadequate. That given by us is much more in harmony with the whole theology of St. Paul.

† Ἦν ἐν Χριστῷ κόσμον καταλλάσσων ἑαυτῷ. 2 Cor. v, 19.

‡ There is no subject more fraught with grave and weighty considerations than that on which we have thus briefly touched. Impar-

The salvation achieved on the cross is consummated by the glorification of the Redeemer. The resurrection is, in Paul's view, an essential condition of our justification.* "If Christ be not risen, then is our preaching vain, and your faith is also vain." 1 Cor. xv, 14. Such is his argument. The resurrection is, in truth, the divine pledge of the acceptance of the redeeming sacrifice. The risen Christ has entered into glory; he is now at the right hand of God the Father, and he carries on his redeeming work by bestowing mediatorily upon us all the graces gained by his death. Rom. xiv, 9; Phil. ii, 11. The grace which comprises all the rest is the gift of the Holy Spirit, the Spirit of the living God, which is also the Spirit of Christ.† The Spirit is sent by the Saviour to his Church by virtue of his death, which has made an open way of access to the Father, cast-

tial men, who are familiar with the history of theology, will admit that the theory of Anselm is so obscurely derivable from the words of St. Paul, that for centuries the Church had no conception of it. We must be on our guard against identifying with the truth of Scripture that which has become a current and popular notion. To do so would be to give a lamentable application to the famous adage, *Vox populi, vox Dei.* This theory has against it the gravest moral objections. It is enough for us at present to show that it is also opposed to the teaching of the Apostles. It has been sustained by a legitimate dread of falling, if it were abandoned, into the rationalistic conception of redemption, according to which the Cross has no significance beyond the simple declaration of the love of God. Clearly, in spite of its exaggerations, Anselm's theory is much more in harmony with the scriptural representation of redemption than the rationalistic idea. But we are not reduced to any such alternative. A thoughtful study of the Scriptures will lead to a conception deeper and more consonant with moral claims, one which is alike honorable to God and satisfying to the conscience.

* Ἠγέρθη διὰ τὴν δικαίωσιν ἡμῶν. Rom. iv, 25; 2 Cor. v, 15.

† Πνεῦμα Χριστοῦ. Rom. viii, 9.

ing down every obstacle and barrier between us and him. Ephes. ii, 18. This Spirit is the "Spirit of adoption," (Gal. iv, 6; Rom. viii, 15;) the great agent in conversion and sanctification. It is he who quickens us, (Ephes. ii, 5,) by him it is we receive power and might from God, (Phil. ii, 13;) it is he, in a word, who helps all our infirmities. Rom. viii, 26.

True righteousness is restored by the new Adam; but we have yet to ascertain how sinful man may become a partaker in it—in other words, how he may be justified. Paul's reply is included in a single word: "The just shall live by faith." * Let us examine more closely this ideal of justification, for it is that which attaches the special seal of originality to the doctrine of Paul. To justify, is, with him, to declare to be just. Rom. ii, 13; iii, 24; Gal. ii, 16. This declaration may be made either as a matter of law or of grace. As a matter of law, it can be obtained only by perfect righteousness. As a matter of grace, it is a gift of God, and may be bestowed on the sinner.† But if justification is gratuitous, it is not unconditional; it is granted only to faith, and we find here the moral element which permeates the whole theology of the Apostle. Rightly to understand what he intends by faith, it is necessary to inquire what is its origin, its nature, its object. Its origin is twofold, according as we regard it in eternity or in time. In eternity it originates, as does the whole of salvation, in the decree of eternal love, that is, in election, of which we have already defined the significance and bearing. Every Christian has been the

* Ὁ δὲ δίκαιος ἐκ πίστεως ζήσεται. Rom. i, 17.

† Δικαιούμενοι δωρεὰν τῇ αὐτοῦ χάριτι. Rom. iii, 24.

object of God's love from all eternity, and the cause of his salvation is not in himself, but in the will of the Father.* In time, faith is necessarily preceded by the divine call: "Faith cometh by hearing, and hearing by the word of God." † But it is only produced in the heart by the Holy Spirit. It "is the gift of God." ‡ We must not, however, for a moment entertain the idea of any magical operation upon man without the participation of his own moral power. A consideration of the nature and object of faith will suffice to exclude any such idea. Faith commences by the drawing of the Spirit, a belief in the promises of God, a knowledge of the truth, (2 Cor. v, 17;) it is in this sense a firm and joyful confidence, to which Christian experience bears most distinct testimony; (2 Cor. iv, 12, 13;) it rests on the assurance that God has forgiven us in his Son. But it does not stop there; in the language of the Apostle it has a deep and mystical meaning. Faith establishes between us and the Saviour a real and mysterious union, which makes him *dwell in our hearts by faith,* which keeps us rooted and grounded in him, § and enables us to say: "It is no more I that live, but Christ who liveth in me." The commencement of the sixth chapter to the Romans shows us Paul's view of this subject. He sees in the act of baptism a true representation of faith. As in baptism the neophyte is plunged beneath the water, soon to come forth again bearing

* *Οὓς προέγνω, καὶ προώρισε.* Rom. viii, 29.

† *Ἡ πίστις ἐξ ἀκοῆς.* Rom. x, 17.

‡ *Οὐκ ἐξ ὑμῶν· Θεοῦ τὸ δῶρον.* Ephes. ii, 8.

§ *Κατοικῆσαι τὸν Χριστὸν διὰ τῆς πίστεως ἐν ταῖς καρδίαις ὑμῶν.* Ephes. iii, 17, 18.

the seal of consecration ; so the soul which embraces salvation is buried, at it were, in the death of Christ, and at once rises again with him into newness of life. It has grown to be one with him in his death and resurrection.* To believe is then to be closely united to Christ, by dying to ourselves, and becoming partakers of his divine life. This does not imply that we may not be assured of our salvation until this union with Christ is complete. No, his righteousness covers us before God so soon as we have accepted the pardon it has procured ; but on the other hand, this acceptance is only real when a bond is formed between our souls and him ; when we have begun to die and to live again with him ; when we have been engrafted into his death and resurrection. We are not justified by the works of the law, but by the work of Christ, inwrought in our hearts by a living and sanctifying faith. Our whole salvation is of grace, and yet God, in order to save us, makes a powerful appeal to the living forces of our moral being. He consents to accept the appropriation of the work of redemption wrought by faith in our hearts, however imperfect it may be, if it be but in reality begun. Thus the very condition imposed upon us is itself an effect of his love, and a proof of the freeness of his gifts.†

The natural consequence of faith is conversion, or the renewing of the inner nature. Thus understood, it is inseparable from sanctification. If St. Paul repudiates strongly justification by works, he does so

* Εἰ *γὰρ σύμφυτοι γεγόναμεν τῷ ὁμοιώματι τοῦ θανάτου αὐτοῦ, ἀλλὰ καὶ τῆς ἀναστάσεως ἐσόμεθα.* Rom. vi, 5.

† See the beautiful analysis of the word *faith* in Reuss, ii, 21.

because the works of the law do not truly realize the righteousness of God, but either cherish pride or lead to despair. Holiness springs from faith ; faith contains it in the germ, for sanctification consists simply in putting on Jesus Christ as sin is more and more put off. Self-mortification pierces the rebellious flesh of the Christian, as it were with the nails which wounded the Saviour on the accursed tree; it is a true crucifixion,* and like that of the Redeemer, it leads to a resurrection. The new man, created in the image of God, takes the place of the old, and is changed from glory to glory into the likeness of Christ. The ideal and the end of holiness is to be able to say, "For me to live is Christ." Phil. i, 21. We know with what strong and solemn eloquence Paul incites Christians to seek this salutary death and blessed resurrection, urging them to identify themselves with that Saviour whose life he himself manifested, and the mark of whose wounds he rejoiced to bear. This is indeed the highest morality; that which comes down from above, which finds its law in the heart of the God who is love, and reads it written afresh in characters of blood upon the cross. Love is its Alpha and Omega. "Be ye imitators of God ;" † this is its principle. "The love of Christ constrains us: if one is dead, all are dead ;" (2 Cor. v, 14;) this is its motive. "The grace of our Lord Jesus Christ be with your spirit ;" (Gal. vi, 18 ;) this is its power. It is as efficacious as it is perfect ; for the love which is its supreme ideal is communicated

* Χριστῷ συνεσταύρωμαι. Gal. ii, 20.

† Γίνεσθε οὖν μιμηταὶ τοῦ Θεοῦ, . . . καὶ περιπατεῖτε ἐν ἀγάπῃ, καθὼς καὶ ὁ Χριστὸς ἠγάπησεν ἡμᾶς. Ephes. v, 1, 2.

as it is revealed. Paul has celebrated this love in language truly sublime. No poetry can surpass his pæan on charity. We feel that this is the highest attainment possible even to inspired human thought, for love in man, responding to the eternal love of God, is the glorious re-establishment of righteousness upon earth ; it is restoration perfected, salvation realized.

The Apostle, however, goes further than a merely individual appropriation of salvation. It being the purpose of God to reconstitute a true humanity in Christ, it was necessary that a new people of God should be formed, and a religious society organized, in which faith and love should be essential elements of the mutual relations between men. This new people of God is the Church. Paul compares it sometimes to a temple of which Christ is the corner-stone ; (1 Cor. iii, 16, 17 ; 2 Cor. vi, 16 ; Ephes. ii, 20, 22 ;) sometimes to a body of which he is the head. Rom. xii, 5 ; 1 Cor. xii, 12 ; Ephes. i, 23. It thus forms a living organism, a holy community, differing widely from such an institution as was the Jewish theocracy. It is entered, not by birth, but by faith ; all external distinctions are thus abolished. Here there is "neither Jew nor Greek, circumcision nor uncircumcision, Barbarian, Scythian, bond nor free, but Christ is all in all." * The Apostle recognizes in all his letters that the Churches to which he writes present a melancholy admixture of good and evil ; but he urges upon them as a duty to purify themselves from all the corrupt elements which defile and bring dishonor upon them. 1 Cor. v, 11–13. The sign of admission into the Church is baptism, which symbolizes the two

* Τὰ πάντα καὶ ἐν πᾶσι Χριστός. Col. iii, 11.

phases of conversion, and thus is no less significant of death unto sin than of the new life to which the Christian is called. Rom. vi, 4. The holy communion is the Lord's Supper, taken in remembrance of his redeeming death. 1 Cor. xi, 25. It draws closer the bonds of brotherhood, for by it all the members of the Church drink of the same cup of blessing. 1 Cor. x, 16, 17. It is at once the solemn symbol of the divine love, and the pledge of Christian oneness. The Church, the holy community of the redeemed of Christ, whose calling it is to strive against sin and to fulfill the law of love, represents to us humanity as it is to be formed anew according to the will of God. It is thus *the fulfillment of Him who fulfills all in us all**—the fulfillment, that is, of that eternal purpose of divine love which was frustrated in the fall and is realized in redemption.

But the kingdom of God extends far beyond this world. The family is in heaven as well as upon earth. Ephes. iii, 15. The angels form, with the redeemed, the heavenly host of which Christ is the Captain, (Col. ii, 10; Ephes. i, 20, 21; iii, 10,) which is perpetually at war with the dark kingdom of evil, with the malignant spirits of the air sent forth on the behests of the prince of this world. Ephes. ii, 2; vi, 12; 2 Cor. iv, 4. These powers of darkness, though vanquished at the cross of Christ, (Col. ii, 15,) continue to fight against the Church, but they are doomed to inevitable defeat. 1 Cor. xv, 24–26.

We shall not dwell at length upon the picture drawn by St. Paul of the last times. He has not done more than paraphrase the prophecies given by

* Τὸ πλήρωμα τοῦ τὰ πάντα ἐν πᾶσι πληρουμένου. Ephes. i, 23.

Christ. He proclaims a wide diffusion of the Gospel light, which is to spread first over the Gentile world, then to return to enlighten also that people of the Jews, who will have thus so strikingly verified in their pride the saying of the Master, "The first shall be last." Even this tardy illumination is to come to them only on condition that they abide not still in unbelief.* Rom. xi, 23–25. The prophecy being that the whole earth shall be filled with the knowledge of the truth as the waters cover the sea, the country which was the cradle of revelation cannot remain forever in darkness. The grief of a temporary rejection, and the privileges granted to the Gentile world, will in the end stir up Israel to jealousy, and bring it back to God. Rom. xi, 31.

When the Gospel shall have thus subdued the obduracy of the Jews its final triumph will be at hand, and the conversion of Israel will be the precursive sign of the glorious consummation of the kingdom of God. Rom. xi, 15. Before this, however, a terrible conflict will take place between the Church and Antichrist personified in the "man of sin;" (2 Thess. ii, 3–8;) and the close of this conflict will be the return of Christ in the clouds to judge the world, and to raise the dead. 1 Thess. iv, 14–18. He is himself the first-fruits of the resurrection; we shall be made like him. Our body, like the grain of corn which dies in the ground to live again as the golden ear, shall be raised glorious and incorruptible. 1 Cor. xv, 42–45. The Christians who shall be living at the coming of the Lord shall be changed without dying.*

* 1 Thess. iv, 13–16. The idea of a first resurrection has no foundation in Paul's epistles. The passage 1 Thess. iv, 16, makes no al-

The judgment will follow immediately on the resurrection; it is spoken of as the great day of the Lord. 2 Cor. v, 10; 2 Tim. iv, 1; Rom. ii, 5. When death, the last enemy, shall have been destroyed, then shall the Son restore the kingdom to the Father, that he may *be all in all.** This expression seems to open before us a boundless view of the compassions of God. It is limited, however, by the words of St. Paul as to the *eternal punishment* of the wicked in the day of the Lord.† We have thus two distinct assertions which we do not find brought into harmony in the theology of the Apostle. He associates nature herself with the grand consummations of redemption; he represents her as groaning and travailing in pain for the deliverance of the sons of God, ‡ and he leads us to anticipate a sort of resurrection of the material world as the abode of glorified humanity.

The views of the Apostle as to the nearness of this closing period of history, which is to be inaugurated by the personal return of Christ, seem to have undergone some modifications. In the first stage of his apostolical career he supposes, with all the Christians of that time, that but a very few years will intervene before the coming of the day of the Lord; he is even persuaded that it will arrive before his own

lusion to it. Πρωτῶς (first in order) applies to the Christians already dead, who shall be raised before the Christians still living are changed; but the two events will transpire on the same day. The judgment is called *παρουσία*. (1 Thess. ii, 19; see 2 Tim. iv, 1, where it is said that Christ will judge the quick and the dead at his appearing.)

* *Ἵνα ᾖ ὁ Θεὸς τα πάντα ἐν πᾶσιν.* 1 Cor. xv, 28.

† *Ὄλεθρον αἰώνιον.* 2 Thess. i, 9.

‡ *Πᾶσα ἡ κτίσις συστενάζει καὶ συνωδίνει ἄχρι τοῦ νῦν.* Rom. viii, 22.

death.* Subsequently, in the Roman prison, on the eve of sealing his testimony with his blood, he receives new light. This is very evident from his Epistle to the Philippians. Phil. i, 20–25. He learns before his death that centuries are to be granted to the Church for the fulfillment of its work, and for sowing the seed of the Gospel in the vast field opened to missionary labor.

This exposition of the doctrine of St. Paul anticipates the solution given by him of the great question of the relation of the two covenants. We have seen that he fully recognizes the divine and preparatory value of the Old Testament; (Gal. iii, 19–23; iv, 1–6;) but he regards it as only the shadow and type of the salvation of which the Gospel brings us the substance. Col. ii, 17. He contrasts the new law with the old. 2 Cor. iii, 6–9. The old law, which includes the whole Mosaic dispensation, was external; it was the law of the letter, the law of precepts regulating the life in detail, but not reaching to the inner nature. It was graven on stone, not in the heart; and it remained external to man, because it could exercise only the ministry of death, and bring man under condemnation. It had no transforming power; its character of terror forbade its being received into the heart. The new law, on the contrary, is a ministry of life, because by it true righteousness (2 Cor. iii, 9) is realized in our salvation; thus it is written on the living table of the heart. It is the ministry of the Spirit which quickens. It has finally taken the place of the law of precepts and of ordinances, which was nailed to the cross of Christ. Col. ii, 14. The Christian is en-

* Ἡμεῖς οἱ ζῶντες. 1 Thess. iv, 15.

tirely set free from that law, but he is so much the more dependent on the law of the Spirit of life, which is in Christ Jesus.* Thus all ceremonial observances, all legal distinctions, are done away; Christianity is settled on its true, broad basis, and all the exclusiveness of the ancient law melts before the manifestation of eternal love. The Apostle of grace raises us to such an elevation that the questions bearing upon the circumcison of converted Gentiles and the observance of the law, which so long engaged the Church, sink out of sight. Christianity appears in its true character; the edifice of doctrine built up by St. Paul is so vast that within it all the revelations of God range themselves in majestic proportions; so that being "rooted and grounded in love, we may be able to comprehend with all saints what is their breadth, and length, and depth, and height." Eph. iii, 18.

The apology of the Apostle is closely connected with his doctrine; it is animated by the same spirit, and in it also grace occupies the foremost place. Truth is alien to the soul in its natural state. "The natural man discerneth not the things of the Spirit of God, for they are foolishness unto him." 1 Cor. ii, 14. The preaching of the Cross is to them that perish foolishness, (1 Cor. i, 18;) but it is none the less the wisdom of God to them that are saved—to those, that is, who have received the Spirit of God, and whose hearts he has opened. Paul, however, while recognizing in every man an element of the divine life, bases his apology for Christianity on the

* *Διακόνους καινῆς διαθήκης, οὐ γράμματος, ἀλλὰ πνεύματος.* 2 Corinthians iii, 6.

need of redemption, of which the soul is painfully conscious, and of which he traces the manifestations even in the midst of the Gentile world. In his discourse at Athens he constantly appeals to this secret aspiration of the human heart after the true God. "*Whom ye ignorantly worship* him declare I unto you." Acts xvii, 23. Thus the Apostle avers, on the one hand, that man cannot, by his own wisdom, arrive at the possession of the truth, and throws down the challenge to all the philosophy of the ancients, in the noble words, "Where is the wise? where is the scribe? where is the disputer of this world? hath not God made foolish the wisdom of this world?" 1 Cor. i, 20. On the other hand, he admits the existence of spiritual cravings in the unconverted man, who is at once desirous and powerless to find God. Hence results a state of sadness and unrest, which should prepare him to receive the Gospel, But he will not receive it unless he suffers himself to be influenced by the Holy Spirit; and we find here, in their indissoluble union, grace and freedom, the operation of God, and the responsibility of man—in one word, the great and legitimate dualism of the teaching of Paul. Let us observe that in addressing the heathen, he dwells more upon the internal than upon the external evidences of his message. He limits himself to relating in its solemn simplicity the fact of redemption, while his great endeavor is to bring the soul into contact with Christ; he even goes so far as to place in the same category the Jew who *requires a sign*, and the Greek who seeks after wisdom.* In

* Ἰουδαῖοι σημεῖα αἰτοῦσι καὶ Ἕλληνες σοφίαν ζητοῦσιν. 1 Corinthians i, 22.

truth, faith founded simply upon miracle is no more faith but sight, quite as much as the faith which is founded only on philosophic reasoning. It is no longer that seeing of the invisible, that mystic union with Christ, which lifts us above the sphere of the outward and sensible into that of the divine life.

In addressing the Jews, Paul based his arguments chiefly on the sacred Scriptures, of which he distinctly acknowledges the full inspiration. 2 Tim. iii, 16. He quotes them with great freedom,* and his exegesis is sometimes very bold, sometimes very minute, sometimes almost rabbinical in its method; (See Gal. iv, 22–26;) but taken as a whole it displays a deep and admirable comprehension of the Old Testament. It is with the exegetical method of St. Paul as with the incorrect language which he speaks; he turns both to the best possible account, and expresses the highest truths of revelation while making use of an instrument for the imperfection of which he was not responsible, since he received it from those who went before him.

We are now in a position to estimate the views of the Tübingen school on the theology of St. Paul. To that school it appears a system entirely new, and differing widely from the doctrine of Christ. To us, on the contrary, it seems evident that the teaching of Paul is based entirely on that of the Master. It would be easy to connect all the essential points in Paul's theology with words of Christ, contained in the first two Gospels. It is, in the first place, universally admitted that his prophetic delineation of the last times is in all points in conformity with the

* See, for example, Gal. iii, 16.

last discourses of the Saviour. We have already shown that his rich and ample tribute to the majesty of Christ as the Son of God is but an expansion of the doctrine contained in germ in the Gospels of Matthew and Mark. The rejection of the Jews as a nation is clearly foretold in the parables. Matt. xix, 30; xx, 16; Mark x, 31. Faith is set forth in the synoptics, no less than in the epistles of Paul, as the condition of the forgiveness of sins. Matt. ix, 28; xxi, 22; Mark xi, 24. Jesus Christ repeatedly insisted on the importance of his death; and the account of the passion is the sublime commentary on his words. We may add that Paul was equally familiar with that portion of evangelical tradition which has come down to us in the fourth Gospel, and that being so near the source, he doubtless drew copiously from it. He does, in fact, quote words of the Master of which we have no record apart from his writings. 1 Cor. vii, 10; Acts xx, 35. Paul never passed the line laid down by Him who said, "I am the truth." But it was given him by the Divine Spirit to discern most important applications of those words; enlightened by a special revelation, he definitively solved the great question of the relation of the two covenants, and he successfully asserted, both by his powerful arguments and by his missionary activity, the complete independence of Christianity. He achieved its recognition as the ultimate religion, which had broken down the wall of partition between man and God, and at the same time had leveled all barriers between man and man—the religion of mankind redeemed by the blood of the cross. Jesus Christ had died to give it birth; Paul in preaching it was the most faithful and the most docile of his disciples.

§ VI. *The Gospel of Luke and the Epistle to the Hebrews.*

The Gospel of Luke bears distinct marks of the mind of St. Paul. It gives special prominence to the character of mercy in the work and teachings of the Master. It is the Gospel which contains the beautiful parables of the lost sheep and of the prodigal son. Luke xv. It carefully records the calling of the seventy disciples, (Luke x, 1,) who, by their symbolic number, represented not simply, like the twelve Apostles, the tribes of Israel, but all the nations of the earth. It traces the genealogy of Christ back to Adam, while Matthew stops at Abraham. It is impossible not to recognize in these various characteristics the idea so strikingly exhibited by Paul, of the abrogation of all national distinctions by the cross of Christ. The book of the Acts of the Apostles is evidently written from the same point of view. The sacred historian concentrates his powers in depicting the life and labors of the great missionary whose disciple he was ; we feel that he is thoroughly imbued with Paul's doctrine, and with that conciliatory breadth of spirit which in Paul was associated with irrefutable force of argument. Luke delights to show that in their work the Apostles acted in concert.

We have already noticed that the Epistle to the Hebrews is also traceable to what may perhaps be called the Pauline school of thought.* It contains the leading principles of Paul's theology, but it pre-

* See Bleek's admirable commentary, "Der Brief an die Hebræer."

sents them in a new aspect and makes entirely new applications of them. This letter, addressed, as we have seen, to Judaizing Christians, is designed to exalt the glory of the new covenant, and to show its superiority to the old economy. The author first compares Moses to Jesus Christ, and proves without difficulty that there is an immeasurable distance between the great Prophet of Israel and the Son of God. He then establishes a parallel between the results obtained by the law and those assured to us by the Gospel. He is thus led to a detailed comparison of the Jewish priesthood with the eternal priesthood of Christ. The Epistle concludes with exhortations often severe, always admirable. The last three chapters are unquestionably among the most beautiful and the most stirring portions of the New Testament.

It is at once obvious that the writer of the Epistle to the Hebrews has a very thorough acquaintance with the Jewish religion; he interprets its types and symbols, and makes very effective use of exegesis as bold as it is learned. Every page shows traces of the Judaism of Alexandria, transfigured, however, by the Spirit of God, as the rabbinic lore of Gamaliel became in the case of Paul. The writer insists not less forcibly than the Apostle on the exalted dignity of Christ. He declares that he is far higher than the angels; he gives to him the name of God. He is the Son, the brightness of the Father's glory, the express image of his person.* These expressions bear a striking analogy to the declarations of St. John concerning the Word; they are more explicit than those

* Heb. i, 3, 4, 8; iii, 6; i, 3—'Απαύγασμα τῆς δόξης καὶ χαρακτὴρ τῆς ὑπυστάσεως αὐτοῦ.

of Paul. The author of the Epistle to the Hebrews dwells with beautiful and touching emphasis on the humiliation of the Son of God: "It behooved him," he says, "to be made like unto his brethren, that he might be a merciful and faithful high priest in things pertaining to God, to make reconciliation for the sins of the people." Heb. ii, 17. The idea of redemption is clearly stated. Jesus Christ is not only our High Priest, he is also the Victim by whose blood we obtain peace. His "blood speaketh better things than that of Abel." Heb. xii, 24. The sacrifice of the Saviour is a perfect sacrifice, which needs not to be repeated; its perfectness proceeds from the spotless holiness of Him who offers it. Heb. vii, 27; ix, 26. The blood of Christ is not simply the pledge of the promise of God, it actually takes away sin. Heb. ix, 20–26. The redeeming sacrifice opens to us the way into the true sanctuary, into which our High Priest has already entered gloriously.* In all these respects the new covenant is incomparably superior to the old. This conception of the sacrifice of Calvary contains no element not already included in the doctrine of St. Paul. The connection is as close between suffering and holiness; but the parallel constantly drawn by the author of the Epistle to the Hebrews between the economy of Moses and the new covenant leads him to make more frequent use of the language of the Old Testament, and to lay more stress on that which we may call the aspect of blood in the redemptive sacrifice. He affirms no less forcibly than Paul the abolition of that old law which made nothing perfect, but he has not formed so deep a conception of its preparatory

* Εἰς ἀθέτησιν ἁμαρτίας.

work. To him it is mainly "the shadow of good things to come," (Heb. x, 1;) the type of blessings already bestowed in part upon Christians, in part reserved for the Church triumphant in the eternal habitations. Neither is the question of the appropriation of salvation treated with the same fullness as in the Epistles to the Romans and the Ephesians. We cannot grant, however, that the sacred writer makes faith to consist in a mere conviction of the mind, when we consider with what urgency he impresses the necessity of holiness.*

To establish that under the economy of grace the justice of God maintains all its rights; to show that the law of love is under a sanction the more tremendous because of the boundlessness of the divine mercy declared in it; (Heb. ii, 1–3;) to set forth that the God of sovereign compassions is also a consuming fire; (Heb. xii, 29;) to prove, in a word, that the superiority of the new covenant over the old renders rebellion more inexcusable, and therefore liable to severer chastisement—such is the substance of the exhortations with which the Epistle to the Hebrews concludes. The author even goes so far as to place those brought into the new covenant under the menace of an irrecoverable fall, so fearful is he that by a terrible profanation of the love of God the sinner may confound grace with impunity.† The teaching of the

* M. Reuss (vol. ii, p. 152) has dwelt too exclusively on passages like Heb. xi, 1. The close of the chapter, which sets forth faith as the source of religious heroism, is the commentary on that passage.

† We can give no other interpretation to the words in Hebrews vi, 4–8. The text is clear, and cannot be evaded. Such expressions as "having tasted of the heavenly gift," being "made partakers of the

Pauline school is thus brought into close correspondence with that of James, and leads to the same result. All shades of doctrine melt and blend, and the unity of the apostolic teaching remains intact.

Holy Ghost," have no doubtful meaning. The sacred writer does not say that such a possibility is realized, but he places it before us.

[But what proof is there that what is always possible does not sometimes, or often, happen?]—AM. ED.

CHAPTER IV.

STATE OF THE CHURCH DURING THIS PERIOD. FIRST SYMPTOMS OF HERESY.

THE picture we have given of the opposition encountered by Paul, from enemies and detractors, has already shown us that this epoch was pregnant with stormy controversy in the Churches. They had to pass through a sharp, but salutary, crisis.

The conferences at Jerusalem had dissipated all misunderstanding among the Apostles, but it was not possible that they should have quieted and reassured all minds in the same degree. The fanaticism of the Judaizing party in the Church was not to be so promptly disarmed by the conciliatory measures adopted in the first Council. It had lost its cause when tried before the highest representative assembly of the Church; it must make its next appeal to the tribunal of popular passions. It began, therefore, to scatter every-where seeds of dissension, and sought to destroy, both by craft and violence, the credit and authority of St. Paul. While this fanatical party succeeded in stirring up the pride of the Jews against the comprehensiveness of the Christian doctrine, it also found means to reach the Gentile converts, whose faith was yet in its infancy. We shall see chiefly in Asia Minor how Jewish prejudices made common cause with oriental dualism, and fostered dangerous errors in the Church under the name of Christianity

Thus, in the very first century, originated the two great heresies which, whether in opposition or in combination, or transfusing their spirit into the doctrine and ecclesiastical organization of the Church, were destined to play a very important part in the history of primitive Christianity. Ebionitism and Gnosticism have their germ in the apostolic age. It is of consequence to note their first appearance, while carefully guarding against confounding the date of their commencement with that of their full development. We must not attribute to them, from the first, the systematic character they afterward assumed; but we must not, on the other hand, fail to mark the earliest indications of these powerful heresies, which, had they gained the ascendency, would have stifled Christianity in its cradle.

They did not originally declare themselves as constituted and organized heresies, altogether distinct from the Church. In the first century they rather sought to undermine it from within than to attack it from without; but it will not be difficult to show that such attempts were frustrated, and that the Church repudiated their dogmas as foreign and dangerous elements.

This important fact will appear very clearly in the rapid sketch we are about to give of the state of the Churches during this period. We shall not adhere strictly to the chronological order of their formation, already sufficiently indicated in our account of the missions of the Apostles, but shall follow the development of the Judaizing tendency through its various phases before describing the inroads of oriental theosophy.

§ I. *The Judaizing tendency in the Churches of Palestine, Galatia, Macedonia, Achaia, and Italy.*

We have seen the Church at Jerusalem forming itself into an organized body, borrowing its principal institutions from the synagogue, but still remaining faithful to the Jewish worship. Judging from these conditions alone we might suppose that it would be especially distinguished by opposition to the work of St. Paul. Such, however, was not the case, as is amply proved by the authority exercised in that Church by James, the brother of the Lord. It is certain that the Christians of Jerusalem rallied around James, and manifested to him on all occasions the most sincere and respectful deference. As he exercised no episcopal function, strictly so called, his influence must have been entirely of a moral character. We have had evidence in the first Council of the breadth of his spirit, since he gave the right hand of fellowship to Paul, and sacrificed without hesitation the narrow notions of the Judaizing Christians. The author of the beautiful epistle we have analyzed was not the man to put salvation by circumcision in place of salvation by Christ. We cannot, then, suppose any open hostility to Paul at Jerusalem during the life-time of James, and it is an ascertained fact that their death took place at the same period. Further, St. Paul always continued in the most friendly relations with the Church at Jerusalem ; he visited it again and again at the close of his missionary journeys ; he himself carried thither the offerings of the converted Gentiles to relieve the poverty of the Christians of Palestine. Acts xi, 30 ;

1 Cor. xvi, 3. The most sincere affection bound him to the Flders who presided over those Churches ; he received unquestionable proofs of their affection; they glorified God for his success. Acts xxi, 19, 20. It is needful, therefore, to show that the Church at Jerusalem was at variance with its representatives in order to establish its hostility to Paul. To assert, as some have done, that the imprisonment of the Apostle was brought about by the intrigues of the party of Judaizing Christians, and not by the party of the Pharisees, is not only to hazard a gratuitous supposition, but also to invalidate the most positive statements of the history of primitive Christianity.*

It would, however, be equally erroneous to suppose that the doctrine of Paul was fully comprehended by the majority of the Christians in Palestine. Thanks to the influence of James, the principles asserted by Paul had not been formally condemned; but they were not generally recognized, either in their real character or in their issues. The first Council had bound Jews by birth to adhere to the prescriptions of the law. The converted Jews, in Gentile cities, who of necessity lived in association with Christians of Greek extraction, had been led to shake off, in many particulars, the Mosaic yoke. At a distance from the religious center of their nation they had no other synagogue than the assemblies of the new worship. Thus their habits became gradually modified, and their spirit enlarged. At Jerusalem it was otherwise. The Church of that city numbered several thousands of Jews zealous for the law, (Acts xxi, 20,) who lived in an atmosphere of Judaism, and

* Baur, "Christ. der drei erst. Jahrhund.," p. 65.

repaired daily to the temple. The greater part had sincerely received the faith in Jesus, and persecution, constantly renewed, raised a barrier between them and the body of their people. But they were still strongly imbued with national prejudices, though they refrained from any intolerant expression of them, and continued in communion with the Churches gathered from among the Gentiles. They are not to be confounded with those teachers in Galatia or Corinth, who placed themselves beyond the arena of conciliation, and openly violated the decisions of the first Council. They were in that intermediate state, which was both natural and legitimate, on the theory of the gradual development of the Church. Undoubtedly, there were at Jerusalem disciples of the narrow school, but the predominating influence was that of the broad and conciliating Christianity of James. It appears, however, probable, that after the death of the latter there may have been a Judaizing reaction among the Christians of Palestine.

We know that the years preceding the fall of Jerusalem were marked by numerous revolts among the Jews. The national spirit was stimulated to fanaticism, and the passions of the people were kept in violent agitation. Some of the converted Jews could not breathe with impunity this heated atmosphere. At their side were ardent champions of the independence of their beloved country; was it strange if, with renewed patriotic zeal, there should have come a revival of those religious ideas which had ever been so closely identified with the glory of their nation? It is possible, also, that in the persecutions which did not cease to rage against the Church, defections may have multiplied. From the Epistle to the Hebrews we learn that the Church at Jerusalem was threatened with apostasies; some had begun to forsake "the assembling of themselves together."* The general tone of the letter, however, proves that the faith of the Christians at Jerusalem rested on the same basis as that of the Churches founded by Paul. The writer has no fear of not being understood when he rises at once to the sublimities of the faith. He would assuredly not have spoken as he does, without preface or comment of the person of Jesus Christ, had he been addressing a company of declared Ebionites. We shall find the Ebionite heresy springing up in the following century on the ruins of the holy city; but if the germ from which it was to grow was already present, it was not yet developed, nor could it be while the influence of a James and an Apollos was still paramount.

The other Churches of Palestine, and those of the neighboring countries, were in a position similar to that of the Church at Jerusalem; being, however, less directly under the influence of the Apostles, they were more accessible to the spirit of intolerance. The Epistle of James, which was written for them, discloses serious irregularities in their conduct. They had evidently allowed themselves to be carried away by stormy contentions; into these they had thrown much bitterness of spirit, much of that wisdom which was earthly, sensual, devilish; and, under pretext of defending the interests of truth, they had forgotten and belied its essential element of love. Jas. iii, 15, 16.

* Heb. vi, 4; i, 5; x, 25. (See Bleek "Brief an die Hebræer," pp. 56, 57.)

Favored by these sharp disputations, formalism had crept into the Church; piety had become a mere sound of words, a deceptive appearance, a purely intellectual belief, with no power over the heart—theory without practice, faith without works. James ii, 16–18. Worldly distinctions had been introduced into the Church; the poor were slighted, while the rich were courted; and we may judge the extent of the evil from the vehement indignation of James. James i, 9–11; ii, 1–7; v, 1–7. It is impossible not to discover in these characteristics a revival of the old Pharisaic spirit, which had only changed its garb, and had insinuated itself among the Christians of these regions through the inlet of their sectarian prejudices. We see reason to think that the Judaizing form of Christianity assumed a more decided character in the small towns of Palestine than at Jerusalem. It is probable that the fanatical adherents of the old law left that city after the Council, and sought to propagate their views wherever they could hope to find credit for them. We have seen emissaries of this party making unfair use of the name of James in their attempt to divide the Church at Antioch, and so far accomplishing their end as to draw Peter into an unworthy concession, and to acquire considerable influence in this early sphere of Christian missions. There is full ground, however, for believing that the effect produced by them was not abiding, and that the Church at Antioch retained its original type. Judæo-Christianity found a stronghold only in the Churches of Galatia, of Corinth, and of Philippi; and even there, though it produced for a time sharp divisions, it achieved no ultimate triumph.

It was a leaven of bitterness which troubled the Churches, but it failed to leaven them altogether, and could not maintain its influence against the irresistible reasoning of Paul.

We have described the first fervent attachment of the Galatians to the Apostle who had preached the Gospel to them. Yielding again to the same remarkable susceptibility to impressions, they soon allowed themselves to be led away, and, as it were, bewitched by false teachers, the declared enemies of Paul. These false teachers, though imbued with all Jewish prejudices, do not appear to have been Jews by birth.* They were proselytes fanatically zealous for the law of Moses, like those Hellenist Jews who had denounced Stephen to the Sanhedrim. They had embraced Christianity in form only, and sought to stifle it under a weight of ritual observances. Some have supposed them to be messengers from Peter and James, because theirs is the authority invoked.† It is evident, however, that by their violent hostility to St. Paul, they placed themselves in opposition to the Apostles at Jerusalem, who had given to him the right hand of fellowship. According to this same Epistle to the Galatians, which is the sole document that can be brought forward to support the theory of a schism in the apostolate, these false teachers used every effort to nullify the influence of Paul. They disputed his authority, and sought to place him in a position subordinate to that of the first witnesses of Christ. Gal. ii, 7, 8. Not content with insisting upon the observance of the law by those who were

* Οἱ περιτετμημένοι. Gal. vi, 13.

† Schwegler, Nachapost. Zeit., i, 16.

Jews by birth, they attempted to lay the same yoke on the Gentile converts. They made circumcision and legal observances the essential and universal conditions of salvation. Gal. v, 2, 3; vi, 12. They thus repudiated the decisions of the Council at Jerusalem; they placed themselves outside the Church of the Apostles; they preached, in truth, "another Gospel." ‡ It is not difficult to draw the line of distinction between these false teachers and the Judaizing Christians of Jerusalem. The latter, when they admitted with James, that Gentile converts could not be compelled to be circumcised, implied by that very concession that the rite of circumcision had lost its positive value, and that it was no longer a saving ordinance; since the Gentile converts could not have been allowed to dispense with a practice really necessary to their entrance into the kingdom of God. Faith in the Lord Jesus was now the one absolute condition of conversion, as it had been declared by Peter in his Pentecostal sermon. Acts ii, 38. This would no longer be the case if circumcision was raised to the height of a universal and permanent obligation. Christianity would be then only the complement of Judaism. The Gospel would be overthrown or rather destroyed. Thus the false teachers of Galatia were innovators and schismatics. They succeeded by guile in acquiring a dangerous ascendency in a young Church, in disseminating the malice of which their own hearts (Gal. v, 15) were full, and in leading timid Christians to seek circumcision in order to escape persecution and the reproach of the Cross. Gal. vi, 12. But their successes were only momentary.

* Εἰς ἕτερον εὐαγγέλιον. Gal. i, 6.

We have evidence, at the close of Paul's career, that the Galatian Church had placed itself again under his influence. He writes to Timothy, in his second epistle, that he has sent Crescens, one of his companions, into Galatia, doubtless there to fulfill the same mission as Titus in Dalmatia, and Timothy himself at Ephesus. 2 Tim. iv, 10. Peter's epistle, which belongs to the same period, is addressed to the Christians of Galatia, and of the countries round about. We may infer from the tone of that letter that the Churches to which it speaks are in a prosperous condition. Peter does not in any way reproach them, nor reason with them, as he would have done if they had been under the influence of these false teachers. He sets forth the vital truths of the Gospel without comment, as confident of being understood. Persecution was imminent in Galatia; the furnace was even then heated. 1 Pet. iv, 12. The Christians had already experienced its salutary effects, and the purifying fire had consumed the dross. They also bore in their body the marks of the Lord Jesus. Gal. vi, 17. Judæo-Christianity, therefore, if it seemed for awhile to flourish among them, took no root. Its influence, though critical, was but transitory. It still hovered in the air, however—a vague, floating spirit of evil—and the day would come when it would take the form of open heresy.

We meet again with these false, Judaizing teachers in that Church which is certainly the most prosperous of those founded by St. Paul. Formed in circumstances of difficulty, early tried by persecution, matured by protracted suffering, (Phil. i, 27, 28,) the Church of Philippi was distinguished by its courageous fidelity and unwavering attachment to the Apostle. Of this attachment it gave him many proofs, sending to him again and again the gifts of its generosity. Phil. iv, 14–16. We gather, however, from the warning words of the Apostle, that a spirit of strife and vainglory had begun to show itself even at Philippi. Phil. ii, 2, 3. It is certain that some seeds of division and some roots of bitterness had found a place in that Church. Phil. iv, 2. The advocates of a Judaizing Christianity were there conspicuously in the minority, but they endeavored to balance the smallness of their numbers by the bitterness of their zeal. Paul speaks of them, therefore, with unusual severity. "Beware of dogs," he says to the Philippians; "beware of evil workers; beware of the false concision." *

The false teachers of Philippi united to their legalism a kind of immorality which went to the length of the grossest materialism, (Phil. iii, 18,) thus proving that when religion is made to consist in forms and outward ceremonies it has no influence on the heart and life, and that bigotry is perfectly compatible with impurity. They were not able to shake the authority of Paul at Philippi, and they were equally unsuccessful at Thessalonica. The Church founded in that city was one of the jewels in the crown of the great missionary. 2 Thess. i, 4. It was early distinguished for its piety, its charity, and its steadfastness under persecution. 1 Thess. iii, 6. We may, perhaps, attribute to the influence of Jewish notions, the false and exaggerated interpretation given by some of the Christians to the teaching of the Apostle. Some members of the Church of Thes-

* Literally, "of mutilation"—τὴν κατατομήν. Phil. iii, 2.

salonica, excited by these erroneous views of evangelical prophecy, felt themselves raised above the normal conditions of ordinary life, and gave up their customary occupations, and even work of any kind, living, as they said, in daily expectation of the return of the Saviour. 1 Thess. iv, 11; 2 Thess. ii, 2; iii, 10. This was the first manifestation of the millenarian doctrine, which became in the second century so widely diffused, and so strongly imbued with Judaistic elements.

Judæo-Christianity did not fail to find its way into the great metropolis of the ancient world. It attempted to creep into the Church at Rome, and there carried on its intrigues and underhand practices. But it has no claim to the honor of having founded that important Church, and modeled it after its own image.* It is quite evident, from the Epistle to the Romans, that the majority of those whom Paul addressed were Gentile converts. He writes to them as being of the number of those Gentiles to whom he was the special embassador. Rom. i, 6; xi, 13. He speaks in that letter of the Jewish people in a general manner, which gives no ground for supposing that many of them were to be among his readers. Rom. x, 1. And, lastly, Roman names abound in the salutations with which the letter closes. *Urbane*, *Apelles*, *Herodion*, *Rufus*, *Hermes*, did not, we may be sure, belong to the synagogue. We do not assert that none of the Christians at Rome were of Jewish extraction. The Jewish colony in that city was a very considerable one; it had its separate quarter,

* See Baur, work quoted, p. 59; Schwegler, work quoted, vol. i, p. 167.

and, in spite of the contempt thrown upon it, had gathered to itself many proselytes.* It is probable that at Rome, as elsewhere, the Gospel was first preached in the synagogues, and that it gained some adherents among the Jews, while it received a far more eager welcome among the Gentiles. It is not known who was the first missionary who proclaimed the name of Christ in the capital of the empire; it is only proved, as we have seen, that it was not the Apostle Peter. The Church at Rome was founded, like that at Antioch, by the preaching of simple evangelists. It, at first, exercised no considerable influence, (though this statement is contradicted by Catholic writers,)† but it largely increased during St. Paul's stay in Rome.

The terrible persecution raised against it by Nero shows how great had been its progress. It was not, however, free from divisions; the fanatical, Judaizing Christians sought there, as elsewhere, to counterbalance the credit of their powerful adversary. They tried to add affliction to his bonds, (Phil. i, 16,) but they failed signally in their attempt, for we find the influence of Paul paramount and almost exclusive at Rome during an entire century.

The great battle between the Judaizers in the Church and the Apostle of the Gentiles was fought at Corinth. The atmosphere of that city was favorable to such a contest. These converted Greeks had brought into the Church the subtle and supple spirit of their race; their old nature was but imperfectly subdued. Great in disputation, they loved to make

* Josephus, "Antiquities," iii, 3.

† See Abbé Cruice, "Etude sur les Philosophoumena," p. 238.

the Gospel, as some of them had been wont to make philosophy, the subject of their dialectic skill. The Church of Corinth had received in large measure the gifts of the Holy Spirit, and especially the more brilliant of those gifts, those which were most distinctly miraculous. It prided itself much on this fact, and was in that dangerous attitude of mind when there is a disposition rather to make use of truth to advance personal glory than to serve it with humility and fidelity. 1 Cor. iv, 18–20. We can understand what an influence would be at once acquired in such a Church by the false teachers who had displayed so much malice and cunning in Galatia. They stirred up sharp contentions at Corinth; piety and charity grew cold, and the voice of God was almost drowned in the babel of discordant words. Serious practical evils were the consequence of this condition of things. The bond of brotherliness was broken by the spirit of envying and pride. The Christians at Corinth began to dispute about their secular interests with as much acrimony as about their religious views; they went to law with one another, and carried their causes before heathen tribunals. 1 Cor. vi, 1. The recognition of the equality of believers in the sight of God was lost as brotherly love declined. Worldly distinctions began to assert themselves, not only in the ordinary worship, as in those Churches so sharply reprimanded by James, but even in the feasts specially designed to show forth the equality and unity of all Christians. The rich began to make a show of their abundance at the tables of the *agapæ*, as it were to mock, instead of to minister to, the wants of their needy brethren. 1 Cor. xi, 20–22. Lastly, in just rebuke of its pride, shameless scandals brought dishonor upon the Church of Corinth. The most unblushing vices of paganism were found, and even tolerated, in its midst. 1 Cor. v, 1.

All these evils were, in truth, the grievous results of that spirit of division which had poisoned at the spring the piety of the Corinthian Christians. From Paul's first epistle to them we gather that there were four parties in the Church—that of Paul, of Apollos, of Cephas, and of Christ. 1 Cor. i, 12. Between the two former the distinction was rather that of personal preference than of difference of doctrine. Apollos professed the same principles as Paul; he regarded Paul as his master, and nothing could be more unjust than to attribute to him the formation of a sect at Corinth. It is probable, that by his great eloquence and his extensive learning he may have given a peculiar charm to the exposition of the truth. The Epistle to the Hebrews shows us with what skill he was able to present it. He placed at the service of Christ that dialectic art, so fertile in ingenious allegorization, which was the glory of the Alexandrine school. He thus acquired a vast influence over a Church which was still far too keenly susceptible to the charms of human wisdom. Apollos made no concession to this their weakness; he preached, no less than Paul, "the foolishness of the cross," but he presented it under a learned and philosophic form. It was this form which enraptured the Corinthians, not the doctrine which it enshrined. There was, therefore, blameable extravagance in their professed enthusiasm for Apollos, and this Paul points out with admirable delicacy, while he casts not the faintest reproach on the innocent object of their fanatic ardor. His penetrating glance fixes at once on the inordinate estimate of human eloquence, the perilous craving for mere intellectual gratification. 1 Cor. ii, 1.

Paul is no less severe, however, upon his own partisans, who were equally guilty of schism. Their attachment was to him rather than to the truth, and they were as passionate in their defense of his personal claims as were his adversaries in their attack upon them. 1 Cor. iii, 4, 5. They had, moreover, drawn false deductions from his principles; they had exaggerated them in practice; they had failed to unite, as Paul did, charity with fidelity; and, in the pride of their intellectual superiority, had wounded the weak consciences of their brethren. The most serious charge against them was, that they had placed themselves in open opposition to the decision of the Council at Jerusalem with reference to meats offered to idols; they had thus refused to conform to the system of mutual concession which was gradually to effect the emancipation of the Church. By such conduct they showed a narrow and sectarian spirit. They carried a carnal mind into the defense of great principles and the support of a noble cause. With larger charity and greater humility they would have formed the true Church at Corinth, instead of adding another to the rival parties by which it was divided and distracted.

The party of Cephas or Peter had at its head the false, Judaizing teachers. They sheltered themselves very unfairly under the revered name of Peter; as the partisans of Apollos, without his own consent, made him their watchword. The Epistle to the Galatians has already initiated us into the system pursued by these false teachers; they set up an opposition between St. Paul and the twelve Apostles, accrediting the latter with far higher authority. The party of Cephas, therefore, attempted at Corinth, as in Galatia, to deny Paul's claims to apostleship. In this way his influence might be most surely undermined, for if Paul's authority were once brought into discredit, it would be easy to revive Jewish prejudices; and Peter was not on the spot to silence those who spoke falsely in his name. The enemies of Paul left no means untried to detach the Corinthians from him. They appear to have been here more personal than elsewhere in their attacks, for his apology has reference rather to himself than to his doctrine; it is plain that he was assailed on all sides at once. The false teachers had endeavored at first to bring his teaching into disfavor on account of its somewhat bald simplicity. They had even spoken scoffingly of his bodily infirmity and suffering. "His letters," say they, "are weighty and powerful, but his bodily presence weak, and his speech contemptible." 2 Cor. x, 10. Not satisfied with calling his apostleship in question from a legal point of view, his detractors had contested it on the ground of Christian virtue, depreciating his missionary labors, (2 Cor. xi, 21–28,) and extorting from his humility the bold protestation: "I suppose I was not a whit behind the very chiefest Apostles." 2 Cor. xi, 5.

Paul names a fourth party, which he calls the party of Christ.* Some have regarded this as only a section of the party of Cephas, distinguished by a yet more

* Ἐγὼ δὲ Χριστοῦ. 1 Cor. i, 12.

unmeasured zeal for Judaism.* But it is impossible to trace so fine a line of demarkation between two schools so closely allied. There is no sect which has not its moderate and its extravagant disciples; and if all these gradations were to be distinguished by separate names, subdivisions might be multiplied indefinitely. Other theologians have regarded the party of Christ as an exclusively Gentile company, formed of converted Greeks, who endeavored to carry the speculations of philosophy into the Church, and who, scornfully rejecting apostolical authority, maintained that they alone comprehended the teaching of Christ, and held their doctrine directly from him.† But this theory has no ground to rest upon; the designation, the party *of Christ*, points to a Hebrew origin; it would be hard to imagine a Hellenist school giving this theocratic title to the Lord. It seems to us that without having recourse to the third hypothesis, which is equally unsustained, that of a transcendental mysticism, laying claim to direct communication with the Saviour‡ by means of visions, the two former may be happily combined.

The party of Christ is in truth of Jewish origin, but it belongs to the eclectic Judaism of the period, in which there was an infusion of Gentile elements, and which was more or less tinged with oriental dualism. It is well known that in these times of universal syncretism, a large number of Jews at Alexandria, in Judæa, and elsewhere, had come, to a

* Schwegler, "Nachapost. Zeit.," i, 161. Baur, "Das Christ. der drei erst Jahrh.," 57, 58. Reuss, "Geschichte des N. T.," p. 55.

† Neander, "Pflanz.," vol. i, p. 383.

‡ De Wette, "Comment. in Corinth. Brief." Einleit., 3, 4. Schenkel, "Inquisitio critica historica de Eccles. Corinth," p. 90.

very considerable extent, under the influence of foreign ideas. We have already given abundant evidence of this, and shall find fresh corroborative proof in the study of the heresies of Colosse and Ephesus. Now Paul tells us that a section of the Church at Corinth had embraced the principles of a false spirituality on the subject of the resurrection of the body,* and inclined to positive asceticism with reference to marriage. 1 Cor. vii, 1–5. These opinions were founded on a dualism more or less logical. These Christians could not be classified with the party of Paul or of Apollos, still less with that of Peter, for their views were in diametrical opposition to Pharisaic legalism. We are led, therefore, to regard them as that fourth party alluded to by the Apostle as the party of Christ. It had probably taken this sacred name to establish its superiority over all the rest; perhaps some of its adherents boasted of being in direct communication with the Lord, or they may have taken hold of some detached portions of his teaching, misunderstood and wrested from their true signification. Thus in this encounter of opposing parties in the Church of Corinth all forms of error came into contact and collision. Roots of bitterness, which were subsequently to bear fruits of death, had struck into this fertile soil, which, for all its refined and brilliant culture, was as yet but imperfectly renovated by the Spirit of God.

The letters of Paul to the Corinthians produced the happiest results. From the second it is evident that he had already regained the leadership in that

* "How say some among you that there is no resurrection of the dead?" 1 Cor. xv, 12–38.

Church, which owed him so large a debt of gratitude. His heroic disinterestedness, which led him to refuse all pecuniary support lest he should give the slightest pretext to his calumniators; his words, now flashing with the fire of love, now falling with the sound of tears, now piercing like the sword of God; his sufferings, described by himself with such eloquence of pathos; every thing, in short, touched upon and appealed to in these inimitable letters, won back to him the hearts of the Corinthians. Was it possible to resist entreaties such as these: "I write not these things to shame you, but as my beloved sons I warn you. For though ye have ten thousand instructors in Christ, yet have ye not many fathers; for in Christ Jesus have I begotten you through the Gospel." 1 Cor. iv, 14, 15. The party of Judaizers was vanquished at Corinth as at Philippi and in Galatia.

We have thus reduced to its true value the assertion that the Church of the first century was divided into two almost equal sections, each with an Apostle at its head; and that to avoid the scandal of such a contest pushed to its full and final issue, the two parties were compelled to seek an approach to reconciliation by a series of diplomatic combinations. Judæo-Christianity was only really powerful in the early period, before it came to a knowledge of itself; that is, before it had been confronted with Christianity in its breadth and comprehensiveness. After the Council at Jerusalem it was not upheld by any Apostle, for all admitted the abrogation of circumcision in the case of Gentile converts. It may have succeeded in raising stormy dissensions in young Churches, which, in their inexperience, were surprised and beguiled ; but it was nowhere able to sustain a resistance to the arguments of St. Paul. At the close of this period, it was already preparing to organize itself as an heretical sect apart from the Church. The history of the second century will clearly establish its complete defeat in the first.

§ II. *Dualistic heresies in Crete, at Colosse, and at Ephesus.*

Judaizing heresy was not the only form of error which presented itself in the path of St. Paul. In the Churches of Crete, of Colosse, and of Ephesus he found himself confronted with the old oriental dualism so powerful at that period, not only because it contained the final utterance of the pagan systems of religion and philosophy, but also because it seemed to hold in reserve precious treasures of wisdom, and to guard under the vail of its mysteries the last resource of humanity. We have elsewhere so fully described this form of dualism that we shall not now do more than exhibit the special aspect it assumes on its first contact with Christianity. The island of Crete was a very favorable sphere for the development of dualistic heresy, for Pythagorean ideas had there obtained much currency. Epimenides, the Cretan poet, quoted by St. Paul, had made them the theme of his muse. Ephesus had become, as we know, the metropolis of Asia Minor, and an important religious center for the confluence of East and West. Of Colosse, we have only to remember that it was a Phrygian city, in order to understand the early appearance of heresy in the Church which had been there founded by a disciple of Paul. Before tracing the history of the false doctrines indicated by the Apostle, we must recall the first-known attempt made to combine Christianity with the theosophy of the East. We refer to the system of Simon Magus. The discovery of the "Philosophoumena" has confirmed the unanimous opinion of the "Fathers," who regarded Simon as the first heretic. We have already analyzed his strange system under its original form, as he had devised it before he became acquainted with the new religion. It only remains for us now to study it in its later aspect, while briefly recalling its fundamental principles. This explanation will help us better to understand the heresies of Colosse and of Ephesus, for they belong to the same current of ideas.

We have seen that the first principle of all things in this extraordinary system is an obscure and mysterious power, a sort of infinite potentiality.* This first principle is fire; it is at first hidden and invisible, purely potential, but it is destined to pass from the virtual to the actual, and to become a reality.† Simon compares it to a tree; the roots going down into the earth correspond to the hidden and potential fire; the trunk, the branches, and the leaves, to the fire in manifestation.‡ In the infinite potentiality are contained all the roots, all the germs of the world, and primarily the two great opposing principles which constitute dualism; the male, active spiritual principle, or the mind; the feminine, receptive principle, or

* Ἀπέραντον δὲ εἶναι δύναμιν ὁ Σίμων προσαγορεύει τῶν ὅλων τὴν ἀρχήν. "Philos.," 163.

† Ἀλλὰ γὰρ εἶναι τὴν τοῦ πυρὸς διπλῆν τινὰ τὴν φυσιν, καῖ τῆς διπλῆς ταύτης καλεὶ τὸ μέν τι κρυπτὸν, τὸ δέ τι φανερόν. "Philos.," 163.

‡ "Philos.," 164.

the idea.* The mind represents the active principle, the idea the passive principle. In passing from the potential to the actual, the *mind* becomes heaven, the *idea* becomes earth. Creation is a necessary manifestation of the former principle ; by it, it passes from possibility to reality ; † if it was not thus realized it would remain in the state of the purely potential, like geometry in the mind of the geometer, or grammar in the mind of the grammarian.‡ There is in every being a blessed and immortal germ *which has been, which is, and which is to be.* It is a particle of that first principle, which was the potential energy, which is power and reality in the world, and which in its essential potentiality perpetually takes an infinity of new forms. This first principle is the one force, diffused above and below, giving birth to itself, seeking, losing, recovering itself ; it is its own mother, father, sister, daughter ; the one sole root of all things, the male and female principle.§ Man is an epitome of the world ; he is a perfect microcosm ; he contains the potential fire, and realizes it in his double element.

It was impossible to give bolder expression to

* *Νοῦν καὶ ἐπὶνοιαν.* Philos.," 116. The mind is the active principle, the idea the passive principle. Simon counted six roots of things divided into couples : the mind and the idea, the voice and the name, conclusion and reflection. In passing from the potential to the actual they take other names, and we have thus three fresh couples : heaven and earth, sun and moon, air and water.

† Τὸ *πνεῦμα ἐὰν μὴ ἐξεικονισθῇ μετὰ τοῦ κοσμου ἀπολεῖται, δυνὰμει μεῖνον μὸνον καὶ μη ἐνεργείᾳ γενόμενον.* "Philos.," 167.

‡ *'Εστὼς ἄνω, ἐν τῇ ἀγεννήτῳ δυνάμει, στὰς κάτω ἐν τῇ ῥοῇ τῶν ὑδάτων, ἐν εἰκονι γεννεθεὶς, στησομενος ἄνω, παρὰ τὴν μακαρίαν ἀπέραντον δύναμιν ἐᾶν ἐξεικονισθῇ.* "Philos.," 171.

§ *'Αυτῆς μήτηρ, ἀυτῆς πατὴρ, ἀυτῆς ἀδελφὴ ἀυτῆς σύζυγος ἀυτῆς θυγάτηρ.* "Philos.," 171. *'Αρσενόθηλυς δύναμις.* "Philos.," 173.

pantheism. Simon Magus clothed these ideas in sacred symbols borrowed from the Old Testament. He endeavored to make his theories accord with the account of the creation. He saw in the six days of the creative work the six roots of the universe comprised in the infinite potentiality. The seventh day represented the first principle when it found itself manifested in the universe. The heaven and the earth expressed the first duality of the mind and the idea.* The description of Paradise became in his view the allegorical history of the creation of man contained in the Pentateuch.† Thus we find in this father of Gnosticism that tendency of all the Gnostic heretics to interpret revelation as a cosmogony. But Simon was not satisfied with distorting the meaning of the Old Testament to sustain his system; he made the same misuse of the words of Christ. It appears that he had blended with his pantheism some ill-digested notions of the emanation theory.

The transition from the virtual to the actual was not, it seems, effected without confusion; after the mind by its union with the idea had given birth to the angels, these in jealousy took possession of their mother, and made her captive in the fetters of the body.‡ Kept a prisoner in the lower world, she is

* "Philos.," 167. † "Philos.," 168, 169.

‡ Here there is a gap in the "Philosophoumena." There are merely these words: *μετενσωματουμένην ὑπο τῶν ἀγγέλων*, (p. 174, I.) Irenæus, whose sketch of the whole system is very incomplete, gives us a commentary on this phrase: "*Eunoiam* generare angelos et potestates a quibus et mundum hunc factum dixit. Posteaquam generavit eos hæc detenta est ab ipsis propter invidiam quoniam nollent progenies alterius cujusdam putari esse." Irenæus, "Contr. Hæres.," I, c. xxiv. Compare Epiphanes, i, 21.

said to have become personified as a woman of remarkable beauty, and reappears in history under various names from time to time. Thus she took the features of the famous Helena, whose fatal beauty occasioned the Trojan war. We have seen that Simon pretended to recognize her in a courtezan of Tyre, whom he made his companion. He declared himself to be the incarnation of the rational principle, whose destiny it was to set her free.* He thus represents the fall to be nothing else than materialization, and redemption to consist in release from the bonds of the body. It does not appear, however, that Simon's doctrine led his followers into asceticism. On the contrary, they allowed themselves the most unbridled license under pretext of celebrating the true eucharistic feast, and they sanctioned their infamous proceedings under the name of perfect love.†

Dualism does in fact thus lead to the two extremes of license and asceticism. Some of its adherents imagine they triumph over the material element by placing themselves beyond all restraint; others seek to annihilate it by the severest mortification of the flesh. Simon Magus adopted the former method, and his disciples were guilty of still greater excesses in the same direction. He set himself forth as the great Deliverer, the true Christ. He said that he had appeared as the Son in Judæa, as the Father in Samaria, and as the Holy Ghost among the nations; ‡ but

* We have already opposed the notion that Simon was the incarnation of the first principle.

† *Μακαρίζουσιν ἑαυτοὺς ἐπὶ τῇ ξένῃ μίξει, ταύτην εἶναι λέγοντες τὴν τελείαν ἀγάπην.* "Philos.," 175.

‡ "Philos.," 175. M. Bunsen ("Hippolytus," i, 38, 39) supposes that Simon spoke in this passage not of himself but of Jesus Christ.

that, under these or other names, he always fulfilled the same mission, which was to set free the idea from the fetters of the body. With this design he took a form like the inferior powers, and submitted to seeming suffering.* The parable of the lost sheep represented, according to Simon, his redeeming work. Did he not, like the good shepherd, seek out the unfortunate Helena, the object of his compassion, who had strayed into the lower world like the sheep into the desert ? † He wrought her salvation by revealing himself to her, and he was to restore her to that higher region from which she had fallen. ‡ This unfortunate Helena, the personification of the idea, held captive in the chains of nature, is found in every man, since man is a perfect microcosm, and contains in himself all the elements of the world. The work of enfranchisement is therefore to be carried on in every individual. Thus Simon promised salvation to all who should believe in him and call upon his name. It is easy to understand the importance of magic in a system in which it was the first essential to fight against the angels by whom the world was created, and to vanquish the powers of the cosmogony. The moral aspect is thus completely sacrificed. Evil does not proceed from a perversion of the human will ; it results from angelic creation, and every man is what

We cannot share this opinion, for evidently Simon sets himself forth as the deliverer of Helen, the saviour of the lost sheep. He then is himself the Christ ; his docetism allowed him to admit indefinitely changes of form and of name.

* Δεδοκηκέναι πεπονθότα. "Philos.," 175.

† Ταύτην τὸ πρόβατον τὸ πεπλανημένον. "Philos.," 174.

‡ Οὔτως τοῖς ανθρώποις σωτηρίαν παρέσχε δία τῆς ἰδίας επιγνώσεως. "Philos.," 175.

he is by that creation;* he is consequently under the yoke of fatality. Simon pretended to be alone capable of procuring deliverance by his doctrine and his sorceries.†

We have no certain information as to the history of Simon Magus or of his school. We have already had occasion to refute the legendary assertion of his stay at Rome and of his contest with St. Peter. It appears to us probable that his disciples were gathered chiefly in Samaria and the surrounding countries.‡ His system is clearly connected with the Phœnician superstitions, as they are made known to us in the "Philosophoumena." We have therefore reason for supposing that his influence had an effect, direct or indirect, on the formation of the heresies alluded to by St. Paul.

These heresies, of which the Apostle carefully points out the various phases, all bear the same impress of Judaism combined with dualism. In Crete, at Colosse, and at Ephesus, we find substantially the same ideas, the same principles, with this difference, that in Crete the false doctrines had not as yet effected the threatened entry into the Church, but were still

* Οὐ φύσει κακὸς ἀλλὰ θέσει. "Philos.," 176.

† It is needful to show that there was a distinction between the system of Simon and the forms given to it by some of his disciples. For instance, the very marked opposition between the Old and the New Testament expressed in these words, "The prophecies were inspired by the angels, creators of the world," ("Philos.," 175,) is rather due to the disciples than to the master. In fact, Simon in many passages makes free use of the Old Testament. Besides, this idea only acquired such precision at a much later period. In the first century dualism sought to shelter itself under the shadow of Judaism.

‡ The fables of the "Clementines," which make Simon pass through the cities of Syria and Phœnicia, may rest upon local traditions.

kept without,* while at Colosse and at Ephesus they had made shipwreck of the faith of many professing Christians.† The future looked even more gloomy than the present, and the Apostle foresaw a terrible growth of these roots of bitterness. 2 Tim. iii, 1–5. But in Crete, as at Colosse and at Ephesus, the false teachers were converts from Judaism, and represented its ascetic and theosophic side. ‡ This is very apparent from the various characteristics by which St. Paul makes us acquainted with them. They are of Jewish origin, and pretend to be deeply versed in the law.§ They are distinguished by their ostentatious austerities. They burden the Christians with ascetic restrictions, repeating perpetually, "Touch not; taste not; handle not." || They thus make a show of wisdom in not sparing the body. Like the party of Christ at Corinth, they condemn marriage,¶ and are led as a natural consequence of their principles to deny the resurrection of the body, and to maintain

* Εἰσὶ γὰρ πολλοὶ . . . μάλιστα οἱ ἐκ περιτομῆς. Titus i, 10.

† Τινες περὶ τὴν πίστιν ἐναυάγησαν. 1 Tim. i, 19; vi, 21.

‡ Compare Titus i, 14 and 1 Tim. iv, 7. See an excellent dissertation on this point in Mangold's pamphlet, "Die Irrlehrer der Pastoralbriefe," Marburg, 1856. He well refutes Credner and Thiersch, who asserted that the heresies combated by St. Paul were manifold. Credner ("Einleit. in N. T.," i, 348) counted four different heresies: first, two in Crete—one Judaizing, one derived from paganism; he based this opinion on Titus i, 10, (μάλιστα οἱ ἐκ περιτομῆς,) but this passage refers only to one single Jewish heresy; second, two heresies at Ephesus—one already formed, one in process of formation; (2 Tim. iii, 1, 2;) but Paul is speaking clearly of one and the same heresy in various stages.

§ Νομοδιδάσκαλοι. 1 Tim. i, 7. The heretics at Colosse are also Jews. 1 Col. ii, 16.

|| Col. ii, 21. Compare Titus i, 14.

¶ Κωλυόντων γαμεῖν. 1 Tim. iv, 3.

that there is no resurrection but that of the soul renewed by Christ.*

This whole system was evidently based on a dualistic philosophy which identified evil with matter. These heretics were not satisfied with carrying out dualism in practice; they gave it formal expression, and endeavored to find a speculative basis for it; they concerned themselves with fables and foolish questions concerning the doctrine of angels. 1 Tim. i, 4; 2 Tim. iv, 4; Col. ii, 18. We know already from the system of Simon Magus, that the doctrine of angels was connected with a theory of emanation as yet confused and chaotic. In these vain speculations we recognize that science, falsely so called, which the Apostle condemned. 1 Tim. vi, 20. These heretics then followed the example of Simon Magus in turning the sacred Scriptures to their own purposes, and wresting them into the confirmation of their peculiar tenets. They gave an allegorical interpretation to the historical portion of the Old Testament, and thus cast a sacred vail over their monstrous errors.†

* *Λέγοντες τὴν ἀνάστασιν ἤδη γεγονέναι.* 2 Tim. ii, 18.

† This is the meaning we attach to the words "endless genealogies." 1 Tim. i, 4. Some have supposed the reference to be to the *genealogies of the eons* in the system of emanations; but this would infer a system of Gnosticism much more advanced than that here described. Mangold shows that the word genealogy has never been taken in this sense in the Gnostic systems. He quotes, after Dæhne, a passage from Philo, which justifies the interpretation we have given. Philo, in fact, after dividing the Pentateuch into two parts—the first comprising the laws and ordinances, the second the historical documents—makes under the latter head two further subdivisions: the historical, properly so called; and the *genealogical* portion: *'Εστὶν οὖν τοῦ ἱστορικοῦ, τὸ μὲν περὶ τῆς τοῦ κόσμου γενέσεως, τὸ δὲ γενεᾶλογικόν· τοῦ δὲ γενεᾶλογικοῦ, τὸ μὲν περὶ κολάσεως ἀσεβῶν, τõ δὲ αὖ περὶ τιμῆς δικαίων.*

The question now before us is to ascertain to what known sect these first heretics belonged. They have been represented as professing Gnosticism in a form already complete and systematized, in all points resembling that of the second century, and this hypothesis has been used as an argument against the authenticity of the Pastoral Epistles.* But the general features pointed out by the Apostle as characteristic of the false teachers at Ephesus, correspond rather to Gnosticism in its first elementary form, than in its full, systematic development as we meet with it in Valentinus and Marcion. It is evident, from the Epistle to the Colossians, that dualistic and ascetic

"Of the genealogies one portion refers to the punishments of the wicked, the other to the rewards of the righteous." Philo, "De Vita Contemplativa," *a. o. θ* § 4. Thus the genealogies, according to him, were to show the punishment of the wicked and the recompense of the just. It is evident that they can only do this under an allegorical system of interpretation. Now, it is known that Philo found in the genealogies a complete psychology. The names represented to him the conditions of the soul, (*τρόποι τῆς ψυχῆς*.) It is easy to imagine what important results the party of Judaizing heretics might derive from the innumerable genealogies of the Old Testament. That which has decided us in favor of this explanation of Dæhne and Mangold is a passage in the "Philosophoumena" not quoted by the latter, and which contains an exact exemplar of this mythical use of the genealogies on the part of those Ophite heretics, who may be regarded as the direct successors of the false teachers described in the pastoral epistles. We there read as follows: "The Sethians (one of the numerous branches of the Ophites) say that Moses upholds their doctrine when he enumerates in Paradise, Adam, Eve, and the serpent, to the number of three, and when he names Cain, Abel, and Seth, or again Shem, Ham, and Japheth; and lastly, when he speaks of the three patriarchs, Abraham, Isaac, and Jacob." Ὅταν λέγῃ τρεῖς πατριάρχας Ἀβραάμ, Ισαάκ, Ἰακώβ. "Philos.," 143.

* Baur, "Die sogenannten Pastoralbriefe." Schwegler, "Nacha-post. Zeit.," ii, 142. See M. Reuss's excellent reply, "Geschichte der Heil. Schr., N. T.," 115, 116.

ideas were agitated in the Churches of that period, as they were universally. This agitation was likely to assume a marked and decided character in cities like Colosse and Ephesus. A movement so important as Gnosticism, must have been, like all the great movements of the human mind, long in preparation. It existed as a tendency long before it was constituted as a school of philosophy. The system of Simon Magus proves the existence of the elements of Gnosticism in the first century.

The heresies of Colosse and Ephesus ought not to be exclusively referred to the ascetic tendency of Judaism.* The influence of pagan ideas had, in our view, a large share in producing the false doctrines denounced in the epistles to Titus and to Timothy. Doubtless, the ascetic direction given to Judaism was due in part to this influence. The Jewish school of Alexandria was a product of Platonism and of the religions of the East. The Essenes transplanted into the soil of Judæa the dualism of Philo, giving it a more practical character. They also held the eternal opposition between spirit and matter ; they regarded the body as the prison of the soul, the true cause of evil ; and, imitating the Therapeutics of Alexandria, they professed the most extreme asceticism.†

We are convinced, however, that the heretics of Colosse, of Ephesus, and of Crete, came under pagan influence not only through the medium of a Jewish sect, but that they also borrowed new elements from paganism, and arrived at a more decided dualism.

* Josephus, "Bell. Judaic," ii, 8–11.
† This is Mangold's hypothesis.

They unquestionably drew their first conceptions from the doctrine of the Essenes, or from that of Philo, for they were of Jewish origin; but they, subsequently, went far beyond this modified pantheism. We cannot regard them either as pure Essenes or as of the pure Alexandrine school. It is not proved that the former attempted any active propagandism beyond Judæa, and the latter existed as a school only in Egypt. The fundamental ideas of both were derived from the moral atmosphere of the age; it was the "power abroad. in the air." These ideas would take various forms of manifestation wherever they found a soil favorable to their growth; and what soil could be more favorable than that of the province of Phrygia, in the middle of which the Church of Colosse was placed? The mysteries of Cybele or of the great goddess, of Atys, of Pan, of Bacchus, were inspired by the dualistic pantheism, which led at the same time to the most infamous licentiousness and the most extravagant asceticism. St. Hippolytus tells us that the heresies of the commencement of the second century—that is to say, the heresies which immediately followed those opposed by St. Paul—had drawn largely from these myths and mysteries.* He declares, at the same time, that long before they came into the light they had been brooding in the shade. "This hydra," he says, "which casts forth so many blasphemies against Christ, has been crouching in the dark for many years." † The system of Simon

* Ζητοῦσι δὲ οὐκ ἀπὸ τῶν Γραφῶν, ἀλλὰ καὶ τοῦτο ἀπὸ τῶν μυστικῶν. "Philos.," 98, 99, 117–119.

† Ὧν πολλοῖς ἔτεσιν ἔλαθεν ἡ κατὰ Χριστοῦ δυσφημία. "Philos.," 123.

Magus, which belongs to the same date, is strongly impregnated with elements borrowed from the pantheism of the East. It appears to us, then, probable that the heretics of Colosse and of Ephesus brought together in hybrid union Jewish and pagan ideas. It is not possible to give an exact account of their system. It is enough for us to know that it led to ascetic practices, and was based upon a medley of idle fables and on emanatist principles, in order to recognize in it a sort of anticipation of Gnosticism. Against such false and vain speculations the Apostle sets the grand and powerful doctrine of Christianity, that between God and the world there is but one Mediator, the Eternal Son, who is the express image of the Divine Person, "by whom and for whom were all things created." Col. i, 15, 16. He points to the cross triumphing over all the malignant powers with which false science sought to fill up the gulf between earth and heaven. Col. ii, 15. He is especially careful to show the dangerous effects of heresy on the Christian life. He represents the false teachers as creeping into houses, leading captive the minds of "silly women" laden with sins, and as pursuing self-interested ends, seeking to satisfy at once their pride and their greed for filthy lucre. Titus i, 11.

The latent immorality, ever characteristic of Gnosticism, thus betrayed itself from the very first. In this its earliest form there is nothing systematic, but it has already broad and well-marked features—its pretensions to profound speculations, which end in "old wives' fables;" its false science, which is ever teaching without leading to any true knowledge; its wild theories concerning angels; its incongruous combination of asceticism and libertinism. It was, doubtless, checked by the severe reprobation of the Apostle ; but, like Judæo-Christianity, it would recover from the blows thus leveled at it, would reunite its scattered elements, repudiate its Jewish origin, and, better organized and better armed, enter on a deadly warfare with the Church.

CHAPTER V.

CONSTITUTION OF THE CHURCHES DURING THIS PERIOD.*

§ I. *General Principles of Ecclesiastical Organization.*

WHILE, during the first period of the apostolic age, the predominance of the miraculous prevents the Church from assuming a definitely organized form, we are able, in this second period, to discern the essential features of its constitution. The first broad outline is shaded and filled up. The thought embodied in the existence of the Church finds fresh and fuller expression. Christians, while they were still held in the bonds of Jewish exclusiveness, did not clearly comprehend that they were called to form a religious society differing altogether from the ancient theocracy. They were conscious of a new and special relation established between those who had been baptized in the name of Christ; but they regarded themselves rather as the true Israel than as the Christian Church. As Christianity extended its conquests among the heathen, their ideas widened, and, as we have seen in the theology of St. Paul, the true con-

* The principal work of reference on this subject is Rothe, "Anfänge der christlichen Kirche." See also Ritschl's work, "Altcatholische Kirche;" and the various histories of the apostolic age already quoted. We refer the reader also to Bingham's "Origines seu Antiquitates ecclesiasticæ." Halæ, 1724. Vitringa, "De Synagog. vetere." Ignatius, "Von Antiochien und seine Zeit." Sieben Zendschreiben. Bunsen, Hamburg, 1847.

ception of the Church, the idea of a willing people gathered out of the whole world, of a regenerated race formed anew in Christ Jesus, was one of the most precious results of the mission of the Apostles. The Church, no longer shut up within a single city, but spreading beyond the gates of Jerusalem far and wide over the Gentile world, could not any more be regarded as identified with any purely local or external conditions. The spiritual reality was disengaging itself from the material form, and through and beyond the visible Churches came the dawning recognition of that invisible Church, the abiding type and ideal of them all.

It is this invisible Church which Paul beholds with the eye of faith when he speaks of the bride of Christ, without blemish and without spot, (Ephes. v, 23–27 ;) it alone possesses in perfection that unity of love, so often marred by failure and sin in the various visible Churches. Ephes. iv, 4, 5. The Apostle assuredly knew only too well the unhappy contentions in those Churches ; he, who had probed their wounds with so unshrinking a hand, would not hold forth any one of them as the glorious, irreproachable Church of which he speaks to the Ephesian Christians. He, who so clearly saw and so strongly rebuked the evils in the Church of Corinth and that of Colosse, while, at the same time, he did not withhold from them the sacred name, evidently recognized the distinction between the visible and the invisible Church. The invisible Church formed, in his view, "the body of Christ, indissolubly united in all its parts, and drawing its nourishment from the divine head." In Churches in which he found divisions and strife, he could not recognize this mystical body in its normal constitution. When writing to the Church at Corinth in rebuke of its contentions, he says, "Is Christ divided?"* Such a Church could not be to him the faithful image of that ideal society in which love is the bond of perfectness. He distinguished, therefore, the invisible Church from the particular Churches in which its characteristics were so imperfectly reproduced. The former was to him the Church of Jesus Christ, the true exponent of his mind and will; it exists upon earth just in the measure in which true faith and charity exist. The invisible is the bright, celestial side of the Church visible. It follows that the invisible Church is found in various degrees in every particular Church, but it is not to be absolutely identified with any.

According to these principles, so simple and so plain, it is obviously a grave error to regard the primitive Church as a vast hierarchical establishment, like the Church of the fourth century. It is no Mother Church—*Mater Ecclesia*—laying the yoke of its external unity on each individual Church. Such an idea is altogether alien to the apostolic age. The one invisible Church is realized or embodied in the particular Churches. These Churches form their own organizations, on the same substantial basis indeed, but with notable differences in all secondary matters. They are united among themselves, but the bond thus formed is purely spiritual; it is never a chain. Each of the Churches is a small republic, a society of believers, an association of Christians, which governs itself without seeking direction or inspiration

* Μεμέρισται ὁ Χριστός. 1 Cor. i, 13.

from any of its sister Churches. Paul never appeals at Corinth, at Ephesus, or in Galatia, to the authority of the Church as a whole. The questions raised are decided fully and finally within each particular Church, and each is considered competent to its own absolute self-government, subject only to the sovereignty of truth. The conferences held at Jerusalem are no violation of this rule. It was necessary that the Apostles should understand each other on questions of such moment. Moreover, we have already shown that the so-called Council did not issue any thing like positive decrees ; it confined itself to recommending a compromise which had no obligatory character.

It is impossible to find in the whole of this period any traces of a general organization of the Churches tending to external unity. There are no general and periodical assemblies ; more significant still, there is no center of unity. Those who regard Rome as having been such a center are guilty of a strange anachronism. We have seen, also, how little prominence really attaches in this period to the part of that Apostle who has been made the head of the pretended ecclesiastical monarchy. If the Churches had sought at this time, as subsequently they did, a religious center, they would unquestionably have chosen Jerusalem, the glorious birthplace of Christianity. But the Church in that city, so far from exerting a wide influence on the development of Christian thought during the period of St. Paul, only followed afar off the movement led by the great Apostle. The Churches founded in the midst of paganism departed without scruple from the customs of Moses ; they felt themselves under no constraint to preserve, for the sake of uniformity, the same form of Jewish worship as was observed by the Christians at Jerusalem; but these minor differences did not prevent the existence of substantial oneness. The theologians, therefore, who assert that these differences took the form of actual opposition and declared hostility, are not less at fault than the advocates of the hierarchy. We have a touching proof of the unity prevailing among the Churches of Asia Minor and Greece and those of Palestine in the generous collections made at the urgent and repeated instance of Paul, even as far as Galatia and Corinth, for the poor brethren in Judæa. The Churches of Asia Minor, of Macedonia, and Achaia, sent messengers to Jerusalem to carry thither their offerings, and, with their gifts, the assurance of their brotherly affection. Never was unity more real than in these times, when it rested on the perfect law of liberty. The harmony which reigned among the Apostles helped to maintain it. Peter writes to the Churches founded by St. Paul in Asia Minor, as Apollos, the disciple of Paul, writes to the Christians at Jerusalem. Thus we have in the first century a true Christianity based upon a common faith, but exercising no constraint but the constraint of love upon the individual Churches, each of which had its distinct and special characteristics. The fiction had not yet arisen of an impersonal Church, distinct from the various local Churches in combination and from the free association of believers, divinely endowed with arbitrary power to rule the people of God, and established and built up by some other means than individual faith. The particular

Church or congregation united by a living link to all Christians throughout the world—such is the visible Church in the age of the Apostles. The grand and holy image of the invisible Church is discerned through the medium of the various local Churches, as the sun through intervening clouds; to behold it in its beauty, the soul must rise above the mists of sin and imperfection which cleave to the earthly embodiment of the heavenly idea. The particular Church or congregation is the only form of the visible Church recognized by the Apostles.*

Thus understood, the Church must be regarded simply as a community composed of Christians. Its gates were opened only to believers, or to those, at least, who professed the true faith. It could not prevent false Christians from creeping in surreptitiously, but, in principle, it owned as members only those who confessed with the mouth the Lord Jesus, and with the heart believed unto righteousness. We cannot doubt, as we read the epistles written by the Apostles to the various Churches, that they were addressed, not to a mixed multitude, among whom indifference and even unbelief found place side by side with piety and living faith, but to an association of Christians—to a self-governing religious society. There is no recognition whatever of the existence in that society of two classes of members—the converted and the unconverted. Serious evils might arise and compromise it; hypocrites might be found among the faithful; but, as we read the epistles, we feel that, as a whole, these Churches were Christian

* "Die Kirchenverfassung war wesentlich Gemeindeverfassung." Bunsen, "Hippolytus," ii, 152.

societies. If it was otherwise, what mean the salutations with which the letters commence? "To all that be in Rome, beloved of God, called to be saints." "Unto the Church of God which is at Corinth, to them that are sanctified in Christ Jesus, called to be saints." "To the saints which are at Ephesus, and to the faithful in Christ Jesus." Rom. i, 7; 1 Cor. i, 2; Eph. i, 1. The general tone of the epistles, the subjects they treat, the discussions they contain of the most delicate points of Christian practice, all absolutely forbid the supposition that such Churches were merely institutions for religious instruction, designed to impose the faith by authority upon men. They are missionary Churches, true centers of evangelization, spreading light all around them. The idea of a mere school into which the unconverted were free to enter is excluded by such words as these: "Dare any of you, having a matter against another, go to law before the unjust and not before the saints?" 1 Cor. vi, 1.

That conception of the Church which regards it as the community of believers arises naturally out of the general views of St. Paul on the relation of the two covenants. While the old economy was a theocracy associated with outward and material facts, the new is essentially spiritual. Before the cross distinctions of nationality or of birth are done away. "There is neither Jew nor Greek, bond nor free, but Christ is all and in all." Col. iii, 11. In other words, the new birth or personal faith alone gives admission to the Church. Paul, by his energetic opposition to the false teachers, who desired to make circumcision compulsory on the Christians, repudiated altogether the idea of an impersonal and traditional religion, dependent on outward circumstances and transmitted by birth. He did not reject circumcision mainly because it was a form and ceremony belonging to Judaism; his protest was against the principle involved in it—that of a national and theocratic religion descending by right of inheritance from generation to generation. To inherit without accepting is of no avail in the Christian Church, while to accept without having inherited suffices for salvation. In a word, personal adherence, that is, faith, is every thing.

Not only did every Church in the apostolic age require a positive and personal act of adherence from all who sought a place among its members, but it was also enjoined to cast out of its midst any impure elements which might have crept into it; and which, coming within the scope of the judgment of man, might be distinguished and expelled. "Purge out the old leaven," wrote the Apostle to the Corinthians, alluding to the notorious sinners who had insinuated themselves into the ranks of the Christians.*

§ II. *Gifts and offices.*

The universal priesthood was fully and practically realized in the apostolic Churches.† Composed of sincere believers, they, in no degree, acknowledged the too common distinction between active and passive members. All the Christians were required to contribute of their zeal and piety to the general

* 1 Cor. v, 7. We shall recur to the subject of apostolical discipline when we come to speak of the Lord's Supper.

† See Baur's excellent observations. "Geschichte der drei erst. Jahrh.," pp. 248, 249.

good. There are special offices, but these are very far from absorbing the whole activity of the Church. They are of less importance at this stage than subsequently, when the gifts of the Holy Spirit have lost their miraculous character, and the supernatural is more closely blended with the natural in the elements of the Christian life. At this period organized forms are perpetually broken through by miraculous manifestations, as the banks of a brimming river are overflowed by its swelling, rushing tide. The line drawn between official service in the Church and the gifts bestowed on all believers is so indistinct that Paul places both in one category. "God hath set some in the Church, first apostles, secondarily prophets, thirdly teachers, after that miracles, then gifts of healings, helps, governments, diversities of tongues." 1 Cor. xii, 28. Let us endeavor to distinguish the variety of gifts in this community of service characteristic of the apostolic age.

Christianity is the religion of grace. It teaches that every good and every perfect gift comes from God, who dispenses all by the same Spirit. James i, 17. The Holy Spirit not only renews the heart in conversion, but he also communicates to the believer the special aptitude he needs to enable him to glorify God. We err, however, if we imagine that there is any absolute incompatibility between the gifts of grace and the gifts of nature. The God of redemption is also the God of creation. Natural gifts are not annulled by the Holy Spirit; on the contrary, he accepts and appropriates them, while, at the same time, he purifies and communicates to them a heavenly virtue, by which they are made of true service to the Church.* They then become spiritual gifts. The proportion of the supernatural element may vary in these gifts ; it may be more or less predominant. Sometimes the natural element seems completely absorbed. This was the case in the commencement of the apostolic era ; but, as early as its second period, there was a sensible diminution of purely supernatural gifts ; they were brought into subjection and subordination, while natural gifts, and aptitude sanctified by grace, acquired constantly increasing importance and prominence.† Taking these general principles as our starting point, it is easy to show the distinction between the divers gifts enumerated by St. Paul.

The gift which is most distinctly miraculous is the gift of tongues.‡ It assumed a modified form in this second period of the apostolic age. Those who spoke in strange languages at Pentecost were understood by their hearers. This was no longer the case in the time of St. Paul. The gift of tongues seems to have been at that period an inarticulate language, a mysterious psalmody, the strange manifestation of that state of ecstacy, in which thought, lost in the ineffable, submerged, as it were, beneath a flood of divine influence, became unutterable. Such is the impression given by Paul's description of the gift of tongues. § "Things without life giving sound, whether pipe or harp, except they give a distinction in the sounds, how shall it be known what is piped

* Διαιρέσεις δὲ χαρισμάτων εἰσί, τὸ δὲ αὐτὸ Πνεῦμα. 1 Cor. xii, 4.

† Neander, "Pflanz.," i, 233, 235.

‡ Γένη γλωσσῶν. 1 Cor. xii, 28.

§ "He that speaketh in an unknown tongue edifieth himself; but he that prophesieth edifieth the Church."

or harped?" 1 Cor. xiv, 7. Abandoning themselves without restraint to religious ecstacy, some Christians might reach a state of ever-cumulating excitement, and take pleasure in a psychological condition not free from peril, and leading to an extravagant use of that gift of tongues which had no useful purpose in the edification of the Church. St. Paul, therefore, urges that it be restrained within due limits. He desires that it be not indulged in, unless there be present in the assembly brethren capable of interpreting the unknown tongues. This gift of interpretation was one of the manifestations of the gift of prophecy, which was also of a miraculous character, although it did not reduce the recipient to a state of entire passivity, as did the gift of tongues. The prophet was the organ of divine inspiration; now he declared events in the future, (Acts xi, 28,) now he made manifest the secrets of the heart, (1 Cor. xiv, 25,) and appointed brethren to their office in the Church; (1 Tim. iv, 14;) again, he taught with a degree of power and efficiency which attested the special co-operation of the divine Spirit. The language of the prophet was not calm, connected, flowing, like the language of reflection. It did not bear the trace of meditation, or seem the labored effort of thought. It was impetuous and abrupt. These prophetic revelations were not to be received absolutely and without reason; St. Paul desires that they be tested by the Church, for it was possible for suggestions of the natural mind to be confounded with those of the Spirit. "Let the prophets speak," he says, "two or three, and let the others judge.* The gift of healing and

* Οἱ ἄλλοι διακρινέτωσαν. 1 Cor. xiv, 29.

of working miracles belong to the same category.* It was largely bestowed on the early Churches, not on the Apostles alone, but indiscriminately among all Christians.

These peculiarly supernatural gifts abounded, for obvious reasons, in the early history of the Church—the period of creation and formation. They may reappear, but in a subordinate degree, in times which have some analogy with the first century; but these miraculous endowments must never be regarded as the necessary manifestations of the divine Spirit upon earth. The gifts which abide are not those of a specially miraculous character; they are those which blend in beautiful harmony, nature, and grace, the human element and the divine—the very gifts by which the Apostles were themselves pre-eminently distinguished. We place in this second category the gift of teaching, (Rom. xii, 7,) and that of government.† The former is applied sometimes to the practical side of Christianity, and then it is called the word of wisdom; sometimes to the theoretical side, and then it is called the word of knowledge.‡ The gift of government must be accompanied by the gift of discernment of spirits; § for, at a period when the manifestations of the supernatural world were so frequent, it was of moment to discern between the true inspirations and

* *Χαρίσματα ἰαμάτων . . . ἐνεργήματα δυνάμεων.* 1 Cor. xii, 9, 10. The gift of faith, spoken of in 1 Cor. xii, 9, must be understood of this gift of miracles. It is evident that the word cannot bear in this passage its ordinary meaning. The faith which saves is not a special gift granted to some Christians; it is needful for all.

† *Κυβερνήσεις.* 1 Cor. xii, 28.

‡ *Λόγος σοφίας, λόγος γνώσεως.* 1 Cor. xii, 8.

§ *Διακρίσεις πνευμάτων.* 1 Cor. xii, 10.

the false. The gift of teaching, like that of government, obviously implied certain natural aptitudes, and could not be exercised without the concurrence of moral and intellectual activity.

Such were the principal gifts bestowed on the Church. They preceded the various offices; it is utterly false to pretend that they depended in any way on those offices, and were manifested only within the limits of a fixed organization. The wind bloweth where it listeth, and the Spirit of God never surrenders its sovereign freeness. The advocates of the hierarchy do not deny that the miraculous gifts were bestowed on the Christians generally; but they assert, on behalf of the ecclesiastics, a monopoly of the gift of teaching, the use of which must, they maintain, be regulated by official and sovereign authority, or doctrinal anarchy will inevitably follow.* This distinction, however, is wholly arbitrary. The synagogue already acknowledged, under certain limitations, the right of every pious Jew to teach.† It is not surprising that this right should have been extended by St. Paul to all Christians, with the exception of women, who were to be silent in public worship. "When ye come together," he says, "every one of you hath a psalm, hath a doctrine, hath an interpretation. Let all things be done unto edifying." ‡ This right was long acknowledged in the Church. We read in the eighth book of the "Apostolical

* This is Thiersch's opinion. "Kirche im Apost. Zeit.," p. 154.

† "Si nec senex sit nec sapiens, constituant aliquem spectatæ formæ integritatisqua virum." ("If there be neither elder nor teacher, let a respectable and upright man speak.") Vitringa, "De Synag. vetere," p. 705.

‡ Διδαχὴν ἔχει ἑρμηνειαν ἔχει. 1 Cor. xiv, 26–35.

Constitutions," "Let him who teaches, if he be a layman, be versed in the Word." * It is impossible, then, to trace a clear line of demarkation between the gift of prophecy and that of teaching. The latter, like the former, belonged to the Church without distinction of clergy. It remains an established fact that all believers had the right to teach in public worship.† All alike took some share in the government of the community. They were summoned, as we have seen, on the occasion of the conferences at Jerusalem, to take a part in important deliberations. The letters of the Apostles laid upon all the duty of caring for the great interests of the congregation. Discipline was an act of the community, not of the clergy. To the Corinthian Christians, Paul writes with reference to the man guilty of incest: "I verily, as absent in body, but present in spirit, have judged already, as though I were present, concerning him that hath so done this deed, in the name of our Lord Jesus Christ, *when ye are gathered together, and my spirit,* with the power of the Lord Jesus Christ."‡ The entire Church is supposed to be assembled with the Apostle as a council of discipline, under the invisible presidency of our Lord Jesus Christ. No distinction is made; all the believers are called together to pronounce, as a sovereign tribunal, the sentence of condemnation. The excommunication is spoken in their name. In the same manner, it is in their name that the repentant sinner is re-admitted

* Ὁ *διδάσκων εἰ καὶ λαϊκος ᾖ.* "Const. Apost.," viii, 35, 1.

† See Ritschl, "Altcath. Kirche.," p. 365.

‡ *Συναχθέντων ὑμῶν καὶ τοῦ ἐμοῦ πνεύματος, σὺν τῇ δυνάμει τοῦ Κυρίου ἡμῶν Ἰησοῦ Χριστοῦ.* 1 Cor. v, 4.

into the Church. The Church, as a body, pardons the wrong he did to it by bringing dishonor upon it, and permits him to return to the communion of the brethren. 2 Cor. ii, 6. The power of the keys thus belongs, according to St. Paul, to all Christians.

The sacraments are equally far from being a monopoly of the clergy. These principles were so deeply rooted in the Church that long after, at a time when it had undergone most important changes, they received striking testimony from the lips of St. Jerome. He says, "The right of the laity to baptize has often been recognized in cases of necessity, for every one may give that which he has received." * We read in the "Commentaries" attributed to Ambrose, that "in the beginning all taught and all baptized on every opportunity."† With reference to the Lord's Supper, Paul attributes to all Christians the breaking of the bread and the blessing of the cup. "The cup of blessing *which we bless*, is it not the communion of the blood of Christ? The bread *which we break*, is it not the communion of the body of Christ?" ‡ From all this, it follows that the idea of a sarcedotal order was altogether foreign to the Churches founded by Paul. §

In those Churches, however, we can discern the commencement of various ecclesiastical offices.

* "Quod enim accepit quis, ita et dare potest." St. Jerome, "Contr. Luciferianos," 4.

† "Primum omnes docebant et omnes baptizabant quibuscumque diebus ut temporibus fuisset occasio."

‡ Τὸ πο·ήριον ὃ εὐλογοῦμεν, τὸν ἄρτον ὃν κλῶμεν. 1 Cor. x, 16. Harnack, though a Lutheran, supports this interpretation. (See his book, "Christengemeinde Gottesdienst," p. 170.

§ See Ritschl, "Altcath. Kirche," p. 378.

These offices acquire gradually increasing importance, without, however, assuming any thing of a priestly character. Paul introduced into the Churches gathered out of heathenism the same simple organization, borrowed from the Jewish synagogues, which flourished in the Churches of Palestine. We find the same democratic constitution at Ephesus as at Jerusalem. A body of elders is nominated by the Church; these are rather its representatives and delegates than its rulers. This is no organization of a Levitical caste; to be convinced of this we need only read the Epistle to the Hebrews. Heb. vii, 26–28. Jesus Christ is there represented as the High Priest of the new covenant, living for evermore—the one Mediator between God and man. He transmits to none a priesthood which is perfect only because it is eternal. Those times foretold by the prophets had arrived, when the law was to be written in the hearts of all the faithful; when each one, being placed in direct communication with Heaven, would no more need authoritative teaching from his brother man.* The ecclesiastical office, from this point of view, can be regarded only as a service, or ministering to the Church.† Those who are invested with it are not to be rulers over their brethren, but their servants. "We are your servants for Jesus' sake," says St. Paul to the Corinthians; showing by words so full of tender humility that, in his view, the apostolate bore no analogy to the ancient priesthood.

Let us bring before our minds the very simple

* Heb. viii, 10, 11. "I will put my laws into their mind. . . . And they shall not teach every man his neighbor."

† Ἑαυτοὺς δὲ δούλους ὑμῶν διὰ Ἰησοῦν. 2 Cor. iv, 5; Rom. xii, 7.

mechanism of the institutions of a Church like that of Corinth or Ephesus. The ecclesiastical office already created elsewhere to meet actual necessities, and to maintain order in the midst of liberty, was there speedily called for. We find, in the epistles of Paul, valuable hints of the manner in which it sometimes originated. The Apostle speaks again and again of the Church in the house of a simple Christian. Rom. xvi, 5; 1 Cor. xvi, 19; Col. iv, 15; Philemon 2. Such a Church, or fraction of a Church, was nothing else than a pious family circle extended, and becoming a religious center for those around. Many believers, converted through the influence of this Christian family, gathered around its hearth, and worshiped beneath its hospitable roof. The master of the house presided, and thus became naturally the elder pastor of the little congregation. If, in the same town, Christianity made many conquests, these small domestic congregations ultimately combined, and, as a matter of course, when an important Church was formed, those elders and teachers were placed at its head, who, in their zeal, had voluntarily filled that office before being regularly appointed to it. Such cases must have been many in the apostolic age. The office grew out of the exercise of the pastoral gift which had preceded it, and which was still often used with perfect freedom side by side with it.

Episcopal pretensions have frequently been founded on the passages in Paul's epistles where the word bishop occurs. But an attentive examination of the texts shows that the two words elder and bishop are used interchangeably, and that, in the language of Paul, they are synonymous, representing one and the same office.* He never mentions three degrees in the ecclesiastical hierarchy; he recognizes two only—the office of elder or bishop and that of deacon.† It is equally clear that several bishops were found at once in the same Church, (see Phil. i, 1; Acts xx, 17; James v, 14,) which is incompatible with the notion of there being one bishop superior to the elders. St. Peter, in his first epistle, carries this identification of the bishop with the elder so far as to charge the latter to use well the episcopal office, taking watchful oversight of the flock.‡

This identity of the office of bishop with that of elder is so very apparent in the New Testament that it was admitted by the whole ancient Church, even at the time of the rise of the episcopate properly so-called. "The elder is identical with the bishop," said St. Jerome, "and before parties had so multiplied under diabolical influence, the Churches were governed by a council of elders." § The name of bishop was more frequently used in the Churches founded among the pagans, because the ancient Greeks were

* Μετεκαλέσατο τοὺς πρεσβυτέρους τῆς ἐκκλησιάς. Acts xx, 17. Compare with verse 28 in same chapter: Ὑμᾶς τὸ Πνεῦμα τὸ ἅγιον ἔθετο ἐπισκόπους. See also Titus i, 5, 7; 1 Tim. iii, 1, 8. On this point we refer to the admirable argument of Rothe. "Anfänge," p. 174.

† 1 Tim. iii, 1 and 13. See also Phil. i, 1: Πᾶσι τοῖς ἁγίοις . . . σὺν ἐπισκόποις καὶ διακόνοις.

‡ Πρεσβυτέρους παρακαλῶ . . . ποιμάνατε τὸ ποίμνιον τοῦ Θεοῦ, ἐπισκοποῦντες. 1 Peter v, 1, 2.

§ "Idem est ergo presbyter quam episcopus, et antequam diaboli instinctu studia in religione fuerent, communi presbyterorum consilio ecclesiæ gubernabantur." St. Jerome, "In Epist. Tit.," vol. iv. We read in the "Ambrosiast," "Primum presbyteri episcopi appellabantur." Comp. Chrysostum, "Homilia i, in Phil. i, 1." See also Theodoret, "Interpretat. ad Phil. iii," 445. Ἐπισκόπους δὲ τοὺς πρεσβυτέρους καλεῖ. "The two offices," he adds, "had the same name."

accustomed thus to designate the magistrates, whose functions in the State had some analogy with those of the elders in the Church, since it was their office to exercise vigilance over the interests of the republic.*

In the failure of the attempt to establish the episcopate upon the words of the Apostles, an effort has been made to uphold it, by giving an exaggerated significance to certain facts of an exceptional and transitory character in the primitive Church. Reference is made to the mission of organizing the Churches committed by Paul to Titus and Timothy; the part taken by James at Jerusalem is urged in confirmation of the same theory. But these facts, rightly understood, ought to tell against hierarchical notions, instead of lending them any support. With reference first to Timothy and Titus, they bear no likeness whatever to bishops governing a diocese; they are missionaries, or, as Paul calls them, evangelists,† whose mission it is to direct the first steps of young and inexperienced Churches; they exercise a truly apostolical power wherever that power is necessary. They derive their exceptional authority from an exceptional situation. They are no apostolical legates, invested with official dignity; ‡ they are simply the representatives of St. Paul, his friends and fellow-workers. §

* "Those who were sent by the Athenians," we read in the "Scholiast" of Aristophanes, "to exercise surveillance in the cities subject to their authority were called bishops and guardians." Ὁι παρ' Ἀθηναίων εἰς τὰς ὑπηκοους πόλεις επισκέψασθαι τὰ παρ' ἑκάστοις πεμπομένοι ἐπίσκοποι καὶ φύλακες ἐκαλοῦντο. Rothe, "Anfange," p. 219.

† Ἔργον ποίησον εὐαγγελιστοῦ. 2 Tim. iv, 5. Comp. with Eph. iv, 11.

‡ This is Thiersch's view.

§ Συνεργός. Rom. xvi, 21; 1 Thess. iii, 2; 2 Cor. viii, 23.

They do the work of missionaries. They exercise over the young Churches the vigilance indispensable in the period of creation and formation, but, as we shall observe, they never infringe the inalienable rights of Christian liberty. They are no more bishops than were the Apostles. They are, like them, the founders of Churches, nothing more and nothing less. Their claim rests on the important duties undertaken by them in connection with those Churches, or rather on the great love they bear them. Their authority is entirely moral, and is vindicated by its effects; it resolves itself into influence. The apostolic missionary cannot acquit himself faithfully of his task without using this authority; he must needs water that which he has planted, and cultivate and cherish that which he has helped to create. He feels bound to uphold the frail plant, which has not yet had time to gather strength to sustain itself unsupported against the shock of storms.

We have already stated our views of the ministry of James at Jerusalem. In spite of the assertions of the "Fathers," we maintain that it presents no analogy to the episcopate of subsequent ages.* He also is an apostle, and one of the most influential, though he can show no formal nomination to the office. He is an apostle, as Paul was, by right of his lofty piety and of the divine power manifested in him. His diocese

* See Hegesippus in Eusebius, ii, 23, Ἰάκωβος Ἱεροσολυμῶν ἐπίσκοπος. "Const. Apost.," Book VI, chap. xiv; Epiphan., "Hæres," lxxxviii, 7. "Jacobus, qui appellatur frater Domini, post passionem Domini, statim ab apostolis Hierosolymorum episcopus ordinatur." August., "Catal. script. eccles." All these testimonies are without weight, because we know that the "Fathers" transferred to the past the ecclesiastical constitution of their own time.

extends as far as his influence and his word can reach. Thus, a careful examination of facts destroys all the chimeras of an episcopal organization in the first century.*

It is very difficult to determine precisely the functions of the elders or bishops. They formed a council † which occupied itself with the general interests of the Church ; its authority was limited, and always exercised with a practical recognition of the universal priesthood. They were, according to the beautiful figure borrowed from Christ himself, the shepherds of the flock.‡ The gift of teaching, freely used by all Christians, was not especially connected with the office of elders ; the only gift required in them was that of government. In his Epistle to the Ephesians Paul names the teachers after the pastors.§ There is no trace of two orders of elders hierarchically constituted ; it is probable, however, that it was soon found necessary to choose as elders men capable of

* Bingham ("Origines," i, 69) regards the Apostles as the first bishops. The Catholic school falls into the same error, already refuted by us.

† Πρεσβυτερίου. 1 Tim. iv, 14.

‡ "Feed the flock of God which is among you, not as being lords over God's heritage, but being ensamples to the flock." 1 Peter v, 2, 3; Acts xx, 28.

§ Ephes. iv, 11. Neander, "Pflanz.," i, 261. Calvin, and, following him, all the adherents of old Presbyterianism, recognize two orders of elders, some not teachers, and others whose office it is to teach, the latter holding a higher position than the former. This idea has no foundation in Scripture. Nowhere do we find such a line of demarkation between two orders of elders. The passage 1 Tim. v, 17 has no such bearing. It forms part of an epistle treating especially of false doctrines, and designed to set forth the great importance of the teaching of the truth. It contains no allusion to hierarchical orders. See Rothe, "Anfänge," 224.

teaching, since false doctrine was rife on every hand. St. Paul demands that the bishop hold fast the faithful word, that he may be able, by sound doctrine, both to exhort and to convince the gainsayers.* Toward the end of this period, the office of elder or bishop shows a general tendency toward a more permanent character. Purely supernatural gifts decrease ; the exercise of the gift of government and that of teaching becomes all the more necessary. Doctrinal and moral anarchy threatens the Churches. It is obviously wise to give them at such a crisis greater fixedness of organization, and by a definite constitution, and a stronger government, to place them in the condition of a society† capable of living and developing itself. We have no right, however, to suppose a substitution, at this period, of the monarchical for the democratic form of Church government ; there is no trace of any such change. There is one single allusion to the ruling of assemblies, (Rom. xii, 28,) but it is too vague to sustain the inference that one of the elders presided permanently over the Council of the Church. Perhaps the presidency was taken by all the elders in turn. As the Churches increased in importance, and made larger claims upon the time of the pastors, it became needful to provide in part for their maintenance, that they might be able to attend, without distraction, on duties which grew daily wider and more weighty. St. Paul frequently insists on the duty of

* Titus i, 9; 1 Tim. iii, 2. Διδακτικός.

† Comp. Hebrews xiii, 17. See Bunsen, "Ignatius und seine Zeit," p. 129. M. Reuss shows very clearly that the ecclesiastical constitution described in the pastoral epistles is not so complicated as has been asserted, with a view to deny their authority. It is in harmony with all we know of the apostolic age.

the Churches to contribute liberally to the support of their elders or bishops. 1 Cor. ix, 11, 13, 14; 1 Tim. v, 17. We see, however, no reason for supposing that these entirely gave up working with their own hands; they did not, at any rate, feel themselves bound to do so by any scruple of conscience, for the distinction between the sacred and the profane found no place in the lives of those who did all in the name of the Lord Jesus, and who had before their eyes the example of Paul, the tentmaker. The contributions of the Churches were perfectly free, no rule or measure of giving was laid down; the care of the poor was regarded as a more pressing claim than the maintenance of the pastors. The elder or bishop was under no more obligation to surrender family ties than any private Christian. Paul says distinctly that an apostle might be married, and might take his wife with him on his missionary journeys. The counsels of moderate asceticism which he gives to the Corinthians are intended for all the members of the Church without distinction. The bishop is to be the ensample of the flock, and is to keep himself with peculiar care from those immoral relations so common in the heathen world. Let him be the husband of one wife; let him show what is true Christian marriage; let him guide his family with firmness and discretion; he will then find in his own home a valuable school for the government of the Church.*

*It is universally admitted that Peter was married. 1 Cor. ix, 5. Eusebius, following Clement of Alexandria, asserts that it was so. Πέτρος μὲν γὰρ καὶ Φίλιππος ἐπαιδοποιήσαντο. Eusebius, "Hist. Eccles.," iii, 30. In spite of the opinion of several distinguished theologians, Reuss, among others, we cannot admit positively that

Next to the office of elders, we find, in all the Churches founded by St. Paul, the office of deacons. This carries us back to the appointment of the seven deacons at Jerusalem; but, like the whole of the ecclesiastical organization, it assumed, at this period, a more decided character. It received its proper name; it was called the diaconate.* Those who were intrusted with it do not seem to have taken part in the missionary work of the Apostles as directly as the first deacons, among whom were Stephen and Philip. They devoted themselves more exclusively to the care of the poor and the sick, and sought to exercise that beautiful gift of helping which St. Paul mentions in his Epistle to the Corinthians.† They were the representatives of the charity of the Church to its suffering and afflicted members. We know that the deacons at Jerusalem were chosen to serve tables. In the second period of the apostolic age there were no common feasts, except the *agapæ*, which were accompanied by the celebration of the Lord's Supper. The deacons were charged with all that related to this part of Christian worship; with their office of mercy was associated the care of all the outward details of public service.

the words "husband of one wife," μιᾶς γυναικὸς ἄνδρα, (1 Tim. iii, 2,) contain a prohibition of second marriages. The exhortation of the Apostle to perfect purity of life was always seasonable in Churches encompassed with heathen corruption, and some members of which might have continued in illicit relations which were hard to break. The condition imposed on widows who would be deaconesses not to have been twice married, (1 Tim. v, 9,) prevents us, however, rejecting peremptorily the sense given by the whole of the ancient Church to the passage. 1 Tim. iii, 2.

* Rom. xii, 7. Διακονίᾳ. Phil. i, 1.

† Ἀντιλήψεις. 1 Cor. xii, 28.

The Churches of the first century also created an office for women, in order to employ for the good of the Church the special gifts bestowed by God upon them. What office could have been better suited to them than the diaconate, the merciful ministry of succor and consolation? It is difficult to ascertain exactly what these deaconesses of the primitive Church were. Rom. xvi, 1. They had, no doubt, their part in the distribution of alms, and in the visiting of the sick; doubtless, they also assisted in the arrangements for the *agapæ*, and lent their aid where-ever it was required by the deacons in matters relating to public worship. We know that the deaconesses of the second century were employed as helpers at the baptism of women.* This custom, so natural and so becoming, must have been introduced into the Church in the first century. The widows, above sixty years of age, whose names were in the Church books, and of whom Paul speaks in his first Epistle to Timothy, were probably deaconesses.† It would be difficult to understand all the conditions required of them in that passage if nothing more than ordinary membership was in view. On the other hand, it is perfectly in harmony with the spirit of the apostolic Church to give employment to the activity of all its members, and to establish a holy relation between the generous gifts bestowed upon poverty and the valuable services which, in return, even poverty can

* "Constit. Apostol.," iii, 16.

† Schaff, 534; Rothe, "Anfänge," p. 253. In the "Apostolical Constitutions," (iii, 1,) widows are raised to the rank of *elders*, πρεσβυτίδες. This is evidently an innovation of the second century. The prohibition of second marriages to the deaconesses is an ascetic rule which gives slight cause for surprise.

render to the Church. The widow was far better adapted than the unmarried woman for the office of deaconess, for she had experience of human life ; she knew its great sorrows, and her position gave her a special fitness for administering consolation.

From whatever point of view we regard it, the ecclesiastical office appears to us always as a ministry, as the service of the Church, not as a priesthood. It has an altogether different origin, it is bestowed by popular election, and thus preserves its representative character. This was the case (as we have seen) with the very first office which arose out of the apostolate. The seven deacons of the upper chamber were chosen by the Church at Jerusalem. "*Choose you out seven men;*" such is the language of St. Peter, and it sanctions the abiding privilege of the Church.* The nature of the office of elder also implied its being elective. The charge given by St. Paul to Timothy and Titus to appoint elders† contains no contradiction to this rule, for it is obvious that in a young and inexperienced Church the influence of the Apostle or of his representative would naturally preponderate. This influence, however, never assumed the form of despotic authority, and Luke shows us how it was exercised in harmony with the elective voice of the Church, when he tells us that Paul and Barnabas caused elders to be chosen in all the Churches.‡ The Apostle presided over the elec-

* *Ἐπισκέψασθε.* Acts vi, 3.

† *Ἵνα καταστήσῃς πρεσβυτέρους.* Titus i, 5 ; 1 Timothy iii, 1.

‡ *Χειροτονήσαντες δὲ αὐτοῖς πρεσβυτέρους κατ' ἐκκλησίαν.* Acts xiv, 23. We see (2 Cor. viii, 18–24) that the member of the Corinthian Church, intrusted to bear the offerings of the brethren into Palestine, was chosen by them.

tion but did not suppress it. It is further certain that this right of election was preserved inviolate during more than two centuries. The Coptic Constitution of the Church of Alexandria witnesses to the continuance of the right of election into the middle of the second century.* Now, as it is incontestable that the second century did not originate the right, its tendency being on the contrary to weaken and depreciate it, it follows that it must be traced back to the first century, and is of apostolical institution.

The laying on of hands which was conferred on the deacons, elders, and evangelists, had not at all the character of ordination.† It was not used exclusively for the investiture of office in the Church. Christ laid his hands on the little children brought to him that he might bless them, (Matt. xix, 15,) and on the sick whom he was about to heal. Luke xiii, 13. The laying on of hands was regarded as a solemn benediction; coincidently with it there was sometimes the communication of the supernatural gifts peculiar to the apostolic age.‡ It was subsequently conferred in the ordinance of Baptism, in the celebration of the Lord's Supper, and on the occasion of the restoration to the Church of those

* Ἐπίσκοπος χειροτονείσθω ὑπὸ παντὸς τοῦ λαοῦ εκλελεγμενός. "Constit. Copt.," canon ii, 31.

† See Ritschl, "Altcath. Kirche., 395.

‡ This is the explanation of the famous passage 1 Timothy iv, 14, in which these supernatural gifts are referred to. Timothy received them in fulfillment of a prophetic revelation, like that which led to the dedication of Paul and Barnabas by the laying on of hands at Antioch. Acts xiii, 2, 3. We must not forget that Timothy had been temporarily invested with the office of an evangelist. Rothe, "Anfänge," 161.

who had been excommunicate.* It was always accompanied with prayer.† St Augustine goes so far as to say, "What is the laying on of hands if not praying over a man?"‡ Prayer was then the essential act. "The neophytes," says Cyprian, § "receive the Holy Ghost through our prayer, and the laying on of hands." The latter had only a symbolic significance like baptism itself. It represented the grace communicated through prayer, and as all Christians stand in need of that grace, it was conferred on all. Nay, more. Prayer cannot, in any point of view, be regarded as a clerical act; it is the expression of the Christian feeling of the whole assembly; it follows that the laying on of hands could no more have a sacerdotal character than the prayer which constituted its essential virtue. It was bestowed in the name of the Church. Tertullian admitted that laymen had a right to baptize; they had, then, an equal right to perform the laying on of hands. We do not deny, however, that the laying on of hands had a special application when received by the deacons or elders. It was the solemn sign of their entry upon office, according to a custom of the synagogue, in the case of new rabbis.|| But between the

* "Egressi de lavacro de hinc manus imponitur per benedictionem advocans Spiritum Sanctum." Tertull., "De Baptismo," 7, 8; Cyprian, "Epist.," lxxxiii, 1, 2.

† Acts vi, 6. *Καὶ προσευξάμενοι ἐπέθηκαν αὐτοῖς τὰς χεῖρας.* This first laying on of hands is the type of all the rest.

‡ "Quid est aliud manuum impositio, quam oratio?" Aug., "De Baptismo," iii, 49.

§ "Per nostram orationem ac manus impositionem Spiritum Sanctum consequantur." Cyprian, "Epist.," lxxxiii, 9.

|| "Ordinatio autem non tantum fit *manu* sed etiam sermone solo, dicendo, ego te promoveo." Vitringa, "De Synag. vetere," p. 838.

imposition of hands in the synagogue and the same ceremonial in the church there was as wide a difference as between the two institutions themselves. It was, in truth, the prayer of the Church which gave value to the outward act ; the Church thus took an active and direct part in the consecration of the man who was to be its minister and representative. It appears, also, to have been customary, from the times of the Apostles, for the individual thus set apart to make an explicit profession of his faith before the Church, which had a right to know with exactness the doctrine of those for whom, as its delegates, it was responsible. 1 Tim. vi, 12. The outward act was so far from being regarded as conferring a sacred and unalterable character, that the same man might receive the laying on of hands on several occasions.* This unquestionable fact sets aside any superstitious notion with reference to it.

In a word, therefore, ecclesiastical offices did not constitute in this second period, any more than in the first, a new order of priesthood. They were not directly and authoritatively instituted by God, but were created one by one as the necessity for them arose in the Church. They are not, like the ancient priesthood, of immediate divine appointment, but they proceed from divine inspiration, and are according to the will of God. We must not, however, allow ourselves to imagine that the Churches of the apostolic age, though of so democratic an organization, suffered their liberty to degenerate into license. Revealed truth exerted a holy authority over them.

* Acts xiii, 3. Paul and Barnabas had long been exercising their ministry in the Church when they received this laying on of hands.

Paul uses the bold and energetic language of an ambassador of Jesus Christ speaking in the name of truth. He does not impose that truth; if the Churches reject it, there are no means to constrain to its reception and to obedience. But he declares that in rejecting the doctrine they reject not the messenger but the God who sent him; and he proves it. He desires also that this truth, once accepted in the Churches, should continue to be to them an infallible test and touchstone for heresy. If in the Christianity of the first century there is no organized external authority, there is nevertheless an authority which is effectual. We are quite free to admit, also, that while each Church has its own distinctive life and character, there is nothing in the primitive ecclesiastical organization adverse to an ulterior federation among the Churches, and a synodal government, provided only that the liberties of the individual assemblies be left intact. We have simply shown that as a matter of fact such a federal government did not exist in the first century. But the Church has the right—and sometimes the right becomes a duty—to modify its organization in course of time, and to depart in more than one point of detail from the type of the apostolic Churches, subject only to this condition—that it remains faithful to the general principles of their constitution; for those principles are unchangeable, and rest upon eternal truths.

CHAPTER VI.

WORSHIP AND THE CHRISTIAN LIFE.

§ I. *Christian Worship during this Period.**

WHILE the Christian converts from Judaism were continually in the temple, and observed all the rites of the religion of their fathers, the converted Gentiles held themselves free from any ceremonial law. In their churches, therefore, we find the true worship of the new covenant first established. The disciples did not comprehend immediately after the Pentecostal effusion of the Holy Spirit that Christianity was a new creation. They supposed that the true worship—public and solemn worship—was still to be celebrated in the temple at Jerusalem, and their adoration in the upper chamber was of a secret and spiritual nature. The case was altogether different in the Churches founded by St. Paul. Their worship was completely distinct from the Jewish. There is no reason to conclude that it was less spiritual than that presented in the earlier days of the Church, or less spontaneous because it was more carefully regulated. We must remember that the adoration offered in the upper chamber had more the character

* Vitringa, "De Synagoga vetere." Bingham, "Origines Ecclesiæ;" Augusti, "Handbuch der Christlichen Archæologie," (1836;) Harnack, "Christliche Gemeinde Goltesdienst," (Erlangen, 1854;) Guericke, "Archæol." (1847.) We need not enumerate again the works on the apostolic age already referred to.

of family worship than of the worship of a Church, and that associated with it was the assiduous attendance of the Christians in the temple. The worship of the Gentile converts, on the contrary, was their public worship ; it had, therefore, a less private character, and more solemnity of form. Its forms, however, are very simple, and significant of the great emancipation wrought by St. Paul ; they are nothing more than the orderly and fitting expression of the ardent piety of the believers. The true idea of worship in spirit and in truth characterizes them all, and is set forth in them with incomparable clearness and beauty.

The worship of the old covenant could not fail to be more or less materialized by its association with outward conditions. It was confined to the walls of the sanctuary ; it set apart times and seasons ; the priestly tribe alone had a right to approach the altar. All these restrictions had one common cause—the separation still existing between guilty man and his offended God. Hence the necessity of sacrifices, which embodied the acknowledgment of guilt, while they contained the prophecy of future reconciliation. The new covenant, which has for its basis the great fact of a finished salvation, at once substitutes for those sacrifices offered daily the sacrifice of Christ once offered for sin,* and abolishes the peculiar priesthood of a class in favor of the eternal priesthood of Christ,† communicated by faith to all believers. In the Church there is no altar, no sacrifice, no priest. To

* Νῦνὶ δὲ ἅπαξ. Heb. ix, 26.

† Ἀπαράβατον ἔχει τὴν ἱερωσύνην. "But this man, because he continueth ever, hath an unchangeable priesthood. Heb. vii, 24.

the material sacrifice has succeeded the reasonable sacrifice of the heart and will, in which every Christian is at once priest and victim.*

All the institutions which were designed to remind man of his state of condemnation prior to redemption are alike abolished. There is no longer any privilege attaching to certain consecrated places and consecrated persons. The Christian Church has no temple in the true sense of the word, or rather, it is itself a spiritual temple, built up of living stones, and founded upon Christ.† Its worship has no other design than the edification of this temple, or its consolidation by the increase of faith and love.‡ Thus religious service is held in private houses, as in the case of Mary, the mother of Mark, at Jerusalem, of Lydia at Philippi, of Jason at Thessalonica. Acts xii, 12; xvi, 40; xvii, 7. In the same manner worship is celebrated under the roof of Justus at Corinth, and of Aquila and Priscilla at Ephesus. Acts xviii, 7; 1 Cor. xvi, 19. In large cities, where there are many Christians, the places of meeting rapidly multiply.§ There is nothing to lead us to infer that the houses in which worship was thus celebrated ceased to be used for other purposes. The name of Church was not given to a sacred edifice, but to the assembly of believers

* "A living sacrifice, a reasonable service." Rom. xii, 1; xv, 16; 1 Peter ii, 5.

† 'Εν ᾧ καὶ ὑμεῖς συνοικοδομεῖσθε εἰς κατοικητήριον τοῦ Θεοῦ ἐν Πνεύματι. Eph. ii, 20–22; 1 Cor. iii, 16; 2 Cor. vi, 16. "Whose house are we." Οὗ οἰκός ἐσμεν ἡμεῖς. Heb. iii, 6.

‡ "Let all things be done unto edifying."—Πάντα πρὸς οἰκοδομὴν γινέσθω.

§ 'Εκκλεσίαι κατ' οἶκον. Rom. xvi, 4, 5, 14, 15; Col. iv, 15; Philemon 2.

gathered within it.* "The Church itself," says an old writer, "or the assembly of the faithful, was the house of God."†

The rapid increase of the Church soon rendered these private houses inadequate for the purposes of worship. At Ephesus Paul taught in a public school. James points out in his epistle abuses which could only have occurred in large assemblies, like those of the Jewish synagogues.‡ To the family gathering succeeded the gathering as a Church, to which all ranks of society furnished their contingent. The rich and the poor met together, and pride and insolence had frequent opportunities of manifesting themselves. But the worship acquired no new character of sacredness by being transferred to a more spacious building. It was only on the ruins of the spiritual that the material temple was subsequently reared. §

The primitive Church recognizes no more distinction between days than between places. The entire life has become the calm and earnest celebration of redemption; ‖ its simplest acts are raised by the

* 1 Cor. xi, 18–22; xiv, 34. Bingham lays stress on these passages as establishing the existence of sanctuaries, properly so called, in the first century, ("Orig.," iii, 143;) but he forgets Christ's positive statement to the woman of Samaria as to the abolition of all holy places.

† "Ipsa Ecclesia, ipse fidelium cœtus est domus Dei." Vitringa, "De Synag. vetere," 446; Augusti, "Archæol.," i, 336.

‡ *'Εὰν εἰσέλθη εἰς τὴν συναγωγὴν ὑμῶν ἀνὴρ.* James ii, 2. We must not, as Vitringa does, ("De Synag. vetere,") make the unfair deduction from this expression, that the worship of the Church resembled in all respects that of the synagogue.

§ We are not speaking of the erection of majestic edifices for worship, but simply of the superstition which introduces into Christianity the notion of a sanctuary, a place in itself exceptionally holy.

‖ "Whether ye eat, or drink, or whatsoever ye do, do all to the glory of God."—*Παντα εἰς δόξαν Θεοῦ ποιεῖτε.* 1 Cor. x, 31.

Christian spirit to the dignity of a religious service. To the believer nothing is common or unclean; every thing is holy.* It is impossible, then, to find in the Gospel a principle with which we can connect the institution of one holy day, as belonging to God, more than the rest. This institution is intimately associated with the old covenant, and ought to have vanished with it like the priesthood and the consecration of special holy places. With regard to the distinction of certain days Paul proclaims the principles of the new covenant with all his wonted clearness and force. "How," he writes to the Galatians, "turn ye again to the weak and beggarly elements, whereunto ye desire again to be brought in bondage? Ye observe days and months, and times and years."† To the Colossians he says: "Let no man judge you in meat or drink, or in respect of a holyday, or of the new moon, or of the *sabbath-days*, which are a shadow of things to come." Such being the prin-

* The advocates of the permanence of the Sabbath appeal to the decalogue. But Paul has already taught us that the decalogue contains the law of holiness in but an incomplete form—a form which has been done away with the whole of Judaism. To trace the Sabbath back to the garden of Eden is to lose sight of the true conditions of innocence, which do not admit a division of the life into the sacred and profane. The blessing pronounced on the seventh day did not imply rest in Paradise; it applied to the whole creation, which for the first time appeared complete. The life of the world before the fall was a blessed life—the whole earth was a temple, and every man a priest. The Jewish Sabbath was a reminder of this happy past, and at the same time a prophecy of its restoration in the future. It was also a witness to the total perversion of human life previous to redemption, since that life needed to be interrupted in some sort, in order that man might serve God.

† Ἡμέρας παρατηρεῖσθε, καὶ μῆνας, καὶ καιροὺς, καὶ ἐνιαυτούς. Gal. iv, 9–11.

ciples of the Apostle, it remains for us to see what was the practice of the Churches. It differed among the various sections of primitive Christianity. The disciples in Palestine scrupulously observed the Sabbath and the Jewish feasts, but they made no distinction between days with regard to their Christian worship, properly so called. The Gentile Churches rejected the Sabbath as they did circumcision. They assembled every day at Ephesus to hear Paul.* This was doubtless also the case in the other mission centers of Greece and Asia.

We do not imagine that the Gentile converts at this period felt themselves bound to observe any of the great Jewish feasts, not even the Passover or the Pentecost. They had received no commandment concerning them. No stress can be laid on Paul's example in repairing to the Holy City to keep the Pentecostal feast, for the case is irrelevant. A Jew by birth, he faithfully observed the conditions laid down by the Council at Jerusalem, and himself adhered to the customs of Moses, though in a broad spirit of tolerance and charitable concession.† We do not condemn the Christian festival in itself; on the contrary, we fully admit its lawfulness and utility. We only desire to show that it is not of directly divine institution. It cannot plead even the practice of the Apostles, since in their observance of the feasts of the Passover and Pentecost they celebrated the ancient Jewish festivals, not the high days of the new covenant. The latter have been freely set apart by the Church under the influence of true Christian feeling.

* "Teaching daily in the school of one Tyrannus." Acts xix, 9.

† This is Schaff's great argument. (P. 546.)

An old ecclesiastical historian says: "Never did the Apostles impose the yoke of bondage on those who came to them for teaching; they left the observance of the Passover and other feasts to the free will of those who thought it well and profitable to keep them. The Lord and his Apostles instituted no feasts by law, nor did they, like Moses, hold any threat of punishment or a curse over those who did not observe them. The aim of the Apostles was not to lay down laws for special seasons, but to lead men's lives back to uprightness and piety." *

During the whole period of St. Paul we find only two very vague indications of the celebration of worship on the first day of the week.† It is impossible to draw from them any certain conclusion. Considering, however, that in the following period that day is already known as the Lord's day, it seems probable that the custom of celebrating worship with more than ordinary solemnity on the first day of the week commenced very early in the apostolic age. The Church did not by this practice depart at all from the principles of Paul; it did not invest that day with an exceptional sanctity, nor lower at all the ordinary level of the Christian life. It had no thought of putting the Lord's day in the place of the Jewish Sabbath. It is certain that for a long time many of the Chris-

* Socrates, "Hist. Ecclesiæ.," v, 22; Augusti, "Archæol.," i, 174.

† *'Εν μιᾷ τῶν σαββάτων, συνηγμένων τῶν μαθητῶν.* Acts xx, 7. The passage 1 Cor. xvi, 2, "Upon the first day of the week let every one of you lay by him in store, as God hath prospered him," does not speak of the public assembly of the Church. (See Neander, "Pflanz.," i, 272.) Bingham, according to his wont, forces the sense of these two passages. "Origines," v, 280.

tians kept the seventh day of the week as the Sabbath. If the Church had been standing on the ground of legalism it would have been impossible for it to transfer the rest of the Sabbath from one day of the week to another without a divine revelation. No such claim to a divine institution of the Lord's day was advanced in the early ages. The Christians were not content with saying that they had neither temple nor altars; they also distinctly avowed by the mouth of Justin Martyr, "We do not sabbatize." *

The worship of the Churches founded by Paul bears the same impress of liberty and spirituality by which their piety was characterized. The liturgical element is completely absent; every thing is spiritual and free. Some organization, however, is found indispensable, that all things may be done decently and in order. The rules which Paul gives refers simply to what is decorous. He desires that while the man has his head uncovered the woman should be covered, thus marking by her appearance the reserve of modesty so becoming to her, and which nature herself suggests

* *Οὐ σαββατιζόμεν.* Justin, "Dial. cum Tryph.," p. 246. There is nothing in the foregoing consideration opposed to the observance of the Sabbath. The Sabbath is a necessity of public worship; it is needed as are the temple and the ministry; but there is, nevertheless, a universal priesthood, as it were, for all days as for all men. This is the essential principle of the new covenant, which is so palpably ignored in what is called Sabbatarianism. The Sabbath is not more holy in itself to the exclusion of other days than the temple to the exclusion of other places. The Sabbath is the Lord's day, as the temple is the Lord's house. This analogy is very striking in the German. The word Church (Kirche) comes from the Greek work *Κυριακή* (Dominica;) the temple is *τὸ κυριακόν*, the place of the Lord. The Church is the Lord's place, as the Sabbath is the Lord's day. Augusti, "Archæol.," i, 35. This analogy solves the question.

by the long hair given her for a vail. The Apostle also forbids a woman to teach in the Christian assembly. 1 Cor. xi, 4, 5 ; xiv, 34. He is anxious that individual inspiration should be controlled, and kept in subjection, that it might not interfere with the general edification.

The essential acts of worship were always the reading of the Holy Scriptures, prayer, teaching, and praise.* The Old Testament was at this period the only canonical book acknowledged by the Church. Interpreted in its deep significance, often, perhaps, used somewhat allegorically, as in the epistles of St. Paul, it opened an inexhaustible mine of Christian instruction.† The words of the Lord Jesus were earnestly meditated upon, and were listened to as the voice of God. Paul reminds the Corinthians that these had formed the basis of his teaching, and that he had quoted to them the words of the Lord Jesus himself, concerning the institution of the Lord's Supper and the resurrection. Col. iv, 16 ; 1 Thess. v, 27. But these words of the Master are not found in the canonical Gospels. They were either handed down by oral tradition, or were contained in some of those anonymous writings which Luke mentions in the prologue to his Gospel. We cannot, therefore, regard the use then made of the discourses of our Lord as part of the reading of Holy Scripture.

Nor can we include under that head the reading of the letters of the Apostles, expressly recommended

* See Harnack, work quoted, pp. 146–164.

† The commandment of Paul to Timothy to give attendance to reading (1 Tim. iv, 13) seems to refer to the public reading of the Scriptures, for in the same passage *exhortation* is spoken of.

by them, (Col. iv, 16; 1 Thess. v, 27,) for there is no indication that this reading was to be regularly and statedly repeated, like that of the Old Testament. These letters were the echo of the living voice of the Apostles. They were received with the same respect paid to their spoken words, and were invested with all apostolical authority. But while the Apostles still lived, the idea was not entertained—because the necessity was not felt—of forming a canon of the New Covenant. It was not until subsequently that this legitimate want sought and found satisfaction.*

Teaching formed an important part of primitive worship, and especially of the worship of the Churches at a distance from Jerusalem. Teaching gained in proportion as ritualism lost. The priest always eclipses the teacher where there is a priesthood and sacrifice to be offered. We need not here repeat the evidence that the right of teaching was granted to all. But if any might teach, they might not teach any thing; the doctrine of the Apostles was to be the standard and rule, because it was the faithful reproduction of the doctrine of Jesus Christ. "Stand fast," writes St. Paul to the Thessalonians, "and hold the traditions which ye have been taught, whether by word or our epistle." 2 Thess. ii, 5; 2 Tim. i, 13; Titus i, 9. Calm and systematic teaching is gradually but steadily substituted for the language of ecstacy, prophecy, and the gift of tongues. Paul seems even to fear that these miraculous gifts may fall into too great dis-

* We have already noticed, in speaking of the origin of the first three Gospels, the preference of the primitive Church for the living word. (See Augusti, "Archæol.," ii, 165.)

credit, for he warns the Thessalonians not to quench the Spirit, nor to despise prophesyings.*

In his discourse at Miletus, however, as in his later epistles, he insists strongly on the importance of teaching. Acts xx, 31–33; 1 Tim. iv, 6; Titus i, 9. At a time when the Apostles were about to be removed, and when, consequently, the control of individual inspiration would be more difficult, it greatly concerned the welfare of the Church that the teaching by which the apostolic doctrine was to be perpetuated should acquire a preponderating influence.

Prayer is the soul of Christian worship, as it is the source of all Christian life. It sprang up freely, as did the word of edification. It contained no admixture of any liturgical element, and there is not a word in the whole of the New Testament in support of the idea that the Lord's Prayer was repeated as a sacred formula.†

St. Paul, however, without desiring at all to infringe this liberty, specifies some points which should not be neglected in Christian prayer, and especially in the prayer of the Church. He desires that prayer be made for all men, especially for kings and those in authority, thus tracing a strong line of demarkation between the religious revolution which he desires to effect, and any thing like a political revolution. Thus even in this free domain of prayer we discern a law

* Προφητείας μὴ ἐξουθενεῖτε. 1 Thess. v, 20.

† Bingham affirms the liturgical use of the Lord's Prayer in the first century, without giving the least proof of the fact. "Origines," v, 125. Vitringa erroneously draws a parallel between the prayers of the Church and those of the synagogue. In reality, on the one hand all is spontaneous; on the other all is fixed and methodical. "De Synag. vet.," p. 162. See Augusti, "Archæol.," ii, 60.

of divine wisdom. Thanksgiving—the *Eucharist*, properly so called—had a very large place in the prayer of the first Christians. Phil. iv, 6. For a long time this preserved its character of a joyous outpouring of adoration and gratitude.* The assembly expressed its concurrence in the spoken petitions by a consentaneous *Amen*.†

The Church does not remain satisfied, as at first, with singing the Psalms. Christian feeling finds expression in its own spiritual song. This utterance, like prayer and the word of edification, proceeds in the first instance from individual inspiration. "If any man hath a psalm," says the Apostle, "let him speak." Ephes. v, 19; Col. iii, 16; 1 Cor. xiv, 26. Here the reference is evidently to a new song given by inspiration of the Spirit of God to one in the assembly. The song is a sort of transition between the gift of tongues and the calm and measured utterance of teaching; it gives vent to those deep and ardent feelings which cannot be restrained within the form of ordinary speech; it bears up to heaven the unutterable yearnings and the inexpressible adoration of primitive Christianity. None of these first psalms of the Christian Church have come down to us, because, like its prayers, they were essentially spontaneous, and were multiplied in such abundance in those days of mighty inspiration.

But though we do not possess any of the hymns of the first century, we find in the Epistles of St. Paul clear traces of what we may call the lyrical inspi-

* See the fragments of ancient liturgies published by Bunsen in his "Anténicœna," vol. iii.

† Πῶς ἐρεῖ τὸ ἀμὴν. 1 Cor. xiv, 16.

ration of the apostolic age. The close of the 8th chapter of the Epistle to the Romans, the 13th chapter of the Epistle to the Corinthians, and many other passages, in which the soaring thoughts of the Apostle rise to the heights of sublime poetry,* give us a conception of what the inspired song was, which was freely heard in the first Christian assemblies.

The idea of the sacraments entertained in the primitive Church was in harmony with its general constitution.† Based upon living faith, this Church was an association of Christians working together for their own edification and for the evangelization of the world. The notion of any intrinsic virtue in a sacrament, the theory of the *opus operatum*, inseparable from the sacerdotal system, could have found no place in these congregations, which had the living Spirit of God in their midst. Every thing in the doctrine of St. Paul is opposed to any such views. The Apostle, who acknowledged no saving virtue in any outward observance of the law, would assuredly not have ascribed such virtue to a purely material act. "The kingdom of God," in his view, "was not in word but in power."‡ In speaking, then, of the sacraments of the primitive Church, we must set aside all notions of sacramental grace by which the operation of God is assimilated to the arts of magic. Such conceptions of divine grace are, as Bunsen eloquently says, borrowed from the lustrations of decaying paganism.§

* See also 1 Tim. iii, 16; Eph. v, 14. (See "Das Kirchenlied in seiner Geschichte und Bedentung," by W. Baur, Frankfort, 1852; Augusti, "Archæol.," ii, 110–123.)

† The word *sacraments* is quite unknown in biblical language in the sense in which it is used by us.

‡ Ἐν δύναμει. 1 Cor. iv, 20.

§ Bunsen, "Hippolytus," ii, 127.

Baptism, which was the sign of admission into the Church, was administered by immersion. The convert was plunged beneath the water, and as he rose from it he received the laying on of hands. These two rites corresponded to the two great phases of conversion, the crucifixion of the old nature preceding the resurrection with Christ. Faith was thus required of every candidate for baptism. The idea never occurred to Paul that baptism might be divorced from faith—the sign from the thing signified ; and he does not hesitate, in the bold simplicity of his language, to identify the spiritual fact of conversion with the act which symbolizes it. "We are buried with Christ by baptism into death," he says. Rom. vi, 4. With such words before us, we are compelled either to ascribe to him, in spite of all else that he has written, the materialistic notion of baptismal regeneration, or to admit that with him faith is so intimately associated with baptism, that in speaking of the latter he includes the former, without which it would be a vain form. The writers of the New Testament all ascribe the same significance to baptism. It presupposes with them invariably a manifestation of the religious life, which may differ in degree, but which is in every case demanded. Acts ii, 38 ; viii, 13–17, 37, 38 ; x, 47 ; xvi, 14, 15, 33. "The baptism which saves us," says St. Peter, "is not the putting away of the filth of the flesh, but the answer of a good conscience toward God, by the resurrection of Jesus Christ." *

In these times, when the organization of the Church

* *Βάπτισμα οὐ σαρκὸς ἀπόθεσις ῥύπου, ἀλλὰ συνειδήσεως ἀγαθῆς.* 1 Peter iii, 21.

was still in many respects undefined, baptism was equivalent to the profession of faith. Administered in the name of the Lord Jesus * as a solemn sign of conversion, it had all the value of an explicit confession of the Christian faith, especially at a time when its observance was sure to bring down reproach and persecution.† It is further probable that before receiving baptism, the convert made a short profession of his faith ; this was that answer of a good conscience toward God spoken of by St. Peter. This custom was quite habitual in the second century, and there is every reason to suppose it originated in the first. This simple and popular confession of faith has been erroneously confounded with the Apostle's Creed, which is of much later date. That Creed is nothing more than an expansion of the baptismal formula, which received gradual additions till it became a rule of faith.

Regarded from the apostolic point of view, baptism cannot be connected either with circumcision or with the baptism administered to proselytes to Judaism. Between it and circumcision there is all the difference which exists between the Theocracy, to which admis-

* There is no example in the New Testament of the employment of the complete formula of baptism. Bingham in vain attempts to deny this fact. "Origines," iv, 163.

† Great importance must have been attached to baptism as the sign of incorporation with the Church, since in some congregations it was held necessary to administer it to Christians already baptized, in the name of catechumens who had died before receiving it. This is in our opinion the only reasonable meaning to attach to those words. 1 Cor. xv, 29. This practice, passingly mentioned by St. Paul, was afterward perpetuated in heretical sects. Epiphanius, "Hæres," chap. xxviii, page 7 ; Tertullian, "De Resurrectione," page 48.

sion was by birth, and the Church, which is entered only by conversion. It is in direct connection with faith, that is, with the most free and most individual action of the human soul. As to the baptism administered to the Jewish proselytes, it accompanied circumcision, and was of like import. It purified the neophyte and his family from the defilements of paganism, and sealed his incorporation and that of his children with the Jewish theocracy; its character was essentially national and theocratic.* Christian baptism is not to be received, any more than faith, by right of inheritance. This is the great reason why we cannot believe that it was administered in the apostolic age to little children. No positive fact sanctioning the practice can be adduced from the New Testament; the historical proofs alleged are in no way conclusive. There is only one case affording any ground for doubt, and those who attach more importance to the general spirit of the new covenant than to the isolated text, unhesitatingly admit that it is of no force.†

* Augustine has erroneously established a complete parallel between Christian baptism and that of the Jewish proselytes. "Archæal.," ii, 326.

† Five baptized households are mentioned in the New Testament. The family of Cornelius was baptized only after the descent of the Holy Ghost upon all its members. Acts x, 44, 47. The family of the jailer at Phillippi had heard the preaching of Paul and Silas: "They spake unto him the word of the Lord, and to all that were in his house." Acts xvi, 32. The house then contained no child incapable of comprehending the Gospel. We read in Acts xviii, 8: "Crispus believed on the Lord with all his house." St. Paul says (1 Cor. i, 16) that he baptized the family of Stephanas; and in the same epistle (xvi, 15) he mentions that this family was the first-fruits of his ministry in Achaia, a statement which implies that all its members

In this second period of the apostolic age the communion is not celebrated at every meal, as in the primitive times. It forms the conclusion of those feasts of brotherly love, known under the name of *agapæ*, at which the rich and the poor sat side by side on equal terms. 1 Cor. xi, 20–22. This was a custom borrowed from the usages of ancient Greece,* and sanctified and transformed by Christian love. The *agapæ* is neither a mere ordinary meal, like those spoken of in the early chapters of the Acts, nor a solemn sacrament, as the Lord's Supper became in the Church in succeeding times. It is an exceptional meal, but still it is a meal. The communion is subsequently altogether merged in the mystical feast of the Church. But, at the time we are now considering, it is still regarded as the Supper of the Lord, and is celebrated around the tables of the *agapæ*. It is observed in the evening.† If its celebration is at a different hour from that of public worship, it is not on the ground that has been assumed of there having already arisen a custom of private and secret worship reserved for Christians alone. It is the love-feast of the Christian family, therefore it is taken in the evening, and in privacy. No conclusion can be drawn from this practice to bear upon times when the Lord's Supper has become a ceremonial of worship

were converted. The single doubtful case is that of the baptism of the family of Lydia, (Acts xvi, 15,) but it loses this character when we connect it with the instances already referred to. It appears to us evident that the family of Lydia was the first-fruits of Macedonia, as the family of Stephanas was of Achaia.

* Xenophon ("Memorabil.," iii, 14) speaks of meals to which each brought his own food.

† Acts xx, 7. Augustine, "Archæol.," ii, 562.

properly so called.* St. Paul presents to us a faithful picture of the celebration of the Lord's Supper, and we find in it no trace of a consecration of the elements. When he calls the eucharistic cup "the cup of blessing which we bless," he is referring to a well-known custom of the paschal feast. The head of the household, when he took the cup, uttered a prayer, blessing God for the gift of the bread and wine.† Jesus Christ, having made the bread and wine the solemn symbols of his body broken and blood shed for our sins, the Lord's Supper recalled at once the benefits of creation and those of redemption. It was thus a feast of thanksgiving, a solemn eucharist. During a long period the Church felt constrained at this moment to bless God for all his gifts, alike for those of nature and of grace.‡ The Lord's Supper was not regarded as a sacrifice or offering; it was the renewal of the paschal feast taken by the Lord with his disciples, and the great memorial of the love of God regarded in all its manifestations, from the most elementary to the most mysterious, and sealed with the blood of Christ.

It is not possible for us to represent to ourselves exactly the mode of celebration of the communion at this period. A prayer of gratitude was doubtless spoken as the cup passed from hand to hand. Hence the name of the eucharistic cup. The bread was

* Harnack attaches an exaggerated importance to this fact. 163–165.

† "Benedictus tu, Domini Deus noster, qui producis panem e terra creans fructum vitis." Harnack, p. 166.

‡ The eucharistic prayers of the second and third centuries which have come down to us give convincing proof of this. "Ecclesiæ Alexandr. Monumenta." Bunsen, "Analecta Antenicœna," iii, 107.

broken in remembrance of the broken body of the Lord. There is every reason to believe a psalm or hymn was sung, as it was by Jesus and his disciples in the upper chamber. It does not appear probable that the words instituting the feast were regularly repeated on every occasion. The manner in which Paul quotes them argues the contrary. He refers to them as to some special teaching which he had given, and not as to an established usage in the Church. 1 Cor. xi, 23.

While the Lord's Supper was thus celebrated with all simplicity and liberty, it was, nevertheless, invested with much solemnity in the eyes of the Church. It summed up in one symbol, chosen by the Lord himself, the whole Christian religion. To partake of it was to make the most solemn profession of faith in Christ. To receive it unworthily was not only to despise the Lord's body in the symbol which spiritually set it forth, but also to make the Church partaker in the sin. Thus serious and severe discipline was appointed not merely to prevent the profanation of the Lord's Supper, but also to repress all kind of irregularities.* This discipline dealt only with scandalous offenses, and made no pretension to guard the visible Church against all contact with evil. Immorality and flagrant heresy were followed by the exclusion of the offenders.† The Christians were enjoined to avoid all contact with the false brother who brought

* Schaff, p. 491.

† The synagogue also had its excommunication, commencing with the rebuke, "peccatores publice confundunt." (Vitringa, "De Synag. vet.," 731,) and ending in exclusion, "Ingressus in synagogam ipsi sit prohibitus." (P. 741.)

dishonor upon the Church. Rom. xvi, 17; 2 Thess. iii, 6, 14; 1 Cor. v, 2. They were not to eat with him; not only was he forbidden to be present at the *agapæ* and the Lord's Supper, but even all social intercourse with him was prohibited. In those days of miracle, when the Holy Ghost still acted in a direct and sensible manner, the discipline of the Church was often confirmed by some exceptional and sudden attestation—the stroke of the divine rod.* The Apostle, by a lively image taken from the book of Job, called this intervention of the justice of God a visitation of Satan. In this sense he delivered great offenders over to Satan, not for their perdition but their amendment, hoping that suffering might bring them to repentance. 1 Tim. i, 20. The anathema pronounced against the false teachers of Galatia has the same significance and bearing. The Apostle earnestly desired the restoration of the offenders, and after their repentance they were restored. But neither in the act of excommunication or of re-admission were the solemn forms of subsequent ages employed in the primitive Church.

There is no trace in the apostolic age of any other sacraments than baptism and the Lord's Supper. The anointing with oil, enjoined by James, (James v, 14, 15,) has none of the characteristics of a sacrament. It does not symbolize any great aspect of the religious life, nor is it of general usage. It can only be regarded as an oriental custom accepted in the Churches of Palestine, and sanctified by prayer. We

* In this way we explain the sicknesses and punishments with which the Corinthians who had unworthily partaken of the Lord's Supper were visited. 1 Cor. xi, 30, 31.

have no particular account of the manner in which the last honors were paid to the dead. It is probable that the Churches founded in Greece and Asia Minor at once abandoned the pagan practice of burning the bodies of the departed, and buried them like the Jews. Belief in the resurrection of the body favored this custom. St. Luke tells us that after the death of Stephen the devout men who carried him to his burial made great lamentation over him.* This is the first instance recorded of any funeral ceremony; it is possible that the practice became general from that time. The ceremonial probably consisted of prayers and exhortations.

§ II. *The Christian Life.*†

Between the worship and the Christian life of the primitive Church there was a close relation. Worship was nothing else than the solemn epitome or concentration of the Christian life, while the entire life was raised to the height of true service to God. This character of sacredness, impressed upon the whole existence, is especially remarkable in the first period of the history of the first century, when the Church lived, as it were, in heaven, raised above earth by its young and ardent enthusiasm, or rather, by the all-powerful influence of the divine Spirit. It seems, for the time, as if all social and family relations were absorbed in the new relation formed among those who had received the baptism of fire; but it was according

* Συνεκόμισαν δὲ τὸν Στέφανον ἄνδρες εὐλαβεῖς, καὶ ἐποιήσαντο κοπετὸν μέγαν ἐπ' αὐτῷ. Acts viii, 2.

† This subject is carefully treated by Schaff; work quoted, pp. 447-500.

to the will of God that human life, with all its numerous and varied natural elements, should re-appear in the Church to be transformed by the new Spirit. Within the Church was to be realized that gradual coalescing of the human and the divine which alone gives to the plan of salvation its full and beautiful development. We must not, however, lose sight of the fact that the human element was at this period deeply defiled by heathenism. It was not possible that it should be at once brought into entire subjection to Christianity. Some spheres of action, which come not only naturally but rightly within the domain of the religion of Christ, were necessarily closed to it, so long as civilization rested upon a pagan foundation. How, for example, could a Christian exercise any magisterial function at a time when religion was so identified with politics that the most simple public act was associated with idolatry? How was it possible for Christians to cultivate any branch of art, so long as art—that great syren of Greece—was at the service of paganism; but it would be a very false conclusion that the domain of public life, or that of art, was to be permanently closed to Christians. Had there been any foundation for such an opinion the Apostles would have expressly stated as a principle the positive incongruity of religion and politics, of Christianity and the æsthetic faculties; but they make no such assertion. St. Paul recognizes the State in itself as a divine institution, necessary for moral development. "Let every soul," he says, "be subject unto the higher powers. For there is no power but of God: the powers that be are ordained of God. Whosoever, therefore, resisteth the power, resisteth the ordinance of God ; and they that resist shall receive to themselves damnation. For rulers are not a terror to good works but to the evil. Wilt thou, then, not be afraid of the power ? do that which is good, and thou shalt have praise of the same : for he is the minister of God to thee for good. But if thou do that which is evil, be afraid ; for he beareth not the sword in vain : for he is the minister of God, a revenger to execute wrath upon him that doeth evil." * The Apostle, in these words, rises from the corrupt manifestations of the civil power which are before his eyes, to its principal and fundamental idea. He acknowledges it to be a divine institution, and, consequently, an essential condition of moral development. 1 Tim. ii, 1, 2. He desires that the Christian, so far from taking a position hostile to the State, should pay to it all due submission and respect ; and he enjoins as a duty the offering of prayers for kings and all in authority. As there is no necessary antagonism between Christianity and the State, the Christian will be in time called upon to fulfill his duties as an active citizen, and to contribute to the general well-being in temporal matters—to uphold, that is, the cause of justice. But, before he can enter on this career, the general conditions of ancient society

* Ὁ *ἀντιτασσόμενος τῇ ἐξουσίᾳ τῇ τοῦ Θεοῦ διαταγῇ ἀνθέστηκεν.* Rom. xiii, 2–4. Paul, in this passage, rises to the ideal conception of the State. He establishes that there is no opposition between Christianity and the State in itself, but he does not teach us, as has been asserted, unreserved submission to existing authority, whatever may be its infringements of moral freedom. This question is not even touched upon by him in this passage. He has been erroneously made to advocate a doctrine which, in its abuse, does away entirely with the true conception of the State, since the State may cease to be the domain of right, and become simply that of blind and iniquitous force.

must be changed under the influence of the new religion.

The question of the relations of Church and State could not come before the apostolic age. Those relations were then very simple; they were those of the persecuted and the persecutor. There was every thing, however, in the general principle of Christianity to set aside any idea of a formal association of the two. The close union between the Church and the State was one of the most characteristic features of pagan society, in which the individual was kept in absolute subordination to the State, his faith being no less under official control than his outward life. Christianity, the religion of the conscience, sought only free and individual adherence. Respect for the individual was born into the world with the respect for conscience. A State religion, however orthodox, will be always a partial resurrection of the pagan idea. Ancient religions were maintained only by coercion, and by the support of wealth—both forces foreign to Christianity, which conquers by none but spiritual weapons. It might well blush to grasp the sword which slays the body, since it has in its hand the sword which can pierce the soul. Its kingdom is not of this world, therefore it can assert its dominion over the whole world. Protection places it in a servile position; it is strong in its own independence. The State is not at variance with the Church—as the flesh with the spirit, the old man with the new. The State, no less than the Church, is of divine institution. The Church is called to act upon it, but only by way of influence, and the more the two spheres are kept distinct, the greater and more penetrating is that influence. The State is the realm of right, and, consequently, of constraint and force, but of force regulated by, and made subservient to, justice.

The Church is pre-eminently the realm of freedom, for it receives its members only by their own free adherence. To combine the two spheres is to confound things that differ, and to move both from their foundations. The union of Church and State reverses the apostolical conception of a religious society; it is a retrogression from Christianity to paganism, or at least to Judaism. But mankind was to purchase this truth, like every other, at the price of long and bitter experience, by which it learned how much it costs the Church to mingle spiritual things with temporal.

The religion of Christ was, therefore, contented with laying down the principles by which the State was to be renovated; and it pursued the same course with reference to art. If, during the apostolic age, and the periods immediately succeeding, it held aloof from these two spheres of human activity, its influence was only the more efficacious in transforming them. In maintaining the independence of conscience in relation to the State, in sanctioning its right to resist all coercion from without, Christianity laid the foundations of all true liberty, and insured the overthrow of all despotic powers. Martyrdom is the mightiest protest against persecution; it shows material force the limit which it cannot pass. On the other hand, by the creation of a new ideal, at once divine and human, the way was prepared for truly Christian art, which should substitute for the calm; emotionless beauty of the Greek marbles, the deeper and more pathetic loveliness of those immortal forms, to which the great artists inspired by the Gospel have given birth.

All the reforms of Christianity have been wrought from within. The great revolution effected by it in the world had its beginning in human souls. Its first aim is to change the individual, that through him it may do its transforming work on society, and, primarily, on the family—that miniature society, source and type of the greater—upon which it has set its seal. The new religion found, in the regeneration of the individual, the lever with which to upheave the old world. It is, then, of great importance that we form a true estimate of the general principles of Christian life in the first century.

Its great principle is the imitation of Jesus Christ. To reproduce the features of his holy image, to feel as he felt, to share his humility, his self-renunciation, his tender compassion, to walk in love as he walked —such is the calling of his disciple.* He finds in his Saviour a living and powerful law, which "gives what it commands," to use the beautiful expression of St. Augustine. If Jesus Christ is the ideal type of the Christian, he is, at the same time, his support; (John vi, 48, 50;) the bread of God coming down from heaven on which he feeds; every member of his mystical body derives his nourishment by prayer from Christ the Head. Eph. iv, 15, 16.

The Christian life of primitive times seems like the life of Christ continued upon earth. Its most striking characteristic is a fervor altogether apart from fanaticism, which sustains it in the ordinary conditions of

* Τοὐτο γὰρ φρονείσθω ἐν ὑμῖν ὃ καὶ ἐν Χριστῷ Ἰησοῦ. Phil. ii, 5; Col. iii, 12, 13; Eph. v, 2.

human life. These men, full of holy zeal for truth, and daily awaiting the return of the Lord, feel themselves under no necessity to go out of the world, and to form for themselves a separate existence, like the Essenes and Therapeutics. Each remains in the position in which he was called,* unless he finds it one of too great temptation. The Christian has no sanction for abandoning work under pretext of yielding himself to pious meditation. 2 Thess. iii, 10, 13. Work itself rests upon a law of God; it is part of man's allotted task. The primitive Churches found the larger part of their members, as we know, among the poorer classes. They contained a large number of artisans, men who supported themselves by the work of their own hands.† In ennobling manual labor, Paul prepared the way for one of the most important reforms effected by Christianity. Toil had been regarded as a degradation in ancient society, which was composed only of victors and vanquished, indolents and slaves. All the conditions of pagan existence were overturned by so simple a reform. The right of conquest and the tyranny of a patrician class were virtually abolished. The Christian artisans of Corinth and of Thessalonica were thus, without knowing it, great social reformers.

This disposition to impress on the entire life a divine seal and a religious character, was blended with a certain asceticism, to which no saving virtue was attributed, but which was of importance in the discipline of the spiritual life. Paul says, that he kept under his body. 1 Cor. ix, 27. He even goes

* Ἕκαστον ὡς κέκληκεν ὁ Θεός, οὕτω περιπατείτω. 1 Cor. vii, 17.

† Ἐργάζεσθαι ταῖς ἰδίαις χερσὶν ὑμῶν. 1 Thess. iv, 11.

so far as to recommend celibacy, as a state in which it is more easy to serve God without hinderance; and there is reason to believe that this counsel, falling from such lips, was frequently followed during the first century.* Fasting was practiced in all the Churches, especially in times of difficulty and trial, when a peculiar need was felt of near approach to God. Acts xiii, 2, 3; xiv, 23. But this asceticism was not made obligatory on any; it was not prescribed by any fixed rules. It was observed with all freedom, never approximating in any degree to oriental dualism, never being regarded as the glorious and exclusive privilege of a sacerdotal class. It is considered a means of sanctification which should not be neglected, and which might render valuable aid in the struggle against the flesh with its desires and lusts. Ever since this primitive age the Church has been carried about on this question from one extreme to the other, passing from monastic Manicheism to the complete repudiation of asceticism. In the first century it was equally removed from both extremes.

One of the most beautiful creations of primitive Christianity was the Christian family, as we see it in the Churches of those days. What the family was in

* See 1 Cor. vii, *passim*. It is evident to us that Paul saw special reasons in the circumstances of the times in which he wrote, rendering celibacy desirable: *διὰ τὴν ἐνεστῶσαν ἀνάγκην*. 1 Cor. vii, 26. He thinks, however, that the state of an unmarried man, who, possessing a special gift, is not exposed to the grossest temptations, is the most favorable to piety. 1 Cor. vii, 32–35. Paul states, that on this point he does not speak a positive command from the Lord, but his own individual conviction. This private opinion of his does not prevent his maintaining intact the great principles of the new covenant. The "forbidding to marry" is set forth by him as one of the most grievous signs of heresy. 1 Tim. iv, 3.

the pagan world we know well. There was no medium for woman between the indolent and stupid captivity of the gynæceum and the part of a courtesan. Christianity raises her from this degraded position, and makes her truly a helpmeet for man. The outward union becomes the symbol of the union of life and soul, and the relation of Christ to his Church is the sublime type of the conjugal relation. Ephes. v, 23. Thus marriage is at once invested with divine purity, and an element of true devotion sanctifies the earthly love. Polygamy is absolutely, though indirectly, abolished. Paul still keeps the wife in a position of subordination to her husband ; he demands from her respect and obedience, but he maintains her rights, those sacred rights of the weaker, which Christianity ever espouses before all others. On the part of the husband he requires protection and love. Ephes. v, 24, 25. Marriage thus regarded is a holy association of man and woman for the common promotion of God's glory. Priscilla and Aquila, Paul's able and efficient fellow-workers in the Gospel of Christ, and the instructors of Apollos, supply a noble type of a Christian couple in the first century. Acts xviii, 2, 26.

A delicate question arose in these young Churches, composed of converts from paganism, as to what was the right course to take when either husband or wife became a Christian. Paul decides that the conjugal bond is not to be broken. The Christian wife may win the husband, or *vice versa*. 1 Cor. vii, 13–16. In any case, the marriage is sanctified by the prayers of the one who is the servant of Christ. Marriage appears to have been consecrated at this time only by the piety and faithfulness of those thus united, for they did not have recourse to any special ceremony.* The right of contracting a fresh union was recognized only in the case of the death of the husband or wife, (1 Cor. vii, 39;) the only exception to this rule was that admitted by Jesus Christ in cases in which marriage had been morally violated by adultery. Second marriages were therefore tolerated, but it is easy to gather from the language of Paul that, in his view, perpetual widowhood was preferable. 1 Cor. vii, 40. This opinion resulted naturally from the principle of asceticism, which was one feature of his individuality.

The relations of parents and children, no less than of husband and wife, assume a new character under the influence of Christianity. The implacable severity of the Roman father is to be tempered by Christian love; he is to train up with all gentleness the frail being so absolutely dependent upon him; and the child, on its part, is bound to a submission the more perfect because not founded on fear. Ephes. v, 1–4. Then appears the sweet and attractive type of the Christian mother. When Paul says of the woman that "she shall be saved in child-bearing," (1 Tim. ii, 15,) he rises, according to his custom, from the particular to the general; he sees in the woman the Eve who gave birth to the blessed Seed that was to bruise the serpent's head, and who brings into the world day by day sons and servants of God, destined to carry on and complete the work of redemption. These she nourishes and cherishes by that Christian education in which she takes so direct and active a

* The nuptial benediction is one of those happy innovations suggested to the Church by the Spirit of God.

part. Thus the Christian family is established on its true basis.

It has been made a reproach to Christianity that it did not at once proclaim the abolition of slavery. It is forgotten by those who bring this charge, that by taking such a course Christianity would have exchanged the religious sphere for the civil, and would thus have confounded two domains, between which a careful distinction is always important, and was especially so on its first introduction to the world. It could not enter into civil matters without exposing itself to all the perils, fluctuations, and chances of external authority. It would have become a political instead of a moral power; it would have abdicated its true throne of royalty, and bartered for an uncertain and hasty revolution that eternal power of reformation, by which it is able from age to age to renew individuals and societies. Christianity no more accepted slavery than it accepted polygamy and Roman legislation as to divorce; and it brought into the world the principle which was to abolish these institutions, so profoundly hostile to the morality of the Gospel. That principle it defined with reference to slavery with so much clearness, that it did in fact morally abolish it, so far as that was possible without going beyond its own domain. For, firstly, Christianity regulates the relations of masters and servants according to the laws of justice. The one are to remember that they also have a Master in heaven, (Ephes. vi, 9,) the other to recover their dignity as men by doing their service as unto God.* Still further, Paul clearly declares that in Christ Jesus there is

* Ὡς δοῦλοι τοῦ Χριστοῦ. Ephes. vi, 6.

"neither bond nor free," that is to say, every human being has equal rights in the sight of God. Col. iii, 11. The possession of one man by another is thus proclaimed to be immoral, an infringement of the rights of the redeemed in Christ, and incompatible with the doctrine of redemption and the equality which is its consequence. Nor was Paul content with a mere theoretical statement of these principles; he gave them practical application. His Epistle to Philemon is morally the deed of enfranchisement of the Christian slave. He sends back Onesimus to his master, as a brother in the faith, as his own son, and asks that he may be received even as himself.* Such words have done more to break the fetters of the slave than the outbursts of rebellion, and the justly indignant cry of those who are unjustly oppressed. Let us only picture to ourselves the slave, who yesterday was grinding at the mill, or serving his master like a beast of burden in the fields, without receiving one look of kindly recognition, to-day sitting with him at the table of the *agapæ*, breaking with him the bread of communion, and drinking the same cup of blessing. Trials and persecutions he now undergoes in common with his master; as a member of the same Church he is treated by him as a brother. Surely this is a vast social revolution, and one which cannot fail to bring in its train many results not at once, realized. We may add, that St. Paul was not satisfied with proclaiming the equality before God of men in Christ; he declared positively that it was desirable that the Christian should be enfranchised in

* Ἐμοῦ τεκνοῦ ὃν ἐγέννησα, αὐτὸν, τοῦτ' ἔστι τὰ ἐμὰ σπλάγχνα. Philemon 10, 12.

fact as well as in spirit. He advised him not to neglect any opportunity that might offer to be made free.* This advice is very significant, especially if we consider what moderation of language was necessary on a question so delicate, which by one imprudent word might be made to trench on social and political problems.

Christianity accepts the natural affections of man's heart, those at least which are normal, and purifying and penetrating them with a supernatural and divine element, it assimilates them to the highest love. The essence of this pure and devoted love is the spirit of sacrifice, and it has received its name, as it received its character, from the Gospel. It is called charity.† We have observed its first manifestation in the inner circle of the family, but it is not confined within these limits. It embraces all men in its arms of compassion, and while the national spirit among the ancients raised high barriers between different peoples, who were to each other as strangers and barbarians, the Christian knows no such exclusive distinctions. To him it is plain that God has made of one blood all nations of men ;‡ and if Tacitus brings against him the charge of hating the human race, it is only because the Christian is erroneously confounded by him with the narrow and prejudiced Jew. The contact into which Jews were brought with converted Gentiles in the Churches founded by St. Paul, contributed effectually to the expansion of heart and

* Εἰ καὶ δύνασαι ἐλεύθερος γενέσθαι, μᾶλλον χρῆσαι. 1 Cor. vii, 21.

† 'Αγαπη. 1 Cor. xiii, 1. This word had quite another meaning prior to Christianity.

‡ 'Εποίησέ τε ἐξ ἑνὸς αἵματος πᾶν ἔθνος ἀνθρώπων. Acts xvii, 26.

mind. By exalting the idea of humanity above that of nationality, Christianity gradually transformed the fierce patriotism of the old world into a nobler feeling. But it is pre-eminently in the Church that Christian affection finds its sphere. A spiritual bond, close and tender, is formed between those who are partakers of the same faith. In token that they form but one family in Christ, they call each other brethren, (Rom. viii, 12; xiv, 10; 1 Cor. vi, 6; Eph. vi, 10; Phil. i, 14; 1 Peter ii, 17,) they "salute one another with a holy kiss," (Rom. xvi, 16; 1 Cor. xvi, 20; 2 Cor. xiii, 12; 1 Thess. v, 26; 1 Peter v, 14,) they are of one heart and one soul. So strange a spectacle constrains both Jews and Gentiles to exclaim, "Behold how they love one another!" When a Christian stranger arrives in a city he is received as the representative of his Church. It is esteemed a privilege to give him lodging; pious widows wash his feet, according to oriental custom, and he receives every token of brotherly affection. The care of the poor and the afflicted becomes, as is natural, one of the chief concerns of Christian love. We know how high a place of honor is given to the poor in the Church of Christ. Poverty has preserved a reflected ray of the glory of Him who humbled himself and became poor; and the poor are lifted up because Christ has identified them with himself. It is not necessary to enumerate here the various offices created especially with a view to succor the poor. The example of Dorcas shows us how large was the love of the first Christians for the poor and needy, even when they acted only in their private capacity. Acts ix, 36. Large and regular collections were also made to provide for the wants of the Churches which were unable to support themselves.

The relations of Christians with the world were regulated by Paul with much wisdom. He was far from desiring that by an extreme and impracticable exclusiveness they should avoid all contact with men not yet converted. 1 Cor. v, 10. He did not blame them for sitting at the table of the heathen. 1 Cor. x, 27. He desired only that they should make no compact with evil and idolatry.

Two opposite tendencies had manifested themselves among the Christians of that time. Some, narrow and timorous, scrupled to eat of meats which had been sacrificed to idols ; others, of a broader spirit, and maintaining that an idol is in truth nothing at all, felt themselves justified in eating any thing that was sold in the market. Paul holds the justness of the latter principle ; (1 Cor. x, 23, 24 ;) but he demands from those who espoused it the largest consideration and respect for the conscience of weaker brethren, and urges on them the exercise of that elevated and delicate charity which can sacrifice a right rather than wound a weak brother, and which will not peril the soul of another for the sake of meat. 1 Cor. viii, 10–13.

Surrounded by all the seductions of paganism, the Churches were to use constant watchfulness. The letters of Paul give glimpses of strange revivals of old pagan corruption among these young Christians ; and a dangerous readiness to fall back into the mire of licentiousness is evidenced by his frequent warnings against the sins of the flesh. 1 Cor. vi, 15–20 ; Col. iii, 5–9. Many other blemishes appear in the picture of Christianity drawn by the Apostle. We have not disguised these in sketching the history of the various Churches. Schisms, heresies, the pride of wealth, the tendency to self-indulgence, all these aberrations which we have pointed out, show us that the Churches of the first century were, not, any more than those of any other age, pure Churches. But in spite of these imperfections—upon which their founders and directors felt bound to speak more strongly than in commendation of the piety of the faithful—the Christianity of that age has all the beauty of a new creation of God, which had not had time to be vitiated by man. "The world," says Bossuet, "believed in holiness as it saw holy men." And what examples of holiness was it not permitted to witness in this period of the apostolic age? The form of St. Paul—severe, earnest, burning with zeal for God, bearing the honorable scars of persecution—stands forth as if to manifest to all eyes what power and moral beauty human nature gains by union with Christ. The great Apostle was pre-eminently a great saint, and it may even be added, (taking the word in its best sense,) a great mystic in the depth of his piety and the fervor of his love to Christ. In the domain of the Christian life, as in that of missionary activity—in the teaching as in the guidance of the Church—he has left traces more profound than any other, and being the last of the Apostles, he is indeed first. Let us hear his own confession made in the holy boldness of humility, of all that he had suffered for Christ: "Are they ministers of Christ?" he says, speaking of the false teachers at Corinth, "(I speak as a fool,) I am more; in labors more abundant, in stripes above measure, in prisons more frequent, in deaths oft. Of the Jews five times received I forty stripes save one. Thrice was I beaten with rods, once was I stoned, thrice I suffered shipwreck, a night and a day I have been in the deep; in journeyings often, in perils of waters, in perils of robbers, in perils by mine own countrymen, in perils by the heathen, in perils in the city, in perils in the wilderness, in perils in the sea, in perils among false brethren; in weariness and painfulness, in watchings often, in hunger and thirst, in fastings often, in cold and nakedness. Besides those things that are without, that which cometh upon me daily, the care of all the Churches. Who is weak, and I am not weak? who is offended, and I burn not? If I must needs glory, I will glory of the things which concern mine infirmities." 2 Cor. xi, 23–30.

Such was an apostle and a saint in the first century. It is not surprising that no power in the world could withstand the influence of lives like this.

BOOK THIRD.

PERIOD OF ST. JOHN, OR CLOSE OF THE APOSTOLIC AGE AND TRANSITION TO THE AGE FOLLOWING.

CHAPTER I.

THE FALL OF JERUSALEM AND ITS CONSEQUENCES.

§ I. *Destruction of the Holy City.*

THIS period opens with a signal catastrophe, the consequences of which were most momentous to the Christian Church. Jerusalem, the Holy City, the religious center of Judaism, is reduced to ashes, and the Temple is but a smoking ruin. With it passes away the whole theocratic and priestly system of the old dispensation. Until this time the Church has been, so to speak, overshadowed by the Temple. Henceforward it has nothing more than a historic connection with Judaism, and a new era commences in its history.

The Jewish people, as we know, never consented to bow beneath the yoke of their conquerors. There was a natural antipathy between the two nations, founded, perhaps, on a certain obstinacy and invincible determination common to both. The Jews could not submit with the softness of the Asiatic, or the suppleness of the Greek, to foreign domination. They displayed as much perseverance in resistance as the

Romans in conquest. Their patriotism assumed the character of fanaticism, from its connection with their religious views. Their beliefs, which had become identified with earthly hopes and closely bound up with national pride, so far from inspiring them with patience and resignation, fostered rebellion in their hearts. It must be acknowledged, also, that to them the Roman dominion appeared only in its most hateful aspects. They had a succession of governors who were veritable brigands ; it seems that Judæa was regarded as a worthless province, and was given in prey to men laden with debts and vices, whose only object was to make a gain of a despised people. The Roman policy, usually so wise, and wont to deal considerately with the national faith and customs of a conquered people, was abandoned in the case of Judæa. Felix and Festus had indulged without restraint in all the caprices and violences of a tyrannic rule, and their successors had outdone even the abominations of their government. Albinus, who succeeded Festus, made shameless traffic of the administration of justice, selling impurity to the most notorious criminals. "There is no manner of evil unpracticed by him,"* says Josephus. Gessius Florus surpassed even Albinus. "It seemed," says the same historian, "as though he had been sent as an executioner to put to death condemned criminals."† The nominal kingship of Herod Agrippa laid no kind of check on these acts of injustice. It was not possible

* Οὐκ ἔστι δὲ ἥντινα κακουργίας ἰδεάν παρέλιπεν. Josephus, "Bell. Jud.," II, xiv, 1.

† Ὥσπερ ἐπὶ τιμωρίᾳ κατακρίτων πεμφθεὶς δήμιος. Josephus, "Bell. Jud.," II, xiv, 2.

that under such a rule peace should long be preserved. A circumstance, in itself unimportant, occasioned a terrible explosion, which had long been threatening and had already thrown out sparks in previous insurrections. The synagogue of the Jews at Cæsarea had been profaned by the Greeks of that city. Gessius Florus justified the act, and the Jews at Antioch and at Jerusalem immediately rose in a rebellion, which spread far and wide. It was stifled in the blood of thousands of Jews at Alexandria, at Damascus, and at Cæsarea. At Jerusalem the Roman garrison was massacred, and Eleazar, the son of the high priest, persuaded the Levites not to receive the offering of any stranger. This was to forbid the sacrifice for Cæsar, and such an act was equivalent to a declaration of war.* The rebellion was scarcely organized when Cestius Gallus, the governor of Syria, marched upon Jerusalem ; but he failed to enter the city, and was compelled to make an ignominious retreat. This triumph stimulated the fanaticism of the Jews, and carried it to its culminating point. Thenceforward it was beyond all control. Rome could not tolerate such contempt of her power. She sent Vespasian, one of her best generals, with a large army to avenge the insult offered to the Roman eagles ; and Galilee, after a sanguinary struggle, was subdued.

The death of Nero and the elevation of Vespasian to the throne gave the Jews a momentary respite ; but the combat recommenced with augmented vigor, under the conduct of Titus, the son of the Emperor, (A. D. 68.) Jerusalem soon became the center of

* Τοῦτο δὲ ἦν τοῦ πρὸς Ῥωμαίους πολέμου καταβολή. Josephus, "Bell. Jud.," II, xvii, 2.

attack, and the siege of that city was laid by the most skillful general of the Roman armies. Thousands of Jews, who had assembled in the interval to celebrate the Passover, were shut up within the walls of the Holy City, and the presence of such numbers contributed to render the defense more difficult, and the final catastrophe more fearful.

Every feature of this siege attests it to be a judgment of God. It is not an ordinary event of history; all the attendant circumstances are marked by an aggravation of suffering and woe; men appear to be led by a mysterious hand, which urges them on to commit acts not within their original intention. They are the instruments of a chastisement as tremendous as was the crime to be visited. Even those who were its victims seem to have felt that it was so. The Jewish historian enumerates the omens by which the catastrophe had been foretold. Many of these are obviously the puerile fables and inventions of popular superstition; but that very superstition reveals a strange presentiment of coming woe. According to Josephus, the Levites officiating in the Temple at the Feast of Pentecost heard a voice, which cried, "Let us depart from this place."* Four years before the war, when the city was enjoying profound peace, a man named Jesus, the son of Ananias, a simple inhabitant of the country, was heard crying in the Temple, at the Feast of Tabernacles: "A voice sounds from the east, from the west, and from the four winds of heaven. This voice is against Jerusalem and the Temple; against husbands and wives; this voice is against the whole nation." They tried to silence

* Josephus, "Bell. Jud.," VII, v, 3.

him ; he was scourged and variously ill-treated ; but still the words burst from his lips, "Woe, woe, to the inhabitants of Jerusalem!" He never ceased his terrible denunciations till the war had broken out. In the siege he fell a victim, still uttering his melancholy cry of woe.*

The condition of the city at this time was indeed one of misery almost without a parallel. Pressed by foreign armies without, it was torn within by three hostile factions, each working for its own ends on popular fanaticism. It had first the faction of the Zealots, under the conduct of Eleazar, who, as their name imported, claimed to be the zealous defenders of the national cause, and under this pretext gave themselves up to all kinds of brigandage.† For a time this faction was strengthened by the Idumeans, whom Eleazar engaged to fight against the high priest Ananias ; but these in the end separated from their allies, and turned against them. John of Giscala, who had fled to Jerusalem after the taking of his native city, and had at first joined the party of Eleazar, in his turn also organized a rival faction.

The unhappy city, closely encompassed by the legions of Titus, became the scene of the most frightful civil war. It was pillaged and sacked by its own sons. That which one faction spared, fell into the hands of another, and the contending parties agreed only in crime. "Such was the terror among the people," says Josephus, "that no one dare mourn for the dead or bury them. Tears must flow in secret, groans must be stifled, for such tokens of lamenta-

* Aἶ, Aἶ. Josephus, "Bell. Jud.," VI, v, 3.

† Josephus, "Bell. Jud.," IV, xiii, 9.

tion were visited with death. A little earth was hastily thrown over the corpses by night."* "O wretched city," adds the historian, "what cause of reproach hast thou against the Romans, who have but purged thee from thine abominations! Thou wast no more the city of God, and thou couldst never again be such, since thou wast become the tomb of thy slaughtered children."† Josephus knew not that Jerusalem was expiating a yet darker crime, and that its soil, once sacred, had been stained by the blood of God.

To the horrors of civil war those of famine were soon added. The small store of food was quickly consumed by the brigands, who went from house to house, laying hands on all they found, and roughly treating those who had nothing to give, in order to make them betray the supposed place of concealment. On the roofs were to be seen women and children, wasted with want, and uttering heart-rending groans; the young people walked about the street pale and lifeless as specters, and constantly sinking to the ground from exhaustion. Deep silence settled over the city; night after night the dead were numbered by thousands, and all these sufferings were slight compared with the atrocities enacted by the brigands.‡

Natural feeling seemed extinguished, and the spectacle—horrible even to the vilest criminals—was seen

* Ἦν δὲ τοσαύτη τοῦ δήμου κὰταπληξις ὡς μηδένα τολμῆσαι μήτε κλαίειν φανερῶς, μήτε θὰπτειν. Josephus, "Bell. Jud.," V, iii, 3.

† Τί τηλικοῦτον, ὦ τλημονεστάτη πόλις, πέπονθας ὑπὸ Ῥωμαίων, οἳ σοῦ τὰ ἐμφύλια μύση περικαθαροῦντες εἰσῆλθον. Josephus, "Bell. Jud.," V, 1, 3.

‡ Βαθεῖα δὲ τῆν πόλιν περιεῖχε σιγὴ καὶ νὺξ θανάτου γέμουσα, καὶ τούτων οἱ λησταὶ χαλεπώτεροι. Josephus, "Bell. Jud.," V, xii, 3.

of a mother killing and eating her own child. The close of the drama was at hand. The city was almost completely invested by the Roman legions, who had erected an encompassing wall, and who, despite the fierce resistance of despair, daily gained ground. The outer city wall was broken down; the fortress Antonina, to the north of the Temple Mount, carried by assault. Both attack and defense were now concentrated on the Temple itself. At length the day came when the conquering eagles floated from the Most Holy Place, and the sacrifices and ceremonies of the ancient law were for ever done away. This was on August 10th, A. D. 70. The people had crowded together in thousands on the holy hill, on the delusive promise of a false prophet, that that very day a sign of salvation should be given in the Temple.* The carnage only ceased when the victors were weary of slaying.

The Temple, contrary to the orders of Titus, was destroyed by fire. A soldier threw into it a burning brand. He did the audacious deed unauthorized, and actuated, says Josephus, by some demoniacal impulse.† We know that that impulse had a higher cause, and that this obscure soldier was the minister of the justice of God. In vain Titus gave orders for the fire to be extinguished; no one listened; on the contrary, every one pressed forward to feed the flames, and they spread with alarming rapidity. Even Roman soldiers, "moved to madness by the demon of war,"‡ forgot their stern discipline. Who cannot see the hand of God in this strange accomplishment of a

* Josephus, "Bell. Jud.," VI, xxv–xxx.

† *Δαιμονίῳ ὁρμῇ ὕλης.*

‡ *Πολεμική τὶς ὁρμὴ λαβροτέρα.*

righteous retribution? The roaring of the flames mingled with the cries of the dying, and from the height of the temple hill and the magnitude of the conflagration, the whole city appeared wrapt in fire. The lamentations of the Jews, as they witnessed the burning of their temple, were loud and terrible beyond description, says Josephus. The cry was proportioned to the greatness of their grief.* In the miserable remnant of God's ancient people was thus fulfilled the mournful prophecy, which but a short time before they had treated as madness. The wailing of a city left desolate was the echo of the words, "Woe, woe to Jerusalem!" The prayer of the murderers of Christ was heard; his blood was upon them, upon their children, and upon the ruins of their temple. God himself had pronounced the final sentence of Judaism.†

According to Eusebius and Epiphanes, the Christians had left the Holy City at the commencement of the troubles, and retired to Pella, in Peræa. Some of them returned into the city after its sack, when the storm was past.‡

§ II. *Consequences to the Church of the Destruction of the Temple.*

The great truths maintained by St. Paul received emphatic sanction from this terrible event. God had cast into the balance the weight of his judgments. The destruction of Jerusalem was to have yet a further effect—it was to enlarge the views of the

* Τοῦ πάθους ἀξιά. Josephus, "Bell. Jud.," VI, iv, 5.

† See Tacitus, "Historia," V, x, 14.

‡ Eusebius, "Hist. Eccles.," iii, 3; Epiphanes, "De ponderibus et mensuris," c. xviii.

Christians as to the future of the Church, and to give indefinite expansion to the horizon of prophecy. They had until now been living in daily expectation of the end of the world, and the immediate return of Christ. In the prophetic picture drawn by the Master they had failed to apprehend the true perspective. They had recognized no distinction between the prophecies relating to the Holy City and those having reference to the final judgments of God; they had not grasped the idea that the condemnation about to fall on Jerusalem was a symbol of the judgments kept in store for the world. This confusion, so natural in the first period of the apostolic age, was no longer possible after Judaism had lost its religious center. It became then distinctly evident that a long future of conflict was before the Church. We have a striking proof of this enlargement of the views of prophecy as resulting from the fall of Jerusalem. Hegesippus relates that the Emperor Domitian, on questioning some Christians in Palestine, who were connected with the Saviour by ties of kindred, as to the kingdom of Christ and his return, received this reply: "His kingdom is not an earthly kingdom or of this world, but a heavenly and angelic kingdom, which will come in the fullness of the ages, when he shall return to judge the quick and the dead." * The second coming of Christ had then at this time ceased to be expected as immediate, and those whose hopes had been most set on its speedy realization had learned to defer indefinitely the appointed time.

* *Οὐ κοσμικὴ μὲν οὐδ' ἐπίγειος ἐπουράνιος δὲ καὶ ἀγγελικὴ τυγχάνει ἐπὶ συντελείᾳ τοῦ αἰῶνος γενησομένη.* Routh, "Reliquiæ Sacræ," i, 219; Eusebius, "Hist. Eccles.," ii, 32.

This revelation, so clear and positive, of the prolongation of the period of struggling and suffering, combined with the destruction of the ancient form of worship, to which so many of the Christians still clung, tended to promote the more settled and permanent organization of the Church. In fact, from the year 70, there is a very marked advance toward a definite form of government and of worship. The Church now realizes its position as the true Israel of God, the religious society approved by him, which has taken the place of the theocracy; and it is thus led to organize institutions which shall permanently substitute those of the past. There was danger, however, lest in replacing these the Church should be led into imitating them. The necessity which was felt, after the destruction of the temple, of a fixed and clearly-defined organization, might lead to a resurrection of Judaism under a new form. The letter of Clement of Rome to the Corinthians gives sufficient evidence of the existence of such a tendency at the close of the first century. He says, "We ought to do all that the Lord has commanded us to do at the times appointed. He has commanded us to present offerings and to celebrate worship, not irregularly and irreverently, but at the times and seasons by him determined. He has revealed, by his most holy will, in what places and by what men the various acts of religious service can be acceptably performed. Special functions are ascribed to the high priest; a particular place is set apart for the priests, and the Levites have their distinct offices. Let each one of you then, my brethren, render honor to God, in his special order, with a good conscience, and without infringing the rule of his ministry. The sacrifices were not offered in all places, but at Jerusalem alone; and in Jerusalem, at the altars in the Temple. Take heed, my brethren, lest we who have been honored with a wider knowledge should bring upon ourselves severer chastisements by violating established rules."*

It would be absurd to infer from this passage that Clement, a disciple of St. Paul, holds the perpetuity of the Levitical worship, but we can clearly mark in it the tendency to transplant into the Church the precise organization of the old law, and to introduce the fixed order of Judaism. Evidently such notions can only have arisen after the destruction of the Temple. The Christians, accustomed to regard that as their religious center, were filled with a sort of alarm after its fall; they felt about for other props; they began to be afraid of the great freedom which, until then, had prevailed in the worship and government of the Church; and thus the event which was designed to set a seal on the spirituality of the new covenant helped, by a not unnatural perversion, to bring it back under the yoke of the old.

We cannot, however, admit, with an illustrious German divine, that in consequence of this great event a second Council was held at Jerusalem, at which the surviving Apostles met and authoritatively instituted the episcopate. A fact of such importance would not have escaped the ancient historians of the Church. The early Fathers would have made more than vague allusions to it. Besides, none of the passages adduced in support of this hypothesis are at all conclusive. Such an apostolical council appears to

* Clement of Rome, "Ad Corinth.," 4.

us inconceivable in the first century; it would suppose a wide modification of the very idea of the apostolate, and a radical revolution in then existing ecclesiastical institutions.*

* The hypothesis to which we allude was brought forward by Rothe ("Anfange," p. 311,) and supported by Thiersch, ("Apost. Zeit.," p. 275.) Rothe takes his ground on the following passage: *Μετὰ τὴν Ἰακώβου μαρτυρίαν καὶ τὴν αὐτίκα γενομενην ἅλωσιν τῆς Ἱερουσαλημ, λόγος κατέχει τῶν ἀποστόλων καὶ τῶν τοῦ Κυρὶου μαθητῶν τοὺς εἰσέτι τῷ βιῷ λειπυμενους ἐπὶ ταῦτα πανταχόθεν συνελθεῖν.* "After the martyrdom of James and the taking of Jerusalem, it is said that the Apostles of the Lord, and his disciples who were yet alive, assembled together." According to Eusebius, the object of this assembly was the choice of a successor to James. Rothe maintains that the opportunity thus offered was embraced for the institution of the episcopate. But, without dwelling on the hypothetical character given by Eusebius himself to this statement, it affords no support to Rothe's idea. In fact, according to Eusebius, who is only the echo of Hegesippus, the foundation of the episcopate is to be traced back, not to Simon, but to James himself, of whom he speaks positively as a bishop. He cannot, then, have intended to speak of the foundation of the episcopate after the death of James. The second passage brought forward by Rothe is taken from the fragment of Irenæus edited by Pfaff. It is as follows: *Οἱ ταῖς δευτέραις τῶν ἀποστόλων διατάξεσι παρηκολουθηκότες ἴσασι τὸν Κύριον νέαν προσφορὰν ἐν τῇ καινῇ διαθήκῃ καθεστηκέναι κατὰ τὸν Μαλαχίαν τὸν πρυφήτην.* "Those who follow the second injunctions of the Apostles know that the Lord appointed a new sacrifice in the new covenant, according to the Prophet Malachi." Rothe supposes these second injunctions to proceed from the second Council at Jerusalem. But there is no evidence that these second injunctions are of a different date from the first; there is nothing more implied than a simple classification of the injunctions of the Apostles. In any case, the passage gives no indication of an episcopate. The third passage is taken from Clement of Rome. "The Apostles," we read in his First Epistle to the Corinthians, xliv, "knowing from the Lord Jesus Christ that there would be disputes in the Church as to the name of bishop, and, having a perfect prevision of the fact, appointed elders, and subsequently gave directions that when these died other tried men should succeed them." *Καὶ μεταξὺ ἐπινομήν δεδώκασιν ὅπως ἐὰν κοιμηθῶσιν διαδέξωνται ἕτεροι δεδοκιμασμένοι ἄνδρες τὴν*

Another consequence of the fall of Jerusalem was the tracing of a broad line of demarkation between Judæo-Christianity and the Church.* So long as the Temple was standing the Christians of Palestine might suppose that it was the will of God that they should continue to practice all the rites of Judaism, as decided by the Council at Jerusalem. This could no longer be the case when the Temple was overthrown. The enforced cessations of sacrifices is a momentous fact, which it has been vainly endeavored to explain away.† This event could not fail to produce a very deep impression on the more liberal section of the Church at Jerusalem, which still retained the tone of feeling imparted by James. This party recognized it

λειτουργίαν αὐτων. Rothe lays stress on the word ἐπινομήν, which he translates *testament*, *testamentary disposition*, on the authority of a single passage in Hesychius, who assimilates ἐπίνομος to κληρονόμος He thus translates the passage from Clement: "The Apostles made this testamentary disposition, that when they (the Apostles) should be dead, other tried men should succeed to their office." To this we reply, the κοιμηθῶσιν does not relate to *apostles*, but to *elders*. The dispute at Corinth related not to the apostolic office, but to the office of elders, and it arose on the occasion of the death of the first elders appointed in that Church. Still further, the root of the word ἐπινομή is νόμος, law. It is, therefore, much better translated, *commandment*, *decision*. We read in an old Latin translation, "Hanc formam tenentes." "Forma" is here the equivalent of decision or ordinance. It is not necessary to have recourse to the arbitrary correction of Bunsen, who substitutes ἐπιμονήν for ἐπινομήν, (Ignatius und seine Zeit.," p. 98,) and who regards it as the consecration for life to the office of elder. We translate the passage thus: "The Apostles determined that when the first elders should be dead others should succeed them." (See Ritschl, "Altcath. Kirche," pp. 424–429.)

* See, on this point, "Das apostolische und nachapostolische Zeitalter," by Lechler, of Stuttgart, pp. 436–¼441; Ritschl, "Altcath.," 238–256.

† Schwegler, work quoted, pp. 192–308.

as the decree of God, finally abrogating the old worship. Under the influence of Simon, the cousin of James, and a man probably of like spirit, these Jewish Christians were gradually brought into closer fellowship with those of Gentile origin. The hatred of the Jews, who were eager to fulminate excommunications against the Christians, and to put them under the ban of their synagogues so soon as these were reconstituted, contributed not a little to enlarge the spirit of the Christians of Palestine.* In fact, a short time after the destruction of Jerusalem a new Sanhedrim was formed at Jabna, which endeavored to rally around it the remnants of the Jewish people. This Sanhedrim assumed the most hostile attitude toward the Christians, whom it called Mineans. The Rabbi Tarpho said, "The Gospels deserve to be burned; paganism is less dangerous than the Christian sects, for the former through ignorance does not receive the truths of Judaism, while the Christians know and yet reject. Salvation may be more readily found in the idol temples than in the assemblies of the Christians." The Jews were forbidden to eat with the Christians, and a form of excommunication against them was introduced by the Rabbi Gamaliel into the daily prayers. Its import was, that there was no hope for apostates. No gulf could be deeper than that by which the Church was thus divided from the synagogue.

In the commencement of the following century we find a flourishing Church, without any Judaistic tendencies, at Ælia-Capitolina, a Roman colony founded on the ruins of Jerusalem, to which, by a decree of

* Lechler, p. 440.

the Emperor, no Jews were admissible. It is certain that a large number of Christians of Jewish origin were among its inhabitants, and that these associated without distinction with Gentiles by birth. There could be no stronger proof of the decay of Judæo-Christianity.* These same Christians were, as we shall presently show, sacrificed in large numbers by Bar Cocheba in the violent persecution which he instigated against the Church. We freely admit, however, that all were not equally enlightened. The existence in the second century of a Nazarite sect distinct from the Ebonites, and treated with tolerance by Justin Martyr, proves that a section of the Jews in Palestine, without breaking with the Church, still retained an exaggerated attachment to the ancient forms.† They could not be charged with any doctrinal error; they did not give formal expression to their views; but they refused to cast off the Mosaic yoke, even after God had himself broken it. The Church at Jerusalem contained within its bosom violent and fanatical men, who even before the siege of the Holy City had begun to fall away from it. These, far from being enlightened by that event, became yet more extravagant in their Judaizing notions. Previously, it might have been supposed that they adhered to the old worship rather from position than conviction; but from the year 70 they substituted for such a modified and transitional form of Judaism, one more decided and emphatic. Thus they became further and further alienated from apos-

* Eusebius's Ecclesiastical History, iv, 6; Ritschl, work quoted, page 247.

† Justin, "Dial. cum Tryph.," c. xlvii.

tolic doctrine, and in combination with the Jewish sects, especially with the Essenes, they constituted a distinct and avowed heresy. To this period, then, we, with Irenæus, trace the obscure commencement of Ebionitism, although the name is of later date.*

* Γέγονε ἡ ἀρχὴ τούτου μετὰ Ἱεροσολύμων ἅλωσιν. Irenæus, xxx, 2.

CHAPTER II.

ST. JOHN THE APOSTLE AND PROPHET.

§ I. *Life of St. John.**

AS in the first period of the apostolic age the principal part is enacted by St. Peter, and in the second by St. Paul, so in the third period the paramount influence is that of St. John. His natural disposition and peculiar gifts account for this delay in the exercise of his apostleship. With a soul meditative and mystical, he had neither the impetuous zeal of Peter nor the indefatigable activity of Paul. On him Christianity had wrought most intensively; he had penetrated into the deepest meaning of the teaching of Christ; or rather, he had read the very heart of the Master. It was his vocation to preserve the most precious jewels in the treasury of Christ's revelations, and to bring to light the most sacred and sublime mysteries of the Gospel. In order to fulfill this mission, he must needs wait until the Church was ready for such exalted teaching. The first storms of division must subside. Just as the prophet heard the still small voice, which was the voice of God, only

* See Lücke's excellent Introduction to his "Commentary on the Fourth Gospel." Bonn, 1840. See also the Introduction to Tholuck's "Commentary on the same Gospel," and the passages referring to St. John in the works already quoted. We cite also an admirable sketch of St. John in Adolphe Monod's Sermon on "La Parole Vivante." Paris, 1858.

after the sound of the tempest and the roaring of the thunder, so the Apostle of supreme love could not speak till a calm had succeeded to the storm stirred up by the polemics of St. Paul. His work was not more important, nor attested with a diviner seal, than that of the great controversialist of the apostolic age ; the two are closely connected, and the latter is the natural sequence to the earlier. The revelation of love could not be complete till Judæo-Christianity had finally succumbed, and had carried with it in its fall all the barriers within which it had sought to limit the grace of God. So true is this, that we find St. Paul himself sounding the first notes of the hymn of love, and thus inaugurating the work of St. John. The former sowed in tears, the latter reaped in joy. The one resisted to blood ; the other received for the Church the prize of the well-fought fight. This diversity in the missions of the two Apostles is manifested in the diversity of the methods employed by them, in order to establish the truth, of which they are the organs. While St. Paul wields the weapons of warfare in his irresistible and impassioned dialectics, St. John is satisfied with expounding doctrine. He does not dispute ; he affirms. It is clear that he has been led into the possession of the truth by a path widely divergent from that of St. Paul—by the path of intuition, of direct vision. His language has the calmness of contemplation. He speaks in short sentences, strikingly simple in form ; but that simplicity, like a quiet lake, holds in its depths the reflection of the highest heaven. "He has filled the whole earth with his voice," says St. John Chrysostom, "not by its mighty reverberations, but by the divine grace, which dwelt upon his lips. That which is most admirable is, that this great voice is neither harsh nor violent, but soft and melting as harmonious music."*

It is very far from the truth, however, to regard St. John as the type of feminine gentleness, as he is represented in legend and in painting, which is only another form of legend. The ancient Church had a far worthier conception of him when it gave to John the Evangelist, the symbol of the eagle soaring to the sun, as though to signify that the mightiest and most royal impulse—that which carries farthest and highest—is love. The soul of the Apostle of Ephesus was as vigorous as that of Paul. He was called the Son of Thunder before grace had subdued his natural vehemence; and something of this early ardor always remained with him. In proportion to his love of truth was his hatred of error and heresy. Such love is a consuming fire, and when it sees its object despised or wronged, it is as ardent in its indignation as in its adoration. The truth which St. John loved and served was no mere abstract doctrine; it was to him incarnate in the person of Jesus Christ. He was ever the beloved disciple of the Master, the disciple admitted to his most tender and intimate friendship; and the Church has ever pictured him in the attitude in which he is represented in the gospels at the Last Supper, leaning on the bosom of the Lord. It was by the power of love so strong and deep that he was enabled to fulfill his mission of conciliation, and to harmonize all the apparent contradictions of the apos-

* Τὸ δὴ θαυμαστὸν ὅτι οὕτω μεγάλη οὖσα ἡ βοὴ, οὐκ ἔστι τραχεῖά τις οὐδὲ ἀηδὴς, ἀλλὰ πάσης μουσικῆς ἁρμονίας ἡδίων. Chrysost., "Procem. in Homel. in Joh."

tolic age in the rich synthesis of his doctrine. Let us now inquire how he was prepared for this glorious vocation.

John was the son of Zebedee, a fisherman of the Lake of Gennesaret, who dwelt at Bethsaida. Matt. iv, 21; Mark i, 19; Matt. x, 2. It is not proved that he was actually poor, as Chrysostom maintained, for his father had "hired servants;" (Mark i, 20;) his mother was among the women who ministered to Jesus of their substance, (Luke viii, 3,) and John himself had a house of his own. John xix, 27. Be this as it may, however, he was of obscure and humble origin. Possibly, as some commentators have thought, he may have owed his first religious impressions to his mother, who was among the earliest followers of the Saviour. John, as well as Peter, was a disciple of the Forerunner; the preaching of John the Baptist answered to the needs of his heart, which was eagerly waiting for the hope of Israel. We have already narrated, on the occasion of the calling of Peter, the circumstances under which this Apostle and John were led to follow Christ. John i, 37. They did not at once leave all to be his disciples. The Master gave time for their first impressions to deepen before he called them to forsake family and fishing-nets, and to come after him. Matt. iv, 18–22; Mark i, 19, 20; Luke v, 1–11. John appears to have been very young at this time; his grave and thoughtful nature peculiarly fitted him to receive the education which Jesus Christ imparted to his disciples, and which consisted in impressing on them the features of his own likeness.

John, Peter, and James were, as we know, admitted

to special intimacy with the Saviour.* There is no reason to suppose that John had a much clearer comprehension than the other disciples of the doctrine of Christ. He shared their carnal conceptions of the earthly kingdom of Messiah, (Matt. xv, 20–28,) and exhibited sometimes the narrow spirit of the sectary. Luke ix, 49, 50. His invocation of wrath upon the Samaritans displays an alloy of human passion, blended with his affection for the Saviour. Luke ix, 54. But this affection was so real and true, that it was sure to lead to all the developments of the religious life. He proved his love in a way not to be mistaken at the time of Christ's passion.† He followed him into the court of the high priest, and even to the foot of the cross. John xix, 26. He is the only one of the Apostles who witnessed the last sufferings of Christ; and possibly for this reason, he was chosen to render the most emphatic testimony to his eternal glory in the bosom of the Father.

We can well imagine what an ineffaceable image of unparalleled love and sorrow would be left on the soul of John by this scene. Who can tell with what feelings he caught those last words of the God-man, spoken almost in his parting agony, which committed to him the mother of his Lord as a sacred legacy. John xix, 27. He was also one of the first to see the risen Christ. John xx, 8. All these memories, and many more connected with them, were to be succes-

* Matt. xvii, 1; xxvi, 37. Lenain de Tillemont ascribes Christ's preference for John to the fact that he had remained unmarried. ("Mémoires," i, p. 330.) Arbitrary criticism can go no further than this.

† It has been justly remarked that while Peter was rather *φιλόχριστος*, John was pre-eminently *φιλοἰήσους*

sively illuminated by the Holy Spirit till they should form in the mind of John a perfect whole. But he was not himself capable, immediately after the Pentecostal effusion of the Spirit, of receiving, in all its fullness, this divine revelation.

During the earlier period of the apostolic age we see John by Peter's side lending him efficient help, but leaving to him the initiative in speech and action. Acts iii, 1; viii, 14, 25. He enjoyed much consideration, but did not exert a preponderating influence; nothing is recorded of his share in the Council at Jerusalem, though he appears to have been present. Gal. ii, 9. At this time he still adhered to the Mosaic law, as did Peter and James—a course of conduct confirmed by the decisions of the conference at Jerusalem.* There are no means of ascertaining in what year he left that city; but he was no longer there in the year 60, when Paul made his last visit. Acts xxi, 17, 18. Nicephorus asserts that he remained at Jerusalem until the death of Mary; but this gives us no exact information, inasmuch as the date of that event is entirely unknown.† There is one whole period of the life of the Apostle of which we possess no details. His supposed journeys to Rome, and into the country of the Parthians, are wholly legendary.‡ But if we

* "Apostoli Petrus et Jacobus et Johannes religiose agebant circa dispositionem legis quæ est secundum Moysem." Irenæus, "C. Hæres.," iii, 12, edit. Feuardentius.

† Nicephorus, "Histor. Eccles.," ii, 42.

‡ This is the opinion of Lenain de Tillemont, i, 355. The legend of the preaching of St. John to the Parthians originated in a false reading of the title of the second Epistle, as "Ad Parthos." (August., "Quæst. Evangel.," ii, 37.) See Lücke's "Commentary on the Epistles of John," p. 28.

have no precise records of his life during these years, his writings give evidence that the time was not lost in reference to his own development. He learned to contemplate one aspect of the person and doctrine of his Master, which had not presented itself to any of the other Apostles with equal distinctness; this was the profound mysterious fact of His eternal divinity, his pre-existence, and incarnation. If we wonder at these differences in the manner of apprehending Christ among his immediate disciples—differences, however, which are never contradictions, but are distinguished by the predominance of one or another element, in conceptions substantially identical—we must bear in mind the important influence of moral affinity in connection with religious truth. The eye of the soul, like the eye of the body, has a wider or narrower range. "There are," says Origen, "various forms under which the Word reveals himself to his disciples according to the degree of light in each, which is proportioned to the measure of their progress in holiness. If he manifested himself on the Mount of Transfiguration in a form much more sublime than that in which he appeared to those who had remained at the foot of the mountain and could not reach its summit, the reason was, that those who were below had not eyes able to behold the glory and divinity of the transfigured Word."* St. John was carried by the Spirit of God up to these blessed heights; thus he saw and heard that which others around him saw not nor heard. The higher he rose in faith and love,

* *Εἰσὶ γὰρ δίαφοροι οἱονεὶ τοῦ λόγου μορφαὶ καθὼς ἑκάστῳ τῶν εἰς ἐπιστήμην ἀγομένων φαίνεται ὁ λόγος ἀναλογον τῇ ἕξει τοῦ εισαγομένου.* Origen, "Contra Cels.," iv, 16, edit. Delarue, i, p. 511.

the more he beheld of the glory and the Godhead of the transfigured Word, and penetrated deeper and deeper into the meaning of the sayings which he had received from the Master's lips, as one by one they became illuminated with heavenly light.

We are free to suppose that the period of his life about which we have no information, was devoted to climbing that spiritual Tabor on the summit of which the only and eternal Son, who is in the bosom of the Father, was to appear to him in all the glory of his divinity. The Apostle, like Mary, pondered in his heart all that he knew of his Master; in the silence of devotion he listened to his living voice, and under the inspiration of the Holy Spirit, discerned more and more of the mystery of his being. St. Augustine says: "While the three other evangelists remained below with the man Jesus, and spoke little of his divinity, John, as though impatient of treading the earth, rose from the very first words of His gospel, not only above the bounds of earth, air, and sky, but above the angels and celestial powers, into the very presence of Him by whom all things were made. Not in vain do the gospels tell us that he leaned on the bosom of the Saviour at the Passover feast. He drank in secret at that divine spring: "*De illo pectore in secreto bibebat.*" * All the life of St. John, during the period when scarcely a trace of him is to be found in the apostolic Church, is summed up in these words.

It is certain that in this interval the Apostle must have come in contact with the philosophic culture so widely diffused at the time among the Jewish synagogues. The comparative correctness of his language

* August., "Tractat. 36 in Johann."

is itself a proof that this was the case ; it is also beyond question that he borrowed from the modified and infinitely diversified Platonism of his age the expression "the Word," which is evidently of Greek origin. Divine truth can speak in all tongues—in the polished tongue of the learned as well as in the simple and rude idiom of the common people ; but through whatever medium conveyed, its substance is still "the things which it hath not entered into the heart of man to conceive."

The time was to come when the Apostle would emerge from his obscurity, and would in his turn exert a wide and deep influence over the Churches of the first century. According to the testimony of Clement of Alexandria and of Irenæus, St. John, after the death of St. Peter and St. Paul, took up his abode at Ephesus.* No city could have been better

* Ἐν Ἐφέσῳ τῆς Ἀσίας διατρίβων. (Irenæus, "Adv. Hæres.," iii, 1, 3.) The existence of another John at Ephesus, called John the Presbyter, has been called in question, though he appears to have played an important part in primitive tradition. This doubt has arisen from the silence of Polycrates (Eusebius, "Hist. Eccles.," iii, 31) and of Irenæus, ("Adv. Hæres.," v, 33,) who make no mention of him. The testimony of Jerome is also appealed to, who asserts that the two tombs, which, according to tradition, were sacred to the memory of John the Apostle and John the Presbyter, were both really consecrated to the Apostle John. "Nonnulli putant duas memorias ejusdem Johannis evangelistæ esse." St. Jerome, "Catal. Script. Eccl.," 9. The evidence of Papias, however, seems to us conclusive in favor of the existence of John the Elder. "I inquired," he says, "what had been said by the Elders—Thomas, James, Peter, or John—and what say the other disciples of the Lord, (ἤ τις ἕτερος τῶν τοῦ Κυρίου μαθήτων,) as Ariston and John the Presbyter." Eusebius, iii, 39. Clearly Papias distinguishes John the Apostle from John the Presbyter. Nothing can be ascertained about the latter beyond the fact that he lived. See Lücke, "Comment. in Johann.," i, 25-31.

chosen as a center from which to watch over the Churches, and follow closely the progress of heresy. At Ephesus the Apostle was in the center of Paul's mission-field in Asia Minor, and not far from Greece. Christianity had achieved splendid conquests in the flourishing cities of that country; but it had also encountered dangerous enemies. It was there that false Gnosticism first of all showed itself, and perpetually sought new adherents. The Apostle Paul had spoken before his death of its rapid progress. In his Second Epistle to Timothy he seems himself to point out Ephesus as the city most threatened with heresy, where, consequently, the presence of an apostle would be especially needed. St. John made this city his settled abode, without, however, devoting himself exclusively to the important Church there founded. Ephesus was the center of his apostolic activity, but that activity extended over a wide area. Clement of Alexandria tells us how the Apostle visited the Churches, presiding at the election of the bishops, and restoring order where it had been disturbed. To one of these journeys of apostolic visitation belongs the striking incident recounted by the same author. This incident helps us more than many explanations to understand why John was the disciple whom Jesus loved.

"Arrived in a town not far from Ephesus, after having comforted and exhorted the brethren, he observed a young man, tall of stature, of a noble countenance and ardent spirit. Addressing himself to the Bishop, John said: "I commit that young man to thy charge, and call the Church and Jesus Christ to witness that I do so." The Elder at first conscientiously fulfilled his task; he received the young man into his house, instructed him, and at length administered baptism to him. The young man allowed himself to be drawn away into immorality, then into theft. He was obliged to flee from the town, and became the chief of a band of brigands. A short time after," adds Clement, "John had again occasion to visit that Church. After fulfilling his mission, he turned to the Bishop, and said, 'Restore to me the trust which I and the Lord committed to thee before the Church over which thou art overseer.' The Bishop did not at once understand to what the Apostle referred. 'I ask,' said John, 'for the young man whose soul I intrusted to thee.'* 'He is dead,' exclaimed the Elder, with many sighs and tears. 'How dead?' asked the Apostle. 'Dead to God; he fell away and was forced to flee for his crimes; he is now a brigand among our mountains, instead of a member of our Church.' Hearing these words, the Apostle rent his clothes and smote on his head, crying: 'What a guardian have I left over the soul of my brother!' He quitted the Church, made his way to the mountains, and gave himself up to the robbers.

"The young man recognized the Apostle, and was about to make his escape. John, forgetting his old age, ran after him, exclaiming: 'My son, why dost thou flee from thy father? I am feeble and far advanced in years; have pity on me, my son; fear not. There is yet hope of salvation for thee. I will stand for thee before the Lord Christ. If need be, I will gladly die for thee, as he died for us. Stop, stop,

* Ἄγε δὲ την πὰρακαταθήκην ἀπόδος ἡμῖν, ἣν ἐγώ τε καὶ ὁ σωτήρ σοι παρακατεθέμεθα ἐπὶ τῆς εκκλεσίας ἧς προκαθέζῃ μάρτυρος.

believe, it is Christ who has sent me.' * The young man listened, with his eyes cast down to the earth; then flung away his weapons and burst into tears. Throwing his arms around the aged saint, he implored his pardon with a flood of tears which were to him as a second baptism. The Apostle raised him up; he prayed and fasted with him; he completely subdued him by his words, and did not leave him till he had restored him to the Church, a great example of penitence, and a living trophy of Christian love." Never since the time of Christ has the parable of the lost sheep received so perfect an application.†

It has been asserted that by his example and practice at Ephesus, John confirmed the principles of Judæo-Christianity, and adopted them in the government of the Churches.‡ Such a supposition is altogether inadmissible, if we accept his gospel and epistles as authentic. Importance has been attached to the singular assertion of Polycrates that John was invested with pontifical attributes; the error here is in giving a severely literal sense to a figurative expression.§ It is evident from his writings, and also

* Τί με φεύγεις, τέκνον, τὸν σαυτοῦ πατέρα, τὸν γὺμνον, τὸν γέροντα; ἐλέησόν με, τέκνον, μὴ φοβου· ἔχεις ἔτι ζωῆς ελπίδα, ἐγὼ Χριστῷ δώσω λογόν ὑπὲρ σοῦ· ἄν δέῃ, τὸν σου θάνατον ἑκὼν ὑπομενω, ὡς, ὁ Κύριος τὸν ὑπὲρ ἡμων· ὑπὲρ σοῦ τὴν ψυχὴν, ἀντιδώσω τὴν ἐμήν. Στῆθι πιστεύων. Χριστός με ἀπέστειλεν.

† Clement of Alexandria: Τὶς ὁ σωζομενὸς πλοῦσιος, 39; Eusebius, "Hist. Eccles.," iii, 42.

‡ Schwegler, "Nachapost. Zeit.," i, 145; ii, 249.

§ Ἔτι δὲ καὶ Ἰωάννης ὁ ἐπὶ τὸ στῆθος τοῦ Κυρίου ἀναπέσων ὃς ἐγενήθη ἱερεὺς τὸ πεταλον πεφορηκως καὶ μάρτυς καὶ διδασκαλος. Eusebius, "Hist. Eccles.," iii, 31. A very little reflection removes all dubiousness from this passage. If John had been a Judaizing Christian, how could he have assumed the insignia of the high priest's office in oppo-

from his immediate disciples, that John continued to guide the Church along the way opened by Paul, and raised it even to a greater height above the specialties of Judaism. We shall also observe, in speaking of the ecclesiastical constitution at the close of the first century, that there is no foundation for ascribing to him the episcopal organization, properly so called.

It is not possible to determine accurately at what date St. John suffered for the Gospel. The "Fathers" differ as to the time of his banishment to Patmos. We are inclined to place it shortly after the death of St. Peter and St. Paul.* His exile may have been protracted during some years. The Revelation appears to us to have been written long before the gospel. It carries us into a period very little removed from the fearful persecution under Nero, which was the great typal war of Antichrist against Christ. The mode of thought, the form of language, the prominent ideas, the historical allusions, all suggest

sition to the most positive prescriptions of the law. It is evident that this expression, which is certainly singular, cannot be taken in a literal sense, but that it relates to the government of the Churches by St. John during this entire period. St. Jerome, who falls into the error of taking literally the expression of Polycrates, sets aside the idea of a Jewish priesthood: "Qui supra pectus Domini recubuit et pontifex *ejus* fuit." "De Script. Eccles.," 45.

* Lücke even asserts that it is not proved that John was directly the subject of persecution. The passage, Rev. i, 9, "I was in the isle which is called Patmos for the word of God" (*διὰ τὸν λογον τοῦ Θεοῦ*) may, he says, refer to a simple mission for preaching. Lücke, "Offenb. Johannes," p. 815. John, however, declares in the same passage that he had a share in the sufferings of those to whom he writes, (*συγκοινωνὸς ἐν τῇ θλιψει.*) We regard as wholly legendary Tertullian's assertion that under Nero John was thrown into a bath of boiling oil. Tertullian, "De Præscript.," 36.

this date; and, in the absence of any decisive external evidence, we are free to give full weight to the internal.*

With reference to the gospel and epistles, tradition is agreed in the date affixed to them. These writings are the slowly-ripened fruit of all the labors of the apostolic age; but, at the same time, like every other good gift, they come down from heaven, and bear the undeniable seal of inspiration. They clearly belong to a period when heresy was rife, and especially those forms of heresy which, denying the corporeal reality of the Saviour's sufferings, contained the first germ of Docetism. John did not, indeed, design his gospel to be a systematic refutation of the errors of Cerinthus, or of any other heretic. He was satisfied with setting forth true Christian Gnosticism in opposition to false oriental or Judaizing Gnosticism; and his gospel is beautifully characterized by Clement of Alexandria as pre-eminently the gospel of the Spirit.† We should do injustice to the fourth gospel were we to regard it as a merely polemical writing, or as only the complement of the synoptics. The latter supposition cannot be reconciled with the admirable unity of composition to be observed in the Gospel of John. It is full of a creative inspiration. The style is altogether unlike that of a mere commentator, who is completing by a gloss a text already given. John epitomises in his gospel the substance of his preaching at Ephesus, and in the other Churches of Asia Minor.‡ According to Jerome, he had no intention at first of preserving his discourses

* See Note L, at the end of the volume.

† Eusebius, "Hist. Eccles.," vi, 14. ‡ Ibid.," iii, 24.

in writing, but agreed to do so at the express request of the Churches.*

We have no detailed information of the last years of the Apostle. Two incidents have come down to us which agree perfectly with what we know of him. Irenæus relates, that going one day into the public baths at Ephesus, and hearing that Cerinthus was also there, he immediately went out, exclaiming, that he feared the house might fall, because of the presence of so great an enemy of the truth.† St. Jerome tells us how the aged Apostle, no longer able to preach at any length, would be carried into the assemblies of the Christians to speak the simple words, "Little children, love one another." To his brethren and disciples, who asked him why he thus repeated himself, he replied, "It is the Lord's commandment, and when it is fulfilled nothing is wanting." ‡ This hatred of error, and this holy love, give us the perfect portraiture of John. It does not appear that he died a violent death. He fell asleep in Christ at a very advanced age, at the commencement of the reign of Trajan.

St. Augustine tells us, that in his time there was a very current belief that the Apostle was not dead, but was only sleeping in his grave. § Evidently, this

* Coactus est ab omnibus pene tunc Asiæ episcopis et multarum ecclesiarum legationibus de divinitate Salvatoris altius scribere." St. Jerome, "Procemium in Matt." See Note M, at the end of the volume, on the authenticity of the gospel and epistles.

† Eusebius, "Hist. Eccles.," iv, 14. Epiphanius substitutes Ebion for Cerinthus without giving any reason. "Hæres.," 30.

‡ Hieronym., "Comment. in Galatos," c. vi.

§ Augustini, "Tractatus 124 in Johann.;" Lemain de Tillemont, i, 371.

impression arose from a wrong interpretation of the words of Christ, spoken to Peter with reference to John: "If I will that he tarry till I come, what is that to thee?" John xxi, 22. Perhaps, also, the Christians may have found it hard to believe that the Apostle whose influence was still so great, had really passed from the world. They were not altogether wrong. As Lücke has said, he lives, and will ever live, by his writings,* and the future belongs to him even more than the past.

§ II. *The Revelation.*

Before entering on the exposition of the doctrine of St. John in its most complete form, as we find it in the gospel and epistles, it will be needful, in order to trace the gradual development of the revelations of the New Testament, that we show what is the fundamental idea of the Apocalypse.

We may observe first, that so far from being in opposition to the other writings of St. John, this book comprehends all the essential points of his theology, but in the condition of germs not yet fully developed. There is no stronger evidence of this agreement than the place given in the Revelation to the person of Jesus Christ. Every thing centers in the Saviour. He is called the "Lion of the tribe of Judah," and the "Root of David"—expressions which point to his humanity. Rev. v, 5; xxii, 16. His divinity is no less distinctly recognized. He is the Alpha and Omega, the first and the last, the beginning and the end.

* Lücke, work quoted, p. 40. In the "Acta Apocrypha" (Tischendorf edit., p. 276) it is said that a spring of living water gushed from the tomb of John.

Rev. i, 17; ii, 8; xxii, 13. Clothed in a vesture dipped in blood, he is called the Word, or the Word of God, and he is followed by the armies of heaven. The Revelation is full of the idea of redemption. It delights in representing the Saviour under the image of the Lamb slain, whose blood cleanses from all sin. Rev. v, 9. The heavenly hosts adore him. The King of humanity, as he was once its victim, he holds the keys of hell and of death. Rev. i, 18; iii, 21. He is the divine Head of the Church, its guide and defense. Rev. iii, 19. The Church, in spite of a Jewish symbolism, which is easy of interpretation, is clearly distinguished from the synagogue. It comprehends a "multitude of every nation and kindred and people and tongue." Rev. v, 9. It is composed of those who have washed their robes in the blood of the Lamb, and who are walking in the way of holiness. Rev. vii, 14, 15; xiv, 3, 4. The Apocalypse rests, therefore, on the same doctrinal basis as the fourth gospel; † and, if it is true that it was written nearly thirty years previously, we may fairly conclude that what is called the system of St. John was not the product of speculation, or of the combination of Jewish and Hellenic elements, but that it was formed in substance before these elements, borrowed from pagan philosophy, could by possibility have entered into the current beliefs of the Church. We must seek, then, some other source than Alexandrian philosophy for the theology of John; and what other source can, at this early

* Καλεῖται τὸ ὄνομα αὐτοῦ, ὁ Λόγος τοῦ Θεοῦ. Rev. xix, 13.

† For the discussion of this assertion see the note on the Apocalypse at the end of the volume. Compare Lechler, "Apost. und Nachapost. Zeit.," 199–201.

period, have been open to him but the teaching of the Master?

The Revelation is not a recital of doctrine—it is primarily a book of prophecy; it opens a wide and glorious horizon to Christian hope, and paints it with glowing colors. It bears the impress of the age in which it was written. It raises the events of that time to the height of solemn symbols; thus, it is at the same time the book of revelations and an important historical record. In it, as has been well said, we breathe the very atmosphere of martyrdom. Written immediately after the first, and, perhaps, the most cruel of all the persecutions—that in which the brutal hatred of Roman paganism spent its first fury—the book of Revelation catches, as it were, the lurid reflection of the flames which consumed the Christians in the gardens of Nero; while, at the same time, it is illuminated throughout with the certainty of triumph. Contrasting the glory of the Church above with the indignities heaped on the Church below, the Revelation seems to drown the cries and the blasphemies of earth in the songs of the blessed and of the angels. After depicting the conflict and sufferings of the saints, and the terrible judgments of God upon their persecutors, it opens a vista of the heavenly places. It is one of the grandest conceptions of the sacred writer, perpetually to link together earth and heaven, and to show in the events of religious history the counterpart of other events, of which the abode of the blessed is the scene. The sealed book which contains the mystery of the destinies of humanity is at the foot of the throne of God. From thence resound the seven trumpets which declare the doom of the wicked; from thence do the angels pour forth their vials of wrath. While, for the visible Church, all is humiliation and suffering or weary waiting, all is glory for the Church invisible; yet never was the mysterious link uniting the two more plainly manifested. The Church triumphant watches the struggle of the Church militant with a tender, unceasing solicitude, and all heaven is attentive to the obscure drama enacted in one corner of the universe. No stronger consolation than this could have been given to the Christians, who were treated by their adversaries as the offscouring of all things. Nor has the assured blessedness of the faithful ever been depicted in a manner more beautiful and touching. If the sacred writer employs for this description the rich coloring of oriental symbolism, we are yet fully conscious that the blessedness he describes is essentially spiritual. "These which are arrayed in white robes, whence came they?" "These are they which came out of great tribulation, and have washed their robes, and made them white in the blood of the Lamb. Therefore are they before the throne of God, and serve him day and night in his temple: and he that sitteth on the throne shall dwell among them. They shall hunger no more, neither thirst any more; neither shall the sun light on them, nor any heat. For the Lamb which is in the midst of the throne shall feed them, and shall lead them unto living fountains of waters: and God shall wipe away all tears from their eyes." Rev. vii, 13–17.

But the sacred writer is not content with proclaiming in a general manner the suffering and triumph of the Church. The further he proceeds in his delineation of the struggle between Christianity and Antichrist, the more definite does he become in detail, though he makes use of a stately symbolism, sometimes strange, and always full of variety. Just as ancient prophecy was subject to rhythmical conditions, and uttered its most passionate inspirations in conformity with the rules of Hebrew poetry, so the prophet of the New Testament arranged his abundant materials in harmonious order. The Apocalypse has a rhythm of its own, taking the word in its wide acceptation. The seven trumpets follow the seven seals, and these again are succeeded by the seven vials. In the three cycles of revelations there is always a pause after the sixth link of the series to prepare for the last link, which is itself destined to bring in a new series.* This series is not immediately introduced. The prophet seems to be lost for awhile in meditation on the history of the world and of the Church.† After the three series, intended to be all prophetic of the same visitations, we have the descriptions of the great conflict, which is itself divided into three acts: 1st. The fall of Babylon. Rev. xviii, xix. 2d. The combat between Antichrist and Satan, terminated by the reign of Christ over his own. Rev. xx, 1–6. 3d. The last struggle and the

* Thus, after the sixth seal, there is an interval during which we are shown the elect around the throne of God. Rev. vii. After the sixth trumpet we have the episode of the book bitter and sweet, and of the measurement of the temple. Rev. xxi. Lastly, after the sixth vial, we hear the solemn warning, "Behold, I come as a thief." Chap. xvi, 15. See Lücke, "Offenbarung," 409–411.

† See Rev. viii, 1; see also chap. xii. From chap. xii to chap. xvi, after the seven trumpets and before the seven vials, the sacred writer describes in detail the enemies of the Church.

last victory, the new heaven and the new earth. Rev. xx, 11 ; xxii. Such is the plan of the Apocalypse. We find in it the same gradation as in the prophecy of Christ referring to the last times. Matt. xxiv, 5. Thus the agonies and convulsions of nature which are to precede the final judgment, the wars, famines, pestilences, earthquakes, the darkening of the sun, the falling of the stars, the universal terror—all these signs given in brief touches by the Master, are dwelt upon by the inspired disciple in bold symbolism. The terrible rider on the red horse, who comes forth at the opening of the second seal to take peace from the earth, is the personification of war ; as the man mounted upon the black horse, and with the pair of balances in his hand, represents famine. The earthquakes and the darkening of the sky are heralded by the opening of the sixth seal.

The first trumpets and the first vials announce the same order of judgments, and both have reference to the commencement of the prophecy of the first gospel. Jesus Christ, after predicting the chastisements and judgments of God in nature, declared his judgments in history, and first of all, the destruction of Jerusalem. St. John, who wrote after the overthrow of the Temple, proclaims another judgment of God. Sentence is to be passed now, not upon Jerusalem, but upon Rome, the impure and bloody Babylon, the incarnation at that time of the genius of evil. What a grand delineation does the evangelical Prophet give of this diabolical paganism—now as the beast with seven heads and ten horns, opening its mouth to pour out blasphemy against God ; now as the great whore, robed in purple and scarlet, making the inhabitants of the earth drunk with the wine of her fornications, herself drunk with blood of the martyrs of Christ, having ascended out of the bottomless pit and going into perdition! What an impression was such a prophetic cry calculated to produce, uttered as it was in the presence of the Roman Colossus still standing in all the pride of its great power! "Babylon is fallen, is fallen, that great city!" Rev. xiv, 8. "Rejoice over her, thou heaven, and ye holy apostles and prophets; for God hath avenged you on her. And a mighty angel took up a stone like a great millstone and cast it into the sea, saying, Thus with violence shall that great city Babylon be thrown down, and shall be found no more at all. And the voice of harpers, and musicians, and of pipers, and trumpeters, shall be heard no more at all in thee; and no craftsman, of whatsoever craft he be, shall be found any more in thee; and the sound of a millstone shall be heard no more at all in thee; and the light of a candle shall shine no more at all in thee; and the voice of the bridegroom and of the bride shall be heard no more at all in thee: for thy merchants were the great men of the earth; for by thy sorceries were all nations deceived. And in her was found the blood of prophets, and of saints, and of all that were slain upon the earth." Rev. xviii, 20–24.

But the Church has not only to fight against Antichrist without; it has also to resist Antichrist within: to do battle, that is, with heresy and false prophecy. "Many false prophets shall arise and shall deceive many," said Jesus Christ. Matt. xxiv, 11. St. John represents false prophecy under the image of a beast coming up out of the earth, in appearance like a lamb, but speaking as a beast, doing great wonders, and deceiving them that dwell on the earth by his miracles. Rev. xiii, 11–14. Behind this visible opponent the Apostle shows us the invisible enemy, the dragon, the old serpent, which gave power to the beast. Rev. xiii, 4. The conflict is unto blood, alike in the prediction of the Saviour and in the Apocalypse. The two witnesses, who are Moses and Elias—types of all the confessors of Christ—are put to death; but the Spirit of life from God enters into them again and they are victorious. Rev. xi, 9–11. The holy of holies of the spiritual temple is never profaned. The Church keeps an inviolable sanctuary. Rev. xi, 1, 2. She herself, in spite of the rage of her adversaries, who are gathered together like wild beasts around a travailing woman, is delivered by God from their violence; her child, the divine fruit of this sore travail, is caught up into heaven. Rev. xii, 5. St. John unites in this beautiful image the old economy and the new; both are set forth in this woman, who, in peril and pain, brings forth a glorious offspring. Of the ancient economy the Christ was born, who now rules in heaven with a rod of iron; while by him the Church, in the midst of her anguish, and encompassed with bitter foes, bears many sons unto glory. Ever persecuted, she is ever by God delivered, and the fruit of her labor is received up into heaven.

Thus, in the Revelation as in the prophecy of Jesus Christ, are unfolded the judgments of God as manifested in nature and in history, and the sanguinary and victorious struggles of the Church with her many adversaries. The inspired writer has added in his picture new features drawn from the historical events of the time and interpreted by the spirit of prophecy, but the words of St. John have not, any more than the words of Christ, an application restricted to his own age. The immediate events which he foretells have all a typical value. Just as with the Master, the destruction of Jerusalem was the symbol of the end of the world, so with the disciple, the destruction of Rome symbolizes and precedes the final judgment of God. Prophecy has thus advanced a step and enlarged its horizon as the conflict itself has become wider. St. John gives us clearly to understand that the drama is far from being finished after the overthrow of the Western Babylon, and that it is to be recommenced on the smoking ruins of Rome. In fact, after the Roman power shall have been broken, ten kings are to rise up against Christ, and to give to the conflict a new character of violence. Rev. xvii, 12–15. These ten kings (strange to say) shall be led forth to the battle by the Roman beast, which appears again to make war upon the mystic Lamb. Rev. xix, 20. We recognize here the depth of prophetic insight in the Revelation. We might have thought that the beast, which represented the savage spirit of Antichrist, was dead with imperial Rome, in which it found its most perfect embodiment. Far otherwise; that spirit is deathless upon earth; it has been; it will still be. The wound of the beast shall be healed. Rev. xiii, 3. In one man—Nero, the fifth Emperor—the spirit of Antichrist was absolutely incarnate; and the Antichrist of the last times* shall so

* It is not possible to determine with certainty whether Antichrist will be simply a diabolical power, or a personality. We incline, however, to the latter interpretation.

closely resemble him that Nero may be said to reappear in him. The name of Nero fills, in the prophetic picture of Antichrist, the same prominent position as the name of Cyrus or of David in the prophetic delineations of Messiah in the oracles of the Old Testament.* The triumph of the Church is connected in the Apocalypse, as in the first gospel, with the return of Christ. To proclaim that triumphant return, and to describe its glorious results, is the great object of the book of the Revelation, as to wait for it is the highest consolation left by the Master to his disciples.

In the Apocalypse two distinct periods are marked in this final triumph of Christianity over Antichrist. The first victory is brought about by the direct and visible intervention of the Saviour, taking up the cause of his people and gloriously establishing the reign of his Church upon earth.† After this period

* See, in reference to this whole subject, Note L at the end of the volume. We know how frequently the prophets proclaim the return of a well-known person, when they intend to signify that a man in all points like him is to appear. We need only to refer to the prophecies concerning Elijah, and to the passage in the Revelation, in which the two witnesses are designated as Moses and Elias.

† The idea of a millennium preceded by a first resurrection is suggested by Rev. xx; but we must not forget the symbolical character of the book. The glorious triumph of the Church is in itself a judgment of the world. The world is judged by the saints whom it had made its victims; their victory is its condemnation. The writer of the Revelation, when he shows us the saints raised from the dead and sitting upon thrones, employs an image analogous to that used by him to describe the triumph of the two faithful witnesses in the Church. Rev. xi, 11. We may observe, that at the close of chap. xx, 12–15, mention is made of a general resurrection of the dead in which all are judged according to their works. The judgment had then yet to take place, and the Christians appointed to salvation were not yet raised.

the old adversary of God will once again prevail to deceive the nations; but this will be his last effort. The drama of history concludes with his condemnation and with the solemn judgment of the children of men, conducted by Him whom once they crucified and who now reappears in all the glory of his power. Then comes the end, and then commences that eternal blessedness of the elect celebrated by St. John in the language of heaven.*

"And there shall be no more curse; but the throne of God and of the Lamb shall be in it, and his servants shall serve him. And they shall see his face, and his name shall be in their foreheads. And there shall be no night there: and they need no candle, neither light of the sun, for the Lord God giveth them light, and they shall reign for ever and ever."

Such is this marvelous book—one of the most sublime gifts of the Spirit of God to the Church; one which would have been its best consolation in all ages, as it was that of the martyrs of Lyons and of Asia Minor, if it had not been too often transformed into an unintelligible cipher, through a misconception of its historical basis. One important truth we learn from it, namely, that history interpreted by God is a great oracle, which, in each of its periods, repeats, with a living comment, the prophecy of Jesus Christ concerning the last times. The struggle which is renewed from age to age between Christ and Antichrist, the partial triumph of the former, and the more and more decisive defeats of the latter, bring us to the final conflict and crowning victory, which will be coincident with the return of Christ in glory. The

* See chapters xxi and xxii of the Revelation.

Church, in the certainty of victory, has a right to cry in presence of any power, however great and glorious, which has lent itself to the service of sin : "Babylon the great is fallen, is fallen!" Its fall will be the reiterated prophecy of that of the Satanic power, which for so many ages has set itself against God. The day is coming when that power shall be forever broken, and the disciples of Christ shall see the end of their day of shame, and shall reign in glory with him after whom they have borne the cross.

How greatly were such consolations needed in the year 71, on the eve of so much suffering and ignominy, when the few disciples gathered around St. John saw all the brutal violence of imperial Rome, and all the seductions of heresy arising out of the pit to fight against them.*

* It is not possible to attempt to give even an outline of the history of the interpretation of the Apocalypse. Its commentators may be divided into two classes : 1st. Those who see the fulfillment of the greater part of its revelations in the past. The Apocalypse is to these an inspired manual of the universal history of the last eighteen centuries. 2d. Those who hold that this book relates exclusively to the last times. This interpretation, which is combined with an unintelligent literalism, is wholly inadmissible. In both theories, however, there is an element of truth. It is true that the great phases of history may be discovered in the Apocalypse, because the key to the whole history of mankind is found in the conflict of Christ and Antichrist. It is also true that a final accomplishment of the prophecies is to be looked for in the last times, and especially the personal return of Jesus Christ. Our interpretation appears to us to combine these two systems in their elements of truth, while setting aside what is false and extravagant in both.

CHAPTER III.

THE DOCTRINE OF ST. JOHN.*

PAUL is, in his statement of doctrine, as in his life, the man of contrasts and antitheses. He aims to show how deep is the gulf between human nature and God, that he may the more exalt the grace which has bridged the chasm ; and he traces vigorously the line of demarkation between the old covenant and the new. It is not so with John. Having attained gradually, and without any sudden shock, the highest elevation of Christian truth, he starts from the summit and gently comes down again. He does not even pause to establish the superiority of the Gospel over the law. With him that is a settled point, an admitted principle from which he deduces the consequences. John does not commence, like Paul, with man and his misery, but with God and his perfection. His doctrine, by this character of sus-

* Schmid maintains that the Apostle's doctrine should be sought only in the prologue to the gospel and in the epistles, not in the gospel itself, because the latter gives us not the theology of the Apostle, but the teaching of the Master. We feel no such hesitation, for while we admit that John faithfully reproduces that divine teaching, it is evident that in the choice made by him of the words which he preserved, there is the clear impress of his own individuality. (See, for the doctrine of John, Schmid, work quoted, pp. 359-395 ; Neander, "Pflanz.," 874 ; Reuss, "Christian Theology of the Apostolic Age," ii, 276 ; Lechler, "Das apostolische und nachapostolische Zeitalter," 195 ; Fromman, "Der Johannische Lehrbegriff," 1857. See also the works quoted from Baur and Schwegler.)

tained elevation, and by the part assigned in it to love and to the direct intuition of divine things, bears the impress of mysticism, but of a mysticism which is essentially moral, in which the great laws of conscience are always maintained, and which is as far removed from oriental pantheism as from Pharisaic legalism.

§ I. *The Father, the Son, and the Holy Spirit.*

At the summit of his doctrine, St. John places the idea of God. God is the Absolute Being, the great I Am, whom no eye hath seen or can see. He is a Spirit.* All perfection dwells in him; he is at once life, light, and love. As he is Absolute Being, so he is Absolute, Eternal Life, the inexhaustible source, the sole principle of every thing that is.† But this life is at the same time light. 1 John i, 5. Light represents perfect knowledge and spotless purity.‡ God knows all things; God is holy. But John does not pause at this abstract conception of moral good. He gives us a concrete notion of it when he tells us that God is love.§ This he is, as essentially as he is life and light. Love is not only a manifestation of his being, it is its very essence. Never before had this sublime thought been expressed with such clearness; it had been discerned only by glimpses. Under the old covenant the love of God was subordinate to his justice. Under the new, this limited view had for a long time prevailed. St. Paul insisted with much force upon the love of God, but he considered it

* Θεὸν οὐδεὶς ἑώρακε πώποτε. John i, 18; iv, 24.

† Ἡ ζωὴ αἰώνιος. 1 John v, 20.

‡ Γινώσκει πάντα. 1 John iii, 20. Ἁγνός ἐστι. 1 John iii, 3.

§ Ὁ Θεὸς ἀγάπη ἐστί. 1 John iv, 16.

rather in its historical manifestation for the salvation of man than in its eternal principle. It is on this eternal principle that St. John dwells. He sees in the cross not only reconciliation between man and God, but also the revelation of the true name of God, of his very being. He is love ; the God who is love is the true God. 1 John v, 20. Love is so assuredly the absolute truth, that he who loveth is "of the truth." He is a partaker of the nature of God.* Thus truth or light is inseparable from love ; it is not simple knowledge, a mere theory. St. John does not recognize the ray of light which has no flame. Truth is, as it were, full of life ; it is life as it is love. It is all that God himself is. To be of the truth is to be born of God, to possess him, to be what he is ; it is, therefore, to have love in one's self. The object of knowledge being the God who is love, it is natural that true knowledge should be inseparable from love.

It must not be supposed, because John dwells especially on the moral attributes of God, that he passes by in silence his metaphysical attributes. These are all comprised in the absolute life which he ascribes to God.† To the Apostle, love is not one of the attributes of God, it is God himself; the metaphysical attributes are the attributes of the divine love. God is holy, infinite, almighty love, knowing every thing, every-where present. John delights, therefore, to give Him the name of the Father—that wondrous name which commands at once tenderness and reverence. John i, 14, 18 ; 1 John iii, 1.

* Πᾶς ὁ ἀγαπῶν ἐκ τοῦ Θεοῦ γεγέννηται καὶ γινώσκει τὸν Θεόν. 1 John iv, 7.

† "The Father hath life in himself." John v, 26.

But how does this invisible God reveal himself? How does He who inhabits the inaccessible light communicate himself to the creature, and what can be the first object of his love? We know the response of ancient philosophy to this question. At one time, finding no means of really bringing together the Infinite Being and the changing and finite creature, it left them face to face as two eternal principles—Uncreated Spirit opposed to uncreated matter. Again it sought in the Infinite Spirit the germ of the finite and perishable being, and arrived at the second by a series of descending steps from the first. Human opinion vacillated between Platonic dualism and the oriental or Alexandrian theory of emanation. Neither of these solutions is that given by St. John. The prologue of his gospel, written distinctly in view of the false philosophies of his age, solves the delicate problem of the relation of the invisible God to the world by the doctrine of the Word—a doctrine absolutely unknown before Christianity, and which, so far from being borrowed from Philo, is in direct opposition to his system. What is here treated of is not an impersonal Word, which is only a scholastic term to designate the world, or rather, the complex of the ideas realized in the innumerable beings of which the universe is composed.* The prologue speaks of a Being distinct from God, and yet God as God himself. He is, like him, life and light in an absolute sense.† The only begotten Son dwelling in the bosom of the Father, he is the eternal object of his love. Eternal

* See our exposition of Philo's doctrine in "The Life and Times of Jesus Christ."

† Ὁ λόγος ἦν πρὸς τὸν Θεον, καὶ Θεὸς ἦν ὁ λόγος. John i, 1.

love has thus an object like itself beyond the world and time.* The Son calls himself the Word, because he is the perfect manifestation of the Father. He reveals him in his person, which is his express image, and becomes the organ of his revelations in the world when it pleases him to create a world. The single fact that he bears this name of the Son and the Word appears to us to imply in the doctrine of St. John, as in that of St. Paul, a relation of subordination to the Father. The Son proceeding eternally from the Father is, in comparison with him, eternally in the relation of him who is begotten to him who begets. Their nature is identical because of this very relationship. He is God with God, but he is God begotten of God from all eternity.† He may nevertheless truly say, "I and my Father are one."‡

After the Son and the Father, John recognizes a third Divine Person—the Holy Spirit, who is sent to the Church by the Father and the Son. John xiv, 26; xv, 26. This Spirit speaks of those things which he

* Ἐν αὐτῷ ζωὴ ἦν. John i, 4.

† Ὁ μονογενὴς υἱὸς, ὁ ὢν εἰς τὸν κόλπον τοῦ πατρὸς. John i, 18. M. Reuss sees in this passage only the idea of the free existence, not of the eternity, of the Word. But is not this eternity implied in the divinity so clearly recognized in the Word by St. John?

‡ Compare John v, 43; vii, 28; viii, 42. According to Fromman, neither the Father nor the Son alone constitutes the Deity. Just as the idea of the State is only realized by the co-existence of the governing and the governed, so the idea of the Deity is only realized by the co-existence of the Father and the Son, necessary to the relation of absolute love. (See Fromman's explanation of the prologue of St. John.) This analogy with the State is not happy, for the relations between the Son and the Father bear no parallel to those between the governing and the governed. But it may reasonably be said that there are ideas involved of complex elements, and of several agents, which are only realized by their co-existence.

has heard. John xvi, 13. Here the subordination is evident. Some have even gone so far as to question the personality of the Holy Spirit, on the ground of certain expressions which seem to contradict it; but the offices attributed to him, such as teaching, consoling, the guidance of the Church, imply a personal existence. This fact appears to us to come out distinctly from the writings of St. John, though we may not be able to deduce from them a clear and complete statement of the doctrine of the Holy Spirit.*

§ II. *The Word and the World.*

The existence of the Eternal Word establishes the divine freedom, for in him absolute love finds its perfect realization.

God is under no constraining necessity to create. If he does so, it can only be by a determination of his free love. According to St. John, the Word takes an important part in creation. As the organ of revelation, by whom alone the light, life, and love emanating from God can be communicated, "all things were made by him, and without him was not any thing made that was made."†

The Word not only created the world. He already, in part, gave himself to the world: "He was in the world."‡ In truth, the moral creature derives from him all the elements of the higher life. Something

* God himself is called a Spirit. John iv, 24. Mention is made of more than one Spirit. 1 John iv, 1, 2; compare John vii, 39, *οὔπω γαρ ἦν Πνεῦμα ἅγιον*, and John xx, 22. See Reuss, work quoted, vol. ii, pp. 413–432.

† *Πάντα δι' αὐτοῦ ἐγένετο, καὶ χωρὶς αὐτοῦ ἐγένετο οὐδὲ ἓν ὃ γέγονεν.* John i, 3.

‡ *'Εν τῷ κόσμῳ ἦν.* John i, 10.

was imparted to it from the Word. The Word is the "light which lighteth every man that cometh into the world."* Thus do we find in St. John a sublime commentary on the noble utterance of St. Paul—"For we are also his offspring." In reason and conscience man has in himself an inner Word, an emanation from the Eternal Word, by which he is rendered capable of perceiving divine things and of possessing God himself. Such a conception raises us far above any dualistic notion ; nor is it possible to conceive a more decided opposition than that which subsists between this doctrine and that of Philo. While John admits an essential and true harmony between human nature and the Godhead, the Alexandrian philosophy declares plainly that it is impossible for man to draw near to God.

This harmony, however, has not been sustained. John recognizes the intrusion of a principle of discord into the world. The power of sin has been let loose. He does not enter into any argument on the origin of evil. He affirms the fact and is content with proving it. A kingdom of darkness has set itself in

* *Ἦν τὸ φῶς τὸ ἀληθινὸν, ὃ φωτίζει πάντα ἄνθρωπον, ἐρχόμενον εἰς τὸν κόσμον.* John i, 9. Notwithstanding the contrary opinion held by many learned exegetes, our translation still seems to us more in harmony with the context and with grammar. In fact, the distance between *ἦν* and *ἐρχόμενον* is too great for the two words to be connected. We know that the rabbis were accustomed to designate man as "him that cometh into the world." Lastly, St. John, in the verse following, speaks not of the illumination of the world by the incarnation, but of the illumination previously given to the world by the Word. Therefore it is said that when He came into the world he came "unto his own." This last expression would indeed itself suffice to establish an essential link between the Word and humanity. See the discussion of this passage in the commentaries of De Wette, Tholuck, and Lücke.

opposition to the kingdom of light, of which God is the sun. The devil has had a great influence upon man, seducing him into evil. He is not indeed to be regarded as Ahriman the eternal, confronted with the eternal Ormuz; no, the principle of light was before the principle of evil. Satan himself was born in the light, for it is said "He abode not in the truth."* It is evident that John supposes a fall in his case no less than in ours, and that consequently, in the origin of things, all was light and purity as became a creation called into being by the Word.† The cause of evil is entirely moral. "Sin," says the Apostle, "is the transgression of the law."‡

There is a law for the creature. It is this law which John calls the old and new commandment, the commandment of love based upon the very being of God. 1 John ii, 5–10. The destiny of the moral creature is to become like his Creator, conformed to his nature. The law implies liberty, for it appeals to the will. Sin, then, was a free violation of the law of God. The creature took part against God; that is to say, he rejected life, love, and light. Thus the world became dark from the day in which it turned from God. It is now plunged in moral night; all the higher elements are stifled in man; the outward and sensible life predominates; the lust of the flesh, the

* 'Εν τῇ ἀληθείᾳ οὐχ ἕστηκεν. John viii, 44.

† M. Reuss (work quoted, II, 380) misconceives John's idea, when he denies that the fourth gospel represents Satan as a fallen angel. Doubtless the fall of Satan does not explain ours; we might rather say, the reverse is true. The trial through which man passed as a free creature reveals itself to us as an indispensable condition of liberty for all moral creatures.

‡ 'Η ἁμαρτία ἐστὶν ἡ ἀνομια. 1 John iii, 4.

lust of the eyes, and the pride of life enshroud it in threefold darkness. 1 John ii, 16, 17. It is given over to a lie because it has set itself against good and love—that is, against God and the Word. Its prince is he who was a liar and murderer from the beginning, (John viii, 44,) and who, having fallen himself, has dragged after him in his descent all those who have freely, and under no external constraint, followed his suggestions.

John does not assert, however, that this darkness which envelopes the world is traversed by no beam of heavenly light. Even now, the Word enlightens the human soul ; all that it possesses of intelligence, of true reason, of divine consciousness, it derives from him. When he comes to man he comes to his own.* If the fall were total—that is to say, if all spiritual capability were dead in man—it would then be irremediable, since there could be no more any point of contact between the heart and God. But if the buried germ of the Word were not fertilized by grace, mankind would be none the less irrevocably lost.

§ III. *The Word and Redemption.*

The Word, which was the organ of creative love, is also the organ of the compassionate love of the Father. The whole work of salvation rests upon him. This work is twofold. It is both internal and external, for it is to effect the reconciliation and reunion of God and man. It is not enough that God should draw near to man by a series of revelations ; it is also necessary that man should be inclined toward God. In truth, that he may come to the fountain of living

* *Εἰς τὰ ἴδια ἦλθε.* John i, 11.

waters, man must be athirst. John vii, 37. He must be born from above in order to receive the Redeemer, who comes down from heaven. Only "he who is of God heareth the words of God." John viii, 23–49. The voice of the Good Shepherd is known only by his sheep. John x, 27. In other words, the soul must have recovered the sense of divine things, and there must be an affinity between it and the truth, in order that it may come to the light.

This religious aptitude, this pre-existing and necessary harmony between the conscience and the Gospel, John calls the drawing of the Father. John vi, 44. To arouse within the soul this thirst after God, to develop this infinite desire, is the inward work of the Word. Thus he is not satisfied with communicating the higher life of the soul to every man that cometh into the world. He sustains, nourishes, and developes this higher life, and shines into the darkness of every soul.* He scrupulously respects, however, the sacred rights of free will—for man's return to God, like his departure from him, must be a moral act. The light which is in us may be relumed or wholly extinguished, according to the attitude we assume toward the revelations given to the world. If man plunges into sin his mind becomes wholly dark, and thus he repels the light, "because his deeds are evil." If, on the other hand, he seeks to do the will of God, if he fosters the love of truth and of good, he comes to the light,† and he recog-

* *Καὶ τὸ φῶς ἐν τῇ σκοτίᾳ φαίνει.* John i, 5.

† *Πᾶς γὰρ ὁ φαῦλα πράσσων, μισεῖ τὸ φῶς καὶ οὐκ ἔρχεται πρὸς τὸ φῶς, ἵνα μὴ ἐλεγχθῇ τὰ ἔργα αὐτοῦ. Ὁ δὲ ποιῶν τὴν ἀλήθειαν ἔρχεται πρὸς τὸ φῶς.* John iii, 20, 21.

nizes it as it beams on him with gentle radiance. "If any man will do the will of God, he shall know of the doctrine whether it be of God." John vii, 17. The rejection of the light is a determination of the will. "Ye will not come to me that ye might have life." * Thus we find in the inner work of the Word the two poles of the moral world—grace and free will.

But this work within is not enough. To the infinite need of the soul there must be a corresponding infinite satisfaction. It returns to God: God must return to it. A positive revelation is necessary. John, like Paul, distinguishes two successive revelations. The first has only a preparatory value, it is but twilight; its rays proceed indeed from the Word, as all light does, but they only herald his appearance. "The law came by Moses," says John, "but grace and truth came by Jesus Christ." † Thus the Apostle solves without discussion the great question which had excited so much controversy. The law was but the shadow of salvation; the new covenant, by communicating to man the grace and pardon of God, alone gives the substance of the good promised to humanity; it alone lifts him into that full light of truth which is inseparable from love. This was to proclaim the abrogation of the Mosaic covenant in unmistakable terms. John does not fail, however, to recognize its divine character. In the fourth gospel Jesus Christ appeals to Moses; (John v, 46;) he declares that "salvation is of the Jews," thus connect-

* *Οὐ θέλετε.* John v. 40.

† Ὁ *νόμος διὰ Μωϋσέως ἐδόθη, ἡ χάρις καὶ ἡ ἀλήθεια διὰ Ἰησοῦ Χριστοῦ ἐγένετο.* John i, 17.

ing his work with the whole series of antecedent revelations.* Like the author of the Epistle to the Hebrews, but with far greater depth of argument, St. John establishes the superiority of the new covenant by the incomparable superiority of its foundation. The last and the greatest Prophet of the old covenant was not himself "that light, but was sent to bear witness of that light, that all men through him might believe." John i, 6–8. Jesus Christ, on the other hand, is the true light; he is that Word who is "God with God," the "Word made flesh." † He is not sent, like John the Baptist, that all men *through him* might believe, but that all might believe *in him.* He is the object of faith. Did he not say, "I am the Way, the Truth, and the Life?" John xiv, 6.

While St. Paul dwelt especially on the work wrought by the Saviour, St. John insists mainly on his nature. The incarnation is, in his view, the capital truth of Christianity. It is not only the necessary condition of redemption, it is the permanent condition of salvation. The proclamation of pardon is only the preliminary and initiative of salvation. For a man to be saved is to possess God—that is, to possess light, life, and truth; and as in the incarnate Word humanity appears closely and indissolubly united to deity, so it is by union with him that salvation is fully realized.

The incarnation thus regarded has an entirely new significance. Instead of being a pallid ray, which sinful man discerns quivering amid his thick darkness, it places him in the fullness of light; it restores him

* Ἡ σωτηρία ἐκ τῶν Ἰουδαίων. John iv, 22.
† Ὁ λόγος σὰρξ ἐγένετο. John i, 14.

to his normal condition. Created by the Word, and for the Word, in the light and for the light, he was destined to walk in the full light of God. The incarnation is the true consummation of creation, while it is at the same time the only effectual reparation of the fall. We know with what emphasis St. John insists upon the reality of the incarnation in opposition to the heresies of his time, which, by a spurious spiritualism, regarded the body of the Saviour as a sort of delusive semblance. " Every spirit," he says, " that confesseth that Jesus Christ is come in the flesh is of God. And every spirit that confesseth not that Jesus Christ is come in the flesh is not of God."* Writing his gospel and epistles in presence of those dualistic tendencies which identified evil with the corporeal element, he felt himself called upon to magnify this glorious aspect of the incarnation. He does not dwell upon the humiliation of Christ as St. Paul does ; but there is no contradiction on this point between the two Apostles.† If the glory of the only-begotten Son of the Father is apparent to John through the vail of mortal flesh, that glory is nevertheless revealed in shrouded splendor. He shows us Jesus Christ as subject to the weaknesses and suffering conditions of human life : he is weary, he groans, he weeps, he dies. This death is undoubtedly a lifting up, in a spiritual point of view,‡ and it was important to prove this in contradiction to Cerinthus,

* *Πᾶν πνεῦμα ὃ ὁμολογεῖ Ἰησοῦν Χριστὸν ἐκ σαρκὶ ἐληλυθότα ἐκ τοῦ Θεοῦ ἐστὶν.* 1 John iv, 2, 3.

† We cannot accept M. Reuss' idea on this point. He maintains that from St. John's stand-point the humiliation of the Word is inconceivable.

‡ *Ὑψοῦσθαι.* John iii, 14.

who regarded his death as only illusory. St. John gives emphasis to the truth that it is both glorious and real: "this is he that came by blood." But death is still death—that is, the depth of humiliation. The Saviour, as we read in the fourth gospel, prays before working his miracles. John xi, 41, 42. He is not, then, in possession of omnipotence on earth as in heaven. He is subject to a certain abasement; but he is subject to it voluntarily; it is an act of his divine freedom. The Son has power to lay down his life, and has power to take it again;* thus, in our aspect, he is glorious in his humiliation. Yet more, to the Apostle of love the highest glory is that which comes from love. For him, as for Pascal, this is the supreme order of greatness. Thus regarded, what glory can be compared with the glory of Him who gave his life for his brethren on the accursed tree?

St. John does not enlarge upon the incarnation itself. There is no trace in his writings of scholastic theories. He does not formally distinguish two natures in Jesus Christ. He is content with affirming that the Word was made flesh, and with showing how deeply his human nature was penetrated with the nature of God. In the eyes of John human nature has a divine capacity or potentiality. *Est capax divinitatis.* Jesus Christ is distinguished from all other men as the "only-begotten Son of the Father," who is like the Father, and, one with Him,† not only by virtue of his holiness, which is without

* Ἐξουσίαν ἔχω θεῖναι αὐτήν, καὶ ἐξουσίαν ἔχω πάλιν λαβεῖν αὐτήν. John x, 18.

† Ἐγὼ καὶ ὁ πατὴρ ἕν ἐσμεν. John x, 30.

blemish,* but by virtue of his origin—that is to say, he is God in a metaphysical as well as in a moral sense.

If the redemptive work of Christ is not fully brought out by St. John under all its aspects, it would be a grave error to see in it simply a revelation of the love of God. Such a revelation would be untrue and incomplete if it were not in harmony with the demands of justice, which are also the requirements of the human conscience. St. John is very far from ignoring this important aspect of Christianity. He ascribes a redeeming virtue to the Saviour's death. He died for us.† "He is the propitiation for our sins, and not for ours only, but for the sins of the whole world."‡ Writing after St. Paul he uses expressions the meaning of which was already clearly defined. The importance which he attaches to the death of Jesus Christ, the necessity which he so clearly recognizes of appropriating him by faith, of eating his flesh, and drinking his blood, § all show that John discerns in him the sacred victim, who offers the sacrifice of perfect love. But he never separates the redeeming virtue of the blood of the cross from its purifying efficacy. The moral aspect is inseparable from the judicial, and is throughout St. John's writings most prominently advanced. ‖ We

* Ἔρχεται γὰρ ὁ τοῦ κόσμου ἄρχων· καὶ ἐν ἐμοὶ οὐκ ἔχει οὐδέν. John xiv, 30.

† Ὁ ποιμὴν ὁ καλὸς τὴν ψυχὴν αὐτοῦ τίθησιν ὑπὲρ τῶν προβάτων. John x, 11.

‡ Αὐτὸς ἱλασμός ἐστι περὶ τῶν ἁμαρτιῶν ἡμῶν, οὐ περί τῶν ἡμετέρων δὲ μόνον, ἀλλὰ καὶ περὶ ὅλου τοῦ κόσμου. 1 John ii, 2.

§ John vi, 53. Compare 1 John v, 6.

‖ Τὸ αἷμα Ἰησοῦ Χριστοῦ τοῦ υἱοῦ αὐτοῦ καθαρίζει ἡμᾶς ἀπὸ πάσης ἁμαρτίας. 1 John i, 7. Compare iii, 5.

are bound, moreover, to set all the particular points of John's doctrine in the light of his central and dominant principle, which is expressed in the words: "God is love." This love is a holy love, which demands satisfaction for wrong committed, and a penitent retractation on the part of mankind; but it knows nothing of vengeance. The crucifixion, as represented by John, is not an infinite compensation for an infinite crime. For him also, as for St. Paul, the cross is only the consummation of redemption. The entire life of the incarnate Word is comprehended in the redeeming work. The free sacrifice of love began to be offered from the time of his coming into the world, and at the very opening of his ministry John the Baptist pointed to him as the Lamb of God which taketh away the sins of the world. John i, 29. The indwelling divine light shines forth with softened luster throughout the whole course of his life. His miracles are but rays more intense and sensible, revealing to men the existence of the sun within; but it is most of all the pure brightness radiating from his entire nature, his ideal holiness, the heavenly love impressed on all his words and actions, which rekindles in human hearts the sparks of the higher life.* The death of Christ is the culminating point of his redeeming work, for it is, first, the supreme surrender, the highest form of sacrifice; and next, it

* Jesus Christ distinguishes between a faith based upon his holiness and a faith based upon his miracles; and he places the former on a higher level than the latter. "If I do not the works of my Father," he says, "believe me not; but if I do, though ye believe not me, believe the works." John x, 37, 38. In other words, you ought to believe me because of my obedience to my Father, and my holihess; if not, believe me at least because of my miracles.

is the necessary condition of the diffusion of salvation. The love of the Word cannot be spread broadly over the world if it is not set free from all that is local and restricted as to space and time in its manifestation upon earth. "Except a grain of wheat fall into the ground and die, it abideth alone; but if it die, it bringeth forth much fruit." John xii, 24.

We thus understand the Master's words to his disciples: "It is expedient for you that I go away."* From the heaven to which he has returned he sends the Divine Comforter, the invisible and almighty Paraclete, who makes his presence real to his people; and in the abode of glory he carries on, by his intercession, his office of Mediator with the Father.†

Such is the work of the Word for the restoration of the world which he created, and which he thus morally re-creates by imparting himself to fallen man in a fullness greater than any to which man could have dared to aspire even in the days of his integrity.

§ IV. *The Word in the Christian and in the Church until the end of time.*

Love being the primary idea in the doctrine of John, and that which gives color to all the rest, we may expect that he will attach great importance to the appropriation of salvation by the individual. Love in fact supposes reciprocity. It is in vain that God has love enough for man to pardon him—it is in vain that the Word has become incarnate, and offered the redeeming sacrifice—if this infinite love obtains no

* *Συμφέρει ὑμῖν, ἵνα ἐγὼ ἀπέλθω.* John xvi, 7.

† *Παράκλητον ἔχομεν πρὸς τὸν πατέρα.* 1 John ii, 1.

response on earth. We have already seen that the Word prepares every man to receive eternal life by vivifying the divine germ within him. This includes the whole preparatory work of grace, and it is during this process, which is often gradual and prolonged, that the capacity for receiving divine things becomes enlarged or contracted. On the first contact with the incarnate Word the condition of souls is revealed. His manifestation is in itself their condemnation or vindication, since they then receive the fruits of their previous determination. They show then to which side they have inclined—whether they have chosen darkness, or have sought the light.* John assigns a very large part to the operation of grace. It is God who first loves; it is the Word who chooses us, not we who choose the Word.† This election is not, however, with him a fixed decree, which takes no account of human freedom. Faith, which is with John as with Paul, the sole means of salvation, or rather, the sole means of appropriating salvation, requires a creative act; it is a new and divine birth, of which the Spirit of God is the agent;‡ but it is at the same time a work, *the* work which contains in germ all other works.§ Faith is, in fact, not simply a trustful acceptance of pardon; it is first of all a spiritual view of God in the incarnate Word, accompanied by an act of submission which leads us to

* Ὁ δὲ μὴ πιστεύων ἤδη κέκριται. John iii, 18, 19.

† Οὐχ ὑμεῖς με ἐξελέξασθε, ἀλλ ἐγὼ ἐξελεξάμην ὑμᾶς. John xv, 16.

‡ Οἳ οὐκ ἐξ αἱμάτων, οὐδὲ ἐκ θελήματος σαρκὸς οὐδὲ ἐκ θελήματός ἀνδρός, αλλ' ἐκ Θεοῦ ἐγεννήθησαν. John i, 13.

§ Τοῦτό ἐστι τὸ ἔργον τοῦ Θεοῦ, ἵνα πιστεύσητε εἰς ὃν ἀπέστειλεν ἐκεῖνος. John vi, 29.

follow Him. John x, 4; xii, 26; xiv, 7–9. It is yet more than this: it unites us so closely to its object that it assures to us its possession; that object becomes one with us, as the bread we eat becomes part of our bodily substance. John vi, 53. It is a real communion with the Son and with the Father; by it we abide in Christ, deriving our nourishment from him as the branch from the vine. John xv, 1–4. Thus comprehended, faith communicates to us the three great attributes of God. By it we are made "of the truth," or children of light, for we possess him who is the Truth, (John xii, 36;) we receive life, eternal and divine life, even before the barrier which divides us from the invisible world is taken away;* and we are finally made perfect in love. To have Christ abiding in us, to enjoy close fellowship with him—is not this love, and love in the deepest and highest sense?

St. John, who never separates theory from practice, idea from fact, the truth from its application, binds closely together justifying faith and holiness. The latter is, indeed, implicitly contained in the former. Thus from the absolute and ideal stand-point, the believer is a saint. "Whosoever is born of God doth not commit sin." 1 John iii, 9. But the Apostle, who will make no compromise in the ideal, nevertheless recognizes the weakness of the actual Christian. All sin is, as he shows, a culpable inconsistency; nevertheless the Mediator still carries on his work of reparation for those who repent. John will lend no sanction to a delusive confidence; a life in sin he plainly declares to be incompatible with faith. He who truly

* Ὁ πιστεύων εἰς τὸν υἱὸν ἔχει ζωὴν αἰώνιον. John iii, 36.

believes is raised into a divine sphere, the sphere of love. To indulge hatred or bitterness is to quit this sphere, and to return into darkness. 1 John iii, 10–15; iv, 8. Having given us the theology of love, John gives us its morality. We ought to become like God, for, as Christians, we are born of him. The light of his love ought to shine within us, and the incarnate Word, who was his express image—made a sacrifice for us—ought to be the light of every regenerated man, as the creative Word was the light of every created man.* A holy society is founded in love—the society of the children of God, or the Church. The Apostle does not enter into any detail as to its constitution and organization. He only assumes the most complete equality among its members, since all have received "the unction of the Holy One, which teacheth all things."† There is no place for a system of external authority in the conception of St. John.

His views of the future of the Church bear the same impress of spirituality. He speaks in the gospel and the epistles as in the Apocalypse, of a general resurrection of the dead, a final judgment, a glorious triumph of Christ, inaugurated by his return, and a terrible conflict with the powers of darkness; but in his gospel he more clearly shows the connection of these great outward facts with the moral facts, which

* Ἐν τούτῳ ἐγνώκαμεν τὴν ἀγάπην, ὅτι ἐκεῖνος ὑπὲρ ἡμῶν τὴν ψυχήν αὐτοῦ ἔθηκε. 1 John iii, 16.

† Καὶ ὑμεῖς τὸ χρίσμα ὃ ἐλάβετε ἀπ' αὐτοῦ, ἐν ὑμῖν μένει, καὶ οὐ χρείαν ἔχετε, ἵνα τις διδάσκῃ ὑμᾶς· ἀλλ' ὡς τὸ αὐτὸ χρῖσμα διδάσκει ὑμᾶς περὶ πάντων, καὶ ἀληθές ἐστι καὶ οὐκ ἔστι ψεῦδος, καὶ καθὼς ἐδίδαξεν ὑμᾶς, μενεῖτε ἐν αὐτῷ. 1 John ii, 27.

are their antecedents.* In a spiritual sense the resurrection, the judgment, and the conflict with Antichrist have already commenced. Those who hear the voice of the Son of man and live, are so many Lazaruses called to the life divine.† The separation of the darkness from the light effected by the preaching of the truth is a solemn judgment, and whosoever denies that Jesus Christ is come in the flesh is Antichrist. Lastly, in a mystical sense, the adorable Master is come again to his own.‡ But so far from these spiritual facts being incompatible with the external facts declared in the Revelation, they prepare the way for them. After so much suffering and strife, endured from the beginning of the world, divine love will at length win a glorious victory on the very scene of its conflicts. Even the brilliant colors of the Apocalypse fail to depict this triumph, for St. John exclaims in his first epistle: "It doth not yet appear what we shall be; but we know that when he shall appear we shall be like him, for we shall see him as he is."§ To be made like God—is not this the highest possibility of the development of the creature? Is it not the realization of the sublime purpose of the redeeming Word? Is it not the fulfillment of the

* See our note on the Apocalypse, in which we refute M. Reuss's idea that there is a positive opposition between the fourth gospel and the Revelation.

† John v, 24–30. We hold with Lücke that it is not possible to give a purely spiritual application to this passage. It presents the point where the external and the moral fact become inseparable. In verse 28, Jesus Christ appeals to the resurrection of the body, which he will effect on the last day, in order to establish his power to quicken and to judge dead souls.

‡ *Πάλιν ἔρχομαι.* John xiv, 3.

§ *'Εὰν φανερωθῇ, ὅμοιοι αὐτῷ ἐσόμεθα.* 1 John iii, 2.

prayer of Christ, "that they all may be one; as thou Father, art in me, and I in thee, that they also may be one in us."* Having ascended to these heavenly heights, the theology of John is complete; no mysticism can soar above it, however bold its flight. The perfect union of the creature with the Creator through the Word, is the ultimate expression of the doctrine of love; beyond it there is nothing. This is, therefore, the closing utterance of the apostolic age; the conclusion, and not the refutation, of all that has gone before; the conciliation of all contradictions in the Church; in a word, the last revelation from heaven, absolute truth, God himself. Freed from all error, comprehended in all its depth, it will ever be the grandest result wrought out by the historian of theology, who, bending over the book in which it was inscribed by the aged saint of Ephesus, seeks to decipher it from age to age.

* Ἵνα καὶ αὐτοὶ ἐν ἡμῖν ἓν ὦσιν. John xvii, 21.

CHAPTER IV.

THE CHURCHES IN THE TIME OF ST. JOHN.

§ I. *External Condition.*

HISTORY finds few events of note to record in the period which extends from the destruction of Jerusalem to the close of the first century. It is a time of internal development, during which the Church is gathering up all the teachings received during the apostolic age. Missions are carried on on a less imposing scale. The propagation of the faith is, however, far from being arrested, for we can prove the existence, at the commencement of the following century, of a large number of new Churches. Instead of losing ground in the countries where it had gained a footing, Christianity became firmly established. We see from the names of the Churches mentioned in the Revelation, that in Asia Minor, for example, the great cities where Paul had first preached the Gospel became centers of proselytism, from which the light spread into the neighboring towns. From Ephesus, Laodicea, and Colosse, the new faith cast forth its roots to Smyrna in Ionia—a commercial and wealthy city—to Philadelphia in Lydia, and in Mysia to Thyatira, and, lastly, to Pergamos, the ancient residence of the kings of Asia, once famous for its noble library. The same expansive movement—the truth spreading itself by contact—was doubtless carried on in Greece, Africa, and Italy.

Persecution from the close of the reign of Nero to the time of Domitian was not of a general character. It was local and intermittent, but it never entirely ceased. The most unimportant occasion was sufficient to make it burst out afresh in a province. It was continuous in Palestine, where Jewish fanaticism had been stimulated by the very chastisements designed to rebuke it. We have cited the decrees of excommunication, the effect of which was to break the last links between the Church and the Synagogue. But, even beyond Judæa, the Jewish faction pursued its adversaries with implacable hatred. At Smyrna, as at Philadelphia, it greatly troubled the Christians, and succeeded in casting some of them into prison. Rev. ii, 9, 10; iii, 9. In spite of this declared hostility on the part of the Jews, the Christians were still often the victims of the antipathy felt for their adversaries. Their cause was constantly confounded with that of the obstinate rebels, who would not bow under the yoke of Rome.* The emperors were particularly vigilant over any movement proceeding from the Jews. They knew that revolt might at any moment burst forth afresh among them, like fire among hot, smouldering ruins. The imperial police was always on the watch to espy the slightest symptom of rebellion. This explains the strange uneasiness manifested by Domitian in relation to the grandchildren of Jude, the brother of the Lord. Hegesippus tells us that the Emperor, hearing that they were of the race of David, and so of the royal family

* Gieseler, "Kirchen-Geschichte," i, 135.

of Judah, caused them to be brought before him. It appears from the narrative, that an attempt had been made to alarm the Emperor by connecting the Christian hope of the second coming of Christ with the intrigues of the Jews for the recovery of their independence. Domitian at once questioned the grandchildren of Jude as to the nature of the glorious kingdom for which they were looking.* He was only reassured by learning how poor they were, and by seeing their horny hands, which proved that these supposed rivals of Cæsar were nothing more than simple laborers.† This sensitive jealousy over his own imperial power led Domitian to revive the persecution of the Christians. The Church had acquired sufficient importance, especially at Rome, no longer to escape observation. It had found adherents in the highest ranks of society, and a kinsman of the Emperor—his own cousin, Flavius Clement—had embraced the Christian faith. Surrounded with spies and informers, suspicious and cruel like all tyrants, emulating Nero in crime, and surpassing him in hypocrisy, Domitian could scarcely fail to persecute a numerous sect, increasing every day, which refused the profane homage demanded by his insensate pride. It is well known that no emperor, not even Caligula, made more overt pretensions than he to be worshiped as God. He caused his statue to be placed in the most venerated sanctuaries, and whole hecatombs were sacrificed before his altars.‡ He commenced

* Ἐφοβεῖτο γὰρ τὴν παρουσίαν τοῦ Χριστοῦ. Eusebius, "Hist. Eccles.," iii, 20.

† Εἶτα τὰς χεῖρας τὰς ἑαυτῶν ἐπιδεικνύναι μαρτύριον τῆς αὐτουργίας. Eusebius, "Hist. Eccles.," iii, 20; Routh, "Reliquiæ Sacræ," i, 213.

‡ Plinius, "Panegyr.," c. lii.

his decrees with these words: "Our Lord and God has commanded that such and such a thing be done."* It was not lawful to speak of him in other terms. It was easy to bring before such a madman the charge of high treason against the worshipers of the true God. Great numbers of the Christians became victims; † and, among others, Flavius Clement. His wife, Flavia Domitelli, was sent into exile in the Isle of Pontia, where she died. "The husband and wife," says the abbreviators of Dio Cassius, "were sentenced as guilty of atheism." Many others came under the same condemnation through their attachment to Judaism, that is, to Christianity regarded as a Jewish sect. Some were put to death, others suffered the confiscation of their goods. ‡ This persecution, of the details of which we have only vague information, must have been very bloody, for it was placed by the Christians of the next generation on a par with that of Nero. § The more firmly Christianity became established, and the more widely it extended its conquests, the more declared became the enmity of the pagan world toward it.

* "Dominus et Deus noster hoc fieri jubet." Suetonius, "Domitian," c. xiii.

† Πολλοὶ δὲ χριστιανων ἐμαρτύρησαν κατὰ Δομετιανόν. Eusebius, "Chron.," Lib. ii, 6–11; "Ad Olymp.," 218.

‡ Ἐπηνέχθη δὲ ἀμφοῖν ἔγκλημα ἀθεότητος. Xiphilini, "Epitome Dion. Cassius.," 67, 14.

§ This we infer from the following passage from the Apologue of Melito of Sardis to Marcus Aurelius: "Μόνοι πάντων ἀναπεισθέντες ὑπό τινων βασκάνων ἀνθρώπων, τὸν καθ' ἡμᾶς ἐν διαβολῇ καταστῆσαι λόγον ἠθέλεσαν Νέρων καὶ Δομετιανός." Of the emperors, Nero and Domitian alone, urged on by the counsel of some malevolent men, have sought to calumniate our religion. Routh, "Reliq. Sacræ," i, 114.

§ II. *Internal Condition of the Churches. Heresies. Church Organization.*

The position of the Churches at the close of the apostolic age was one full of peril and temptation To the period of first enthusiasm, when no difficulty seemed to damp the ardor of zeal and love, had succeeded a period when the obstacles to be overcome became more and more apparent, when numerous defections cast a doubt upon the fairest promises, when, finally, evils which had seemed completely subdued sprang again into life. We see, in fact, from the picture drawn in the Revelation of the seven Churches in Asia Minor, that shortly after the death of Peter and Paul, influences from without had effected a wide entrance in their midst.* There was not, in the case of these Churches, any violent crisis, as at Corinth, where the elements alien to Christianity came into strong collision, and the evil, like the good, was of a decided character. Such crises give hope of restoration to the truth as speedy as the aberration. But the case was very different to which St. John addressed himself in the book of the Revelation. The sap had almost ceased to circulate in the branches ; first love was ready to die,† and luke-

* One of the most astonishing examples of the arbitrary criticism which has been used in the interpretation of the Apocalypse is the symbolical explanation frequently given of the names of the seven Churches, which are regarded as the types of seven periods of the history of the Church. This is a pure invention, without any basis in exegesis. Of these seven Churches two only are in a prosperous condition—those of Smyrna and Philadelphia ; (Rev. ii, 9 ; iii, 8 ;) two are in a most deplorable state—those of Sardis and Laodicea ; (iii, 2, 15 ;) at Ephesus, (ii, 4–6,) at Pergamos, (ii, 13–15,) and at Thyatira, (ii, 19,) good and evil are nearly balanced.

† Τὴν ἀγάπην σου τὴν πρώτην ἀφῆκας. Rev. ii, 4.

warmness was taking the place of ardor and zeal. Rev. iii, 15. Such a condition is all the more perilous, because it is unconscious and easily accompanied with serious self-deception. Since the time of their foundation the Churches had considerably increased; they were still constantly gaining in external importance. Many of the first generation of Christians—those who had taken the decisive step, and forsaken their idols for the true God—were dead. Nominal Christianity had crept into the Churches. Thus, some of them thought themselves rich while they were really in the deepest spiritual poverty. Rev. iii, 17. The world had joined hands with the Church, and as the world in those rich and voluptuous cities of Asia Minor represented oriental corruption, scandalous falls were sure to result from this fatal association of Christians with the heathen. The former did not always maintain in their relations with the latter the prudent reserve so necessary in contact with a social system deeply defiled by paganism and its shameful practices. They were too often found taking their place at feasts, which were naturally and almost inevitably accompanied by sinful and impure indulgences. The very ties of kindred and friendship became serious temptations.* Nor were there wanting more subtle snares than those of sensuality. The spirit of rivalry was provoked, and men like Diotrephes found scope for their ambition

* *Φαγεῖν εἰδωλόθυτα καὶ πορνεῦσαι.* Rev. ii, 14. Baur sees in this passage a clear condemnation of the ideas of St. Paul; but it must be observed, that John does not speak simply of eating things offered to idols; he alludes, at the same time, to pagan debauch. He is not treating here a question of principle, but rebuking the melancholy inroads of pagan corruption in the Church.

in Churches which had acquired considerable importance. 3 John 9, 10. This desire for pre-eminence is, as yet, kept within bounds, but it gives a presage of the assumptions of clerical domination in the age succeeding that of the Apostles. Nevertheless, faith and love still bear their fair fruits even in these Churches. They contain a nucleus of sincere believers, who, like Gaius, display all the Christian virtues, (3 John 5, 6,) and give full proof of their broad charity by heartily welcoming to their homes brethren from far countries, or the faithful missionaries who go from place to place. Many young Christians are also to be found who have overcome the evil one. 1 John ii, 13. The general condition of the Churches, however, fills John with just anxiety, because he sees clearly what will be the issue of this outward and nominal Christianity, which is, as yet, restrained within certain limits, but which will ultimately stifle so many noble impulses in the Church, and will so often impede its progress.

Heresy, during the period of John, is no longer vague and floating as in the preceding age; it takes a more decided form. We have traced this process of transformation with reference to the Judaizing heresies which do not come within the scope of the Apostle, but which, from the time of the fall of Jerusalem, gradually assumed a settled form. A similar change is passing upon the heresies arising out of paganism, the first manifestations of which we noted in Asia Minor, where the double current of Western philosophy and Eastern theosophy met. Gnosticism is just emerging from its formative state. We cannot yet give a general description of the system, for we should be in danger of committing an anachronism, and attributing to the apostolic age that which really belongs to a much later period. When we come in contact with the systems of Valentinus and Basilides we shall give a summary of all the various features of Gnosticism as they were successively developed. We shall then have a complete idea of this important reaction of the spirit of paganism on the Church. We know already that Gnosticism is essentially dualistic; it rests upon that antagonism between matter and spirit which was a fundamental element of Greek philosophy and of all oriental religions. In the time of St. Paul, heresy terminated in an exaggerated asceticism, founded upon a false spirituality; it had even gone so far as to deny the resurrection of the body. In the time of St. John the doctrine of the Gnostics took a wider range; it tended more and more toward *Docetism*, that is, to the theory which holds the bodily existence of Christ to have been a mere semblance.* From the dualistic stand-point, in fact, the body, as the material element, is infected with evil; it was impossible, therefore, to suppose that He who was to overcome evil could have brought a body with him into the world. The natural consequence of these ideas was the doctrine that Jesus Christ had possessed only a semblance, a shadow of corporeal life. It would be erroneous, however, to suppose that in the time of St. John Docetism had assumed a thoroughly systematic form; it was a tendency rather than a doctrine; but it was constantly gaining ground. It is for this reason the Apostle insists with so much emphasis upon the incarnation: "Every spirit," he

* Docetism comes from the verb δοκεῖν, to appear.

says, "which confesseth not that Jesus Christ is come in the flesh is not of God; this is that spirit of Antichrist."* We should note also the urgency with which he dwells on the essentially practical character of the truth—of that truth which needs not only to be known but to be fulfilled, and which implies absolute submission to the commands of God.† We perceive that even the partially developed Gnosticism of his day tended to reduce Christianity to a mere intellectual theory without influence upon the moral life, and that it fostered the serious inconsistencies of conduct to which we have alluded. It is not surprising, that as it reinstated the fundamental principle of paganism, it should have justified its works and shielded its corruption.

Like the prophet Balaam, and wicked Jezebel, who led the ancient people of God to make a league with the idolators, the heretics sought to lower the barrier between the Christians and the heathen. Thus the Revelation speaks of them in symbolic phrase, under those well-known names which so accurately characterized their conduct. Rev. ii, 14–20. It appears that these dangerous persons had found a leader in the ranks of those who, standing nearest to the Apostles, should have been the surest guardians of purity of doctrine and of life.‡ According to Hippolytus and

* *Πᾶν πνεῦνα, ὃ μὴ ὁμολογεῖ τὸν Ἰησοῦν, ἐκ τοῦ Θεοῦ οὐκ ἔστι· καὶ τοῦτό ἐστι τὸ τοῦ ἀντιχρίστου.* 1 John iv, 3.

† *Ὁ λέγων· ἔγνωκα αὐτόν' καὶ τὰς ἐντολὰς αὐτοῦ μὴ τηρῶν, ψεύστης ἐστὶ, καὶ ἐν τοὺτῳ ἡ ἀλήθεια οὐκ ἔστιν.* 1 John ii, 4.

‡ *Ἔχεις καὶ σὺ κρατοῦντας τὴν διδαχὴν τῶν Νικολαϊτῶν.* Rev. ii, 15. The majority of German theologians maintain that the Nicolaitans were identical with the Balaamites. They argue from the etymology of the two words. Balaam, according to them, comes from the

Irenæus, the Deacon Nicholas asserted that the Christians were not bound to abstain from heathen practices, and that they might, without scruple, allow themselves sensual indulgence.* St. John characterizes such doctrine as the "depths of Satan."†

Already, in the heresies of this age, an idea began to gain currency which became widely diffused in the second century—the idea, namely, that the world was not created by the Supreme God, but by an inferior and antagonistic deity, known as the *demiurge*,‡ the spirit of evil and controller of matter. Cerinthus, the adversary of St. John, accepted this hypothesis of an inferior and evil creator; not, perhaps, with all the clearness of precision attributed to him by Irenæus and Hippolytus, but, at least, in substance. It was a natural consequence from dualism, and seemed to guard the holiness of God much more effectually than the theory of emanations, since it supposed no contact on his part with evil and with matter. The two

Hebrew verb בָּלַע, which signifies to swallow, to destroy, and from the substantive עָם, people. Balaam thus signifies, he who destroys the people. On the other hand, Nicolaitans comes from the two Greek words νικᾶν λαόν, which mean to subdue, to seduce the people. We have thus two synonyms conveying one idea. (Hengstenberg,) "Balaam," 23.) This explanation seems to us very erudite and very subtle. The writer of the Apocalypse, however, distinguishes between those who hold the doctrine of Balaam and the Nicolaitans, (verse 15 is connected with verse 14 of chap. ii, by a καὶ.) The testimony of Hippolytus, so well versed in the sources of heresy, appears to us conclusive. "Philosoph.," p. 258. Comp. Irenæus, "Contr. Hæres.," i, 27; "Epiphanes, Hæres.," xxv.

* Ἐδίδασκεν ἀδιαφορίαν βιοῦ. "Philosoph.," p. 258.

† Τὰ βαθέα τοῦ Σατανᾶ. Rev. ii, 24.

‡ *Demiurge* comes from δημιουργὸς, fabricator. It is the name of the inferior deity, creator of the material world.

principles being opposed to each other as eternally hostile, it was better to suppose that the evil principle had worked without any participation on the part of the spiritual. Cerinthus was by birth a Jew, but imbued with Alexandrian Gnosticism * and oriental Theosophy. The power which created the world was, according to him, a force separate from the Supreme God, and acting without his concurrence.† Jesus Christ was not born of a virgin; he was the son of Joseph and Mary, like other men, but distinguished from others by his righteousness and holiness. At his baptism the divine power, which is above all, descended upon him in the form of a dove.‡ From that time he wrought miracles, and revealed to men the unknown God. But, at the close of his life, this invisible power, which was the Christ, or the divine element in him, returned into heaven, and it was the man Jesus alone who suffered and rose again, while the celestial Christ was subject to no suffering because of his spiritual nature.§ This ingenious system skillfully combined the Gospel narrative with the principles of dualism. We meet, again and again, both in the fourth gospel and in the epistles of John, with allusions to these false doctrines, which were equiva-

* Κήρινθος δέ τις αὐτὸς Αἰγυπτίων παιδείῳ ἀσκηθείς. Hipp., "Philosoph.," p. 256.

† Ὑπὸ δυνάμεως τινὸς κεχωρισμένης, τῆς ὑπὲρ τά ὅλα εξουσίας. Hipp., "Philosoph.," p. 257.

‡ Καὶ μετὰ τὸ βάπτισμα κατελθεῖν εἲς αὐτὸν τὸν τῆς ὑπὲρ τὰ ὅλα αἰθεντίας τὸν Χριστὸν. Hipp., "Philosoph.," p. 256.

§ Προς δὲ τῷ τὲλει, ἀποστῆναι τὸν Χριστὸν ἀπὸ τοῦ Ἰησοῦ. "Philosoph.," p. 257. Comp. Irenæus, i, 25. Cerinthus united the most exaggerated millenarian notions with this absolute dualism. He reverted by a circuitous path to materialism.

lent to the negation of Christianity. The prologue of the fourth gospel is designed to establish that there is no separation between the Jesus and the Christ; that the man Jesus was in very truth the Word made flesh. We read in the first epistle: "Whosoever believeth that Jesus is the Christ is born of God. Who is he that overcometh the world, but he that believeth that Jesus is the Son of God?" 1 John v, 1, 5. John has evidently in view the fatal errors of Cerinthus in reference to the baptism of the Saviour and his crucifixion, when he says: "This is he that cometh by water and blood, even Jesus Christ; not by water only, but by water and blood." * In other words, he wrought out our salvation no less when he shed his blood than when he came up out of the waters of Jordan. It is not true that in the hour of his death his divinity had forsaken him. Thus, at the close of the apostolic age, John, like Paul, plants with a firm hand the standard of the cross, to be a beacon of light shining through all the darkness of coming storms. The folly of the cross is to be for ever the wisdom of the Church, and against this rock all the surges of heresy will break in vain.

Many causes contribute at this period to strengthen ecclesiastical organization. We may point, in the first place, to the development of heresy, and the sensible diminution in the miraculous gifts bestowed on the Church. Less miracles are cited of the Apostle John than of any of the rest. A new era is opening; the first full burst of waters from the divine spring is to be succeeded by the steady flow of the river between

* Οὐκ ἐν τῷ ὕδατι μόνον ἀλλ' ἐν τῷ ὕδατι καὶ τῷ αἵματι. 1 John v, 6.

its banks. The miraculous does not cease; on the contrary, it assumes a permanent character, but it bears less and less the appearance of prodigy. In such a condition of things the organization of the Church would naturally take a more definite form. It is erroneous, however, to attribute to St. John the institution of episcopacy, properly so called. For a long time yet to come we find only two orders in the hierarchy; deacons and elders or bishops are alone mentioned as governing the Church. The angels of the seven Churches, to whom are addressed the solemn exhortations of the opening chapters of the Revelation, are not bishops, as has been asserted. Each one is the symbolic personification of a Church, or its guardian angel.* The name elder or bishop is still used interchangeably, and we gather from the beautiful account of St. John, given by Clement of Alexandria, that the ecclesiastical constitution of that time is eminently democratic. The Apostle calls the assembly to witness of the trust he has committed to one of its directors, so as to make the latter feel that he is in no way above his brethren, and that he is responsible to them for the manner in which he fulfills

* M. Bunsen supports the old interpretation; ("Ignatius und seine Zeit.," p. 133;) as does Thiersch; (work quoted, p. 278;) and Rothe, "Anfänge," p. 423. But Ritschl points out, with justice, that the notion of an ideal representation of the Church is far more in harmony with the symbolism of the Revelation than the notion of a typical representation of bishops; (work quoted, p. 417.) No stress can be laid on what is said about Diotrephes as establishing the existence of the episcopate at this period, (3 John 9, 10;) for John speaks reprovingly of Diotrephes' ambition. Thiersch regards the superscription of the second epistle, Ἐκλεκτῇ κυρίᾳ, as the designation of a metropolitan Church, not of an elect lady (work quoted, p. 282.) It is not needful to refute such a supposition.

his duties. St. John gives explicit recognition to the inalienable rights of Christian people, when he declares that every believer receives for his guidance the anointing of the Holy Spirit. 1 John ii, 27, 28. This exalted view held by the Apostle of Christian freedom was still borne in mind in the second century, for in the Coptic constitutions of the Egyptian Church we find these words addressed in his name to all the Christians: "You have also the Holy Spirit for your guide, if any thing is wanting in our exhortations."*

The worship of the Church retained the same character of freedom as in the preceding century. The narrative of Clement of Alexandria shows us that no hesitation was felt in freely discussing the interests of the Church in the sacred assemblies. The conversation between St. John and the bishop with reference to the young apostate took place at a time when the whole Church was gathered together. The Revelation, however, puts us on the track of a gradual transformation even then commencing. The glowing description given by St. John of the heavenly worship is an indirect invitation to the Church on earth to conform to this ideal. That Church would, doubtless, delight to repeat or to paraphrase some of those sublime songs which gave such glorious expression to the religious feeling. Nothing could be more alien to the spirit of this grand epoch than the work of determining liturgical formularies. Nevertheless, as one by one the miraculous gifts were withdrawn, the great monuments of apostolic inspiration would naturally

* Εἰ δέ τι παρήκαμεν, τὰ πράγματα δηλώσει ὑμῖν, ἔχομεν γὰρ πάντες τὸ πνεῦμα τοῦ Θεοῦ. "Const. Eccles. Ægypt.," canon 44.

become the models and types of Christian adoration. We catch the echo of the anthems of the Revelation in those remarkable prayers of the Church of the second century, which have come down to us.

With reference to Christian festivals, the observance of the Lord's day becomes more marked than formerly. It was already so called in commemoration of the resurrection.* But we find no trace of any formal substitution of the Christian for the Jewish Sabbath, nor any legal appointment of its observance. The only great annual feast of which mention is made is the Passover. The Churches of Asia Minor, following the example of St. John, celebrated the anniversary of the Lord's death on the 14th of Nisan, at the same time as the Jews partook of the Paschal lamb. The anniversary of the resurrection thus fell on various days of the week, since it was always fixed for the third day after the 14th of Nisan. The Western Churches, on the other hand, always made the Easter, the closing day of the Passover fast, coincide with the Sunday.† This difference of practice produced in the following century a violent controversy, which we shall trace through its various phases. In the first century the peace of the Church was not so lightly broken. There is no ground for regarding as a concession to Judaism the fact that St. John fixed on the 14th of Nisan, in determining the date of the great Christian festival. The Apostle recognized in Jesus Christ the true Paschal Lamb, who had taken the place of the prophetic lamb, as the reality substitutes the type. By

* Κυριακῇ ἡμέρᾳ. Rev. i, 10.

† Eusebius, "Hist. Eccles.," v, 23.

celebrating the anniversary of the Redeemer's death on that very day, he proclaimed the abrogation of the old covenant. It is further proved that this celebration was not at all Jewish in character, but was thoroughly in harmony with the spirit of Christian worship.*

With St. John the apostolic age closes.

Revelation is before us in all its wealth, in its inexhaustible freshness, its infinite variety, and mighty unity. The various types of apostolic doctrine succeeded and supplemented one another. But there is not one of these elements which the Church is not bound to make its own, and its whole history will be but a progressive appropriation of the true Christ—of him whose image in all its divine lineaments the first century of the Church faithfully preserved.

That eventful and checkered history is about to begin. The last of the Apostles has passed away. The Church will no longer have that visible protection, that gentle and firm guidance, which has hitherto saved it from so many perils; but these very perils are necessary to its earnest appropriation of the truth. Though the Apostles are removed, He who gave the Apostles remains, and in him the Church will find light in all darkness, lifting up after every fall—victory over every foe.

* Hippolytus says of the observers of the 14th day, who, in the second century followed the practice of John in the celebration of the Passover, that, on all other points, they were in agreement with the Church, (ἐν τοῖς ἑτέροις συμφωνοῦσι.) "Philosoph.," 275. This proves that some observed the 14th of Nisan without being Judaizers.

NOTES.

A. [See page 23.]

LITERATURE OF THE SUBJECT.

WE shall not do more here than indicate the principal works on the apostolic age, those, at least, which have come under our particular notice. It is scarcely needful to say that our fountain-head is the New Testament. We shall treat, in the course of this work, of the title of each of its books to our confidence. Christian Antiquity presents to us also a wealth of information. The "Ecclesiastical History" of Eusebius;* the writings of the "Fathers" of the first three centuries, especially the "Philosophoumena" of St. Hippolytus; the treatise of St. Jerome, "De Viris illustribus Ecclesiæ;" the fragments of the early "Fathers" contained in the "Spicilegium" of Grabe, and in Routh's "Reliquiæ Sacræ,"† have been constantly consulted by us. If we pass on to the various memorials of Christian antiquity, we should refer first of all, for the old Catholic school, to the "Annals" of Baronius, the vast repertory of Catholic tradition, in which the erudition equals the lack of criticism;‡ and next, to the "Mémoires" of Lèmain de Tillemont, which, while they are not at all more critical, are more conscientious, and are always valuable for reference. § The Catholicism of our day in France offers very few works on the history of the apostolic age. The crude medley, dignified by Rohrbacher with the name of "Ecclesiastical History," is beneath serious notice; it is the most senseless of compilations. Germany has given to Catholicism a distinguished historian in Döllinger, but he is too much fettered by a preimposed system to judge of facts with impartiality. A recent work of the same school, "The History

* Eusebii Pamphili, "Eccles. Hist.," libri decem.

† Joannes Ernestus Grabe, "Spicilegium S. Patrum," Oxoniæ, 2 vols. Routh, "Reliquiæ Sacræ," 5 vols., 1846.

‡ C. Baronii, "Annales Ecclesiastici," 1588–1609.

§ "Mémoires pour servir à l'histoire ecclésiastique des six premiers siècles." Paris, 1693, 16 vols.

of Revelation," by Mesmer,* Professor of Theology, attempts to defend the hierarchy on historical grounds, with great moderation of language and ingenuity of thought, but always evidently under the influence of preconceived ideas. M. Albert de Broglie, in the preliminary chapter of his History of the Fourth Century, has drawn a striking sketch of the first age of Christianity, but it is wanting in any scientific demonstration, to which, indeed, it makes no pretense.†

We need not enumerate here all the historical memorials of early Protestantism. We will content ourselves with mentioning only the "Centuries of Magdeburg" in Germany, and in France, the learned "Ecclesiastical History" of Basnage.‡ This erudite author occupies too much the controversialist's stand-point to set forth with sufficient breadth the destinies of the primitive Church. In England, Church histories abound, but few are remarkable for criticism or historical connection. The history of the early ages of the Church has received large contributions from Puseyism, and also from the narrow dogmatism which persistently traces its own likeness in the theology of the Apostles. Some progress, however, has been already made under the influence of Germany. We may refer to the noble works of Howson, on the Life and Writings of St. Paul,§ (somewhat too diffuse and broken up by episodes ;) also to the commentaries of Dean Stanley and Professor Jowett on the epistles of the same Apostle. These distinguished divines have discovered the true secret of awakening interest in exegetical studies, by taking their stand on historic ground. Among the principal writings in France, up to the present time, we may mention M. Rillet's "Commentary on the Epistle to the Philippians," and M. Arnaud's on the "Epistle of St. Jude." There are also valuable suggestions in the "Sermons on St. Paul," by A. Monod, and in many recent treatises. The "Revue de Théologie," founded at Strasburg by M. Colani, has touched on most of the great problems arising out of the apostolic age. We have given careful consideration to these works, even when we differed from their conclusions. We must not omit to note a series of articles by M. Réville on "The First Century of the Church," published in the journal "Le Lien," (years 1856–7.) The learned work of M.

* "Geschichte der Offenbarung," von Aloïs Messmer, Freiburg in Brisgau, 1857.

† "L'Eglise et l'Empire Romain au Quatrième Siècle," par A. de Broglie, Paris, 1856.

‡ "Histoire de l'Eglise depuis Jésus Christ," par Basnage. La Haye, 1724.

§ "The Life and Epistles of St. Paul," by W. J. Conybeare and J. S. Howson, 2 vols., London, 1856.

Reuss on the "History of the Theology of the Apostolic Age," which we have constantly before us, either for purposes of consultation or of refutation, forms a kind of link between France and Germany, leading us into the much-tilled field of German criticism.*

It would be useless to attempt to catalogue the works which have accumulated during the last fifty years in Germany—that fatherland of modern theology. We will only cite the most characteristic. Let us point first to the vast treasures of exegesis—De Wette's exegetical manuals, so full and so exact; the graphic commentaries of Olshausen and Tholuck; the great works of Lücke on the "Writings of St. John," and of Bleek on the "Epistle to the Hebrews," and many other monuments of learning, so solid and so reliable that they furnish inexhaustible resources to the student of the primitive age of the Church. Passing on to the history of the period, properly so called, we place in the first rank Neander's "History of the Foundation of the Apostolic Church," † of which there is a French translation by M. Foutanès, but which is better consulted in the last German edition. In it we find all the profound piety, the breadth of view, the elevated spirituality, the historical acumen, which characterize the great historian. We owe him much, though we feel that he no longer meets all the necessities which have arisen out of the incessant discussions of the last few years. We mention, as another work belonging to the same class, the book of Dr. Philip Schaff, Professor at Mercersburg, in the United States. It displays much learning, and a remarkable talent for exposition, but, perhaps, too much theological caution, and a sort of timidity in coming to clear conclusions on delicate questions.‡ Lange's "Apostolic Age," lately published, combines the merits and the faults of this original and fertile theologian, who is as bold as he is scholarly, and who needs to be consulted with sympathy, and, at the same time, criticised with care.§ "The History of the Apostles, or the Progress of the Church from Jerusalem to Rome," by Baumgarten, is notable for attentive and searching study of the sacred documents, and as an animated exposition, which draws copiously from original sources.|| The author enables us to watch with great clearness the

---

* "Historie de la Théologie Chrétienne au Siècle Apostolique," par Ed. Reuss, Strasburg, 1852.

† "Geschichte der Pflanzung und Leitung der Christlichen Kirche durch die Apostel," von Aug. Neander, 4th edition, Hamburg, 1847.

‡ "Geschichte der Apost. Kirche," von Ph. Schaff, Leipzig, 1854.

§ "Die Geschichte der Kirche. Das Apostolische Zeitalter," von J. P. Lange, 1853.

|| "Die Apostel-Geschichte oder der Entwickelungsgang der Kirche von Jerusalem bis Rom," von Baumgarten, 1852.

transformations wrought in the apostolic Church, between its early days and the triumph of Christian universalism, without, however, exaggerating the divergences, and without representing two opposing Churches in the bosom of primitive Christianity.

The sacerdotal and hierarchical views, or rather the Irvingite idea, is represented by Thiersch. In spite of the narrowness of his principles, his "History of the Apostolic Age" is written with so much piety, skill, and delicacy that it constantly sustains the interest in his theme. Thiersch is an adversary to be opposed only with feelings of sympathy and gratitude.*

The Tübingen school has its most eminent representative in Baur, its learned head. His book on "St. Paul," and his "History of the First Three Centuries,"—especially the pages treating of the first century—comprise the whole programme of that theological school, which, after having outdone itself in Schwegler's book on the "Times Succeeding the Age of the Apostles,"† has pursued a more moderate track in the works of Hilgenfeld, and still more of Ritschl, of whom we would say, as of Thiersch, he is a useful adversary, from whom there is much to learn.‡ Ewald occupies a place apart in these discussions on the New Testament, as in those on the Old.§ We may notice, also, a polemical work by Lechler, in opposition to the Tübingen school; ‖ the "History of the Sacred Writings of the New Testament," by M. Reuss; ¶ and for Biblical theology, the excellent book of Schmid, of Tübingen.** Beyond these general indications we have carefully noted, at the foot of each page, the works quoted.

B. [See page 23.]

The Chronology of the Acts.

It is extremely difficult to fix with precision the detailed chronology of the apostolic age. It is necessary very carefully to guard against any

* "Die Kirche vom Apostolischen Zeitalter," von W. J. Thiersch, 1852.

† "Das Nachapostolische Zeitalter," von Albert Schwegler, 2 vols., Tübingen, 1846.

‡ "Entstehung der Altkatholischen Kirche," von Ritschl. Bonn, 1830. A second edition has just appeared.

§ "Die Sendschreiben des Apost. Paulus," von Ewald, 1857.

‖ "Das Apostolische und das Nachapostolische Zeitalter," von Lechler, second edition, 1857.

¶ "Die Geschichte der Heiligen Schriften des Neuen Testaments," von Ed. Reuss, second edition, 1853.

** Schmid, "Biblische Theologie," 1853.

thing arbitrary, and to be satisfied, apart from some certain data, with approximate results. Wieseler, in his learned work on the "Chronology of the Acts,"* has been, in our opinion, too much carried away by his desire to fix the date of all the principal events. He multiplies ingenious combinations, but he does not succeed in determining with certainty the order of time, because his calculations are too often based upon hypothesis. There are, however, certain fixed points to which we can hold fast, and which serve as pole-stars for the history of the primitive Church; these are its points of contact with general secular history. We thus obtain four precise dates: 1. That of the death of Herod Agrippa. Acts xii, 23. 2. The famine under Claudius. Acts xi, 28. 3. The expulsion of the Jews from Rome. Acts xviii, 2. 4. The entry of Festus upon his office.

Herod Agrippa died in the year 44, according to Josephus, ("Antiquities," books xix, ix, 2.) The same author places the great famine, which took place in the reign of Claudius, under the proconsulate of Caspius Fadus and of Tiberius Alexander. Josephus, "Antiquities," xx, v, 2. Now Caspius Fadus, having been sent into Judea after the death of Agrippa, the famine could not have commenced earlier than the end of the year 44. Indeed, it only reached Judæa some time after the death of the King, for at that time the Sidonians, under stress of the dearth, came to the Jews to be succored out of the abundance in their country. It was, then, only in the course of the year 45 that Judæa was reached by the scourge, and that Paul and Barnabas carried up to Jerusalem the offerings of the Church at Antioch.

The expulsion of the Jews from Rome Suetonius ("Claudius," 25) ascribes to Claudius. Tacitus, ("Annals," xii, 52,) who, under the name of "Mathematici," includes all the abettors of Eastern superstitions, places this expulsion in the year 52.† It would be at this time that Priscilla and Aquila quitted Rome.

The date of the entry of Festus on his office is determined in the following manner. According to Josephus, ("Antiquities," viii, xxii,) Felix, deposed for his exactions, only escaped condemnation through the intercession of Pallas. If this be so, then Pallas himself could not yet have fallen into disfavor. Now his disgrace and death took place in the year 62. But a year does not suffice for all that was accomplished during the proconsulate of Festus. Festus's entry upon his office must then be carried back at least to the year 60.

The date of the death of Herod Agrippa gives us the date of the

* "Chronologie des Apostolischen Zeitalters," von Karl Wieseler, 1848.

† "Wieseler," p. 125.

death of James, and fixes it in the year 44. The date of the famine supplies that of the journey of Paul and Barnabas to Jerusalem, to bear thither the collection made at Antioch. Clearly, the conversion of the Apostle must be placed several years earlier; for, according to Galatians i, 16–24, Paul waited three years after his conversion before he went up to Jerusalem. After that, he stayed for a time at Cæsarea and at Tarsus, (Acts ix, 30,) and then at Antioch. Acts xi, 26. These various sojourns, of which we have no precise details, may have occupied several years. The conversion of St. Paul must then be placed between the years 38 and 40. The journey to Jerusalem, of which he speaks in the Epistle to the Galatians, (Gal. ii, 1,) and which he states to have been fourteen years after his conversion, cannot be relied upon as fixing the date of the latter, since the chronological indications given by the Apostle are very vague. Compare Gal. i, 21, with Gal. ii, 1. The expulsion of the Jews from Rome, coinciding with his meeting with Priscilla and Aquila at Corinth, enables us to fix his arrival in that city in the year 52, and his appearance before Festus between 58 and 60. Thus the first period of the apostolic age extends from the year 30 to 48 or 50. The conversion of Paul took place about the year 38, and the death of Stephen about 37. The first missionary journey of Paul commences after the year 45, probably in 46, and must have concluded about 50. About this time commences the second period. The sojourn of Paul at Corinth takes place in 52, and between 52 to 58 he makes his last great journey. We shall see presently that the second period of the apostolic age probably finishes with the life of the Apostle, about the year 56.

C. [See page 23.]

On the Principal Source of the History of the Primitive Church.

Our principal source is the book known under the name of the "Acts of the Apostles." Of this book we must, first of all, prove the credibility. Its authenticity was generally acknowledged in the early Church, from the time of Irenæus. "Quoniam autem is Lucas inseparabilis fuit a Paulo, et cooperarius ejus in Evangelio, ipse fecit manifestum." Acts xvi, 10. (Irenæus, "Adv. Hæres," Book III, chap. xiv, 1.) The letter of the Church at Lyons to the Churches in Asia Minor quotes the Acts. (See Eusebius, "Hist. Ecc.," V, chap. xi.) Clement of Alexandria ascribes the Acts to Luke: *Καθὼς* καὶ ὁ Λουκᾶς ἐν ταῖς πράξεσι τῶν ἀποστόλων ἀπομνημονεύει τὸν Παῦλον λέγοντα ἄνδρες Ἀθηναῖοι. ("Stromat.," v, 588.) See also Tertullian: "Cum in eodem commentario Lucæ tertia hora orationis demonstretur." ("De jejun.," chap. x, "De Baptismo," chap. x.) Earlier than Irenæus, we find allusions in the Apostolic Fathers and in Justin Martyr to passages in the Acts. There is a striking agreement between the narrative of Luke and the manner in which these Fathers speak of the first century of the Christian Church. We may then say that the external evidence is in favor of the authenticity of the Acts. It remains to be seen if the internal evidence is as unfavorable as has been asserted. The Tübingen school has given a categorical denial to the authenticity of the book of the Acts. It regards it as a production of the second century, the object of which is to facilitate the combination of Judaizing Christians with the Christian disciples of Paul. It is not a history; it is a compromise attempted in the form of history. The author has endeavored to effect a sort of retrospective reconciliation between Peter and Paul; in doing so he has only carried out the impulse of the Church of his time, which felt it needful to efface the memory of irritating controversies. In order to attain this end, he could not do better than put into the mouth of Peter the doctrines of Paul, and tone down all that was most emphatic in the discourses of the latter. Schwegler and Baur assert, that the Paul of the Acts is not the Paul of the Epistles, who, in their view, is much more powerful in controversy.* M. Reuss, who is never untrue to his critical sagacity, assigns, as also does De Wette, its traditional date to the book of Acts; but he appears to us to make too large a concession to the Tübingen school in allowing that the history of the first century has been made to undergo, in the Acts, more or less modification, to subserve the interests of a reconciliation subsequently effected between the parties.†

Baur and Schwegler ground their theory on a supposed deep division between the Apostles, a division which they hold to have continued until their death. The refutation of this error will become apparent from the history. We shall show that there were no sharp and bitter polemics, except between St. Paul and the false teachers of Corinth and Galatia, and that if his proclamation that the Gospel was as wide as the world caused at first a certain degree of surprise, the agreement

---

* Schwegler, "Nachapostolisches Zeitalter," ii, 111. Baur, "Paulus," p. 5. "Das Christenthum, der drei erst. Jahr.," p. 112.

† Reuss, "Histoire de la Théologie Chrétienne au Siècle Apostolique," II, p. 591. "Geschichte der Heiligen Schriften des N. T.," § 210.

between him and the other Apostles was immediately realized. No place is left, therefore, for a subsequent reconciliation of men who had never been enemies. So long as the genuineness of the first Epistle of St. Peter is admitted, it will be impossible to maintain that there is any radical opposition between the two Apostles. There was no occasion for a falsification of facts on their behalf in order to show, after their death, that a good understanding had existed between them during their life. The author of the book of Acts is not an unintelligent chronicler, who does no more than furnish, as it were, the mere material, the bare facts of the history. He is a thoughtful historian, who grasps the connection of events. The picture which he paints has perspective and a horizon; the present is illuminated by the future; from the very commencement of his book, he leads us to look for the solution of disputed problems. This solution he finds in the substitution of Christian universalism for that which was peculiar to the Jewish dispensation; but if we are right in our idea, that this solution marks in reality the close of the first period of the history of the apostolic Church, he fulfilled his duty, as a historian, in leading our expectations toward it. We can discern no trace of falsification in his narrative. He does not attempt, in any way, to disguise the Judaistic character of the worship of the Church at Jerusalem; he lets us see it fairly, in its devotion to the Temple-services and adherence to all the observances of the ceremonial law. The first sermons of Peter are strongly tinged with Old Testament coloring; they show no trace of the broad spirit of Christianity; salvation appears to him still to belong first to the seed of Abraham. Acts ii, 39. The objection drawn from the difference of language used by St. Paul in the Acts and in the Epistles presents no serious difficulty. The book of the Acts purports rather to give a narration of the foundation of the Churches than to give a picture of their inner life and conflicts. It was natural that the language of Paul, the missionary, should differ somewhat from that of Paul, the controversialist. But how many times in the Acts does not his speech wax warm and eloquent, and remind us of some passages in the letters to the Corinthians and Galatians. Acts xiii, 38–42, 46–48; xxiii, 3; xxviii, 25–28.

It has been asserted that the Acts are a compilation of several documents. To us, however, there appears throughout a unity of style and of composition too striking to allow us to suppose it the work of more than one hand, and *that* the very hand which penned the third gospel.* We see no sufficient ground for granting the hypothesis

* See De Wette, "Apostol. Geschichte Einleit.," p. 4, and also the article "Lucas," in the "Encyclopédie Herzog."

that Timothy may have been the narrator of the second part of the Acts, that in which the narrator speaks as the direct witness of the events he records. Clearly the manner in which the writer speaks of Timothy contradicts such a supposition. Acts xix, 22; xx, 4.

The voice of tradition, which ascribes to Luke the composition of the Acts, appears to us the best sustained opinion; it is well known that he was one of the companions of Paul in his last journeys. Col. iv, 14; Phil. 24; 2 Tim. iv, 11. We are quite prepared to admit that he made use for the Acts, as for his Gospel, of various documents. The letters and discourses inserted in the history were probably not written from memory. The date of the composition it is impossible to fix with certainty. It appears to us that the book which closes so abruptly, must have been written before or shortly after the death of St. Paul.

D. [See page 32.]

The Miracle of Pentecost.

It is not to be denied that the narrative of St. Luke presents some serious difficulties. It is not easy, in the first place, to understand the object of the miracle, for the foreign Jews who were at Jerusalem all understood the Aramaic tongue. In the next place, the extraordinary outpouring of the Spirit does not appear in other passages of the Acts, to be accompanied with the gift of tongues. Acts x, 44. In the third place, the *γλώσσαις λαλεῖν* which is mentioned in 1 Cor. xiv, 2, is very different from the gift of tongues at the Pentecost; for the person speaking with tongues at Corinth, so far from having the privilege of being understood by strangers, needs an interpreter in his own Church. Explanations have been multiplied of this difficult problem of sacred criticism. Some, like Bilroth, have seen in the gift of tongues at the Pentecost the recovery for the moment of the primitive language of mankind. Others, like Bunsen,* suppose that the first Christians at the Pentecost spoke the usual Aramaic language, which all would comprehend, instead of the sacred tongue, the ancient Hebrew, which had till then been specially used for purposes of worship. The astonishment of the hearers would be excited by this fact, so entirely new, and, it may be added, so much in harmony with the spirit of the gospel covenant. But, in order to admit this supposition, it is necessary to set aside the sacred narrative, the purport of

* Introduction to the second English edition of Hippolytus.

which is evidently something different. Olshausen, in his commentary, likens the gift of tongues to a magnetic phenomenon. The Apostles, reading the hearts of their hearers, employed for them their own language; a strange theory, which places the inspired teacher in absolute dependence on those whom he is to teach. Neander identifies the gift of tongues at Pentecost with the gift of tongues at Corinth, and sets down as errors on the part of St. Luke those details of the narrative which do not accord with this explanation.*

For ourselves, we should be very slow to admit that, on a fact of such importance, the primitive tradition of the Church can be erroneous or inexact. We see no difficulty in believing that the miracle of the gift of tongues assumed a special character on the day of Pentecost. It was the language of ecstacy, and in this respect resembled the gift of tongues at Corinth, but was distinguished from the latter by its intelligibility. Why should not the same miracle have assumed various forms in the apostolic age? Its extraordinary and unique character on the day of Pentecost is explained by supposing that the miracle reached on that day, as it were, its mightiest development. It was a glorious completion of the divine symbolism, which we have recognized in the marvelous circumstances accompanying the first outpouring of the Spirit.

E. [See page 140.]

The Council at Jerusalem.

The question of the Council and the Conference at Jerusalem is one of those which has called forth in modern times the most lively discussions. The Tübingen school, starting with the supposition that the narrative of the Acts, (chap. xv,) and that of the Epistle to the Galatians, (chap. ii,) refer to the same fact, naturally draw conclusions adverse to St. Luke. Two leading important contradictions are pointed out between the two accounts. 1st. In the Acts the conferences are public; in the Epistle to the Galatians they are private. Baur, "Paulus," p. 115. "Das Christenth. der drei erst. Jahrhund.," pp. 52, 53. We have already replied to this objection by showing that the very nature of the questions under debate explains the coincidence of public and private conferences, When Baur declares that the silence of Paul, in the Epistle to the Galatians, as to the decision at Jerusalem, is inexplicable, he forgets that the Apostle had to treat in

* Neander, "Pflanz.," i, p. 28.

Galatia only of the question touching his own apostleship, and that, consequently, the result of the private conferences alone concerned him. Let us remember, also, that the decree issued from Jerusalem was only of transitional force. 2d. Schwegler says, that according to the account in Acts the Apostles are perfectly agreed ("Nachapost. Zeit.," i, 126,) while in the Epistle to the Galatians they appear greatly at variance among themselves. Both assertions are equally inexact. The Apostles, in the Acts, show a broad and conciliatory spirit, but it is incontestible that there is, nevertheless, a wide distance between the view of Paul and that of James. On the other hand, it is impossible to find in the Galatians any trace of a serious opposition among the Apostles. We see them, on the contrary, giving each other the right hand of fellowship. Gal. ii, 9. Great stress is laid on the slightly ironical expressions of Paul: *'Απὸ δὲ τῶν δοκούντων εἶναι τι. Οε δοκοῦντες στῦλοι εἶναι.* Gal. ii, 6–9. But the irony here is directed not against the Apostles themselves, but against those who, from a party spirit, exaggerated their apostolic authority to the depreciation of that of Paul. 3d. The Tübingen school, in order to discredit utterly the narrative of Luke, seeks to establish a contradiction between the speeches made at the Council at Jerusalem, and the results obtained. These speeches, it is said, are animated by a liberal spirit, while the result of the council sanctions the triumph of the Judaizing party. But our adversaries forget that the speech of James is not identical with that of Peter. The former represented at that time the majority of the Church; he retained more than one Jewish scruple, while at the same time strongly desiring union and conciliation. In what deliberative assembly do we not often see the vote given to the middle party, though the most advanced liberalism may have found a voice? We do not admit, however, that the council did insure a triumph to the Judaizing party. That party received a death-blow from the decision, which declared that circumcision was no longer obligatory on proselytes brought out of paganism. The Tübingen school has supported itself mainly on the second of the conditions, which were imposed on the neophytes from foreign countries—the abstaining from all impurity. While Schwegler ("N. A. I.," 127) sees in the word *πορνειά* the prohibition of second marriages, Ritschl, in his learned work, ("Entstehung der Altcatholisch. Kirche," pp. 115–126,) sees in it the interdiction of those consanguineous marriages forbidden by the Levitical law. Leviticus xviii.* But this is

* A second edition has just appeared. In it the author shows himself still further removed from the views of the Tübingen school.

attaching a very remote meaning to a very simple expression. The able theologian endeavors to show that in its essence, the decree of the Jerusalem Council forms the foundation of the "Clementines" and of the Ebionite system. But it is evident to us that the renunciation of the rite of circumcision, after the lapse of a century or more from the time of the Council, was a matter of small importance. For the Council at Jerusalem it was a large concession; a century later it was an established fact; and the significance of the victory could not be revived. Ritschl's idea appears to us, then, only admissible, supposing the discussions at the Council to be inventions, and the decree itself alone authentic. The deliberation seems to us in perfect harmony with the result. We have already replied to the objection drawn from the quarrel between Peter and Paul at Antioch.

F. [See page 203.]

On the Supposed Second Captivity of Paul.

A large number of writers, both ancient and modern, have admitted a second captivity of the Apostle Paul. Eusebius* and Jerome† support it with their testimony. Among modern writers Neander ("Pflanz.," i, 538) holds the same opinion. We are not prepared to admit it, and we adopt in this respect the views of M. Reuss‡ and of Wieseler.§ We shall confine ourselves to a refutation of Neander, who has presented with great ability all the arguments in favor of the second captivity of Paul. The learned historian does not attach much importance to the testimony of Eusebius, thus expressed:

"It is reported that after having presented his defense, the Apostle departed to continue his apostolic mission, and that he returned a second time to Rome, there to suffer martyrdom. At that time, while in bonds, his second letter to Timothy must have been written." It is clear that Eusebius does not affirm the fact; he merely says, "It is reported." It is only the echo of a tradition, of which he does not assume the responsibility. This tradition rests evidently on the famous passage of Clement of Rome, in his epistle to the Corinthians. It runs thus:

"Paul, having preached righteousness through the whole world, and

* Eusebius, "Hist. Eccles.," ii, 21.

† Hieronym., "In Esaiam," xi, 14.

‡ "Geschichte der Heiligen Schriften, N. T.," p. 125. "Revue de Théologie," 2d vol., 3d part, p. 150.

§ Wieseler, "Chronol. des Apost. Zeit.," p. 521.

having reached the uttermost parts of the West, suffered martyrdom under the emperors, thus departed from their world."* This passage appears conclusive to Neander. He insists strongly on the expression, "The uttermost parts of the West." This appears to him to point to Spain, where Paul declared his intention to preach the Gospel. Rom. xv, 24. The latter declaration does not appear to Neander as irrefragable proof, for he admits, as we do, that Paul, though an Apostle, might form a project and yet be prevented from carrying it out. Combining this declaration, however, with the testimony of Clement, he draws the conclusion that Paul was actually enabled to fulfill it. But it is necessary to ascertain if the passage of Clement has in truth the signification attached to it. Wieseler has well shown that the text bears evident traces of interpolation, and cannot be relied upon with certainty. Then, also, the tone of Clement in this portion of his first letter to the Corinthians is not that of the historian, but of the orator, who uses hyperboles of speech. When he says that Paul preached the Gospel through the whole world, he makes no claim to be taken literally, and to affirm that Paul went into Gaul or Britain. He is not less hyperbolic when he uses the expression, "The uttermost parts of the West." Was not Rome the metropolis of the Western world? To preach the Gospel at Rome, was not this to preach it to the whole of the West? The vague expression of Eusebius, already quoted, ὀγόλος ἔχει, proves that in his time it was not considered permissible to take the passage of Clement literally. It does not seem to us needful to have recourse to the too ingenious explanation of M. Reuss, who sees in this passage a bold and poetic image—a comparison of the career of Paul to that of the sun.†

The other proof adduced by Neander is founded on exegesis. He bases it on the second Epistle to Timothy, in which Paul seems to speak of his deliverance. 2 Tim. iv, 16. We see no necessity for admitting this explanation, since the deliverance of which the Apostle

* Clement, "Ep. ad Corinth.," chap. 5.

† A fragment from the canon of Muratori is also called in evidence. It runs thus: "Sed profectionem Pauli ad urbe id Spaniam proficiscentis." Bunsen, "Analecta Antinicæna," i, 139. But it is not possible to draw conclusions of any certainty from so mutilated a text. All that can be inferred from it is, that at a period even then remote, the tradition of a journey of Paul into Spain was current in the Church. It was founded evidently upon the passage Rom. xv, 24. The passage of Dionysius of Corinth, quoted by Eusebius, ("Hist. Eccles.," ii, 25,) which states that Peter and Paul founded the Church at Corinth, and then came to Rome together, has clearly no historic value.

speaks may very well be understood of the good effect produced by his first appearance before the imperial tribunal. Neander maintains that the manner in which Paul points out the heresies of Ephesus implies a recent journey to that place. 2 Tim. ii, 17. But we know how easy it was for him in the early stages of his captivity to obtain exact and frequent information as to the state of the Churches. The most plausible reason adduced by Neander is drawn from some perplexing features of the epistle, which seem to point to a recent journey of the Apostle in Asia Minor. For instance, he asks for his cloak and the parchments left at Troas. 2 Tim. iv, 13. But this may have reference to the journey from Troas, of which we read in Acts xx, 5. The parchments might be required by Paul for his defense, and he might not until this time have had an opportunity of having them brought to him. When he says (2 Tim. iv, 20) "Trophimus have I left at Miletum sick," it does not necessarily imply that he had been there himself. May we not suppose, with Wieseler, that Trophimus accompanied Paul in his journey from Asia Minor to Rome, and that when the travelers stopped at Myra in Lycia, (Acts xxvii, 5,) a town very near to Miletum, Trophimus was compelled by sickness to stop, and went on to Miletum? Paul's reference to the fact in his second letter to Timothy may be accounted for by supposing that he had need of the witness of Trophimus in the preparation for his trial, and it may be for the same reason that he speaks of Erastus, who "abode at Corinth," (2 Tim. iv, 20,) for the latter, who, we learn from Rom. xvi, 23, was one of the chamberlains of the city, might be able to render him valuable service on his trial. With reference to the reasons drawn by Neander from the date of the First Epistle to Timothy, and from that of the letter to Titus, we have already set these aside by accepting the hypothesis of a journey made by Paul into Europe, during his stay at Ephesus. We have also obviated the objection founded on the growth of heresies in Asia Minor, by proving the antiquity of those heresies, as shown in Paul's farewell address at Miletum. Thus we hold none of the arguments in favor of a second captivity of Paul to be conclusive. We see two serious objections to this hypothesis: 1. The difficulty of supposing that Paul can have obtained a regular trial from Nero, after the terrible persecution recorded by Tacitus. 2. The small probability that the main facts of the first captivity, such as the appeal to Cæsar, should have been repeated in the very same manner in the second.

G. [See page 204.]

The Epistles of St. Paul.

We admit the full authenticity of all the epistles to which the name of Paul is attached, with the exception of the Epistle to the Hebrews, which we attribute to Apollos. There are some about which no question at all is raised. The Epistles to the Galatians, to the Romans, and those to the Corinthians, are beyond a doubt. Baur himself admits their authenticity. The two Epistles to the Thessalonians have been attacked by some on the ground that they are insignificant, wanting in special interest, and give in detail, and without occasion, specific views of prophecy.* We have already replied to the second objection by showing that the unhealthy excitement of some Christians at Thessalonica—who, under pretext of looking for the return of Jesus Christ, abandoned themselves to indolence—required from Paul some enlarged reference to prophecy. He must needs guard against one of the most serious abuses of his doctrine. We disallow utterly the objection founded on the want of interest and originality in these epistles—an objection which Baur urges in a general manner against all the minor epistles of the Apostle. A mere impression cannot be discussed. We appeal to the witness of the Christian conscience. The Epistle to the Ephesians is rejected by the same critic, because of its resemblance to the Epistle to the Colossians.† But M. Reuss has perfectly shown that their resemblance is not as complete as is asserted. "Geschichte H. Schr., N. T.," p. 102. It is not surprising that the Apostle, writing to Churches placed in similar circumstances, should have addressed to them the same counsels. Baur urges, in objection to the genuineness of these letters, certain Gnostic tendencies, which he believes he discovers in the writer.‡ He thus characterizes the metaphysical expansion of the doctrine as to the person of Jesus Christ; he makes much of the word πλήρωμα. Col. i, 20. But in its essence the doctrine set forth in these letters is as far removed as possible from Gnostic dualism, and from the doctrine of emanation. Jesus Christ is not the first emanation of the Godhead; he possesses it in its fullness. Baur makes the same objection to the Epistle to the Colossians as to the pastoral epistles;§ he asserts that the heresies pointed out by the author of these letters do not appear till the second century. Let us observe, first, that the learned critic finds in these

* Baur, "Paulus," pp. 250–259.

† Ibid, p. 481.

‡ Ibid., pp. 423, 424.

§ Ibid., p. 493.

epistles that which is not there. He sees in them a complete description of Gnosticism, while the writer confines himself entirely to general features, such as belong to a nascent heresy. The discovery of the "Philosophoumena" has thrown a flood of light on this much controverted point, and the picture which we have presented of the Churches founded by St. Paul is the best reply we can make to the attacks of the Tübingen school. Too much attention cannot be bestowed on that part of M. Reuss's "History of the New Testament" which takes up this delicate question. In our opinion, it is a masterpiece of wise and learned criticism. (See "Gesch. der H. Schr., N. T.," page 113.)

The objections brought against the epistles of Paul are drawn, as we have seen, from internal evidence. No one denies that their authenticity was unanimously recognized in the third century. Placing ourselves on the ground occupied by our adversaries, it is impossible to us to discover in the disputed epistles a single point not in accordance with the character of the Apostle, and with the history of his life. What shall we say of the extravagance of a criticism which goes so far as to assert that Paul's comparison of the Christian to a soldier, (2 Tim. ii, 3,) being peculiarly in agreement with the taste of the writers of the second century, (by whom it is frequently used,) cannot belong to the first? One is surprised to see a man so sagacious as De Wette bringing the charge of pride against the sublime close of the Second Epistle to Timothy. De Wette's "Commentary on 2 Tim. iv, 8."

H. [See page 206.]

On the Epistles of James and of Jude.

The epistles of James and of Jude have been placed by Eusebius ("Hist. Eccles.," iii, 25) among the "Antilegomena," or disputed writings. But we see no sufficient reason for this assertion, and the external evidence is entirely in their favor. The doubts must have arisen later from doctrinal causes, probably in the case of James from the supposed opposition between his doctrine and that of Paul, and in that of Jude from his quotation from the apocryphal book of Enoch. The Church of Syria had admitted the epistle of the former into its canon. Clement of Rome seems to refer to it: "Epistle to the Corinth.," chap. x. Origen quotes it: "Commentar. in Joannem," vol. xix, iv, 406. Clement of Alexandria quotes the Epistle of Jude. "Stromat.," iii, 434; "Pædagog," iii, 239; Origen, "Commentar. in Matth.," iii, 463. (See, for the Epistle of Jude, the very complete "Commentary" of M. Arnaud.)

I. [See page 213.]

ON THE SECOND EPISTLE OF PETER.

We have spoken of only one Epistle of Peter, because it seems to us impossible to admit, with any certainty, the authenticity of the second. It is noteworthy that it is only mentioned for the first time by Clement of Alexandria, and even that quotation is not direct. Eusebius, "Hist. Eccles.," vi, 24. Origen, who cites it, ("Comment. in Joannem," iv, 135,) is the first and only one of the "Fathers" of the third century who clearly appeals to its authority. The Church of Syria, the testimony of which is of great value, did not acknowledge this epistle, and Eusebius ("Hist. Eccles.," iii, 55) quotes it among the "Antilegomena." The doubt was current as late as the fourth century, for Jerome says, "Scripsit Petrus duas Epistolas, quæ Catholicæ nominantur, quarum secunda a plerisque ejus esse negatur propter styli cum priore dissonantiam." "De Viris illustribus," c. i.

On the other hand, the First Epistle of Peter has in its favor the highest possible testimony. Eusebius, "Hist. Eccles.," iii, 39; iv, 14; Irenæus, "Contr. Hæres," iv, 9, 2; Clement of Alexandria, "Stromat.," iii, 73; Tertull., "C. Scorp.," i, 2.

If we proceed to the examination of the internal evidences, they are very unfavorable to the authenticity of the Second Epistle of Peter. 1st. The style has scarcely any analogy to that of the first epistle. 2d. The dependent relation of this epistle to that of Jude is very marked; the author constantly takes up the text of Jude as a theme to be worked out. (See the parallelism of the two epistles in M. Arnaud's "Commentary on Jude.") 3d. The writer insists upon his apostolic degree with a strange mannerism, resembling that of the apocryphal writings, (i, 13–18.) 4th. He quotes the collection of Paul's epistles as forming part of the canon of the New Testament, which had no existence at this time, (2 Peter iii, 16;) in the year 64 or 65, he speaks of these epistles as being among the number of canonical Scriptures; this is an extraordinary anachronism.

There is nothing incredible in the pretension of the unknown author to pass for Peter. The whole apocryphal literature of the second and third centuries is full of fictitious scriptures, and the name of Peter is that most commonly employed. May we not suppose that an orthodox Christian, at the close of the second century, indignant at the supposed opposition between Peter and Paul, appealed to in the "Clementines," composed this epistle to set forth their deep harmony, making use, perhaps, of some fragments of the preaching of Peter which tradition may have preserved, for the commencement of the epistles? Calvin, in his embarrassed comments on this letter, betrays a doubt, which he is unable to dispel from his own mind or from the minds of his readers: "Cæterum," he says, in his introduction, "de auctore non constat, nunc Petri nunc apostoli nomini promiscue mihi permittam." "As there is no certainty about the author, I shall permit myself to say indifferently, Peter or the Apostle." Let us observe that there is nothing in this epistle in contradiction to other canonical writings; it contains no special or new revelation. It is better frankly to express a doubt as to its authenticity than to sanction the idea that Christian belief is bound absolutely to the traditional canon fixed by the Church of the fourth century.

J. [See page 232.]

On the Author of the Epistle to the Hebrews.

It is not disputed by any, that, while the Western Church for nearly three centuries denies that Paul is the author of the Epistle to the Hebrews, the doctors of the Church of Alexandria are almost unanimous in attributing the epistle to him. But the opinion of the West, and of Rome in particular, has great weight in the question, since that Church must be supposed to have had most authentic information of all that related to the Apostle Paul, and especially of every thing connected with his captivity. Clement of Rome, makes constant allusions to the Epistle to the Hebrews. How would it be possible that he should never have named its author, if he had known who he was, and especially if he had known him to be the Apostle Paul? It is easy to understand how the Church of Alexandria should have arrived by a philosophical synthesis, natural to its genius, at the conclusion that Paul was the writer of an epistle which bears the impress of his thought. The internal evidences which vindicate the judgment of the Western Church are admirably set forth in Bleek's "Commentary." The following are the principal: 1st. The striking difference of style; the diversity of opinion on this point seems to us inexplicable. 2d. The relation of dependence, in which the author places himself, upon the immediate witnesses of Jesus Christ. Heb. ii, 3. Now, Paul never took this position. One of the great objects of his polemics against his adversaries always was to establish that he was in the same rank with the first Apostles. 3d. If the ideas of the writer have much in common with those of Paul, they, nevertheless, bear, in the detail of their exposition, the impress of a different individuality. In favor of the hypothesis which ascribes the Epistle to the Hebrews to Paul, the two following passages are quoted: 1st. *Γινωσκετε τὸν ἀδελφὸν ἡμῶν Τιμόθεον ἀπολελυμένον.* Heb. xiii, 23. It is inferred, from the close relations of Paul and Timothy, that the former was the writer of these words. But it is impossible to base a whole argument on so trifling a point of detail. For Paul was not the only person who was in connection with Timothy. One of Paul's other disciples might very naturally use such an expression. The sense given to the word *ἀπολελυμένον* is of very little weight, whether it signify that *Timothy is absent*, or whether it contain the idea that *he is just set at liberty*, this difference of interpretation in no way affects the solution of the question. 2d. The second passage adduced as an argument is Heb. xiii, 24. It is asserted that the expression, "They of Italy salute you," shows that the epistle was written at Rome; but do not these words, on the contrary, seem to convey the idea that the writer is not in Italy, since he sees in the qualification, *οἱ ἀπὸ τῆς Ἰταλίας*, a special designation?

The hypothesis, which ascribes the Epistle to the Hebrews to Apollos, is the most plausible. He was certainly a warm advocate of Paul's principles; he was well versed in the Scriptures; he was at Alexandria, where great prominence was given to the typical and allegorical style. He was a man eloquent and learned. All these various characteristics are remarkably displayed in the Epistle to the Hebrews.

K. [See page 235.]

Diversity of Opinions as to the Theology of the Apostolic Age.

We have presented the system of the Tübingen school under its most moderate form, as it is set forth in the last book of Baur, "Das Christenthum der drei ersten Jahrhunderte." Tübingen, 1853, pp. 43-151.

The book of Schwegler, often quoted by us, "Das Nachapostolische Zeitalter," (Tübingen, 1840,) is much more arbitrary in the use of internal evidence. His fundamental idea is, that the Christian doctrine of the third century was formed by successive transformations of Ebionitism. Another disciple of Baur—Ritschl—in his book entitled, "Entstehung der altcatholischen Kirche," (Bonn, 1850,) starts from a hypothesis quite opposed to that of Schwegler. In his view, the dogmatic system of the third century was not formed by Ebionitism, but by Paulinism, the normal development of the doctrine of Jesus Christ. He supposes Judæo-Christianity, on the other hand, to have been smitten with absolute dogmatic sterility, and those of its adherents, who did not fall in with Paulinism, to have formed the Ebionite sect—a party in the rear of advancement, and not the nucleus of the Church. A second edition of this learned work has just appeared, in which there is a very perceptible modification of the author's views, more especially, however, with reference to the teaching of Christ, No one can place M. Reuss's learned book, "The History of Christian Theology in the Second Century," (2d vol., Strasburg, 1852,) under the banner of the Tübingen school. The author, whose conscientious works we have already often mentioned, appears to us to have made too many concessions to the system, which supposes a complete ecclesiastical and dogmatical polity in the first century. He has exaggerated the difference between Judæo-Christianity and Paulinism. The great complaint which we make of M. Reuss's book is, that he misconceives the unique, exceptional, and creative character of the apostolic theology. We have endeavored to show how we can, with the Church of every age, admit this without falling into mechanical theopneustics. The work of Schmid, "Biblische Theologie des N. T.," (Stuttgart, 1853,) has been a useful aid to us, as also Neander's "Apostolic Age," 2 vols. The portion of Schaff's book, which refers to apostolic doctrine, (pp. 606–638,) is only an extract from Neander.

L. [See page 428.]

On the Authenticity and the Date of the Apocalypse.

Notwithstanding the able and learned dissertations of Lücke on the passages of "the Fathers" which support the authenticity of the Apocalypse, those passages appear to us conclusive. Either external evidence must be denied all value, or it must be admitted to be conclusive in this case. Setting aside the passages of the writings of the apostolic "Fathers," which, in a general way, remind us of the Apocalypse, (for instance, the sixth chapter of Polycarp's "Epistle to the Ephesians," where mention is made of the prophets, who had declared the coming of the Lord Jesus Christ,) it is clear to us that Papias sought in it support for his millenarian views. Andreas, a writer of the fifth century, quoted, in explanation of Papias, Rev. xii, 7. Andreas, "Præf. ad Comment. in Apoc." Justin Martyr, who wrote about the year 139, cites it positively as the Revelation of John. "Dial. cum Tryph.," p. 179. According to Eusebius, ("Hist. Eccles.," iii, 26,) Melito must have written a commentary on the Revelation. The allusions to this book are plain in the letter of the Church of Lyons to the Churches of Asia Minor. Eusebius, "Hist. Eccles.," v, 1. The testimony of Irenæus, ("Contr. Hæres.," iv, 20;) of Clement of Alexandria, ("Stromat.," vi, 66;) of Tertullian, ("Adv. Marc.," iii, 14;) and of Origen, (see Eusebius, "Hist. Eccles.," vi, 25,) is, without any sort of hesitation, in favor of the authenticity of the Apocalypse.

The first doubts on this subject were expressed by the sect of the *Alogi*, who denied the divinity of Jesus Christ. These doubts were carried further by Caius, and finally by Dionysius of Alexandria, (Eusebius, vii, 25,) and more or less confirmed by Eusebius. But it is only needful to study the grounds taken up by Dionysius, in order to be convinced that he reasons entirely from *à priori* arguments, and that it is fear of the *chiliasts*, or millenarians, which leads him to throw doubt upon the book of the Revelation.

Is the internal evidence in truth as adverse as is asserted? We think not. We admit that there are great differences in substance and in form between the Gospel of John and the Revelation, but there are also striking analogies. The differences seem to us to have been exaggerated by Lücke and Reuss,* as well as by the Tübingen school, which exults in the asserted Judaism of St. John, in order to dispute the authorship of the fourth gospel. Baur † goes so far as to see in it a sort of Judaistic libel on St. Paul. Hengstenberg falls into the opposite extreme.‡

Stress is laid first on the difference of style and on the Hebraic coloring of the Apocalypse. This difference is real; it is explained in part by the fact that the Book of the Revelation is, from its very

* Lücke, "Offenbarung Johannes," pp. 707–744. Reuss, "Théologie du Siècle Apostolique, vol. i, p. 303.

† Baur, "Das Christenthum der drei erst. Jahrh.," p. 75; Schwegler, work quoted, ii, p. 247.

‡ Hengstenberg, "Offenbarung des Heiligen Johannes." Berlin. 1849.

nature, much more dependent on Old Testament prophecy, the vivid images of which it constantly reproduces. This explanation, however, is not alone sufficient, and we are fully convinced that the Revelation cannot have been written at the same date as the Gospel and Epistles.

Three points are especially insisted upon in proof of the difference between the Revelation and the other writings of John. 1st. The prophecy, properly so called, or the view of the future, is different. In the one case, it is said, every thing is materialized—resurrection, judgment, triumph, condemnation, Antichrist; to the author of the Apocalypse, all this is earthly and external, while to the Evangelist every thing is spiritual. Resurrection in the fourth gospel stands for conversion; judgment is the separation of light and darkness. Opposition to Christ is not personified in the form of a man. It is a condition of mind.* Lücke himself does not admit this strongly-marked opposition. He allows that there is, in the Gospel, an element corresponding to apocalyptic prophecy. He thinks, firstly, that even the Evangelist refers to a resurrection, a judgment in the true sense, which is to be the actual close of the religious history of mankind.† John v, 21; vi, 39; xi, 24. Only in the Gospel and in the Epistles this closing scene is not directly external, as, in the Apocalypse, it is in its first significance spiritual; the moral precedes the final judgment. We have here, then, a progression in revelation, but we deny that there is any contradiction. 2d. It is asserted that the Gospel is anti-Judaic, while the Apocalypse is said to be of a profoundly Judaizing tendency.

The opposition of the Gospel of John to Judaism must not be exaggerated. Do we not read in it these words, "Salvation is of the Jews?" John iv, 22. Has it not been often remarked with what scrupulous care the fourth Evangelist endeavors to show the harmony of Old Testament prophecy with the facts to which it refers? In this respect John almost rivals Matthew. It has been far too much forgotten, in speaking of the Judaism of the Revelation, that the symbolism of a prophet of the first century must necessarily be borrowed from the Old Testament. The colors which he must use were, so to speak, already prepared for him. Besides, the author of the Apocalypse recognizes very distinctly Christian universalism, and was not that the essential point? The twelve tribes of which he speaks (vii, 5-9) cannot represent exclusively the chosen people, since the great multitude around the throne of the Lamb belongs to every tribe,

* This opinion is maintained by M. Réville, "Revue de Théologie," 1855; pp. 361, 362.

† Lücke, "Offenbarung," p. 178.

and nation, and kindred, and tongue. Paul had already designated the Church "the Israel of God." Gal. vi, 16.*

3d. It is maintained that the doctrine of the author of the Revelation is totally at variance with that of the author of the Gospel. And first, Jesus, it is said, is not represented as the Word of God, but only as the great revealer; but what, then, is conveyed by those hymns to the Lamb, which blend his name in common adoration with that of God? Rev. v, 13; xiv, 3, 4.

Even those who pretend to discover in the Apocalypse the notion of salvation by works, as opposed to the true Christian doctrine, are constrained to admit that there are few books of the New Testament in which redemption by the blood of Christ is more clearly taught. Rev. i, 5; vii, 14. How is it possible to reconcile such declarations with the idea of a simple recompense for good works? The Judaizing character of the Apocalypse is especially pointed out in that part of the book in which the martyrs are represented as crying to God to be avenged for their blood shed upon the earth. Rev. vi, 10; xiii, 10; xiv, 10, 11. How, it is asked, can this idea of vengeance be harmonized with the conception of love so beautifully set forth in the Gospel and Epistles? Let it not be forgotten that love implies holiness, and that the law of the universe, to which a sanction is attached, cannot be violated with impunity. Condemnation is spoken of in almost every page of the gospel, and we cannot forget the mysterious words of the first epistle as to the unpardonable sin. 1 John v, 16, 17. We admit that this element of justice is set forth in the Apocalypse under the form of ancient prophecy; but it embodies, nevertheless, an immortal verity, though without giving it its highest and most complete expression. This is one of the reasons which convince us that the Revelation cannot have been written at the same period as the Gospel. With reference to the immediate expectation of the return of the Lord, (i, 3; xii, 12; xxii, 10,) this does not at all go beyond that which was common in the writings of St. Paul, and among all the Christians of the first century. There is, then, no contradiction between John the Evangelist and the writer of the Apocalypse, and we do not find ourselves in the dilemma stated by M. Reuss, that if St. John wrote the one, he cannot have written the other. "Gesch. Schr., N. T.," p. 147. On the contrary, there are striking analogies between the two books; in both we note the tender and pathetic, often melancholy tone, which renders the writings of John so touching; the same love for the person of Jesus Christ, the same hatred of

* Lücke, "Offenbarung," p. 739.

heresy. Can we not recognize the son of thunder, the impassioned opponent of Cerinthus, in every page of the book of Revelation?

Though we concur in the belief of the authenticity of the Apocalypse, we are not, however, prepared to admit the traditional date for its composition. We have already pointed out several reasons which, from a doctrinal point of view, make us demur to this. We shall not recur to these. It is not, as we have shown, that we charge the writer of the Revelation with a rude Judaism, as has been done by others.* No, we discern in it a divine revelation full of wealth and beauty. Let us not forget, however, that the revelations of God have been progressive, even in the new covenant. It is clear, for example, that as regards doctrinal fullness, there is a wide disparity between the Epistle of James and that of Paul to the Ephesians. God always takes account of human receptivity. There is, then, no reason for surprise if the revelations granted to the same man, at two different periods of his life, manifest a progression of light, while they, nevertheless, rest on the same basis of truth. We admit, however, without hesitation, that if the testimony of history compelled us to place the Apocalypse in the reign of Domitian, we should at once accept the traditional date, setting aside our own judgment. But there is no such necessity; the sole testimony of the second century in favor of this hypothesis is that of Irenæus. "The Apocalyptic vision," he says, "took place not long before our day, but a short time before our generation, under Domitian."† Clement of Alexandria speaks only of some tyrant, under whom John was exiled to Patmos.‡ Origen calls him the King of the Romans.§ Eusebius and St. Jerome echo the statement of Irenæus.|| Epiphanius is the first who differs from Irenæus as to the name of the tyrant or king who persecuted St. John. According to him it was Claudius who banished the Apostle to Patmos.¶ Tertullian places the exile of John under the reign of Nero, who, he says, after having him plunged in a bath of boiling

---

* This is the opinion of M. Réville, who, placing the composition of the Apocalypse before the destruction of Jerusalem, lays the strangest illusions of Judæo-Christianity to the charge of St. John.

† *Οἰδὲ γαρ πρὸ πολλοῦ χρονοῦ ἑώραθη, πρὸς τῷ τέλει τῆς Δομετιανοῦ ἀρχῆς.* Irenæus, "Contr. Hæres.," v, 30.

‡ *Ἐπειδὴ γὰρ τοῦ τυράννου τελευτησαντος.* Clement of Alexandria, "Quis dives," § 42.

§ Origen, "Opera," III, p. 719.

|| Eusebius, "Hist. Eccles.," iii, 18, 20, 23. St. Jerome, "De viris illustr.," IX.

¶ *Μετὰ τὴν αὐτοῦ ἀπὸ τῆς Πάτμου ἐπάνοδον τὴν επὶ Κλαυδίου γενομένην Καισαρος.* Epiphanius, "Ad. Hæres.," li, 12.

oil, banished him to Patmos.* The last two writers are evidently misinformed, but they prove to us that the tradition as to the date of John's exile was not generally accepted by the Church in their time. Nor was it so several centuries later; for Andreas, in his commentary on Rev. vi, 12, observes that some interpreters saw in this passage a prophecy of the destruction of Jerusalem. Hengstenberg, in order to prove that the Revelation was written under Domitian, dwells upon the internal condition of the seven Churches. He thinks it impossible to suppose such a growth of heresies before the close of the apostolic age. i, 13. But what, then, does he make of the pastoral epistles, and how does he not see that he is thus furnishing negative criticism with weapons to attack them?

From the study of the question we draw the conclusion that it is not possible to determine with exactness, by means of external evidence, the date of the composition of the Apocalypse. We are, therefore, compelled to give full weight to the internal evidence. We have already observed that the doctrinal character of the book is adverse to its traditional date. If, now, we sum up its historical statements, we shall find that they give some indications as to the time of its composition. Lücke and Reuss see one such indication in the eleventh chapter, where the sacred writer is bidden to measure the temple.† In their view, this passage should be taken literally, and would imply that Jerusalem could not then have been destroyed; whence it would follow that the book must have been written before the year 70. But it seems to us impossible to be satisfied with a literal interpretation. We think, with Thiersch,‡ that it is not possible to suppose John giving such flagrant contradiction to the prophecies of the Saviour, which declared the destruction of Jerusalem and of the temple. Matt. xxiv, 1, 2. Then has not Lücke himself admitted that, with John, the Church is the Israel of God? Does not the temple, then, represent the Church itself in its outward constitution? That the temple has this symbolic value appears from Rev. i, 13, where the seven candlesticks of the sanctuary at Jerusalem represent the seven Churches to which Jesus Christ addresses himself. The date of the Apocalypse is not to be sought in the eleventh chapter of the book, but rather in its general coloring.

It is to us evident that the Apostle wrote a few years after the terrible persecution under Nero. It is idle to draw any parallel between the persecutions under Domitian, and that first truly infernal explo-

* "In insulam relegatus." Tertullian, "De Præscript.," xxxvi.
† Lücke, "Offenbar.," p. 827.
‡ Thiersch, book quoted, p. 237.

sion of pagan hatred against the Church. Let it be observed, further, that the sacred writer speaks only of Roman persecutions; he has ever in view the city of the seven hills. Now, was it not under Nero that in the first century Babylon the impure became drunk with the blood of the saints? The thirteenth and seventeenth chapters of the Apocalypse carry us into the midst of the Roman world. The beast in those two chapters represents the Roman power, for it is ridden by the "woman arrayed in purple and scarlet," who is the great harlot of the ancient world; and the seven heads of the beast correspond evidently to the seven hills of Rome. It is, then, in our opinion, a grave mistake to see in these seven heads a succession of monarchies, as in the book of Daniel. They might rather represent the succession of various forms of Roman government, but even this would be a forced interpretation. The seven heads, after representing the seven hills, represent seven kings, seven Roman kings, that is, seven emperors. One of these heads has a peculiar power, this is the Antichristian power, *par excellence*, antichrist in person. Now, this head, which has been mortally wounded, can be nothing else than an emperor who has fallen by a violent death. It is the fifth emperor, Nero. *He was and is not.* "Wounded to death," this head is yet to be healed and to reappear with greater power than before. xiii, 3. This feature recalls the opinion so prevalent in the Roman empire and in the Church, that Nero was not dead, but was to appear again. The ancient Church long regarded him as Antichrist.* This is a very important fact for the interpretation of the Revelation. Does it signify that the sacred writer thus sanctioned an absurd legend so soon to be falsified by fact? Assuredly not; but, as Thiersch† has observed, he has made use of the element of truth lurking in the

* "Nero primus omnium persecutus Dei servos, dejectus itaque fastigio imperii nusquam repente compariuit; ut ne sepulturæ quidem locœs in terra tam malu bestiæ appareret. Unde illum quidam deliri credunt esse translatum ac vivum reservatum, sibylla dicente matricidum profugum a finibus esse venturum ut qui primus persecutus est idem etiam persequatur et Antichristi præcedat adventum." Lactantius, "De Morte persecut.," chap. ii; Augustin, "Civ. Dei," xx, 19; Jerome, "In Daniel," xi, 28. See also the fourth book of the "Sibylline Oracles," v, 106, and the vision of Isaiah in Ethiopia. Victorinus, (2d century,) and Commodianus, (3d century,) think that Nero will be himself Antichrist. The idea of the return of Nero is further expressed in pagan writers. Suetonius, "Nero," 40, 57; Tacitus, "Historia," i, 2; Dio Cassius, lxiv, 9. See Reuss's "Theology of the Apostolic Age," i, 324. Lücke, "Offenbar.," p. 834.

† "In der Volksage selbst liegt eine Wahrheit." Thiersch, work quoted, p. 243.

legend, which was inspired by a sort of prophetic instinct. Opposition to Christianity in one period is the type of that in another. That which the Church saw in Nero it will see again; Nero, or rather the spirit of Nero, (brutal hatred of the Gospel,) will reappear.

The combat is not finished, it has only commenced, and the first century is a faint image of the true Antichrist. What is there here unworthy of the Revelation? Is not the symbol admirably chosen? Do we not know that prophecy has always a primary signification, which, however, is capable of progressive and indefinite expansion? It is certain that the idea that Nero was Antichrist was widely diffused throughout the ancient Church; the expectation of his return took a materialized form, but its origin may be traced to this passage in the Apocalypse. It is not more surprising to find John bringing out the true meaning of a legend, than to find Jude quoting the Apocrypha, or Job speaking of the crooked serpent. xxvi, 13. That which is of importance here is to avoid a literalism which would make John the mere echo of a popular superstition. Of little consequence are the symbols employed by the prophet, provided only his prophecy be true. Did not the last prophets of the New Testament use without hesitation the symbolism of Chaldæa? and did they not convey through this medium divine ideas? We have now before our eyes, in Paris and in London, those huge animals of monstrous forms which were the objects of absurd superstition at Babylon and the sublime types of Jewish prophecy.

We have not yet spoken of the ingenious hypothesis of M. Reuss on the number of the beast, (666,) in which he says:

"We think with Lücke* and De Wette† that it is more natural to look for a Greek than a Hebrew name in a book written in Greek. The ancient hypothesis of Irenæus, who read in it *Latinus*, is very satisfactory; it is sustained also by the relation of the numbers to the letters. Nero is not considered solely as an individual, but as the personification of the Roman power. The spirit of Nero, which is the true genius of paganism and of the Roman empire, the eighth king who comes of the seven, the *Latinus par excellence*, is to reappear among them, more terrible still. This prophecy received its first realization in the persecutions excited by the succeeding emperors; it is to be yet more fearfully fulfilled in the end of time. John is not in error."

Several commentaries on the Apocalypse have recently appeared in

---

* Lücke, "Offenb.," p. 833.
† De Wette, "Commentar. in Apoc."

Germany. The most important is that of Auberlin, "Der Prophet Daniel und die Offenbarung Johannis in ihrem gegenseitigen Verhältniss betrachtet," von Carl Aug. Auberlin. Second ed., Basel, 1857. The writer follows the præterist system, which pretends to find all modern history narrated in anticipation in the Apocalypse. He displays much learning, piety, and subtilty in the exposition of his theory. The woman of the twelfth chapter is in his system the Church, surrounded with the divine light under the figure of the sun, and having under her feet the light of this world, set forth by the moon, which receives light without possessing it. This Church, under her ancient form in Judaism, has given birth to the Christ, who has driven the demons out of heaven, these having hitherto occupied one of its regions. She extends her power in the pagan world, which is represented by the desert. Rev. xii, 6. The devil raises a fearful persecution, (xii, 13;) vanquished the first time, he casts forth upon her the floods of the barbarian invasion, like a great inundating stream. xii, 15. But the earth opens her mouth and swallows this flood; the barbarous peoples are brought into the Roman empire and are Christianized by the Church.

The beast of the thirteenth chapter is the temporal power. If the Apocalypse gives it seven heads, it is to represent its attempt to imitate the divine power, of which seven is the symbolic number. But it fails in this attempt, for in chap. xiii, 11, an eighth head is added; this is enough to denote its incapacity to reproduce the divine power. The number 666 pronounces its condemnation. In fact, the number six always symbolizes the judgment of God, for in the scene of the seven cups, the seven trumpets, and the seven thunders, the sixth link introduces the most terrible visitations of Heaven, which assure the triumph of truth. Further, the number six is the half of the number twelve, the symbolic number of the Church, and it indicates the divided condition of the temporal power. The number 666, by multiplying the number six, prophesies a terrible access to the condemnation of the world. The author sees in the seven hills and the seven heads the succession of monarchies. The fallen Church is set forth in the harlot of the thirteenth chapter. The beast, the image of modern powers, seemed vanquished when it was wounded. xiii, 3. This indicated a check to the evil power, and the Christianization of the world. But its healing shows that the modern, like the ancient world, has fallen again under the power of the devil. One last victory will be permitted to this diabolic power, (xiii, 7,) and the drama of history shall close with the millennium taken in the real sense.

Such a system seems to us to refute itself; the symbolism of numbers on which it hinges, carries the arbitrary beyond all limit. Proceeding thus, we may see any thing or any body in the Revelation.

Ebrard, in the commentary which he published last year, upholds the old Protestant view. The Roman power is depicted in the thirteenth and fourteenth chapters, and Papal Rome in the seventeenth chapter. The system of MM. Elliot and Gaussen is found complete in Grübe's commentary on the Apocalypse. "Versuch einer historischen Erklärung der Offenbarung Johannis." Heidelberg, 1857.

M. [See page 429.]

AUTHENTICITY OF THE GOSPEL AND EPISTLES OF JOHN.

We cannot here go over the whole discussion that has arisen as to the author of the fourth gospel. Its authenticity was impugned with some reserve by Bretschneider in his "Probabilia." That theologian maintained that between the gospel of John and the synoptics the difference was absolute, especially in reference to the discourses of the Saviour. Strauss, in his "Life of Christ," proceeded to set forth three differences in support of his hypothesis of an evangelical mythology. Baur and his school have taken other ground in attacking the authenticity of the fourth gospel. It is, in their view, the last result of the struggle between Paulinism and Ebionitism, and, as it were, a treaty of peace between the two systems, signed upon the heights of Alexandrine Gnosticism. Baur, "Das Christ., der drei erst. Jahrh., 133. Such a reconciliation could only take place at an advanced date, when the combatants had become exhausted, that is to say, about the end of the second century. The most remarkable work in favor of its authenticity is Lücke's introduction to his commentary on the Gospel. All that M. Reuss has written on this subject, whether in his book, "The History of the New Testament," or in his "History of Christian Theology in the Apostolic Age," or in a separate dissertation, has great value. For ourselves, no point of sacred criticism seems to us better established than the authenticity of the fourth gospel. Lücke, in his commentary, had already shown how much favor is in its eternal testimony. Pp. 41–81. It appears to us evident that Justin Martyr makes numerous allusions to passages of the fourth gospel. "Dial. cnm Tryph.," 88, 114, 108. His treatment of the doctrine of the "Word" reminds us of the prologue of John's gospel. He even goes so far as to call Jesus Christ μονογενής, the only Son.

Id. 105. Comp. "Apol.," i, 33. There is an equally evident allusion in the "Apology of Athenagoras," written about the year 177. It is only necessary to read the tenth chapter to be convinced of this. The allusions are also numerous in the letter of the Church of Lyons to the Churches of Asia Minor. Eusebius, "Hist. Eccles.," v, 1. The rejection of the Gospel of John by the *Alogi* was exclusively founded on doctrinal grounds. Origen tells us that Celsus, who wrote about the middle of the second century, sought, in the fourth gospel, for weapons to use against the Christians. "Contr. Celsum," v, 52; i, 67; allusion to John ii, 18.

The first direct testimony is that of Theophilus of Antioch, who lived in the year 168. We read in his book to Antolicus, ii, 22: Ὅθεν διδάσκουσιν ἥμας ἅγιαι γραφαὶ καὶ πάντες όι πνευματοφόροι, ἐξ ὧν Ἰωάννης λέγεί Ἐν ἀρχῃ ἦν ὁ λόγος. The testimony of Irenæus is not less precise. "Contr. Hæres.," iii, 1. Comp. Tertullian, "Adv. Marconem," iv, 2, 5. The mention of the Apocalypse in the canon of Muratori proves to us that the Gospel was received into the canon of the Church of Rome at the commencement of the third century. From that time, all the "Fathers," without exception, confirm the apostolic origin of the fourth gospel. Origen, about the year 222, comments on it. The Peshito version translates it, and Eusebius ("Hist. Eccles.," iii, 24, 25) places it, without hesitation, among the "Homologoumena."

The external evidence derived from the testimony of the orthodox Church is, then, very strongly in favor of the authenticity of the fourth gospel. It will appear decisive and irrefragable, if we take also into account the testimony of heresy itself. The discovery of the "Philosophoumena" has decided the question. St. Hippolytus makes us acquainted with the first "Ophites," who are the immediate successors of the heretics of the apostolic age, and who lived in the first quarter of the second century. All know the doctrine of the "Word;" it occupies a prominent place in the rough outlines of their systems; all quote positively the fourth gospel. Thus Hippolytus attributes to the "Naassenians," the most ancient of the Ophites, declarations like this: Τὸ γεγεννημένον ἐκ τῆς σαρκὸς, σάρξ ἐστι, καὶ τὸ γεγεννημένον ἐκ τοῦ πνεύματος, πνεῦμά ἐστιν. "Philosoph.," p. 106; quotation from John iii, 16. The Ophites *Perates* made the same use of the Gospel of John: Τõυτό ἐστι, φησὶ, τὸ εἰρημένον. A quotation of John iii, 17, follows. "Philosoph.," p. 125. Basilidès, the famous heretic, who wrote between the years 120 and 130, quotes St. John positively in the fragment reproduced by Hippolytus: Τοῦτο, φησὶν, ἐστι τὸ λεγόμενον ἐν τοῖς εὐαγγελίοις Ἦν τὸ φῶς το ἀληθινόν. "Philosoph., p. 232. (See Bunsen on this point; "Hippolytus," i, 33, 36.) We cannot comprehend how the significance of such passages can be questioned, and how the hypothesis of the Tübingen school can stand against them.*

Let us proceed to the internal evidence. It appears to us, first, that there is a striking analogy between what we know of St. John and the character of the fourth gospel. One feels that the writer is a Jew by birth, for the allusions to the customs of his nation are many; but he is also acquainted with Greece and its lofty culture. An allusion to the heresies of Docetism is evident from the commencement, and is in harmony with what is known of the adversary of Cerinthus. The fourth gospel bears the mark of a date subsequent to the first three, and this again brings us to the time of John's abode at Ephesus. It is pre-eminent for accuracy, and shows throughout an eye-witness in the historian. Lastly, how can we avoid recognizing in every page the disciple whom Jesus loved, the apostle of love, who, as Clement of Alexandria says, "discerned like by like, love by love." Objection is taken to the marked difference between the discourses of the Saviour in the synoptics, and in the fourth gospel. It has even been said that John gives us another Christ than the first three evangelists. We admit that he presents him under another aspect, precisely because of his own moral affinity for that which was transcendent in the Master; but the Christ is essentially the same Christ. We have already observed that the writers of the synoptics also discerned the Son of God in the Son of man. It is not just to assert that the element of parable is completely absent from the gospel of John while we can point to the tenth and fifteenth chapters. The uniformity of the discourses is undeniable, and belongs to the more metaphysical character of the gospel of John. Evidently language has less variety when it touches on the highest points of religious teaching. We admit that John has given a certain sameness of color to the words of the Saviour, the same color which we find in his epistle; but the point to be ascertained is, whether John himself

* If it were admitted with Lücke, ("Comment.," ii, p. 826,) and with Reuss, ("Geschichte Schr., N. T.," p. 227,) that the twenty-first chapter of the fourth gospel is not by John, though it is of very ancient date, since it is quoted by Origen and Clement of Alexandria, the gospel of John would bear with it, in its closing verses, the certificate of its origin. The question appears to us insoluble if we take the whole of the chapters; but we think, with Olshausen, that the hyperbola of the last two verses is a gloss. The very antiquity of this gloss makes it a most important witness in favor of the authenticity of the fourth gospel.

is molded by Jesus Christ, or whether the teaching of Jesus Christ is subsequently thrown into a certain form by John. Between the two alternatives we do not hesitate one moment. By admitting the first, the subjective share of the historian is considerably lessened. As regards the differences in the narration of facts between the first three gospels and the fourth, these differences, though real in one respect, do not rise to the height of an absolute incompatibility in narrative, taken as a whole. The synoptics, while they especially relate that which transpired in Galilee, nevertheless contain evident allusions to journeys of the Saviour to Jerusalem. Luke x, 38–42; Matt. xxiii, 37.

When the Tübingen school sets against our statement the asserted Judaism of the author of the Apocalypse, we are prepared to reduce this objection to its true value. (See the preceding note.) Nor can any argument against the authenticity of the fourth gospel be drawn from the fact that St. John, who, in his gospel, places the last supper of Christ with his disciples on the 13th of Nisan, kept the Passover on the 14th, for he might think that the death of the true Lamb of God at that date was of more weight in fixing the paschal feast than the celebration of the same feast on the 13th of Nisan in the upper chamber.

As to the epistles of John, the first is evidently written by the author of the fourth gospel. Never was internal evidence more conclusive. Let us add that it has the most ancient testimony in its favor: "Papias in Eusebius," iii, 39; Polycarp, "Ad. Philipp.," 7; Comp. Irenæus, "Contr. Hæres.," iii, 16; Clement of Alexandria, "Stromat.," ii, 389; Tertullian, "Adv. Praxeam," 15. It has always been classed among the "Homologoumena." There is no reason of any weight for disputing the authenticity of the two smaller epistles of John. They strikingly resemble his style and manner. They also have external evidence on their side, though some doubt was entertained by Origen. Eusebius, vi, 25; vii, 28. Dionysius of Alexandria recognized their authenticity; (Eusebius, vi, 25;) so also did Irenæus, ("Contr. Hæres.," i, 163,) who speaks positively of the second as being by John.

INDEX OF SUBJECTS.

PASSAGES OF SCRIPTURE QUOTED OR REFERRED TO.

1 *Corinthians.*

INDEX OF AUTHORS QUOTED OR REFERRED TO,

AND OF THE SUBJECTS OF QUOTATION OR REFERENCE.

Works by the Same Author.

I.

Jesus Christ: His Times, Life, and Work.

Translated by Annie Harwood. 12mo., pp. 496. $3 75.

One of the most valuable additions to Christian literature which the present generation has seen.—*Contemporary Review.*

M. de Pressensé is not only brilliant and epigrammatic, but his sentences flow on from page to page with a sustained eloquence which never wearies the reader. The life of Christ is more dramatically unfolded in this volume than in any other work with which we are acquainted.—*Spectator.*

The successive scenes and teachings of our Lord's life are told with a scholarly accuracy and a glowing and devout eloquence which are well presented to the English reader in Miss Harwood's admirable translation.—*British Quarterly Review.*

The work of an able and excellent author, whose appreciation of our Lord Jesus Christ, both in his person and in his work, is at once profound and discriminating, and whom no doubts or difficulties hinder from claiming the honor due to the Name that is above every name. In point of learning, intellectual power, and that charm of brilliancy of diction for which the French language is so remarkable when wielded by a master, the merit of this work is remarkably high.—*Sunday Magazine.*

Its arguments are sound, clear, and well illustrated. Of its learning there can be but one opinion, as its pages every-where abound with the results of thorough, well-digested, and extensive research.—*The Rock.*

It is a book eminently adapted to be useful.—*Christian Work.*

II.

The Mystery of Suffering, and Other Discourses.

New Edition.

In these sermons we recognize the same intellectual power, the same exquisite felicity of diction, the same sustained and dignified eloquence, and the same persuasive invigorating Christian thought which are conspicuous in that work—["Jesus Christ: His Times," etc.]—*British and Foreign Evangelical Review.*

. . . The tone of the discourses is so tenderly beautiful that a reader who did not believe one word of the Christian mysteries might be affected by it.—*London Review.*

Sermons brimming up and running over with truth and beauty.—*Weekly Review.*

These are very remarkable discourses. They are distinguished by all the nice analysis of thought and glow of feeling so characteristic of Dr. Pressensé's ministry and writings.—*Evangelical Magazine.*

A volume of beautiful and thoroughly Christian sermons.—*London Quarterly Review.*

They are not ordinary sermons, but replete with valuable thoughts, often beautifully expressed, and are characterized by true pathos and holy unction.—*United Methodist Free Church Magazine.*

Works by the Same Author.

III.

The Church and the French Revolution.

A History of the Relations of Church and State from 1789 to 1802. In crown 8vo.

M. de Pressensé is well known and deservedly respected as one of the leading divines of the Evangelical section of the French Protestant Church. He is a learned theologian, and a man of cultivated and liberal mind. In the present monograph he comes before us as the historian of a period which he rightly judges to have a more than local and temporary interest in the fortunes of the national Church of France. And, on the whole, he has done his work not only ably, but impartially. . . . We are not aware that any previous writer has treated the subject from the purely ecclesiastical point of view.—*Saturday Review.*

IV.

Early Years of Christianity.

Translated by Annie Harwood. 12mo.

This is a sequel to Dr. Pressensé's celebrated book on the "Life, Work, and Times of Jesus Christ." We may say at once that, to the bulk of liberal Christians, Dr. Pressensé's achievement will be very valuable.—*Athenæum.*

De Pressensé tells the glorious narrative with singular force and clearness of expression.—*British Quarterly Review.*

The great theme on which he has labored with the utmost earnestness and zeal suffers no loss of color or life. He holds his brilliant intellectual gifts and his profound learning subordinate to his fervent and absolute faith in the divinity of his Lord and Saviour; but he is well entitled to our credit when he declares that the feeling which has inspired the book has laid no fetters on his freedom of examination.—*Daily Telegraph.*

It is impossible to part from these graphic and learned representations of the purest ages of Christianity without a deep reverence for the ability of the author as a scholar, and his zealous advocacy of the truth as a Christian.—*The Rock.*

V.

The Land of the Gospel:

Notes of a Journey in the East.

He gives us his first and freshest impressions as entered in his journal upon the spot; and these will be found full of interest, especially to every thoughtful reader of the New Testament.—*Evangelical Christendom.*

www.ingramcontent.com/pod-product-compliance
Lightning Source LLC
LaVergne TN
LVHW021300110826
845150LV00003B/446

* 9 7 8 1 4 2 5 5 6 0 2 9 4 *